Breast Cancer

SOURCEBOOK

Fifth Edition

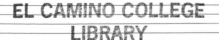

Health Reference Series

Fifth Edition

Breast Cancer
SOURCEBOOK

Basic Consumer Health Information about the Prevalence, Risk Factors, and Symptoms of Breast Cancer, including Ductal and Lobular Carcinoma in Situ, Invasive Carcinoma, Inflammatory Breast Cancer, and Breast Cancer in Men and Pregnant Women

Along with Facts about Benign Breast Changes, Breast Cancer Screening and Diagnostic Tests, Treatments Such as Surgery, Radiation Therapy, Chemotherapy, and Hormonal and Biologic Therapies, Tips on Managing Treatment Side Effects and Living with Breast Cancer, a Glossary of Terms, and a Directory of Resources for Additional Help and Information

OMNIGRAPHICS
615 Griswold, Ste. 901, Detroit, MI 48226

Bibliographic Note
Because this page cannot legibly accommodate all the copyright notices, the Bibliographic
Note portion of the Preface constitutes an extension of the copyright notice.

* * *

Omnigraphics, Inc.
Editorial Services provided by Omnigraphics, Inc.,
a division of Relevant Information, LLC

Keith Jones, *Managing Editor*

* * *

Copyright © 2016 Relevant Information, LLC
ISBN 978-0-7808-1462-2
E-ISBN 978-0-7808-1461-5

Library of Congress Cataloging-in-Publication Data

Names: Omnigraphics, Inc.

Title: Breast cancer sourcebook : basic consumer health information about the
prevalence, risk factors, and symptoms of breast cancer, including ductal and
lobular carcinoma in situ, invasive carcinoma, inflammatory breast cancer, and
breast cancer in men and pregnant women; along with facts about benign breast
changes, breast cancer screening and diagnostic tests, treatments such as surgery,
radiation therapy, chemotherapy, and hormonal and biologic therapies, tips on
managing treatment side effects and complications, a glossary of terms, and a
directory of resources for additional help and information.

Description: Fifth edition. | Detroit, MI: Omnigraphics, [2016] | Series: Health
reference series | Includes bibliographical references and index.

Identifiers: LCCN 2016012498 (print) | LCCN 2016014570 (ebook) | ISBN
9780780814622 (hardcover: alk. paper) | ISBN 9780780814615 (ebook) | ISBN
9780780814615 (eBook)

Subjects: LCSH: Breast--Cancer--Popular works.

Classification: LCC RC280.B8 B6887 2016 (print) | LCC RC280.B8 (ebook) | DDC
616.99/449--dc23

LC record available at http://lccn.loc.gov/2016012498

Table of Contents

Part III: Risk Factors, Symptoms, and Prevention of Breast Cancer

Part IV: Screening, Diagnosis, and Stages of Breast Cancer

Part V: Breast Cancer Treatments

Part VI: Managing Side Effects and Complications of Breast Cancer Treatment

Part VIII: Breast Cancer Research and Clinical Trials

Part IX: Additional Help and Information

Preface

About This Book

Breast cancer is one of the most commonly diagnosed cancers in women, and an estimated one in eight U.S. women (about 12%) will eventually develop an invasive form of this disease. In 2016, an estimated 246,660 new cases of invasive breast cancer are expected to be diagnosed in women in the United States, along with 61,000 new cases of non-invasive (in situ) breast cancer. In 2015, an estimated 40,450 women in the U.S. were expected to die from breast cancer. However thanks to treatment advances, earlier detection and screening techniques, and increased awareness of symptoms, the number of deaths attributable to breast cancer each year has declined since 1989.

Breast Cancer Sourcebook, Fifth Edition, provides updated information about breast cancer and its causes, risk factors, diagnosis, and treatment. Readers will learn about the types of breast cancer, including ductal carcinoma in situ, lobular carcinoma in situ, invasive carcinoma, and inflammatory breast cancer, as well as common breast cancer treatment complications, such as pain, fatigue, lymphedema, hair loss, and sexuality and fertility issues. Information on preventive therapies, nutrition and exercise recommendations, and tips on living with cancer are also included, along with a glossary of related terms and a directory of organizations that offer additional information to breast cancer patients and their families.

How to Use This Book

This book is divided into parts and chapters. Parts focus on broad areas of interest. Chapters are devoted to single topics within a part.

Part I: Introduction to Breast Cancer identifies the parts of the breasts and lymphatic system, discusses common changes in the breast that pose no threat to health, and offers general information about breast cancer in young women, men, and children. It also examines the link between breast and ovarian cancer. Statistical information on the prevalence of breast cancer in the United States is also provided.

Part II: Types of Breast Cancer identifies the most common types of breast cancer, including ductal carcinoma in situ (DCIS), lobular carcinoma in situ (LCIS), invasive carcinoma of the breast, inflammatory breast cancer, Paget disease of the nipple, and triple-negative breast cancer.

Part III: Risk Factors, Symptoms, and Prevention of Breast Cancer provides information about factors that increase the risk of developing breast cancer, including age, alcohol consumption, reproductive risk factors, obesity, and the use of hormone replacement therapy, personal care products, and oral contraceptives. Genetic counseling for breast cancer risk is discussed, along with information about preventing breast cancer in people who are susceptible.

Part IV: Screening, Diagnosis, and Stages of Breast Cancer identifies tests and procedures used to screen, diagnose, and stage breast cancer, including breast examinations, mammograms, and breast biopsies. Information about other breast imaging procedures, including breast magnetic resonance imaging, and breast ultrasound, is also included. The part concludes with FAQs about breast cancer diagnosis.

Part V: Breast Cancer Treatments discusses how to find a treatment facility or doctor and offers information about considerations to make before undergoing breast cancer treatment. Surgical treatments for breast cancer, such as mastectomy, lumpectomy, and breast reconstruction are discussed, and facts about radiation therapy, chemotherapy, hormone therapy, biologic therapies, and complementary and alternative medicine treatments for breast cancer are provided. The part also includes a discussion on treatment of breast cancer in men, treatment during pregnancy, and patients with recurrent breast cancer.

Part VI: Managing Side Effects and Complications of Breast Cancer Treatment describes fatigue, infection, lymphedema, pain, sexual and fertility issues, and hair loss associated with breast cancer treatment. Information about complementary and alternative therapies that may relieve physical discomfort or emotional anxiety is also provided.

Part VII: Living with Breast Cancer discusses strategies for coping with the difficult emotions produced by a breast cancer diagnosis and offers information about body changes, getting back to work, and follow-up medical care. In addition, the part identifies nutrition and exercise recommendations after cancer treatment, tips for dealing with cancer in the workplace, and information on the Women's Health and Cancer Rights Act.

Part VIII: Breast Cancer Research and Clinical Trials provides information on the latest breast cancer research, as well as provides information on current clinical trials related to breast cancer

Part IX: Additional Help and Information provides a glossary of important terms related to breast cancer and a directory of organizations that offer information and financial assistance to people with breast cancer.

Bibliographic Note

This volume contains documents and excerpts from publications issued by the following U.S. government agencies: Centers for Disease Control and Prevention (CDC); Centers for Medicare and Medicaid Services (CMS); Equal Employment Opportunity Commission (EEOC); Health and Human Services (HHS); National Cancer Institute (NCI); National Center for Complementary and Integrative Health (NCCIH); National Institute of Biomedical Imaging and Bioengineering (NIBIB); National Institute of Environmental Health Sciences (NIEHS); National Institute on Aging (NIA); National Institutes of Health (NIH); Office of Disease Prevention and Health Promotion (ODPHP); U.S. Department of Energy (DOE); U.S. Department of Labor (DOL); and U.S. Food and Drug Administration (FDA).

It may also contain original material produced by Omnigraphics, Inc. and reviewed by medical consultants.

About the Health Reference Series

The *Health Reference Series* is designed to provide basic medical information for patients, families, caregivers, and the general public. Each volume takes a particular topic and provides comprehensive coverage. This is especially important for people who may be dealing with a newly diagnosed disease or a chronic disorder in themselves or in a family member. People looking for preventive guidance, information about disease warning signs, medical statistics, and risk factors for health problems will also find answers to their questions in the *Health Reference Series*. The *Series*, however, is not intended to serve as a tool for diagnosing illness, in prescribing treatments, or as a substitute for the physician/patient relationship. All people concerned about medical symptoms or the possibility of disease are encouraged to seek professional care from an appropriate health care provider.

A Note about Spelling and Style

Health Reference Series editors use *Stedman's Medical Dictionary* as an authority for questions related to the spelling of medical terms and the *Chicago Manual of Style* for questions related to grammatical structures, punctuation, and other editorial concerns. Consistent adherence is not always possible, however, because the individual volumes within the *Series* include many documents from a wide variety of different producers, and the editor's primary goal is to present material from each source as accurately as is possible. This sometimes means that information in different chapters or sections may follow other guidelines and alternate spelling authorities.

Medical Review

Omnigraphics contracts with a team of qualified, senior medical professionals who serve as medical consultants for the *Health Reference Series*. As necessary, medical consultants review reprinted and originally written material for currency and accuracy. Citations including the phrase, "Reviewed (month, year)" indicate material reviewed by this team. Medical consultation services are provided to the *Health Reference Series* editors by:

Dr. Vijayalakshmi, MBBS, DGO, MD
Dr. Senthil Selvan, MBBS, DCH, MD

Our Advisory Board

We would like to thank the following board members for providing initial guidance on the development of this series:

- Dr. Lynda Baker, Associate Professor of Library and Information Science, Wayne State University, Detroit, MI

- Nancy Bulgarelli, William Beaumont Hospital Library, Royal Oak, MI

- Karen Imarisio, Bloomfield Township Public Library, Bloomfield Township, MI

- Karen Morgan, Mardigian Library, University of Michigan-Dearborn, Dearborn, MI

- Rosemary Orlando, St. Clair Shores Public Library, St. Clair Shores, MI

Health Reference Series *Update Policy*

The inaugural book in the *Health Reference Series* was the first edition of *Cancer Sourcebook* published in 1989. Since then, the *Series* has been enthusiastically received by librarians and in the medical community. In order to maintain the standard of providing high-quality health information for the layperson the editorial staff at Omnigraphics felt it was necessary to implement a policy of updating volumes when warranted.

Medical researchers have been making tremendous strides, and it is the purpose of the *Health Reference Series* to stay current with the most recent advances. Each decision to update a volume is made on an individual basis. Some of the considerations include how much new information is available and the feedback we receive from people who use the books. If there is a topic you would like to see added to the update list, or an area of medical concern you feel has not been adequately addressed, please write to:

Managing Editor
Health Reference Series
Omnigraphics, Inc.
615 Griswold, Ste. 901
Detroit, MI 48226

Part One

Introduction to Breast Cancer

Chapter 1

Breast and Lymphatic System Basics: Understanding Breast Health

Breast and Lymphatic System Basics

To better understand breast changes, it helps to know what the breasts and **lymphatic system** are made of.

What Are Breasts Made Of?

Breasts are made of **connective tissue, glandular** tissue, and fatty tissue. Connective tissue and glandular tissue look dense, or white on a mammogram. Fatty tissue is non-dense, or black on a mammogram. **Dense breasts** can make mammograms harder to interpret.

Breasts have **lobes, lobules, ducts**, an areola, and a nipple.

- Lobes are sections of the glandular tissue. Lobes have smaller sections called lobules that end in tiny bulbs that can make milk.

- Ducts are thin tubes that connect the lobes and lobules. Milk flows from the lobules through the ducts to the nipple.

This chapter includes text excerpted from "Understanding Breast Changes," National Cancer Institute (NCI), February 2014.

- The nipple is the small raised area at the tip of the breast. Milk flows through the nipple. The areola is the area of darker-colored skin around the nipple. Each breast also has **lymph vessels**.

What Is the Lymphatic System Made Of?

The lymphatic system, which is a part of your body's defense system, contains lymph vessels and lymph nodes.

- Lymph vessels are thin tubes that carry a fluid called **lymph** and **white blood cells.**

- Lymph vessels lead to small, bean-shaped organs called **lymph nodes**. Lymph nodes are found near your breast, under your arm, above your collarbone, in your chest, and in other parts of your body.

- Lymph nodes filter substances in lymph to help fight **infection** and disease. They also store disease-fighting white blood cells called **lymphocytes**.

Check with Your Healthcare Provider about Breast Changes

Check with your healthcare provider if you notice that your breast looks or feels different. No change is too small to ask about. In fact, the best time to call is when you first notice a breast change.

Breast Changes to See Your Healthcare Provider About

A Lump (Mass) or a Firm Feeling

- A lump in or near your breast or under your arm

- Thick or firm tissue in or near your breast or under your arm

- A change in the size or shape of your breast

Lumps come in different shapes and sizes. Most lumps are **not** cancer.

If you notice a lump in one breast, check your other breast. If both breasts feel the same, it may be normal. Normal breast tissue can sometimes feel lumpy.

Some women do regular **Breast self-exams**. Doing breast self-exams can help you learn how your breasts normally feel and make it easier to notice and find any changes. Breast self-exams are not a substitute for mammograms.

Always get a lump checked. Don't wait until your next mammogram. You may need to have tests to be sure that the lump is not cancer.

Nipple Discharge or Changes

- Nipple discharge (fluid that is not breast milk)
- Nipple changes, such as a nipple that points or faces inward (inverted) into the breast

Nipple discharge may be different colors or textures. Nipple discharge is not usually a sign of cancer. It can be caused by birth control pills, some medicines, and infections.

Get nipple discharge checked, especially fluid that comes out by itself or fluid that is bloody.

Skin Changes

- Itching, redness, scaling, dimples or puckers on your breast

If the skin on your breast changes, get it checked as soon as possible.

Finding Breast Changes

Here are some ways your health care provider can find breast changes:

Clinical Breast Exam

During a clinical breast exam, your health care provider checks your breasts and nipples and under your arms for any abnormal changes.

Ask your healthcare provider at what age and how often you should have a clinical breast exam. During the visit, it's important to share your personal medical history and your family medical history. This includes problems or diseases that you or family members have had.

Mammogram

A mammogram is an X-ray picture of your breast tissue. This test may find tumors that are too small to feel. During a mammogram, each breast is pressed between two plastic plates. Some discomfort is normal, but if it's painful, tell the **mammography** technician.

The best time to get a mammogram is at the end of your menstrual period. This is when your breasts are less tender. Some women have less breast tenderness if they don't have any caffeine for a couple of days before the mammogram.

After the X-ray pictures are taken, they are sent to a **radiologist**, who studies them and sends a report to your health care provider.

Both film and digital mammography use X-rays to make a picture of the breast tissue. The actual procedure for getting the mammogram is the same. The difference is in how the images are recorded and stored. It's like the difference between a film camera and a digital camera.

- **Film mammography** stores the image directly on X-ray film.

- **Digital mammography** takes an electronic image of the breast and stores it directly in a computer. Digital images can be made lighter, darker or larger. Images can also be stored and shared electronically.

A research study sponsored by the National Cancer Institute (NCI) showed that digital mammography and film mammography are about the same in terms of detecting breast cancer. However, digital mammography may be better at detecting breast cancer in women who are under age 50, have very dense breasts, or are **premenopausal** or **perimenopausal** (the times before and at the beginning of menopause).

Talk with your healthcare provider to learn more about what is best for you.

Mammograms Are Used for Both Screening and Diagnosis.

- **Screening Mammogram**

A **screening mammogram** is the kind of mammogram that most women get. It is used to find breast changes in women who have no signs of breast cancer.

- **Diagnostic Mammogram**

If your recent screening mammogram found a breast change, or if a lump was found that needs to be checked, you may have a **diagnostic mammogram**. During a diagnostic mammogram, more X-ray pictures are taken to get views of the breast tissue from different angles. Certain areas of these pictures can also be made larger.

Mammograms and Breast Implants

When you make your appointment, be sure to tell the staff if you have **breast implants.** Ask if they have specialists who are trained in taking and reading mammograms of women with breast implants. This is important because breast implants can make it harder to see cancer or other abnormal changes on the mammogram. A special technique called **implant displacement views** is used.

- If you have breast implants for cosmetic reasons, you may have either a screening mammogram or a diagnostic mammogram. This will depend on the facility that does the mammogram.

- If you have breast implants after having a **mastectomy** for breast cancer, talk with your breast surgeon or oncologist to learn about the best screening test for you.

Magnetic Resonance Imaging (MRI)

MRI uses a powerful magnet, radio waves, and a computer to take detailed pictures of areas inside the breast. MRI is another tool that can be used to find breast cancer. However, MRIs don't replace mammograms. They are used in addition to mammograms in women who are at increased risk of breast cancer.

MRIs have some limits. For example, they cannot find breast changes such as **microcalcifications**. MRIs are also less **specific** than other tests. This means that they may give **false-positive test results**—the test shows that there is cancer when there really is not.

Sometimes doctors recommend MRI for women who are at increased risk of breast cancer due to:

- Harmful changes (**mutations**) in the **BRCA1** or **BRCA2** gene

- A family history of breast cancer

- Your personal medical history

Getting Your Mammogram Results

You should get a written report of your mammogram results within 30 days of your mammogram, since this is the law. Be sure the mammography facility has your address and phone number. It's helpful to get your mammogram at the same place each year. This way, your current mammogram can be compared with past mammograms.

If Your Results Were Normal:

- Your breast tissue shows no signs of a **mass** or **calcification**.

- Visit your healthcare provider if you notice a breast change before your next appointment.

If Your Results Were Abnormal:

- A breast change was found. It may be benign (not cancer), pre-malignant (may become cancer) or cancer.

- It's important to get all the follow-up tests your healthcare provider asks you to.

If You Don't Get Your Results, Call Your Healthcare Provider

Keep in mind that most breast changes are not cancer. But all changes need to be checked, and more tests may be needed.

What Can a Mammogram Show?

Mammograms can show lumps, calcifications, and other changes in your breast. The radiologist will study the mammogram for breast changes that do not look normal and for differences between your breasts. When possible, he or she will compare your most recent mammogram with past mammograms to check for changes.

Lump or Mass

The size, shape, and edges of a lump give the radiologist important information. A lump that is not cancer often looks smooth and round and has a clear, defined edge. Lumps that look like this are often **cysts**. However, if the lump on the mammogram has a jagged outline and an irregular shape, more tests are needed.

Depending on the size and shape of the lump, your healthcare provider may ask you to have:

- Another clinical breast exam

- Another mammogram to have a closer look at the area

- An **ultrasound** exam to find out if the lump is solid or is filled with fluid

- A test called a **biopsy** to remove cells, or the entire lump, to look at under a **microscope** to check for signs of disease

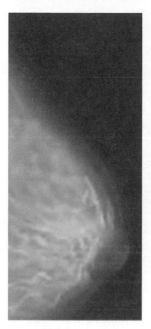 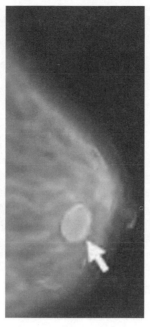 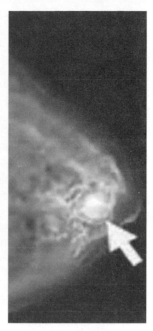

Figure 1.1. *Normal Mammogram*

Figure 1.2. *Benign Cyst (Not Cancer)*

Figure 1.3. *Cancer*

Calcifications

Calcifications are deposits of **calcium** in the breast tissue. They are too small to be felt, but can be seen on a mammogram. There are two types:

- **Macrocalcifications** look like small white dots on a mammogram. They are common in women over 50 years old. Macrocalcifications are not related to cancer and usually don't need more testing.

- **Microcalcifications** look like tiny white specks on a mammogram. They are usually not a sign of cancer. However, if they are found in an area of rapidly dividing cells, or grouped together in a certain way, you may need more tests.

Depending on how many calcifications you have, their size, and where they are found, your healthcare provider may ask you to have:

- Another mammogram to have a closer look at the area

- A test called a biopsy to check for signs of disease

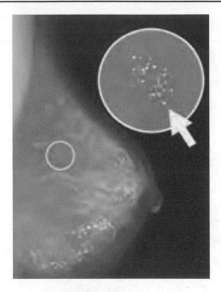

Figure 1.4. *Calcifications in the Breast*

Calcium in your diet does not cause calcium deposits (calcifications) in the breast.

Are Mammogram Results Always Right?

Mammography is a good tool to find breast changes in most women who have no signs of breast cancer. However, it does not detect all breast cancers, and many changes it finds are not cancer. See your healthcare provider if you have a lump that was not seen on a mammogram or notice any other breast changes.

Follow-Up Tests to Diagnose Breast Changes

An ultrasound exam, an MRI, a biopsy, or other follow-up tests may be needed to learn more about a breast change.

Ultrasound

An ultrasound exam uses sound waves to make a picture of breast tissue. This picture is called a **sonogram**. It helps radiologists to see if a lump or mass is solid or filled with fluid. A fluid-filled lump is called a cyst.

MRI

Magnetic resonance imaging, also called MRI, uses a powerful magnet, radio waves, and a computer to take detailed pictures of areas inside the breast. Sometimes breast lumps or large lymph nodes are found during a clinical breast exam or breast self-exam that were not seen on a mammogram or ultrasound. In these cases, an MRI can be used to learn more about these changes.

Breast Biopsy

A breast biopsy is a procedure to remove a sample of breast cells or tissue, or an entire lump. A **pathologist** then looks at the sample under a microscope to check for signs of disease. A biopsy is the only way to find out if cells are cancer.

Biopsies are usually done in an office or a clinic on an **outpatient** basis. This means you will go home the same day as the procedure. **Local anesthesia** is used for some biopsies. This means you will be awake, but you won't feel pain in your breast during the procedure. **General anesthesia** is often used for a **surgical biopsy**. This means that you will be asleep and won't wake up during the procedure.

Below are common types of breast biopsies:

- **Fine-needle aspiration biopsy**

A **fine-needle aspiration biopsy** is a simple procedure that takes only a few minutes. Your health care provider inserts a thin needle into the breast to take out fluid and cells.

- **Core biopsy**

A **core biopsy**, also called a core needle biopsy, uses a needle to remove small pieces or cores of breast tissue. The samples are about the size of a grain of rice. You may have a bruise, but usually not a scar.

- **Vacuum-assisted biopsy**

A **vacuum-assisted biops**y uses a probe, connected to a vacuum device, to remove a small sample of breast tissue. The small cut made in the breast is much smaller than with surgical biopsy. This procedure causes very little scarring, and no stitches are needed.

- **Surgical biopsy**

A surgical biopsy is an operation to remove part, or all, of a lump so it can be looked at under a microscope to check for signs of disease. Sometimes a doctor will do a surgical biopsy as the first step. Other times, a doctor may do a surgical biopsy if the results of a needle biopsy do not give enough information.

When only a sample of breast tissue is removed, it's called an **incisional biopsy**. When the entire lump or suspicious area is removed, it's called an **excisional biopsy**.

If the breast change cannot be felt, **wire localization**, also called **needle localization**, may be used to find the breast change. During wire localization, a thin, hollow needle is inserted into the breast. A mammogram is taken to make sure that the needle is in the right place. Then a fine wire is inserted through the hollow needle, to mark the area of tissue to be removed. Next, the needle is removed, and another mammogram is taken. You then go to the operating room where the surgeon removes the wire and surrounding breast tissue. The tissue is sent to the lab to be checked for signs of disease.

Your doctor may use ultrasound or mammography during a breast biopsy to help locate the breast change.

More about This Cancer

Cancer and the Female Breast

Inside a woman's breast are 15 to 20 sections, or lobes. Each lobe is made of many smaller sections called lobules. Fibrous tissue and fat fill the spaces between the lobules and ducts (thin tubes that connect the lobes and nipples). Breast cancer occurs when cells in the breast grow out of control and form a growth or tumor. Tumors may be cancerous (malignant) or not cancerous (benign).

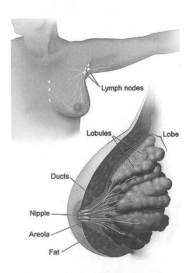

Figure 1.5. *Breast and Adjacent Lymph Nodes*

Chapter 2

Benign Breast Changes

Breast Changes during Your Lifetime That Are Not Cancer

Most women have changes in their breasts during their lifetime. Many of these changes are caused by **hormones**. For example, your breasts may feel more lumpy or tender at different times in your **menstrual cycle**.

Other breast changes can be caused by the normal aging process. As you near **menopause**, your breasts may lose tissue and fat. They may become smaller and feel lumpy. Most of these changes are not cancer; they are called benign changes. However, if you notice a breast change, don't wait until your next mammogram. Make an appointment to get it checked.

Young women who have not gone through menopause often have more dense tissue in their breasts. Dense tissue has more glandular and connective tissue and less fat tissue. This kind of tissue makes mammograms harder to interpret—because both dense tissue and tumors show up as solid white areas on **X-ray** images. Breast tissue gets less dense as women get older.

Before or during your menstrual periods, your breasts may feel swollen, tender, or painful. You may also feel one or more lumps

This chapter includes text excerpted from "Understanding Breast Changes," National Cancer Institute (NCI), February 2014.

during this time because of extra fluid in your breasts. These changes usually go away by the end of your menstrual cycle. Because some lumps are caused by normal hormone changes, your healthcare provider may have you come back for a return visit, at a different time in your menstrual cycle.

During pregnancy, your breasts may feel lumpy. This is usually because the glands that produce milk are increasing in number and getting larger.

While breastfeeding, you may get a condition called **mastitis**. This happens when a milk duct becomes blocked. Mastitis causes the breast to look red and feel lumpy, warm, and tender. It may be caused by an infection and it is often treated with **antibiotics**. Sometimes the duct may need to be drained. If the redness or mastitis does not go away with treatment, call your healthcare provider.

As you approach menopause, your menstrual periods may come less often. Your hormone levels also change. This can make your breasts feel tender, even when you are not having your menstrual period. Your breasts may also feel more lumpy than they did before.

If you are taking hormones (such as menopausal hormone therapy, birth control pills, or injections) your breasts may become more dense. This can make a mammogram harder to interpret. Be sure to let your healthcare provider know if you are taking hormones.

When you stop having menstrual periods (menopause), your hormone levels drop, and your breast tissue becomes less dense and more fatty. You may stop having any lumps, pain, or nipple discharge that you used to have. And because your breast tissue is less dense, mammograms may be easier to interpret.

Breast Changes and Conditions: Getting Follow-Up Test Results

Breast Changes That Are Not Cancer

These changes are not cancer and do not increase your risk of breast cancer. They are called benign changes.

Adenosis: Small, round lumps, or a lumpy feeling that are caused by enlarged breast lobules. Sometimes the lumps are too small to be felt. If there is scar-like tissue, the condition may be painful and is called **sclerosing adenosis**.

Cysts: Lumps filled with fluid. Breast cysts often get bigger and may be painful just before your menstrual period begins. Cysts are most common in premenopausal women and in women who are taking menopausal hormone therapy.

Fat necrosis: Round, firm lumps that usually don't hurt. The lumps most often appear after an injury to the breast, surgery, or radiation therapy.

Fibroadenomas: Hard, round lumps that may feel like a small marble and move around easily. They are usually painless and are most common in young women under 30 years old.

Intraductal papilloma: A wart-like growth in a milk duct of the breast. It's usually found close to the nipple and may cause clear, sticky, or bloody discharge from the nipple. It may also cause pain and a lump. It is most common in women 35–55 years old.

Breast Changes That Are Not Cancer, but Increase Your Risk of Cancer

These conditions are not cancer, but having them increases your risk of breast cancer. They are considered risk factors for breast cancer. Other risk factors include, for example, your age and a family history of breast cancer.

Atypical hyperplasia:

- Atypical lobular hyperplasia (ALH) is a condition in which abnormal cells are found in the breast lobules.

- Atypical ductal hyperplasia (ADH) is a condition in which abnormal cells are found in the breast ducts.

Lobular carcinoma in situ (LCIS) is a condition in which abnormal cells are found in the breast lobules. There are more abnormal cells in the lobule with LCIS than with ALH. Since these cells have not spread outside the breast lobules, it's called " in situ," which is a Latin term that means "in place."

15

The abnormal cells found in these conditions are not cancer cells. If you have ALH, ADH, or LCIS, talk with a doctor who specializes in breast health to make a plan that works best for you. Depending on your personal and family medical history, it may include:

- Mammograms every year

- Clinical breast exams every 6 to 12 months

- **Tamoxifen** (for all women) or **raloxifene** (for postmenopausal women). These drugs have been shown to lower some women's risk of breast cancer.

- **Surgery**. A small number of women with LCIS and high risk factors for breast cancer may choose to have surgery.

- **Clinical trials**. Talk with your healthcare provider about whether a clinical trial is a good choice for you.

Breast Changes That May Become Cancer

Ductal carcinoma in situ (DCIS): DCIS is a condition in which abnormal cells are found in the lining of a breast duct. These cells have not spread outside the duct to the breast tissue. This is why it is called "in situ," which is a Latin term that means "in place." You may also hear DCIS called Stage 0 breast carcinoma in situ or noninvasive cancer.

Since it's not possible to determine which cases of DCIS will become invasive breast cancer, it's important to get treatment for DCIS. Talk with a doctor who specializes in breast health to learn more. Treatment for DCIS is based on how much of the breast is affected, where DCIS is in the breast, and its grade. Most women with DCIS are cured with proper treatment.

Treatment choices for DCIS include:

- **Lumpectomy**. This is a type of **breast-conserving surgery** or **breast-sparing surgery**. It is usually followed by **radiation therapy.**

- **Mastectomy**. This type of surgery is used to remove the breast or as much of the breast tissue as possible.

- **Tamoxifen**. This drug may also be taken to lower the chance that DCIS will come back, or to prevent invasive breast cancer.

- **Clinical trials**. Talk with your healthcare provider about whether a clinical trial is a good choice for you.

Breast Cancer

Breast cancer is a disease in which cancer cells form in the tissues of the breast. Breast cancer cells:

- Grow and divide without control

- Invade nearby breast tissue

- May form a mass called a **tumor**

- May **metastasize**, or spread, to the lymph nodes or other parts of the body

- After breast cancer has been **diagnosed**, tests are done to find out the extent, or **stage**, of the cancer. The stage is based on the size of the tumor and whether the cancer has spread. Treatment depends on the stage of the cancer.

Getting the Support You Need

It can be upsetting to notice a breast change, to get an abnormal test result, or to learn about a new condition or disease. We hope that the information in this booklet has answered some of your questions and calmed some of your fears as you talk with your healthcare provider and get the follow-up care you need.

Many women choose to get extra help and support for themselves. It may help to think about people who have been there for you during challenging times in the past.

- Ask friends or loved ones for support. Take someone with you while you are learning about your testing and treatment choices.

- Ask your healthcare provider to:

  - Explain medical terms that are new or confusing

  - Share with you how other people have handled the types of feelings that you are having

  - Tell you about specialists that you can talk with to learn more

Breast Conditions and Follow-Up Care

Table 2.1. Breast Conditions and Doctor's Recommendations

Condition	Features	What your doctor may recommend
Adenosis	Small round lumps, lumpiness, or you may not feel anything at all • Enlarged breast lobules • If there is scar-like fibrous tissue, the condition is called sclerosing adenosis. It may be painful. • Some studies have found that women with sclerosing adenosis may have a slightly increased risk of breast cancer.	• A core biopsy or a surgical biopsy may be needed to make a diagnosis.
Atypical lobular hyperplasia (ALH)	• Abnormal cells in the breast lobules • ALH increases your risk of breast cancer.	Regular follow-up, such as: • Mammograms • Clinical breast exams Treatment, such as: • Tamoxifen (for all women) or raloxifene (for postmenopausal women)
Atypical ductal hyperplasia (ADH)	• Abnormal cells in the breast ducts • ADH increases your risk of breast cancer.	Regular follow-up, such as: • Mammograms • Clinical breast exams Treatment, such as: • Tamoxifen (for all women) or raloxifene (for postmenopausal women)
Breast cancer	• Cancer cells found in the breast, with a biopsy • A lump in or near your breast or under your arm • Thick or firm tissue in or near your breast or under your arm • A change in the size or shape of your breast • A nipple that's turned inward (inverted) into the breast	Treatment depends on the extent or stage of cancer. Tests are done to find out if the cancer has spread to others parts of your body. Treatment may include: • Surgery • Chemotherapy • Radiation therapy

Table 2.1. Continued

Condition	Features	What your doctor may recommend
	• Skin on your breast that is itchy, red, scaly, dimpled, or puckered • Nipple discharge that is not breast milk	• Hormonal therapy • Biological therapy Clinical trials may be an option for you. Talk with your doctor to learn more.
Cysts	• Lumps filled with fluid • Often in both breasts • May be painful just before your menstrual period begins • Some cysts may be felt. Others are too small to be felt. • Most common in women 35–50 years old	• Cysts may be watched by your doctor over time, since they may go away on their own. • Ultrasound can show if the lump is solid or filled with fluid. • Fine needle aspiration may be used to remove fluid from the cyst.
Ductal carcinoma in situ (DCIS)	• Abnormal cells in the lining of a breast duct • Unlike cancer cells that can spread, these abnormal cells have not spread outside the breast duct. • May be called noninvasive cancer or Stage 0 breast carcinoma in situ.	Treatment is needed because doctors don't know which cases of DCIS may become invasive breast cancer. Treatment choices include: • Lumpectomy. This is a type of breast- conserving surgery or breast-sparing surgery. It is usually followed by radiation therapy. • Mastectomy. Surgery to remove the breast. • Tamoxifen. This drug may be taken to lower the chance that DCIS will come back after treatment or to prevent invasive breast cancer. • Clinical trials. Talk with your doctor about whether a clinical trial is a good choice for you.

Table 2.1. Continued

Condition	Features	What your doctor may recommend
Fat necrosis	• Round, firm lumps that usually don't hurt • May appear after an injury to the breast, surgery, or radiation therapy • Formed by damaged fatty tissue • Skin around the lump may look red, bruised, or dimpled • A benign (not cancer) breast condition	• A biopsy may be needed to diagnose and remove fat necrosis, since it often looks like cancer. • Fat necrosis does not usually need treatment.
Fibroadenoma	• Hard, round lumps that move around easily and usually don't hurt • Often found by the woman • Appear on a mammogram as smooth, round lumps with clearly defined edges • The most common benign breast tumors • Common in women under 30 years old • Most fibroadenomas do not increase your risk of breast cancer. However, complex fibroadenomas do slightly increase your risk.	• A biopsy may be needed to diagnose fibroadenoma. • A minimally invasive technique such as ultrasound-guided **cryoablation** or an excisional biopsy may be used to remove the lumps. • These growths may be watched by your doctor over time, since they may go away on their own.
Intraductal papilloma	• A wart-like growth inside the milk duct, usually close to the nipple • May cause pain and a lump • May cause clear, sticky, or bloody discharge • Most common in women 35–55 years old • Unlike single papillomas, multiple papillomas increase your risk of breast cancer.	• A biopsy may be needed to diagnose the growth and remove it.

Table 2.1. Continued

Condition	Features	What your doctor may recommend
Lobular carcinoma in situ (LCIS)	• A condition in which abnormal cells are found in the breast lobules • LCIS increases your risk of breast cancer.	Regular follow-up, such as: • Mammograms • Clinical breast exams Treatment choices: • Tamoxifen (for all women) or raloxifene (for postmenopausal women) may be taken. • A small number of women with LCIS and high risk factors for breast cancer may choose to have surgery. • Clinical trials may be an option for you. Talk with your doctor to learn more.
Microcalcifications	• Calcium deposits in the breast that look like small white dots on a mammogram • Often caused by aging • Cannot be felt • Usually benign (not cancer) • Common in women over 50 years old	• Another mammogram may be needed to have a closer look at the area. • Treatment is usually not needed.
Microcalcifications	• Calcium deposits in the breast that look like tiny white specks on a mammogram • Not usually a sign of cancer. However, if found in an area of rapidly dividing cells or grouped together in a certain way, they may be a sign of DCIS or invasive breast cancer.	• Another mammogram or a biopsy may be needed to make a diagnosis.

21

Chapter 3

What You Need to Know about Breast Cancer

Basic Information about Breast Cancer

Cancer is a disease in which cells in the body grow out of control. When cancer starts in the breast, it is called *breast cancer*. Except for skin cancer, breast cancer is the most common cancer in American women.

Breast cancer *screening* means checking a woman's breasts for cancer before she has any symptoms. A *mammogram* is an X-ray picture of the breast. Mammograms are the best way to find breast cancer early, when it is easier to treat and before it is big enough to feel or cause symptoms.

Can Men Get Breast Cancer?

Men can get breast cancer. In men, breast cancer can happen at any age, but is most common in men who are between 60 and 70 years old. Male breast cancer is not very common. Less than 1% of breast cancers occur in men.

For men, signs of breast cancer and treatment are almost the same as for women.

This chapter includes text excerpted from "Basic Information about Breast Cancer," Centers for Disease Control and Prevention (CDC), November 18, 2013.

What Is Breast Cancer?

Cancer is a disease in which cells in the body grow out of control. When cancer starts in the breast, it is called breast cancer. Except for skin cancer, breast cancer is the most common cancer in American women.

A breast is made up of three main parts: glands, ducts, and connective tissue. The glands produce milk. The ducts are passages that carry milk to the nipple. The connective tissue (which consists of fibrous and fatty tissue) connects and holds everything together.

Lumps in the Breast

Many conditions can cause lumps in the breast, including cancer. But most breast lumps are caused by other medical conditions. The two most common causes of breast lumps are fibrocystic breast condition and cysts. Fibrocystic condition causes noncancerous changes in the breast that can make them lumpy, tender, and sore. Cysts are small fluid-filled sacs that can develop in the breast.

What Is a Normal Breast?

No breast is typical. What is normal for you may not be normal for another woman. Most women say their breasts feel lumpy or uneven. The way your breasts look and feel can be affected by getting your period, having children, losing or gaining weight, and taking certain medications. Breasts also tend to change as you age.

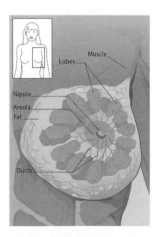

Figure 3.1. *Anterior View of the Breast*

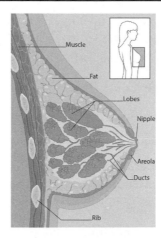

Figure 3.2. *Cross-Section View of the Breast*

What Are the Symptoms of Breast Cancer?

Different people have different warning signs for breast cancer. Some people do not have any signs or symptoms at all. A person may find out they have breast cancer after a routine mammogram.

Some warning signs of breast cancer are —

- New lump in the breast or underarm (armpit).
- Thickening or swelling of part of the breast.
- Irritation or dimpling of breast skin.
- Redness or flaky skin in the nipple area or the breast.
- Pulling in of the nipple or pain in the nipple area.
- Nipple discharge other than breast milk, including blood.
- Any change in the size or the shape of the breast.
- Pain in any area of the breast.

Keep in mind that some of these warning signs can happen with other conditions that are not cancer.

If you have any signs that worry you, be sure to see your doctor right away.

What Are the Risk Factors for Breast Cancer?

The main factors that influence your risk for breast cancer include being a woman, being older (most breast cancers are found in women who are 50 years old or older), and having changes in certain breast cancer genes (BRCA1 and BRCA2). In addition, studies have shown that some other factors may also influence your risk.

Factors That Decrease Your Risk

- Being older when you first had your menstrual period.

- Starting menopause at an earlier age.

- Giving birth to more children, being younger at the birth of your first child, and breastfeeding your children.

- Getting regular exercise.

- Maintaining a healthy weight.

Factors That Increase Your Risk

- Long-term use of hormone replacement therapy.

- Personal history of breast cancer or non-cancerous breast diseases.

- Family history of breast cancer (on either your mother's or father's side of the family).

- Treatment with radiation therapy to the breast/chest.

- Exposure to diethylstilbestrol (DES) (for example, if you took DES during pregnancy or your mother took DES during her pregnancy with you).

- Dense breasts by mammogram.

- Drinking alcohol.

- Night-shift work.

Some women will develop breast cancer even without any known risk factors. Having a risk factor does not mean you will get the disease, and not all risk factors affect your risk to the same extent. Most women have some risk factors and most women do not get breast cancer. If you have breast cancer risk factors, talk with your doctor about ways you can lower your risk and about screening for breast cancer.

What Can I Do to Reduce My Risk of Breast Cancer?

Many factors can influence your breast cancer risk, and most women who develop breast cancer do not have any known risk factors or a history of the disease in their families. However, you can help lower your risk of breast cancer in the following ways—

- Keep a healthy weight.

- Exercise regularly (at least four hours a week).

- Get enough sleep.

- Don't drink alcohol, or limit alcoholic drinks to no more than one per day.

- Avoid exposure to chemicals that can cause cancer (carcinogens).

- Try to reduce your exposure to radiation during medical tests like mammograms, X-rays, CT scans, and PET scans.

- If you are taking, or have been told to take, hormone replacement therapy or oral contraceptives (birth control pills), ask your doctor about the risks and find out if it is right for you.

- Breastfeed your babies, if possible.

Although breast cancer screening cannot prevent breast cancer, it can help find breast cancer early, when it is easier to treat. Talk to your doctor about which breast cancer screening tests are right for you, and when you should have them.

If you have a family history of breast cancer or inherited changes in your BRCA1 and BRCA2 genes, you may have a higher breast cancer risk. Talk to your doctor about these ways of reducing your risk—

- Antiestrogens or other medicines that block or decrease estrogen in your body.

- Surgery to reduce your risk of breast cancer—

  - Prophylactic (preventive) mastectomy (removal of breast tissue).

  - Prophylactic (preventive) salpingo-oophorectomy (removal of the ovaries and fallopian tubes).

It is important that you know your family history and talk to your doctor about screening and other ways you can lower your risk.

What Screening Tests Are There?

Breast cancer screening means checking a woman's breasts for cancer before there are signs or symptoms of the disease. Three main tests are used to screen the breasts for cancer. Talk to your doctor about which tests are right for you, and when you should have them.

Mammogram

A mammogram is an X-ray of the breast. Mammograms are the best way to find breast cancer early, when it is easier to treat and before it is big enough to feel or cause symptoms. Having regular mammograms can lower the risk of dying from breast cancer. The United States Preventive Services Task Force recommends that if you are 50 to 74 years old, be sure to have a screening mammogram every two years. If you are 40 to 49 years old, talk to your doctor about when to start and how often to get a screening mammogram.

Clinical Breast Exam

A *clinical breast exam* is an examination by a doctor or nurse, who uses his or her hands to feel for lumps or other changes.

Breast Self-Exam

A *breast self-exam* is when you check your own breasts for lumps, changes in size or shape of the breast, or any other changes in the breasts or underarm (armpit).

Which Tests to Choose

Having a clinical breast exam or a breast self-exam have not been found to decrease risk of dying from breast cancer. At this time, the best way to find breast cancer is with a mammogram. If you choose to have clinical breast exams and to perform breast self-exams, be sure you also get mammograms regularly.

Where Can I Go to Get Screened?

Most likely, you can get screened for breast cancer at a clinic, hospital, or doctor's office. If you want to be screened for breast cancer, call your doctor's office. They can help you schedule an appointment. Most health insurance companies pay for the cost of breast cancer screening tests.

What Is a Mammogram and When Should I Get One?

A *mammogram* is an X-ray picture of the breast. Doctors use a mammogram to look for early signs of breast cancer.

Regular mammograms are the best tests doctors have to find breast cancer early, sometimes up to three years before it can be felt. When their breast cancer is found early, many women go on to live long and healthy lives.

When Should I Get a Mammogram?

The United States Preventive Services Task Force recommends that women should have mammograms every two years from age 50 to 74 years. Talk to your health professional if you have any symptoms or changes in your breast, or if breast cancer runs in your family. He or she may recommend that you have mammograms before age 50 or more often than usual.

How Is a Mammogram Done?

You will stand in front of a special X-ray machine. A technologist will place your breast on a clear plastic plate. Another plate will firmly press your breast from above. The plates will flatten the breast, holding it still while the X-ray is being taken. You will feel some pressure. The other breast will be X-rayed in the same way. The steps are then repeated to make a side view of each breast. You will then wait while the technologist checks the four X-rays to make sure the pictures do not need to be re-done. Keep in mind that the technologist cannot tell you the results of your mammogram.

What Does Having a Mammogram Feel Like?

Having a mammogram is uncomfortable for most women. Some women find it painful. A mammogram takes only a few moments, though, and the discomfort is over soon. What you feel depends on the skill of the technologist, the size of your breasts, and how much they need to be pressed. Your breasts may be more sensitive if you are about to get or have your period. A doctor with special training, called a radiologist, will read the mammogram. He or she will look at the X-ray for early signs of breast cancer or other problems.

When Will I Get the Results of My Mammogram?

You will usually get the results within a few weeks, although it depends on the facility. A radiologist reads your mammogram and then reports the results to you or your doctor. If there is a concern, you will hear from the mammography facility earlier. Contact your health professional or the mammography facility if you do not receive a report of your results within 30 days.

What Happens If My Mammogram Is Normal?

Continue to get regular mammograms. Mammograms work best when they can be compared with previous ones. This allows your doctor to compare them to look for changes in your breasts.

What Happens If My Mammogram Is Abnormal?

If it is abnormal, do not panic. An abnormal mammogram does not always mean that there is cancer. But you will need to have additional mammograms, tests, or exams before the doctor can tell for sure. You may also be referred to a breast specialist or a surgeon. It does not necessarily mean you have cancer or need surgery. These doctors are experts in diagnosing breast problems.

Tips for Getting a Mammogram

- Try not to have your mammogram the week before you get your period or during your period. Your breasts may be tender or swollen then.

- On the day of your mammogram, don't wear deodorant, perfume, or powder. These products can show up as white spots on the X-ray.

- Some women prefer to wear a top with a skirt or pants, instead of a dress. You will need to undress from your waist up for the mammogram.

How Is Breast Cancer Diagnosed?

Doctors often use additional tests to find or diagnose breast cancer.

- **Breast ultrasound.** A machine uses sound waves to make detailed pictures, called sonograms, of areas inside the breast.

- **Diagnostic mammogram.** If you have a problem in your breast, such as lumps, or if an area of the breast looks abnormal on a screening mammogram, doctors may have you get a diagnostic mammogram. This is a more detailed X-ray of the breast.

- **Magnetic resonance imaging (MRI)**. A kind of body scan that uses a magnet linked to a computer. The MRI scan will make detailed pictures of areas inside the breast.

- **Biopsy**. This is a test that removes tissue or fluid from the breast to be looked at under a microscope and do more testing. There are different kinds of biopsies (for example, fine-needle aspiration, core biopsy, or open biopsy).

Staging

If breast cancer is diagnosed, other tests are done to find out if cancer cells have spread within the breast or to other parts of the body. This process is called staging. Whether the cancer is only in the breast, is found in lymph nodes under your arm, or has spread outside the breast determines your stage of breast cancer. The type and stage of breast cancer tells doctors what kind of treatment you need.

How Is Breast Cancer Treated?

Breast cancer is treated in several ways. It depends on the kind of breast cancer and how far it has spread. People with breast cancer often get more than one kind of treatment.

- **Surgery**. An operation where doctors cut out cancer tissue.

- **Chemotherapy**. Using special medicines to shrink or kill the cancer. The drugs can be pills you take or medicines given in your veins, or sometimes both.

- **Hormonal therapy**. Blocks cancer cells from getting the hormones they need to grow.

- **Biological therapy**. Works with your body's immune system to help it fight cancer or to control side effects from other cancer treatments. Side effects are how your body reacts to drugs or other treatments.

- **Radiation therapy**. Using high-energy rays (similar to X-rays) to kill the cancer.

Doctors from different specialties often work together to treat breast cancer. Surgeons are doctors who perform operations. Medical oncologists are doctors who treat cancer with medicine. Radiation oncologists are doctors who treat cancer with radiation.

Which Treatment Is Right for Me?

Choosing the treatment that is right for you may be hard. Talk to your cancer doctor about the treatment options available for your type and stage of cancer. Your doctor can explain the risks and benefits of each treatment and their side effects.

Sometimes people get an opinion from more than one cancer doctor. This is called a "second opinion." Getting a second opinion may help you choose the treatment that is right for you.

Complementary and Alternative Medicine

Complementary and alternative medicines are medicines and health practices that are not standard cancer treatments. Complementary medicine is used in addition to standard treatments, and alternative medicine is used instead of standard treatments. Meditation, yoga, and supplements like vitamins and herbs are some examples.

Many kinds of complementary and alternative medicine have not been tested scientifically and may not be safe. Talk to your doctor before you start any kind of complementary or alternative medicine.

Chapter 4

The Role of Estrogen in Breast Cancer Development

Overview

Estrogen refers to three related hormones—estrone, estradiol, and estriol—that are primarily responsible for female sexual and reproductive development. Like all hormones, estrogen is a chemical substance that circulates in the bloodstream, binds to receptors on certain cells, and carries messages that influence the growth and function of organs and tissues. In women, estrogen is produced in the ovaries, adrenal glands, liver, and fat tissues. Estrogen plays an important role in breast development, menstruation, pregnancy, lactation, bone growth, and many other processes. Although males do produce some estrogen, its role in the male body is not well understood.

Importance of Estrogen

The role of estrogen in the female body changes throughout the lifespan. Estradiol is mainly produced in the ovaries and is the dominant form of estrogen during the reproductive years. Estriol is produced by the placenta during pregnancy and controls many of the bodily changes that support childbearing. Estrone becomes the most abundant form of estrogen in the bodies of women who have reached menopause,

"The Role of Estrogen in Breast Cancer Development," © 2016 Omnigraphics, Inc. Reviewed April 2016.

when menstruation stops and estrogen production declines. Some of the major functions of estrogen include:

- developing breasts and other secondary sex characteristics at the onset of puberty

- regulating the menstrual cycle (the ovaries produce estrogen during the first part of the cycle to prepare the lining of the uterus to receive a fertilized egg; if fertilization does not occur, estrogen levels drop sharply, causing the uterine lining to break down and menstruation to occur)

- controlling lactation and other changes to the breasts during pregnancy

- breaking down and rebuilding bones

- maintaining vaginal lubrication and the strength and thickness of the vaginal wall

- regulating brain chemistry that affects mood and helping to control inflammation in the brain that leads to neurodegenerative disorders

- affecting blood clotting and cholesterol levels

Changes in Estrogen Levels

Estrogen levels in the bloodstream change naturally over time. They increase at puberty and during pregnancy, for instance, and they decrease while breastfeeding and after menopause. The decline in estrogen production that occurs with menopause can cause a variety of symptoms, including:

- irregular menstrual cycles

- hot flashes and night sweats

- vaginal dryness

- loss of sex drive

- bone loss (osteoporosis)

- trouble sleeping

- anxiety and mood swings

Declining estrogen levels can also result from other health conditions besides menopause, such as diminished function of the ovaries (hypogonadism), polycystic ovary syndrome, nonalcoholic fatty liver disease, or anorexia nervosa.

Estrogen Therapy

Estrogen is used in a number of different medications. It can be found in most oral contraceptives, for instance, because maintaining steady estrogen levels throughout the menstrual cycle prevents ovulation from occurring. Birth control pills containing estrogen are also prescribed to help regulate menstrual cycles and relieve menstrual cramps. Estrogen hormone therapy is also used to treat delayed onset of puberty, and to help transgender women achieve the physical changes that are important in the transition from male to female.

Hormone replacement therapy was once used extensively to relieve the symptoms of menopause and reduce the risk of chronic health conditions related to decreasing estrogen levels, such as osteoporosis and heart disease. In the early 2000s, however, studies showed that hormone replacement therapy led to an increased the risk of breast cancer, stroke, and blood clots. The U.S. Food and Drug Administration (FDA) responded by changing its guidelines regarding hormone replacement therapy. Doctors are now encouraged to prescribe estrogen at the lowest possible dose and for the shortest possible length of time to achieve treatment goals.

Experts saw a significant drop in cases of breast cancer in postmenopausal women over age 50 as soon as the new guidelines went into effect. They attributed the change to the role of estrogen in breast cancer development. Like many other cells, some potentially cancerous cells contain estrogen receptors. When estrogen circulating through the bloodstream attaches to these cells, it causes them to divide and grow. Without estrogen, the cells would stop growing and eventually die.

Estrogen and Breast Cancer

Since the majority of breast cancers are estrogen-receptor positive, researchers believe that increasing estrogen levels through hormone replacement therapy may promote tumor growth. Conversely, treatments aimed at blocking estrogen production or reducing estrogen levels may help slow the progression of breast cancer or prevent recurrence following surgery.

Given the relationship between estrogen and breast cancer, doctors have identified a number of circumstances that tend to raise estrogen levels or extend exposure to estrogen over the lifespan, and thus may increase the risk of developing breast cancer. Some of these circumstances include:

- Early onset of menstruation (before age 12)

- Taking oral contraceptives

- Never becoming pregnant, or giving birth to a first child after age 35

- Not breastfeeding

- Late onset of menopause (after age 55)

- Using hormone replacement therapy during menopause

- Being overweight, especially after menopause

- Exposure to synthetic estrogens in the environment, through absorption of chemicals found in some plastics, cleaning products, pesticides, herbicides, skin creams, and sunscreens

References

1. Bradford, Alina. "What Is Estrogen?" Live Science, March 29, 2016.

2. "Estrogen and Breast Cancer." Cancer Compass, 2016.

3. Manson, JoAnn E. "Estrogen." HealthyWomen, July 28, 2015.

Chapter 5

The Link between Breast and Ovarian Cancer

Overview of Genetics of Breast and Gynecologic Cancers

Inheritance and Risk

Factors suggestive of a genetic contribution to both breast cancer and gynecologic cancer include

1. an increased incidence of these cancers among individuals with a family history of these cancers;

2. multiple family members affected with these and other cancers; and

This chapter contains text excerpted from the following sources: Text beginning with the heading "Overview of Genetics of Breast and Gynecologic Cancers" is excerpted from "Genetics of Breast and Gynecologic Cancers–Health Professional Version (PDQ®)," National Cancer Institute (NCI), March 4, 2016; Text under the heading "Study Reveals Genomic Similarities between Breast and Ovarian Cancers" is excerpted from "Study Reveals Genomic Similarities between Breast and Ovarian Cancers," National Cancer Institute (NCI), September 24, 2012. Reviewed April 2016; Text beginning with the heading "Breast and Ovarian Cancer and Family Health History" is excerpted from "Breast and Ovarian Cancer and Family Health History," Centers for Disease Control and Prevention (CDC), June 17, 2014; Text under the heading "Breast and Ovarian Cancer and Family History Risk Categories" is excerpted from "Breast and Ovarian Cancer and Family History Risk Categories," Centers for Disease Control and Prevention (CDC), June 17, 2014.

3. a pattern of cancers compatible with autosomal dominant inheritance. Both males and females can inherit and transmit an autosomal dominant cancer predisposition gene.

Additional factors coupled with family history—such as reproductive history, oral contraceptive and hormone replacement use, radiation exposure early in life, alcohol consumption, and physical activity—can influence an individual's risk of developing cancer.

Risk assessment models have been developed to clarify an individual's

1. lifetime risk of developing breast and/or gynecologic cancer;

2. likelihood of having a mutation in BRCA1 or BRCA2; and

3. likelihood of having a mutation in one of the mismatch repair genes associated with Lynch syndrome (LS).

Associated Genes and Syndromes

Breast and ovarian cancer are present in several autosomal dominant cancer syndromes, although they are most strongly associated with highly penetrant germline mutations in BRCA1 and BRCA2. Other genes, such as PALB2, TP53 (associated with Li-Fraumeni syndrome), PTEN (associated with Cowden syndrome),CDH1 (associated with diffuse gastric and lobular breast cancer syndrome), and STK11(associated with Peutz-Jeghers syndrome), confer a risk to either or both of these cancers with relatively high penetrance.

Inherited endometrial cancer is most commonly associated with LS, a condition caused by inherited mutations in the highly penetrant mismatch repair genes MLH1, MSH2, MSH6, PMS2, and EPCAM. Colorectal cancer (and, to a lesser extent, ovarian cancer and stomach cancer) is also associated with LS.

Additional genes, such as CHEK2, BRIP1, RAD51, and ATM, are associated with breast and/or gynecologic cancers with moderate penetrance. Genome-wide searches are showing promise in identifying common, low-penetrance susceptibility alleles for many complex diseases, including breast and gynecologic cancers, but the clinical utility of these findings remains uncertain.

Clinical Management

Breast cancer screening strategies, including breast magnetic resonance imaging and mammography, are commonly performed in BRCA mutation carriers and in individuals at increased risk of breast cancer. Initiation of screening is generally recommended at earlier ages and at more frequent intervals in individuals with an increased risk due to genetics and family history than in the general population. There is evidence to demonstrate that these strategies have utility in early detection of cancer. In contrast, there is currently no evidence to demonstrate that gynecologic cancer screening using cancer antigen 125 testing and transvaginal ultrasound leads to early detection of cancer.

Risk-reducing surgeries, including risk-reducing mastectomy (RRM) and risk-reducing salpingo-oophorectomy (RRSO), have been shown to significantly reduce the risk of developing breast and/or ovarian cancer and improve overall survival in BRCA1 and BRCA2 mutation carriers. Chemoprevention strategies, including the use of tamoxifen and oral contraceptives, have also been examined in this population. Tamoxifen use has been shown to reduce the risk of contralateral breast cancer among BRCA1 and BRCA2 mutation carriers after treatment for breast cancer, but there are limited data in the primary cancer prevention setting to suggest that it reduces the risk of breast cancer among healthy female BRCA2 mutation carriers. The use of oral contraceptives has been associated with a protective effect on the risk of developing ovarian cancer, including in BRCA1 and BRCA2 mutation carriers, with no association of increased risk of breast cancer when using formulations developed after 1975.

Psychosocial and Behavioral Issues

Psychosocial factors influence decisions about genetic testing for inherited cancer risk and risk-management strategies. Uptake of genetic testing varies widely across studies. Psychological factors that have been associated with testing uptake include cancer-specific distress and perceived risk of developing breast or ovarian cancer. Studies have shown low levels of distress after genetic testing for both carriers and non carriers, particularly in the longer term. Uptake of RRM and RRSO also varies across studies, and may be influenced by factors such as cancer history, age, family history, recommendations of the health care provider, and pretreatment genetic education and counseling. Patients' communication with their family members about an inherited risk of breast and gynecologic cancer is complex; gender, age, and the degree of relatedness are some elements that affect disclosure of this information. Research is ongoing to better understand and address psychosocial and behavioral issues in high-risk families.

Study Reveals Genomic Similarities between Breast and Ovarian Cancers

One subtype of breast cancer shares many genetic features with high-grade serous ovarian cancer, a cancer that is very difficult to treat, according to researchers supported by the National Institutes of Health. The findings suggest that the two cancers are of similar molecular origin, which may facilitate the comparison of therapeutic data for subtypes of breast and ovarian cancers.

The researchers, using data generated as part of The Cancer Genome Atlas (TCGA), described new insights into the four standard molecular subtypes based on a comprehensive characterization of samples from 825 breast cancer patients.

The study, a collaborative effort funded by the National Cancer Institute (NCI) and the National Human Genome Research Institute (NHGRI), both part of NIH, was published online September 23, 2012, and in print Oct. 4, 2012, in the journal Nature.

"TCGA's comprehensive characterization of their high-quality samples allows researchers an unprecedented look at these breast cancer subgroups," said NIH Director Francis S. Collins, M.D., Ph.D.

Analyses of genomic data have confirmed that there are four primary subtypes of breast cancer, each with its own biology and survival outlooks. These TCGA findings are based on a large number of breast cancer specimens that capture a complete view of the genomic alterations. The four groups are called intrinsic subtypes of breast cancer: HER2-enriched (HER2E), Luminal A (LumA), Luminal B (LumB) and Basal-like. A fifth type, called Normal-like, was observed, but because of small numbers (only eight specimens) the researchers were unable to rigorously study it.

The TCGA Research Network uncovered marked genomic similarities between the Basal-like subtype and serous ovarian cancer. The mutation spectrum, or types and frequencies of genomic mutations, were largely the same in both cancer types. Further analyses identified several additional common genomic features, such as gene mutation frequency, suggesting that diverse genomic aberrations can converge into a limited number of cancer subtypes.

Computational analyses show that Basal-like breast cancer and serous ovarian cancer might both be susceptible to agents that inhibit blood vessel growth, cutting off the blood supply to the tumor, as well as to compounds that target DNA repair, which include chemotherapy drugs such as cisplatin.

The Basal-like subgroup has also been called Triple Negative Breast Cancer because many, though not all, Basal-like tumors are negative when tested for three receptors: the estrogen receptor, the progesterone receptor and human epidermal growth factor receptor 2 (HER2). These receptors can trigger potent cell growth responses and act like a nametag, identifying the cell to the environment. The absence of these receptors means that treatments that target them will most likely be ineffective.

"The molecular similarity of one of the principal subtypes of breast cancer to that found in ovarian cancer gives us additional leverage to compare treatments and outcomes across these two cancers," noted Harold Varmus, M.D., NCI director. "This treasure trove of genetic information will need to be examined in great detail to identify how we can use it functionally and clinically."

According to the World Health Organization, there are approximately 1.3 million new cases of breast cancer and 450,000 deaths worldwide annually. Breast cancer is the most common cancer among women. The majority of cases are sporadic, meaning there is not a family history of breast cancer, as opposed to genetic, where genes predispose a person to the disease. Men can also develop breast cancer, but it accounts for less than 1 percent of breast cancer cases.

Breast cancer tumors that have the HER2 receptor are called HER2-positive, and those that don't are called HER2-negative. When researchers analyzed the genomic findings from tumors determined to be HER2-positive by standard cellular tests, they found that only half of the samples could be characterized as belonging to the HER2E subtype. The other half were characterized as Luminal subtypes, suggesting that there are at least two types of clinically defined HER2-positive tumors.

In general, the Luminal subtypes had the lowest overall mutation rate, but by contrast, had the largest number of genes observed to be significantly mutated. This suggests that each of the genes identified as significantly mutated in the Luminal subtypes is more likely to be important in fueling cancer progression. The Luminal subtypes are characterized by the specific expression signature of multiple so-called transcription-factor genes, including ESR1, GATA3, FOXA1, XBP1 and cMYB. These genes have a complex interaction, cooperating in an orchestrated series of activations. GATA3 and FOXA1 are frequently mutated, but those mutations are mutually exclusive, meaning that mutations were observed in either GATA3 or FOXA1 but never in both. However, ERS1 and XBP1 are highly expressed but infrequently mutated.

The scale of the TCGA program allows researchers to perform the integrative analyses that detect these complex patterns of genomic changes and interactions. This close inspection of the cancer genome has led to a deeper understanding of the mutations essential for cancer progression, and several new candidates were identified in this study. The authors hope that discovery of these mutations will be a crucial step toward improving breast cancer therapies.

Breast and Ovarian Cancer and Family Health History

Breast cancer is the most common form of cancer in women. About 7 out of 100 women (or 7%) will get breast cancer by age 70; about 1 out of 100 women (or 1%) will get ovarian cancer by age 70. While ovarian cancer is less common, it is much harder to detect and often more serious. Most breast and ovarian cancers occur in women after the age of 50.

The Importance of Family Health History

Family health history is an important factor affecting a woman's risk for developing breast and ovarian cancer. Every woman should be aware of these cancers in her family. In general, the more close relatives who have had breast or ovarian cancer, and the earlier their ages of diagnosis, the greater a woman's risk. Close relatives include parents, sisters, brothers, children, aunts, uncles, grandparents, nieces, nephews, and grandchildren.

The majority of women in the general population have family histories that mean they are at average risk. Some women with breast or ovarian cancer in their families will have a somewhat increased or moderate risk. Only about 2% of women will have a family history that is considered strong. In some families with a strong history, genetic testing may be helpful.

Breast and Ovarian Cancer and Family History Risk Categories

This chart provides information about average, moderate and strong family histories of breast and ovarian cancer. This may help you understand if you have an increased risk for these cancers based on your family history.

Note: Not all families may be found in this table. If you have concerns about your family history of breast or ovarian cancer please talk to your doctor.

Table 5.1. Breast and Ovarian Cancer and Family History Risk Categories

Risk Category	Family History	Example	Effect on Cancer Risk	What You Can Do
Average	No first- or second-degree relatives with breast or ovarian cancer or Just one second-degree female relative with cancer of one breast diagnosed after age 50	Grandmother with breast cancer diagnosed at age 75	Typically not increased, similar to the general population risk	• Mammograms or other breast exams (learn more) • Make choices to reduce your risk (learn more) • Discuss any concerns with your healthcare provider **Genetic testing is not typically useful for this type of family**
Moderate	Mammograms or other breast exams (learn more) Make choices to reduce your risk (learn more) Discuss any concerns with your healthcare provider or Two first- or second-degree relatives (female) with cancer of one breast diagnosed after age 50 or Just one first- or second-degree relative with ovarian cancer	Mother with breast cancer diagnosed at age 68 and maternal aunt (mother's sister) with breast cancer diagnosed at 62 or Sister with ovarian cancer	Somewhat higher than the general population risk, but most women from these types of families will not develop breast or ovarian cancer	Taking action may be of greater benefit for women with a moderate versus average risk family history. • Mammograms or other breast exams • Make choices to reduce your risk • Discuss any concerns with your healthcare provider **Genetic testing is unlikely to be useful for this type of family** Exception for families of Jewish ancestry

Table 5.1. Continued

Risk Category	Family History	Example	Effect on Cancer Risk	What You Can Do
Strong	One (or more) first- or second-degree relative(s) with: • Primary cancer of both breasts • Both breast and ovarian cancer in the same relative • Male breast cancer or Two or more first- or second-degree relatives with: • Breast cancer, if at least one breast cancer was diagnosed before age 50. • Breast and ovarian cancer in different relatives. • Ovarian cancer, diagnosed at any age. or Three or more first- or second-degree relatives with breast cancer at any age.	Sister with breast cancer diagnosed at age 40, paternal aunt (father's sister) with breast cancer diagnosed at age 45, paternal grandmother (father's mother) with ovarian cancer	Not all women in these families will develop breast or ovarian cancer, but risk is much higher than general population	• Talk with your healthcare provider about genetic counseling for cancer risk Genetic testing may be useful for this type of family.

Chapter 6

Breast Cancer in Young Women

Young Women Can and Do Get Breast Cancer

Most breast cancers are found in women who are 50 years old or older, but breast cancer also affects younger women. About 11% of all new cases of breast cancer in the United States are found in women younger than 45 years of age.

Who Has a Higher Risk?

Some young women are at a higher risk for getting breast cancer at an early age compared with other women their age. If you are a woman under age 45, you may have a higher risk if you have

- Close relatives who were diagnosed with breast or ovarian cancer when they were younger than 45, especially if more than one relative was diagnosed or if a male relative had breast cancer.

- Changes in your BRCA1 or BRCA2 genes, or close relatives with these changes.

- An Ashkenazi Jewish heritage.

This chapter includes text excerpted from "Breast Cancer in Young Women," Centers for Disease Control and Prevention (CDC), October 15, 2015.

- Been treated with radiation therapy to the breast or chest during childhood or early adulthood.

- Had breast cancer or certain other breast health problems.

- Been told that you have dense breasts on a mammogram.

What Can I Do to Lower My Risk?

It is important that you

- **Know how your breasts normally look and feel.** If you notice a change in the size or shape of your breast, feel pain in your breast, have nipple discharge other than breast milk (including blood), or other symptoms, talk to a doctor right away.

- **Make healthy choices.** Keeping a healthy weight, getting enough physical activity and sleep, and breastfeeding your babies can help lower your overall risk. If you are taking, or have been told to take, hormone replacement therapy or oral contraceptives (birth control pills), ask your doctor about the risks.

- **Talk to your doctor if you have a higher risk.** If your risk is high, your doctor may talk to you about getting mammograms earlier and more often than other women, whether other screening tests might be right for you, and medicines or surgeries that can lower your risk. Your doctor may also suggest that you get genetic counseling to determine if you should be tested for changes in your BRCA1, BRCA2, and other genes related to breast cancer.

Chapter 7

Breast Cancer in Men

How Common Male Breast Cancer Is

Breast cancer is a disease usually associated with women, as reflected by pink ribbons and gear, but men get it too, albeit rarely.

Because male breast cancer is rare, the U.S. Food and Drug Administration (FDA) doesn't have very good clinical trial data on treatments. "We tend to treat men the same way we treat women," says Tatiana M. Prowell, MD, a medical oncologist and breast cancer scientific lead at FDA's Office of Hematology and Oncology Products.

"Men have historically been excluded from breast cancer trials," she adds. "We are actively encouraging drug companies to include men in all breast cancer trials unless there is a valid scientific reason not to. The number of men in breast cancer trials will still be small because male breast cancer is a rare condition, but any information to help men facing this disease is better than none."

Men versus Women

Each year, about 2,000 cases of male breast cancer (1% of all cases) are diagnosed in the United States, resulting in fewer than 500 deaths, according to the National Cancer Institute. Although it can strike at any age, the disease is usually diagnosed in men 5 to 10 years older than in women and is found most often among men ages 60 to 70.

This chapter includes text excerpted from "Breast Cancer—Men Get It Too," U.S. Food and Drug Administration (FDA), June 27, 2014.

Prowell says one reason for the late-age (and later stage) diagnosis may be that men don't think of themselves as being at risk of breast cancer. "You'd think that because men have smaller breasts they would notice a lump instantly," Prowell says. "But men don't expect a breast lump to be cancer, whereas most women who feel a breast lump immediately assume the worst."

Most men with breast cancer have painless lumps they can feel. The lumps can develop anywhere on the breast but often are underneath the nipple and areola complex—right in the center. Because men don't have regular mammograms, their breast cancer is usually discovered when they feel sore, such as from a fall or injury.

"Men often attribute breast lumps to some sort of injury. The mass was already there, but they didn't notice it until it got sore," Prowell says.

Men and women share some similar risk factors for breast cancer: high levels of estrogen exposure, a family history of the disease and a history of radiation to the chest. Although all men have estrogen in their bodies, obesity, cirrhosis (liver disease) and Klinefelter's syndrome (a genetic disorder) increase estrogen levels. All are known risk factors for male breast cancer.

If a first-degree relative—their mother, father, brother, sister, children—has breast cancer, men are also at slightly higher risk to develop the disease themselves. Men who have a BRCA mutation (a mutation or change in a gene that predisposes them to breast cancer) are at a greater risk. While their chance of developing breast cancer is still low (only about 5% to 6%), men with a mutation in BRCA2 have a 100-fold greater risk of developing breast cancer than men in the general population.

"In men and women, having a tumor with estrogen and progesterone hormone receptors is more common than not—but that appears to be even more true in men," Prowell adds.

Treating Male Breast Cancer

Treatment options for men are similar to women's: mastectomy (surgery to remove the breast) or in some cases lumpectomy, radiation, chemotherapy, targeted therapies and hormone therapy.

"Our data on treatments for men are largely based from trials that were conducted in women, or they are retrospective data from a collection of men who were treated over a period of time. We don't have large randomized trials or high-level evidence for treatment of breast cancer in men as we do for women," Prowell says.

Hormonal drug treatments include tamoxifen, a selective estrogen receptor modulator (SERM) that inhibits estrogen receptors, and aromatase inhibitors, which block the production of estrogen from androgens such as testosterone.

"For postmenopausal women, we preferentially use aromatase inhibitors as first-line treatment for early stage breast cancer, and regard tamoxifen as an alternative. It's the opposite for men because what data we have suggest that aromatase inhibitors don't work as well in men. So for men, aromatase inhibitors are usually an alternative or second-line treatment, after tamoxifen," Prowell says.

For men with larger tumors, positive lymph nodes or cancer that has spread, chemotherapy is often recommended in addition to hormonal treatment, just as it is for women. And men with tumors that are HER2-positive are recommended to receive treatment with trastuzumab, an antibody that targets HER2, just as women are.

Genetic Counseling Is a Must

All men with breast cancer should be referred for genetic counseling, Prowell advises.

That's another difference from women, who are not automatically referred to a genetic counselor for genetic testing, such as for mutations in BRCA-1 or 2. These "tumor suppressor genes" allow breast and other types of cancer to develop when they fail to function normally. Only women with a significant family history or certain other characteristics, such as being young or having triple-negative breast cancer (which don't have estrogen, progesterone or HER2 receptors), are recommended to have genetic testing.

Even among men there are differences. African American men are more likely than white men to have advanced stage tumors at diagnosis and to develop triple-negative cancers. Their types of tumors are more likely to recur and have fewer treatment options.

People should tell their healthcare provider if any man in their family has had breast cancer. Prowell says. "Even if your grandfather is deceased, if he had breast cancer, that's important for your health care provider to know. Because male breast cancer is so rare, seeing just one man in a family lineage raises concerns about hereditary breast cancer."

Chapter 8

Breast Cancer among Children and Adolescents

Fibroadenoma

The most frequent breast tumor seen in children is a fibroadenoma. These tumors can be observed and many will regress without a need for surgical resection. However, rare malignant transformation leading to phyllodes tumors has been reported. Sudden rapid enlargement of a suspected fibroadenoma is an indication for needle biopsy or excision.

General Care for Fibroadenoma

Phyllodes tumors can be managed by wide local excision without mastectomy.

Incidence and Outcome

Breast cancer has been reported in both males and females younger than 21 years. A review of the Surveillance, Epidemiology, and End Results (SEER) database of the National Cancer Institute shows that 75 cases of malignant breast tumors in females aged 19 years or younger were identified from 1973 to 2004. Fifteen percent

This chapter includes text excerpted from "Unusual Cancers of Childhood Treatment–Health Professional Version (PDQ®)," National Cancer Institute (NCI), March 8, 2016.

51

of these patients had *in situ* disease, 85% had invasive disease, 55% of the tumors were carcinomas, and 45% of the tumors were sarcomas—most of which were phyllodes tumors. Only three patients in the carcinoma group presented with metastatic disease, while 11 patients (27%) had regionally advanced disease. All patients with sarcomas presented with localized disease. Of the carcinoma patients, 85% underwent surgical resection, and 10% received adjuvant radiation therapy. Of the sarcoma patients, 97% had surgical resection, and 9% received radiation. The 5- and 10-year survival rates for patients with sarcomatous tumors were both 90%; for patients with carcinomas, the 5-year survival rate was 63% and the 10-year survival rate was 54%.

Breast tumors may also occur as metastatic deposits from leukemia, rhabdomyosarcoma, other sarcomas, or lymphoma (particularly in patients who are infected with the human immunodeficiency virus).

Risk Factors

Risk factors for breast cancer in adolescents and young adults include the following:

1. **Previous malignancy.** A retrospective review of the American College of Surgeons National Cancer Database from 1998 to 2010 identified 106,771 patients aged 15 to 39 years with breast cancer. Of these patients, 6,241 (5.8%) had experienced a previous histologically distinct malignancy. Patients with breast cancer as a subsequent neoplasm had a significantly decreased 3-year overall survival (79% versus 88.5%, P <.001), with subsequent neoplasm status identified as an independent risk factor for increased mortality (hazard ratio, 1.58; 95% confidence interval, 1.41–1.77).

2. **Chest irradiation.** There is an increased lifetime risk of breast cancer in female survivors of Hodgkin lymphoma who were treated with radiation to the chest area; however, breast cancer is also seen in patients who were treated for any cancer that was treated with chest irradiation. Carcinomas are more frequent than sarcomas. Mammograms with adjunctive breast magnetic resonance imaging (MRI) start at age 25 years or 10 years postexposure to radiation therapy (whichever came last).

Treatment of Breast Cancer in Adolescents and Young Adults (AYA)

Breast cancer is the most frequently diagnosed cancer among AYA women aged 15 to 39 years, accounting for about 14% of all AYA cancer diagnoses. Breast cancer in this age group has a more aggressive course and worse outcome than in older women. Expression of hormone receptors for estrogen, progesterone, and human epidermal growth factor 2 (HER2) on breast cancer in the AYA group is also different from that in older women and correlates with a worse prognosis.

Treatment of the AYA group is similar to that of older women. However, unique aspects of management must include attention to genetic implications (i.e., familial breast cancer syndromes) and fertility.

Chapter 9

Statistics on Breast Cancer in the United States

Statistics at a Glance

Number of New Cases and Deaths per 100,000: The number of new cases of female breast cancer was 124.8 per 100,000 women per year. The number of deaths was 21.9 per 100,000 women per year. These rates are age-adjusted and based on 2008-2012 cases and deaths.

Lifetime Risk of Developing Cancer: Approximately 12.3 percent of women will be diagnosed with female breast cancer at some point during their lifetime, based on 2010-2012 data.

Prevalence of This Cancer: In 2012, there were an estimated 2,975,314 women living with female breast cancer in the United States.

This chapter contains text excerpted from the following sources: Text beginning with the heading "Statistics at a Glance" is excerpted from "SEER Stat Fact Sheets: Female Breast Cancer," National Cancer Institute (NCI), October 2013; Text beginning with the heading "Breast Cancer Rates by Race and Ethnicity" is excerpted from "Breast Cancer Rates by Race and Ethnicity," Centers for Disease Control and Prevention (CDC), August 20, 2015; Text under the heading "Analysis on Breast Cancer Subtypes and Annual Report on Mortality and Incidence Rates of Cancer" is excerpted from "New Analysis of Breast Cancer Subtypes Could Lead to Better Risk Stratification; Annual Report to the Nation Shows That Mortality and Incidence for Most Cancers Continue to Decline," National Cancer Institute (NCI), March 30, 2015.

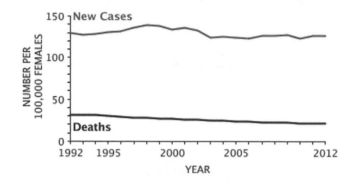

Figure 9.1. *Statistics at a Glance (a)*

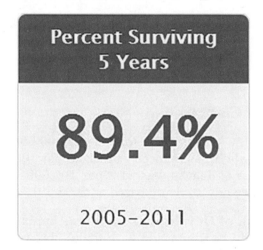

Figure 9.2. *Statistics at a Glance (b)*

Survival Statistics

How Many People Survive 5 Years or More after Being Diagnosed with Female Breast Cancer?

Relative survival statistics compare the survival of patients diagnosed with cancer with the survival of people in the general population who are the same age, race, and sex and who have not been diagnosed with cancer. Because survival statistics are based on large groups of people, they cannot be used to predict exactly what will happen to an individual patient. No two patients are entirely alike, and treatment and responses to treatment can vary greatly.

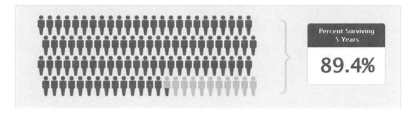

Figure 9.3. *Relative Survival Statistics*

Based on data from SEER 18 2005-2011. Dark figures represent those who have survived 5 years or more. Gray figures represent those who have died from female breast cancer.

Survival by Stage

Cancer stage at diagnosis, which refers to extent of a cancer in the body, determines treatment options and has a strong influence on the length of survival. In general, if the cancer is found only in the part of the body where it started it is *localized* (sometimes referred to as stage 1). If it has spread to a different part of the body, the stage is *regional* or *distant*. The earlier female breast cancer is caught, the better chance a person has of surviving five years after being diagnosed. For female breast cancer, 61.1% are diagnosed at the local stage. The 5-year survival for localized female breast cancer is 98.6%.

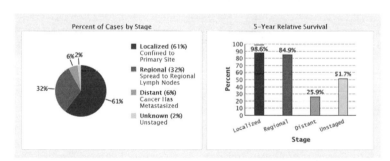

Figure 9.4. *Percent of Cases and 5-Year Relative Survival by Stage at Diagnosis: Female Breast Cancer*

SEER 18 2005-2011, All Races, Females by SEER Summary Stage 2000

Number of New Cases and Deaths

How Common Is This Cancer?

Compared to other cancers, female breast cancer is fairly common.

Common Types of Cancer	Estimated New Cases 2015	Estimated Deaths 2015
1. Breast Cancer (Female)	231,840	40,290
2. Lung and Bronchus Cancer	221,200	158,040
3. Prostate Cancer	220,800	27,540
4. Colon and Rectum Cancer	132,700	49,700
5. Bladder Cancer	74,000	16,000
6. Melanoma of the Skin	73,870	9,940
7. Non–Hodgkin Lymphoma	71,850	19,790
8. Thyroid Cancer	62,450	1,950
9. Kidney and Renal Pelvis Cancer	61,560	14,080
10. Endometrial Cancer	54,870	10,170

Female breast cancer represents 14.0% of all new cancer cases in the U.S.

14.0%

Figure 9.5. *Incidence of Breast Cancer Compared to Other Cancer Types*

Who Gets This Cancer?

Female breast cancer is most common in middle-aged and older women. Although rare, men can develop breast cancer as well. The number of new cases of female breast cancer was 124.8 per 100,000 women per year based on 2008-2012 cases.

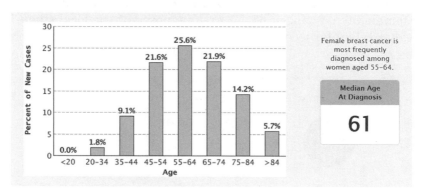

Female breast cancer is most frequently diagnosed among women aged 55–64.

Median Age At Diagnosis

61

Figure 9.6. *Percent of New Cases by Age Group: Female Breast Cancer*

SEER 18 2008-2012, All Races, Females

Who Dies from This Cancer?

Overall, female breast cancer survival is good. However, women who are diagnosed at an advanced age may be more likely than younger women to die of the disease. Female breast cancer is the fourth leading cause of cancer death in the United States. The number of deaths was 21.9 per 100,000 women per year based on 2008–2012.

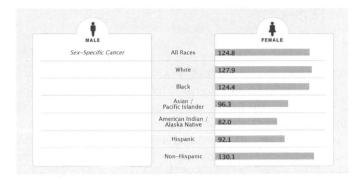

Figure 9.7. *Number of New Cases per 100,000 Persons by Race/Ethnicity: Female Breast Cancer*

SEER 18 2008-2012, Age-Adjusted

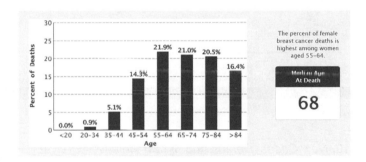

Figure 9.8. *Percent of Deaths by Age Group: Female Breast Cancer*

U.S. 2008-2012, All Races, Females

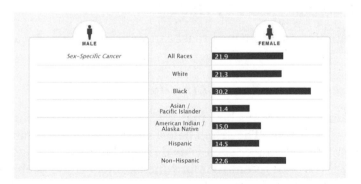

Figure 9.9. *Number of Deaths per 100,000 Persons by Race/Ethnicity: Female Breast Cancer*

U.S. 2008-2012, Age-Adjusted

Trends in Rates

Changes over Time

Keeping track of the number of new cases, deaths, and survival over time (trends) can help scientists understand whether progress is being made and where additional research is needed to address challenges, such as improving screening or finding better treatments.

Using statistical models for analysis, rates for new female breast cancer cases have been stable over the last 10 years. Death rates have been falling on average 1.9% each year over 2003-2012. 5-year survival trends are shown below the figure.

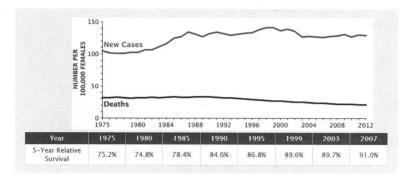

Year	1975	1980	1985	1990	1995	1999	2003	2007
5-Year Relative Survival	75.2%	74.8%	78.4%	84.6%	86.8%	89.6%	89.7%	91.0%

Figure 9.10. *New Cases, Deaths and 5-Year Relative Survival*

SEER 9 Incidence and U.S. Mortality 1975-2012, All Races, Females. Rates are Age-Adjusted.

Breast Cancer Rates by Race and Ethnicity

The rate of women getting breast cancer or dying from breast cancer varies by race and ethnicity.

Incidence Rates by Race / Ethnicity

"Incidence rate" means how many women out of a given number get the disease each year. The graph below shows how many women out of 100,000 got breast cancer each year during the years 1999–2012. The year 2012 is the most recent year for which numbers have been reported. The breast cancer incidence rate is grouped by race and ethnicity.

The graph below shows that in 2012, white women had the highest rate of getting breast cancer, followed by black, Hispanic, Asian/Pacific Islander, and American Indian/Alaska Native women.

Death Rates by Race / Ethnicity

From 1999–2012, the rate of women dying from breast cancer has varied, depending on their race and ethnicity. The graph below shows that in 2012, black women were more likely to die of breast cancer than any other group, followed by white, Hispanic, Asian/Pacific Islander, and American Indian/Alaska Native women.

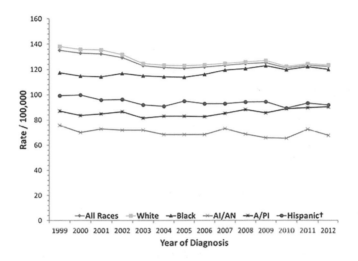

Figure 9.11. *Female Breast Cancer: Incidence Rates* by Race and Ethnicity, U.S., 1999–2012*

Incidence source: *Combined data from the National Program of Cancer Registries as submitted to CDC and from the Surveillance, Epidemiology and End Results program as submitted to the National Cancer Institute in November 2014. *Rates are per 100,000 and are age-adjusted to the 2000 U.S. standard population (19 age groups – Census P25-1130). Incidence rates are for state registries that meet USCS publication criteria for all years, 1999–2012. Incidence rates cover about 92% of the U.S. population.*
†Hispanic origin is not mutually exclusive from race categories (white, black, Asian/ Pacific Islander, American Indian/Alaska Native).

Analysis on Breast Cancer Subtypes and Annual Report on Mortality and Incidence Rates of Cancer

For the first time, researchers have used national data to determine the incidence of the four major molecular subtypes of breast cancer by age, race/ethnicity, poverty level, and several other factors. These four subtypes respond differently to treatment and have different survival rates. The new data will help researchers more accurately stratify breast cancer by clinically relevant degrees of risk and potentially have an impact on breast cancer treatment. Moreover, armed with this information, women will be able to better understand the implications for their health based on their breast cancer subtype.

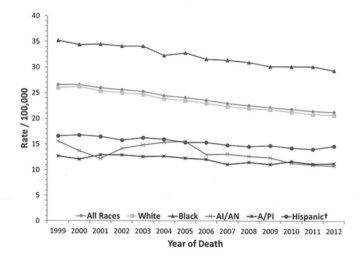

Figure 9.12. *Female Breast Cancer: Death Rates* by Race and Ethnicity, U.S., 1999–2012*

Mortality source*: U.S. Mortality Files, National Center for Health Statistics, CDC. *Rates are per 100,000 and are age-adjusted to the 2000 U.S. standard population (19 age groups – Census P25-1130). Death rates cover 100% of the U.S. population. †Hispanic origin is not mutually exclusive from race categories (white, black, Asian/ Pacific Islander, American Indian/Alaska Native).*

These findings, along with statistical analyses of the most common types of cancer, were reported today in JNCI. "The Annual Report to the Nation on the Status of Cancer, 1975-2011" showed continuing declines in cancer deaths for both men and women, for children, and for nearly all major cancer sites. The report was co-authored by experts from the North American Association of Central Cancer Registries (NAACCR), the American Cancer Society (ACS), the Centers for Disease Control and Prevention (CDC), and the National Cancer Institute (NCI) at the National Institutes of Health.

Breast cancer subtypes have major implications for determining treatment and may hold important clues to the origins of breast cancer. There are four molecular subtypes, which can be approximated by their hormone receptor (HR) status and expression of the

HER2 gene: Luminal A (HR+/HER2-), Luminal B (HR+/HER2+), HER2-enriched (HR-/HER2+), and triple negative (HR-/HER2-). These subtypes are now being recorded by cancer registries across the nation, giving statisticians the ability for the first time to comprehensively examine breast cancer rates based on clinically meaningful subtypes.

The new report suggests that some of the differences in rates of breast cancer incidence and mortality across racial and ethnic groups are related to differences in the incidence of different subtypes. Geographic variation in rates that the authors observed were based on multiple factors, including underlying demographic patterns, regional cultures and associated behaviors, as well as access to care.

The researchers found unique racial/ethnic group-specific patterns by age, poverty level, geography, and by specific tumor characteristics. Rates of HR+/HER2- breast cancer, the least aggressive subtype, were highest among non-Hispanic whites, aligning with previously reported findings. Rates of HR+/HER2- breast cancer decreased with increasing levels of poverty for every racial and ethnic group. Also consistent with prior studies, non-Hispanic blacks had higher incidence rates of the most aggressive breast cancer subtype, triple negative, than other racial/ethnic groups.

Non-Hispanic blacks also had the highest rates of late-stage disease and of poorly/undifferentiated pathology among all the subtypes. All of these factors are associated with lower survival and correspond with blacks having the highest rates of breast cancer deaths.

"In addition to confirming the largely encouraging trends in cancer mortality rates for men, women, and children, this year's report assesses breast cancer as four molecularly defined subtypes, not as a single disease. This is a welcome step, depending on medically important information that already guides therapeutic strategies for these subtypes," said NCI Director Harold Varmus, M.D. "Further, it is a harbinger of the more rigorous classification of cancers based on their molecular features that is now being aggressively pursued under the President's Precision Medicine Initiative. The new diagnostic categories now being defined will increasingly support our ability to prevent and treat breast and many other kinds of cancer, as well as monitor their incidence and outcomes more rigorously over time."

The report also details trends in incidence and death rates of many major cancers and all cancers combined. Overall cancer incidence -- new cases of cancer—continued to decrease in men, remained stable in women, and increased in children. The authors also found that there has been a relatively consistent decline in overall cancer mortality rates since the early 1990s, with rates from 2002 to 2011 decreasing by about 1.8 percent per year among males and by 1.4 percent per year among females. Among children up to 19 years old, mortality rates have continued to decrease since 1975, with the exception of the period between 1998 and 2003.

"The continued decline in cancer death rates among men, women, and children is encouraging, and it reflects progress we are making in cancer prevention, early detection, and treatment," said CDC Director Tom Frieden, M.D. "However, the continuing high burden of preventable cancer, and disparities in death rates among races and ethnicities, show that we still have a long way to go."

For the most recent reporting period, the rate of decline in lung cancer incidence and mortality has accelerated in both men and women, most likely reflecting sustained public health efforts to decrease smoking rates. Colorectal cancer incidence and mortality among both men and women, and prostate cancer incidence and mortality in men, continue the downward trends seen in previous years.

"The drop in incidence in lung and colorectal cancers shows the lifesaving impact of prevention," said John R Seffrin, Ph.D., American Cancer Society Chief Executive Officer. "But we have a long way to go, not only in these two cancers but in the many other cancers where the trend has not been so positive."

Overall cancer incidence rates decreased by 0.5 percent per year from 2002 to 2011. Among men, incidence rates decreased an average of 1.8 percent per year from 2007 to 2011; incidence rates were stable in women from 1998 to 2011. Among children up to 19 years of age, incidence rates have increased by 0.8 percent per year over the past decade, continuing a trend dating from 1992 whose cause remains uncertain.

The report also noted some trends that require greater evaluation:

- Incidence rates of thyroid and kidney cancers are increasing among both men and women. Increases in rates for new cases of thyroid and kidney cancers may be due to several factors, but no increase in mortality has been noted for these diseases.

- Incidence and mortality rates of liver cancer are increasing among both men and women. These increases may reflect, in part, increasing rates of hepatitis C and/or behavioral risk factors, such as alcohol abuse, for which there are opportunities for intervention

- Unlike the declines in incidence of other tobacco-related cancers, incidence rates are increasing for oral/oropharyngeal cancers overall among white men. This may be associated with increased

HPV-associated oropharyngeal cancers, despite a decline in those oral cancers that are more closely associated with tobacco use.

- Incidence and mortality rates are increasing for uterine cancer among white, black, and Asian Pacific Islander women, with the largest increase seen in black women. The cause of these increases is unknown.

Part Two

Types of Breast Cancer

Chapter 10

Breast Cancer and Its Types

What Is Breast Cancer, and What Type Do I Have?

Cancer is a disease in which cells become abnormal and form more cells in an uncontrolled way. With breast cancer, the cancer begins in the tissues that make up the breasts. The cancerous cells may form a mass of tissue called a malignant tumor. The cells of a malignant tumor may spread to other parts of the body and threaten life. (*Benign tumors* are abnormal growths that are not cancer. The cells of a benign tumor do not spread to other parts of the body and do not threaten life.)

The most common types of breast cancer are:

- **Lobular carcinoma**—Cancer that begins in the glands of the breast that make milk. These milk-making glands are called *lobules*. About 1 in 10 breast cancers are this type.

- **Ductal carcinoma**—Cancer that begins in the milk ducts of the breast. Milk ducts are thin tubes that carry milk from the lobules to the nipple. About 8 in 10 breast cancers are this type.

In addition, there are two types of breast tumors that are not cancer but increase the risk of breast cancer:

- **Ductal carcinoma in situ (DCIS)**—DCIS is a condition in which abnormal cells are found in the lining of breast ducts.

This chapter includes text excerpted from "Early-Stage Breast Cancer Treatment Fact Sheet," Office on Women's Health (OWH), U.S. Department of Health and Human Services (HHS), July 16, 2012. Reviewed April 2016.

These cells have not spread outside the duct to the surrounding breast tissue. But some cases of DCIS become breast cancer over time. So DCIS is sometimes called Stage 0 breast cancer. Since it's not possible to know which cases of DCIS will become breast cancer, it's important to get treatment for DCIS. Women with DCIS often are treated with breast-sparing surgery and radiation therapy. Radiation therapy lowers the chance that DCIS will come back or develop into breast cancer. If a large area of DCIS is found or it is found in more than one location, some women will choose to have a mastectomy. Underarm lymph nodes usually are not removed in the treatment of DCIS. The drug tamoxifen, which stops the growth of breast tumors that depend on estrogen, is also sometimes used in the treatment of DCIS. Tamoxifen may decrease the risk of a breast cancer developing in the same breast after treatment or in the opposite breast.

- **Lobular carcinoma in situ (LCIS)**—LCIS is a condition in which abnormal cells are found in breast lobules. In contrast with DCIS, there is no evidence that the abnormal cells will become cancerous. However, having LCIS means that a woman has an increased risk of developing breast cancer in either breast. Despite this increased risk, most women with LCIS will never get breast cancer. Most women with LCIS are followed closely with regular checkups and mammograms. Some women choose to take tamoxifen to decrease their risk of developing breast cancer. Rarely, women with LCIS choose to have both breasts removed as a preventive measure, but most doctors think this approach is inappropriate.

What Does "Early-Stage" Breast Cancer Mean?

Breast cancer is categorized as Stage I, II (A or B), III (A, B, or C), or IV. The stage is based on the size of the tumor and whether the cancer has spread. Stages I, IIA, IIB, and IIIA are considered "early-stage" breast cancer and refer to cancers that may have spread to nearby lymph nodes but not to distant parts of the body.

How Does Breast Cancer Spread?

If cancer spreads to other parts of the body, it's called metastasis. Breast cancer can spread to other parts of the body in 3 ways:

1. Invading nearby healthy tissue, such as the chest wall.

2. Invading the lymphatic system. This system, which is part
    of the immune system, contains a network of lymph nodes
    (small, bean-shaped glands) and lymph vessels (thin tubes)
    that are found throughout the body. Lymph vessels carry a
    fluid called lymph to the lymph nodes, where it is filtered and
    checked for signs of infection and disease. Cancer cells can
    enter into lymph vessels in the breast and travel to the lymph
    nodes and other parts of the body. The first place breast cancer
    usually spreads is to the lymph nodes under the arms, called
    axillary lymph nodes. That is why after breast cancer has been
    diagnosed, the underarm lymph nodes are often removed and
    examined to see if breast cancer has spread.

3. Invading blood vessels in the breast. Cancer cells can travel
    through the blood-stream to other parts of the body, such as
    the lungs or bones.

When cancer cells spread, they can cause tumors to grow in other
parts of the body. Breast cancer that forms tumors in other parts of
the body, such as the lungs, is still breast cancer. The good news is
that most breast cancers can be found and treated and do not come
back in distant parts of the body.

Chapter 11

Ductal Carcinoma in Situ (DCIS)

Overview

Ductal carcinoma in situ (DCIS) is a noninvasive condition. DCIS can progress to invasive cancer, but estimates of the probability of this vary widely. Some reports include DCIS in breast cancer statistics. In 2015, DCIS is expected to account for about 16% of all newly diagnosed invasive plus noninvasive breast tumors in the United States. For invasive and noninvasive tumors detected by screening, DCIS accounts for approximately 25% of all cases.

The frequency of a DCIS diagnosis has increased markedly in the United States since the use of screening mammography became widespread. Very few cases of DCIS present as a palpable mass, with more than 90% being diagnosed by mammography alone.

This chapter contains text excerpted from the following sources: Text beginning with the heading "Overview" is excerpted from "Breast Cancer Treatment–Health Professional Version (PDQ®)," National Cancer Institute (NCI), February 2, 2016; Text beginning with the heading "Talk with Your Doctor" is excerpted from "Surgery Choices for Women with DCIS or Breast Cancer," National Cancer Institute (NCI), January 19, 2015; Text under the heading "Risk of Breast Cancer Death Is Low after a Diagnosis of Ductal Carcinoma in Situ" is excerpted from "Risk of Breast Cancer Death Is Low after a Diagnosis of Ductal Carcinoma in Situ," National Cancer Institute (NCI), August 26, 2015.

DCIS comprises a heterogeneous group of histopathologic lesions that have been classified into the following subtypes primarily on the basis of architectural pattern:

- Micropapillary
- Papillary
- Solid
- Cribriform
- Comedo

Comedo-type DCIS consists of cells that appear cytologically malignant, with the presence of high-grade nuclei, pleomorphism, and abundant central luminal necrosis. Comedo-type DCIS appears to be more aggressive, with a higher probability of associated invasive ductal carcinoma.

Learn about the Types of Surgery

Most women with DCIS or breast cancer that can be treated with surgery have three surgery choices.

Breast-Sparing Surgery, Followed by Radiation Therapy

Breast-sparing surgery means the surgeon removes only the DCIS or cancer and some normal tissue around it. If you have cancer, the surgeon will also remove one or more lymph nodes from under your arm. Breast-sparing surgery usually keeps your breast looking much like it did before surgery. Other words for breast-sparing surgery include:

- Lumpectomy
- Partial mastectomy
- Breast-conserving surgery
- Segmental mastectomy

After breast-sparing surgery, most women also receive radiation therapy. The main goal of this treatment is to keep cancer from coming back in the same breast. Some women will also need chemotherapy, hormone therapy, and/or targeted therapy.

Mastectomy

In a mastectomy, the surgeon removes the whole breast that contains the DCIS or cancer. There are two main types of mastectomy. They are:

- Total (simple) mastectomy. The surgeon removes your whole breast. Sometimes, the surgeon also takes out one or more of the lymph nodes under your arm.

- Modified radical mastectomy. The surgeon removes your whole breast, many of the lymph nodes under your arm, and the lining over your chest muscles.

Some women will also need radiation therapy, chemotherapy, hormone therapy, and/or targeted therapy.

If you have a mastectomy, you may choose to wear a prosthesis (breast-like form) in your bra or have breast reconstruction surgery.

Mastectomy with Breast Reconstruction Surgery

You can have breast reconstruction at the same time as the mastectomy, or anytime after. This type of surgery is done by a plastic surgeon with experience in reconstruction surgery. The surgeon uses an implant or tissue from another part of your body to create a breast-like shape that replaces the breast that was removed. The surgeon may also make the form of a nipple and add a tattoo that looks like the areola (the dark area around your nipple).

There are two main types of breast reconstruction surgery:

1. Breast Implant

Breast reconstruction with an implant is often done in steps. The first step is called tissue expansion. This is when the plastic surgeon places a balloon expander under the chest muscle. Over many weeks, saline (salt water) will be added to the expander to stretch the chest muscle and the skin on top of it. This process makes a pocket for the implant.

Once the pocket is the correct size, the surgeon will remove the expander and place an implant (filled with saline or silicone gel) into the pocket. This creates a new breast-like shape. Although this shape looks like a breast, you will not have the same feeling in it because nerves were cut during your mastectomy.

Breast implants do not last a lifetime. If you choose to have an implant, chances are you will need more surgery later on to remove or replace it. Implants can cause problems such as breast hardness, pain, and infection. The implant may also break, move, or shift. These problems can happen soon after surgery or years later.

2. Tissue Flap

In tissue flap surgery, a reconstructive plastic surgeon builds a new breast-like shape from muscle, fat, and skin taken from other parts of your body (usually your belly, back, or buttock). This new breast-like shape should last the rest of your life. Women who are very thin or obese, smoke, or have serious health problems often cannot have tissue flap surgery.

Healing after tissue flap surgery often takes longer than healing after breast implant surgery. You may have other problems, as well. For example, if you have a muscle removed, you might lose strength in the area from which it was taken. Or, you may get an infection or have trouble healing. Tissue flap surgery is best done by a reconstructive plastic surgeon who has special training in this type of surgery and has done it many times before.

Talk with Your Doctor

Talk with a breast cancer surgeon about your choices. Find out what happens during surgery:

- the types of problems that sometimes occur

- any treatment you might need after surgery

Be sure to ask a lot of questions and learn as much as you can. You may also wish to talk with family members, friends, or others who have had surgery.

Get a Second Opinion

After talking with a surgeon, think about getting a second opinion. A second opinion means getting the advice of another surgeon. This surgeon might tell you about other treatment options. Or, he or she may agree with the advice you got from the first doctor.

Some people worry about hurting their surgeon's feelings if they get a second opinion. But, it is very common and good surgeons don't mind. Also, some insurance companies require it. It is better to get a second opinion than worry that you made the wrong choice.

If you think you might have a mastectomy, this is also a good time to learn about breast reconstruction. Think about meeting with a reconstructive plastic surgeon to learn about this surgery and if it seems like a good option for you.

Check with Your Insurance Company

Each insurance plan is different. Knowing how much your plan will pay for each type of surgery, including reconstruction, special bras, prostheses, and other needed treatments can help you decide which surgery is best for you.

Risk of Breast Cancer Death Is Low after a Diagnosis of Ductal Carcinoma in Situ

A new study suggests that women who are diagnosed with abnormal cells in the lining of a breast duct—a noninvasive condition called ductal carcinoma in situ, or DCIS—generally have a low risk of dying from breast cancer. In addition, treating these lesions may help prevent a recurrence in the breast but does not appear to decrease the already-low risk of dying from the disease, even after 20 years of follow-up.

The findings, from an observational study involving more than 100,000 women, were published August 20 in JAMA Oncology. Steven A. Narod, M.D., of the Women's College Hospital, Toronto, and his colleagues used data from NCI's Surveillance, Epidemiology and End Results (SEER) program to estimate the death rate from breast cancer among women diagnosed with DCIS.

DCIS refers to abnormal cells in the breast duct that form characteristic patterns detectable on mammography. In some cases, DCIS may become invasive cancer and spread to other tissues. At this time, because of concerns that a small proportion of the lesions could become

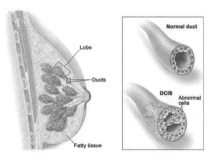

Figure 11.1. *Ductal Carcinoma In Situ (DCIS)*

Ductal carcinoma in situ, or DCIS, is a noninvasive condition in which abnormal cells are found in the lining of a breast duct.

invasive, nearly all women diagnosed with DCIS currently receive some form of treatment.

In the current study, most women received either a lumpectomy (with or without radiation therapy) or a single or double mastectomy. The overall death rate from breast cancer at 20 years after diagnosis was 3.3 percent, a rate similar to that of the general population. The death rates did not vary with the type of treatment used, the researchers noted.

"DCIS has extremely favorable outcomes irrespective of the type of therapy used," said Barry Kramer, M.D., director of NCI's Division of Cancer Prevention, who was not involved in the study. He noted that treatments for DCIS are associated with potential harms. For instance, exposure to radiation therapy increases the risk of developing secondary cancers in the future, and mastectomy can cause serious health problems as well.

Some women with DCIS may be at an increased risk of dying from breast cancer, including those diagnosed at a younger age and African Americans, the study showed. Death rates were higher for women diagnosed before age 35 than for older women (7.8 percent versus 3.2 percent), and higher for African Americans than for Caucasians (7 percent versus 3 percent).

The mean age at diagnosis among women in the study was 54 years old, and less than 1.5 percent of the women with DCIS were under age 35.

The authors of an accompanying editorial said the study's large numbers and long-term follow up provide a compelling case to reconsider how DCIS is treated.

"Given the low breast cancer mortality risk, we should stop telling women that DCIS is an emergency and that they should schedule definitive surgery within 2 weeks of diagnosis," wrote Laura Esserman, M.D., and Christina Yau, Ph.D., of the University of California, San Francisco.

The finding of greatest clinical importance, the study authors noted, was the observation that preventing the development of invasive breast cancer in women diagnosed with DCIS did not reduce the chances of dying from breast cancer. For example, among women who had a lumpectomy, radiation therapy reduced the risk of a recurrence in the same breast compared with women not treated with radiation (2.5 percent versus 4.9 percent), but it did not reduce the risk of death from breast cancer 10 years later (0.8 percent versus 0.9 percent).

"The study showed that even though a lumpectomy can reduce the risk of a recurrence developing in the same breast, it does not change the risk of dying from the disease," said Dr. Kramer. "This suggests that what you do locally to treat DCIS may not affect the risk of dying, which is the most important outcome."

This observation, Dr. Kramer added, "gives us important insights into the biology of DCIS."

In another finding, 517 women diagnosed with DCIS died of breast cancer without ever developing an invasive cancer in the same or other breast prior to death. Some cases of DCIS may have "an inherent potential" to spread to other parts of the body, the study authors wrote.

The finding, Drs. Esserman and Yau concluded, suggests that "our current approach of surgical removal and radiation therapy may not suffice for the rare cases that lead to breast cancer mortality and thus new approaches are needed."

Dr. Kramer agreed that new approaches to managing DCIS are needed and said the new results help set the stage for this work. He cited a potential parallel with prostate cancer and the development of careful follow-up, rather than initial surgery, to manage screen-detected early stage cancers.

"Years ago, it was considered terribly ill advised not to treat prostate cancer," he observed. But as the evidence grew that some prostate cancers detected through screening were slow-growing and better left alone, researchers began to test approaches such as watchful waiting and, later, active surveillance."We are starting to build the evidence to justify these kinds of studies in DCIS," Dr. Kramer said. "We may not be there yet, but this kind of evidence helps us to justify studies to explore new approaches."

Chapter 12

Lobular Carcinoma in Situ (LCIS)

Overview

Lobular carcinoma in situ (LCIS) describes abnormal cell growth that occurs in the lobules, which are tiny milk-producing glands located at the ends of milk ducts in the breasts. Although the term "carcinoma" refers to a cancer in the lining of an organ, LCIS is not technically considered a form of cancer. Left untreated, LCIS does not spread beyond the lobules to surrounding tissues to become invasive carcinoma. As a result, some healthcare professionals prefer the term "lobular neoplasia," which refers to a group of abnormal cells in the lobules. "In situ" means that the abnormal cells are confined to the area where they originally began growing, as is generally found in the earliest forms of breast cancer.

Although LCIS is not considered pre-cancer, studies have shown that women diagnosed with LCIS have an increased risk of developing invasive breast cancer later in life. LCIS is thus viewed as a marker or indicator of higher-than-average breast cancer risk. While the average woman faces an approximately 12.5% risk of developing an invasive breast cancer in her lifetime, a woman with LCIS is estimated to have a 30% to 40% lifetime risk. Other studies suggest the risk is 7 to 11

---

times higher for women with LCIS. When women with LCIS develop breast cancer, however, it typically occurs years or even decades later. The invasive cancer is equally likely to develop in the breast with LCIS or the other breast.

Diagnosis

LCIS can be difficult to diagnose because it does not usually present any obvious symptoms, such as a lump or visible change to the breast. In addition, LCIS may not appear on a mammogram because the abnormal cells often lack microcalcifications, the tiny specks of calcium that form within most breast cancer cells. As a result, experts believe that many cases of LCIS are never diagnosed and never cause any problems.

When LCIS is diagnosed, it usually occurs through a biopsy that is performed to diagnose a different breast problem, such as an abnormal mammogram result or a suspicious lump. A biopsy is a procedure used to remove samples of tissue for examination under a microscope by a pathologist. In a fine needle aspiration biopsy, a small, hollow needle is inserted into the breast tissue to remove a sample of suspicious cells. In an incisional biopsy, a surgeon makes an incision to remove a small piece of tissue for further examination. In an excisional biopsy, the entire lump or abnormal area is removed from the breast.

A challenge for the pathologist examining cell samples is to differentiate between LCIS and ductal carcinoma in situ (DCIS), which is found in the milk ducts rather than the lobules. Although they may appear similar, DCIS is considered to be cancer and can spread without treatment. More than half of women diagnosed with LCIS will have abnormal cell growth in multiple lobules, while about one-third of women will have both breasts affected by LCIS.

Some factors that increase a woman's likelihood of being diagnosed with LCIS include having a history of breast cancer in her immediate family, having taken hormone replacement therapy for menopausal symptoms, and being in her early forties. LCIS is most commonly found in women between the ages of 40 and 50 who have not yet undergone menopause.

Treatment Options

Since LCIS does not become invasive, it does not require traditional cancer treatments, such as chemotherapy and radiation therapy. In some cases, doctors may recommend removing the abnormal cells with an excisional biopsy. In most cases, however, the main forms of treatment for women who are diagnosed with LCIS involve strategies to reduce the risk of developing invasive breast cancer in the future.

One option is to monitor for signs of breast cancer through careful observation. This treatment approach typically includes adhering to a schedule of frequent breast self-examinations, biannual clinical examinations, annual mammograms, and other imaging techniques if there is a family history or additional risk factors to consider. The goal of careful observation is to find and treat invasive breast cancer before it spreads.

A second treatment option involves taking medication to reduce the risk of developing breast cancer. Hormonal therapy drugs like Tamoxifen and Raloxifene (Evista) block estrogen receptors in breast tissue, which helps prevent cancer cells from receiving the estrogen they need to grow. Studies have shown that these medications can reduce a woman's risk of developing breast cancer by 50%. However, they are not recommended for women who have heart disease or multiple risk factors for heart disease because they increase the risk of stroke. Another option for postmenopausal women is exemestane (Aromasin), which reduces the risk of breast cancer in high-risk women by decreasing the production of estrogen in the body.

Finally, some women opt for preventative surgery to eliminate the risk of developing invasive breast cancer. Prophylactic mastectomy involves the surgical removal of both breasts. It is considered as an option for women who have LCIS as well as other factors that increase their risk of breast cancer, such as a strong family history or a BRCA gene mutation.

References

1. "LCIS—Lobular Carcinoma in Situ." BreastCancer.org, February 18, 2016.

2. "Lobular Carcinoma in Situ." American Cancer Society, June 10, 2015.

3. "Lobular Carcinoma in Situ (LCIS)." Mayo Clinic, 2016.

Chapter 13

Invasive Carcinoma of the Breast

Invasive Breast Cancer

Invasive breast cancer is cancer that has spread from where it began in the breast to surrounding normal tissue. The most common type of invasive breast cancer is invasive ductal carcinoma, which begins in the lining of the milk ducts (thin tubes that carry milk from the lobules of the breast to the nipple). Another type is invasive lobular carcinoma, which begins in the lobules (milk glands) of the breast. Invasive breast cancer can spread through the blood and lymph systems to other parts of the body. It is also called infiltrating breast cancer.

Changing Patterns in Survival for U.S. Women with Invasive Breast Cancer

Breast cancer mortality rates have been declining among women in many western countries since the 1970s. Overall, breast cancer survival rates following diagnosis have improved for all women diagnosed

This chapter contains text excerpted from the following sources: Text under the heading "Invasive Breast Cancer" is excerpted from "NCI Dictionary of Cancer Terms," National Cancer Institute (NCI), May 15, 2015; Text under the heading "Changing Patterns in Survival for U.S. Women with Invasive Breast Cancer" is excerpted from "Changing Patterns in Survival for U.S. Women with Invasive Breast Cancer," National Cancer Institute (NCI), July 20, 2015.

with local and regional (area around the tumor) disease. Women diagnosed before age 70 have experienced lower short-term (less than 5 years) death rates, even for metastatic disease. And the long-term death rates (survival beyond the first 5 years) have improved among those with local and regional disease in all age groups. Tumor size at diagnosis has shrunk since the 1980s, but new evidence shows that changes in tumor size within each stage at diagnosis explain only a small proportion of the improvement in breast cancer mortality in women under the age of 70. However, changes in tumor size account for about half of the improvements for women diagnosed with local or regional breast cancer at age 70 and older. This conclusion comes from an analysis of data from NCI's Surveillance, Epidemiology, and End Results (SEER) database.

The study also found that changes in estrogen receptor (ER) status explain little of the improvement after adjustment for tumor size, except for women age 70 and older within 5 years after diagnosis. Results of this study, by Mitchell H. Gail, M.D., Ph.D., and William F. Anderson, M.D., both with the NCI Division of Cancer Epidemiology and Genetics, and their colleague, Ju-Hyun Park, Ph.D., Dongguk University-Seoul, appeared online July 20, 2015, in the Journal of Clinical Oncology.

The investigative team analyzed data that included: age at breast cancer diagnosis; year of diagnosis; tumor size; lymph node status (negative or positive); stage of breast cancer (localized, regional, or metastasized); and ER status (positive, negative, unknown). These data revealed the pattern of changes in survival following diagnosis, and allowed the researchers to determine the contribution of tumor size and ER status to improvements in individual survival outcomes among women with a first primary invasive breast cancer. Their analysis showed that the hazard of breast-cancer-specific death declined over the period from 1973-2010, not only in the first five years following diagnosis, but also thereafter. They found that smaller tumor size within each stage explained less than 17 percent of these positive trends, except for women over age 70. In the older women with local disease, smaller tumor size explained 49 percent of improvement; for those with regional disease it explained 38 percent of improvement. They also found that tumor size usually accounted for more of the improvement in the first five years after diagnosis than in later years, regardless of age.

While treatments seem to account for much of the improvement in breast cancer survival after diagnosis, more favorable tumor biology may also have an influence on trends. Experts have established that rates of harder-to-treat estrogen receptor-negative tumors have been declining since 1990. Some of the stage-specific survival improvements may also be due to changes in diagnostic procedures over time that tend to increase the proportion of women with more favorable prognoses within each stage. Findings from this large-scale study help clarify factors associated with breast cancer survival in women of all ages, according to the investigators.

Chapter 14

Inflammatory Breast Cancer

What Is Inflammatory Breast Cancer?

Inflammatory breast cancer is a rare and very aggressive disease in which cancer cells block lymph vessels in the skin of the breast. This type of breast cancer is called "inflammatory" because the breast often looks swollen and red, or inflamed.

Inflammatory breast cancer is rare, accounting for 1 to 5 percent of all breast cancers diagnosed in the United States. Most inflammatory breast cancers are invasive ductal carcinomas, which means they developed from cells that line the milk ducts of the breast and then spread beyond the ducts.

Inflammatory breast cancer progresses rapidly, often in a matter of weeks or months. At diagnosis, inflammatory breast cancer is either stage III or IV disease, depending on whether cancer cells have spread only to nearby lymph nodes or to other tissues as well.

Additional features of inflammatory breast cancer include the following:

- Compared with other types of breast cancer, inflammatory breast cancer tends to be diagnosed at younger ages.

This chapter includes text excerpted from "Inflammatory Breast Cancer," National Cancer Institute (NCI), January 6, 2016.

- Inflammatory breast cancer is more common and diagnosed at younger ages in African American women than in white women.

- Inflammatory breast tumors are frequently hormone receptor negative, which means they cannot be treated with hormone therapies, such as tamoxifen, that interfere with the growth of cancer cells fueled by estrogen.

- Inflammatory breast cancer is more common in obese women than in women of normal weight.

Like other types of breast cancer, inflammatory breast cancer can occur in men, but usually at an older age than in women.

What Are the Symptoms of Inflammatory Breast Cancer?

Symptoms of inflammatory breast cancer include swelling (edema) and redness (erythema) that affect a third or more of the breast. The skin of the breast may also appear pink, reddish purple, or bruised. In addition, the skin may have ridges or appear pitted, like the skin of an orange (called peau d'orange). These symptoms are caused by the buildup of fluid (lymph) in the skin of the breast. This fluid buildup occurs because cancer cells have blocked lymph vessels in the skin, preventing the normal flow of lymph through the tissue. Sometimes the breast may contain a solid tumor that can be felt during a physical exam, but more often a tumor cannot be felt.

Other symptoms of inflammatory breast cancer include a rapid increase in breast size; sensations of heaviness, burning, or tenderness in the breast; or a nipple that is inverted (facing inward). Swollen lymph nodes may also be present under the arm, near the collarbone, or both.

It is important to note that these symptoms may also be signs of other diseases or conditions, such as an infection, injury, or another type of breast cancer that is locally advanced. For this reason, women with inflammatory breast cancer often have a delayed diagnosis of their disease.

How Is Inflammatory Breast Cancer Diagnosed?

Inflammatory breast cancer can be difficult to diagnose. Often, there is no lump that can be felt during a physical exam or seen in a screening mammogram. In addition, most women diagnosed with inflammatory breast cancer have dense breast tissue, which makes cancer detection in a screening mammogram more difficult. Also, because inflammatory breast cancer is so aggressive, it can arise between scheduled screening mammograms and progress quickly. The symptoms of inflammatory breast cancer may be mistaken for those of mastitis, which is an infection of the breast, or another form of locally advanced breast cancer.

To help prevent delays in diagnosis and in choosing the best course of treatment, an international panel of experts published guidelines on how doctors can diagnose and stage inflammatory breast cancer correctly. Their recommendations are summarized below.

Minimum criteria for a diagnosis of inflammatory breast cancer include the following:

- A rapid onset of erythema (redness), edema (swelling), and a peau d'orange appearance (ridged or pitted skin) and/or abnormal breast warmth, with or without a lump that can be felt

- The above-mentioned symptoms have been present for less than 6 months

- The erythema covers at least a third of the breast

- Initial biopsy samples from the affected breast show invasive carcinoma

Further examination of tissue from the affected breast should include testing to see if the cancer cells have hormone receptors (estrogen and progesterone receptors) or if they have greater than normal amounts of the HER2 gene and/or the HER2 protein (HER2-positive breast cancer).

Imaging and staging tests include the following:

- A diagnostic mammogram and an ultrasound of the breast and regional (nearby) lymph nodes

- A PET scan or a CT scan and a bone scan to see if the cancer has spread to other parts of the body

Proper diagnosis and staging of inflammatory breast cancer helps doctors develop the best treatment plan and estimate the likely outcome of the disease. Patients diagnosed with inflammatory breast cancer may want to consult a doctor who specializes in this disease.

How Is Inflammatory Breast Cancer Treated?

Inflammatory breast cancer is generally treated first with systemic chemotherapy to help shrink the tumor, then with surgery to remove the tumor, followed by radiation therapy. This approach to treatment is called a multimodal approach. Studies have found that women with inflammatory breast cancer who are treated with a multimodal approach have better responses to therapy and longer survival. Treatments used in a multimodal approach may include those described below.

- **Neoadjuvant chemotherapy:** This type of chemotherapy is given before surgery and usually includes both anthracycline and taxane drugs. Doctors generally recommend that at least six cycles of neoadjuvant chemotherapy be given over the course of 4 to 6 months before the tumor is removed, unless the disease continues to progress during this time and doctors decide that surgery should not be delayed.

- **Targeted therapy:** Inflammatory breast cancers often produce greater than normal amounts of the HER2 protein, which means that drugs such as trastuzumab (Herceptin) that target this protein may be used to treat them. Anti-HER2 therapy can be given both as part of neoadjuvant therapy and after surgery (adjuvant therapy).

- **Hormone therapy:** If the cells of a woman's inflammatory breast cancer contain hormone receptors, hormone therapy is another treatment option. Drugs such as tamoxifen, which prevent estrogen from binding to its receptor, and aromatase inhibitors such as letrozole, which block the body's ability to make estrogen, can cause estrogen-dependent cancer cells to stop growing and die.

- **Surgery:** The standard surgery for inflammatory breast cancer is a modified radical mastectomy. This surgery involves removal of the entire affected breast and most or all of the lymph nodes under the adjacent arm. Often, the lining over the underlying chest muscles is also removed, but the chest muscles are preserved. Sometimes, however, the smaller chest muscle (pectoralis minor) may be removed, too.

- **Radiation therapy:** Post-mastectomy radiation therapy to the chest wall under the breast that was removed is a standard part of multimodal therapy for inflammatory breast cancer. If a woman received trastuzumab before surgery, she may continue to receive it during postoperative radiation therapy. Breast reconstruction can be performed in women with inflammatory breast cancer, but, due to the importance of radiation therapy in treating this disease, experts generally recommend delayed reconstruction.

- **Adjuvant therapy:** Adjuvant systemic therapy may be given after surgery to reduce the chance of cancer recurrence. This therapy may include additional chemotherapy, hormone therapy, targeted therapy (such as trastuzumab), or some combination of these treatments.

What Is the Prognosis of Patients with Inflammatory Breast Cancer?

The prognosis, or likely outcome, for a patient diagnosed with cancer is often viewed as the chance that the cancer will be treated successfully and that the patient will recover completely. Many factors can influence a cancer patient's prognosis, including the type and location of the cancer, the stage of the disease, the patient's age and overall general health, and the extent to which the patient's disease responds to treatment.

Because inflammatory breast cancer usually develops quickly and spreads aggressively to other parts of the body, women diagnosed with this disease, in general, do not survive as long as women diagnosed with other types of breast cancer.

It is important to keep in mind, however, that survival statistics are based on large numbers of patients and that an individual woman's prognosis could be better or worse, depending on her tumor characteristics and medical history. Women who have inflammatory breast cancer are encouraged to talk with their doctor about their prognosis, given their particular situation.

Ongoing research, especially at the molecular level, will increase our understanding of how inflammatory breast cancer begins and progresses. This knowledge should enable the development of new treatments and more accurate prognoses for women diagnosed with this disease. It is important, therefore, that women who are diagnosed with inflammatory breast cancer talk with their doctor about the option of participating in a clinical trial.

What Clinical Trials Are Available for Women with Inflammatory Breast Cancer?

NCI sponsors clinical trials of new treatments for all types of cancer, as well as trials that test better ways to use existing treatments. Participation in clinical trials is an option for many patients with inflammatory breast cancer, and all patients with this disease are encouraged to consider treatment in a clinical trial.

Chapter 15

Paget Disease of the Breast

What Is Paget Disease of the Breast?

Paget disease of the breast (also known as Paget disease of the nipple and mammary Paget disease) is a rare type of cancer involving the skin of the nipple and, usually, the darker circle of skin around it, which is called the areola. Most people with Paget disease of the breast also have one or more tumors inside the same breast. These breast tumors are either ductal carcinoma in situ or invasive breast cancer.

Paget disease of the breast is named after the 19th century British doctor Sir James Paget, who, in 1874, noted a relationship between changes in the nipple and breast cancer. (Several other diseases are named after Sir James Paget, including Paget disease of bone and extramammary Paget disease, which includes Paget disease of the vulva and Paget disease of the penis. These other diseases are not related to Paget disease of the breast. This fact sheet discusses only Paget disease of the breast).

Malignant cells known as Paget cells are a telltale sign of Paget disease of the breast. These cells are found in the epidermis (surface layer) of the skin of the nipple and the areola. Paget cells often have a large, round appearance under a microscope; they may be found as single cells or as small groups of cells within the epidermis.

This chapter includes text excerpted from "Paget Disease of the Breast," National Cancer Institute (NCI), April 10, 2012. Reviewed April 2016.

Who Gets Paget Disease of the Breast?

Paget disease of the breast occurs in both women and men, but most cases occur in women. Approximately 1 to 4 percent of all cases of breast cancer also involve Paget disease of the breast. The average age at diagnosis is 57 years, but the disease has been found in adolescents and in people in their late 80s.

What Causes Paget Disease of the Breast?

Doctors do not fully understand what causes Paget disease of the breast. The most widely accepted theory is that cancer cells from a tumor inside the breast travel through the milk ducts to the nipple and areola. This would explain why Paget disease of the breast and tumors inside the same breast are almost always found together.

A second theory is that cells in the nipple or areola become cancerous on their own. This would explain why a few people develop Paget disease of the breast without having a tumor inside the same breast. Moreover, it may be possible for Paget disease of the breast and tumors inside the same breast to develop independently.

What Are the Symptoms of Paget Disease of the Breast?

The symptoms of Paget disease of the breast are often mistaken for those of some benign skin conditions, such as dermatitis or eczema. These symptoms may include the following:

- Itching, tingling or redness in the nipple and/or areola
- Flaking, crusty or thickened skin on or around the nipple
- A flattened nipple
- Discharge from the nipple that may be yellowish or bloody

Because the early symptoms of Paget disease of the breast may suggest a benign skin condition, and because the disease is rare, it may be misdiagnosed at first.

People with Paget disease of the breast have often had symptoms for several months before being correctly diagnosed.

How Is Paget Disease of the Breast Diagnosed?

A nipple biopsy allows doctors to correctly diagnose Paget disease of the breast. There are several types of nipple biopsy, including the procedures described below.

- **Surface biopsy:** A glass slide or other tool is used to gently scrape cells from the surface of the skin.

- **Shave biopsy:** A razor-like tool is used to remove the top layer of skin.

- **Punch biopsy:** A circular cutting tool, called a punch, is used to remove a disk-shaped piece of tissue.

- **Wedge biopsy:** A scalpel is used to remove a small wedge of tissue.

In some cases, doctors may remove the entire nipple. A pathologist then examines the cells or tissue under a microscope to look for Paget cells.

Most people who have Paget disease of the breast also have one or more tumors inside the same breast. In addition to ordering a nipple biopsy, the doctor should perform a clinical breast exam to check for lumps or other breast changes. As many as 50 percent of people who have Paget disease of the breast have a breast lump that can be felt in a clinical breast exam. The doctor may order additional diagnostic tests, such as a diagnostic mammogram, an ultrasound exam, or a magnetic resonance imaging scan to look for possible tumors.

How Is Paget Disease of the Breast Treated?

For many years, mastectomy, with or without the removal of lymph nodes under the arm on the same side of chest (known as axillary lymph node dissection), was regarded as the standard surgery for Paget disease of the breast. This type of surgery was done because patients with Paget disease of the breast were almost always found to have one or more tumors inside the same breast. Even if only one tumor was present, that tumor could be located several centimeters away from the nipple and areola and would not be removed by surgery on the nipple and areola alone.

Studies have shown, however, that breast-conserving surgery that includes removal of the nipple and areola, followed by whole-breast radiation therapy, is a safe option for people with Paget disease of the breast who do not have a palpable lump in their breast and whose mammograms do not reveal a tumor.

People with Paget disease of the breast who have a breast tumor and are having a mastectomy should be offered sentinel lymph node biopsy to see whether the cancer has spread to the axillary lymph nodes. If cancer cells are found in the sentinel lymph node(s), more extensive axillary lymph node surgery may be needed. Depending on the stage and other features of the underlying breast tumor (for example, the presence or absence of lymph node involvement, estrogen and progesterone receptors in the tumor cells, and HER2 protein overexpression in the tumor cells), adjuvant therapy, consisting of chemotherapy and/or hormonal therapy, may also be recommended.

What Is the Prognosis for People with Paget Disease of the Breast?

The prognosis, or outlook, for people with Paget disease of the breast depends on a variety of factors, including the following:

- Whether or not a tumor is present in the affected breast

- If one or more tumors are present in the affected breast, whether those tumors are ductal carcinoma in situ or invasive breast cancer

- If invasive breast cancer is present in the affected breast, the stage of that cancer

The presence of invasive cancer in the affected breast and the spread of cancer to nearby lymph nodes are associated with reduced survival.

According to NCI's Surveillance, Epidemiology, and End Results program, the 5-year relative survival for all women in the United States who were diagnosed with Paget disease of the breast between 1988 and 2001 was 82.6 percent. This compares with a 5-year relative survival of 87.1 percent for women diagnosed with any type of breast cancer. For women with both Paget disease of the breast and invasive cancer in the same breast, the 5-year relative survival declined with increasing stage of the cancer (stage I, 95.8 percent; stage II, 77.7 percent; stage III, 46.3 percent; stage IV, 14.3 percent).

What Research Studies Are under Way on Paget Disease of the Breast?

Randomized controlled clinical trials, which are considered the "gold standard" in cancer research, are difficult to perform for Paget disease of the breast because very few people have this disease. However, people who have Paget disease of the breast may be eligible to enroll in clinical trials to evaluate new treatments for breast cancer in general, new ways of using existing breast cancer treatments, or strategies for preventing breast cancer recurrence.

Chapter 16

Triple-Negative Breast Cancer

Overview

Triple-negative breast cancer is a relatively rare form of the disease in which the cancer cells test negative for the three most common types of receptors that promote tumor growth: estrogen receptors, progesterone receptors, and hormone epidermal growth factor receptor 2 (HER-2). Receptors are proteins that are found both on the surface and inside of cells throughout the body. They enable cells to receive the chemical messages that control their growth and function.

All three types of receptors are normally present in healthy breast cells, and they can be found in most breast cancer cells as well. Estrogen and progesterone support the growth of more than 60% of breast cancer tumors, while 20-30% of tumors have an excess of HER-2 receptors, which stimulates the cancer cells to divide and grow quickly. Only 10-20% of breast cancer cases are diagnosed as triple negative.

Since triple-negative tumor cells lack estrogen, progesterone, and HER-2 receptors, they do not respond to many common treatments—like hormone therapy—that interfere with the receptors' work in order to slow the growth of the cancer cells. Chemotherapy has proven effective in treating triple-negative breast cancer, however, and research is underway to find new treatment methods and medications.

"Triple-Negative Breast Cancer," © 2016 Omnigraphics, Inc. Reviewed April 2016.

Risks of Triple-Negative Breast Cancer

Unlike most other types of breast cancer, which primarily affect older women, triple-negative breast cancer is more likely to occur before age 40 to 50. It is most common among African-American women, who are three times more likely to be affected than white women. Hispanic women also have an elevated risk of developing triple-negative breast cancer compared to white women and Asian women. Although anyone can develop triple-negative breast cancer, it is also the type of cancer that usually affects people with an inherited BRCA1 genetic mutation, especially if they develop breast cancer before age 50.

Studies have shown that triple-negative breast cancer tends to be more aggressive than other types of breast cancer. It is more likely to recur following treatment and to spread beyond the breast to other parts of the body. These risks are highest within the first three years after treatment, however, and decline to the same rates as other types of breast cancer after that time. Similarly, the five-year survival rates for women with triple-negative breast cancer are lower, at 77%, than for women with other types of breast cancer, at 93%. But this increased risk of death only pertains for the first five years following diagnosis and then begins to decline.

Triple-negative breast cancer also tends to be a higher grade at diagnosis than other types of breast cancer. The grade of the tumor refers to the degree to which its cells resemble healthy cells, with a higher grade having less resemblance. Finally, triple-negative breast cancer cells are often a specific subtype called basal-like, meaning that they resemble the basal cells that line the breast ducts. Basal-like cancers are more likely to be aggressive, higher-grade varieties.

Treatment of Triple-Negative Breast Cancer

Since triple-negative breast cancer cells are not fueled by hormones, this type of cancer does not typically respond well to hormone therapy. The drugs commonly used in hormone therapy—such as tamoxifen, Arimidex (anastrozole), Aromasin (exemestane), Faslodex (fulvestrant), and Femara (letrozole)—are designed to alter the levels of estrogen and progesterone in the body or interfere with the action of receptors in the cells. Likewise, patients with triple-negative breast cancer are not good candidates for medications like Herceptin (trastuzumab) or Tykerb (lapatinib) that target HER-2.

The main forms of treatment for triple-negative breast cancer include surgery, chemotherapy, and radiation therapy. On the plus side, research suggests that breast cancers that test negative for hormone receptors may respond better to chemotherapy than other types of breast cancer. Some studies have also shown positive results for women with triple-negative breast cancer who have neoadjuvant therapy, which involves undergoing chemotherapy prior to surgery. The results indicated that two-thirds of patients with locally advanced triple-negative tumors had no evidence of disease following the initial chemotherapy. In addition, their survival rates were similar to those of women with other types of breast cancer.

Research is ongoing to find new and better approaches to treating triple-negative breast cancer. Clinical trials of some targeted therapies have shown promising results. Unlike traditional therapies like radiation and chemotherapy that affect all fast-growing cells—both healthy cells and cancer cells—targeted therapies are designed to interfere with a specific process that fuels the growth of cancer cells without affecting healthy cells. Although hormone therapy is not effective for triple-negative breast cancer, some of the other targeted therapies that are under development include:

- **Poly ADP-ribose polymerase (PARP) inhibitors**

  PARP is an enzyme that repairs damage to DNA in cells. By interfering with this process, PARP inhibitors make it more difficult for cancer cells to repair the damage done by chemotherapy drugs, thus making the treatment more effective. Research suggests that women with advanced triple-negative breast cancer may benefit from taking PARP inhibitors such as iniparib or olaparib in combination with chemotherapy.

- **Vascular endothelial growth factor (VEGF) inhibitors**

  VEGF is a protein that stimulates the creation of new blood vessels—a process known as angiogenesis. Cancer tumors rely on angiogenesis to obtain the oxygen and nutrients they need to grow. VEGF inhibitors like Avastin (bevacizumab) and Sutent (sutinib) block the interaction between VEGF and receptors on blood vessels, thus preventing angiogenesis and tumor growth.

- **Epidermal growth factor receptor (EGFR) therapies**

  EGFR is a protein that receives signals that stimulate cell growth. An excess of EGFRs is typical of triple-negative breast cancer cells. Treatments that target EGFRs, such as Erbitux (cetuximab), attach to the receptors and prevent growth signals from reaching the cancer cells.

101

Since new medications are still being developed for triple-negative breast cancer, it is important to seek opinions from several doctors and compare their recommendations before choosing a course of treatment.

References

1. "Triple-Negative Breast Cancer." BreastCancer.org, October 23, 2015.

2. "Triple-Negative Breast Cancer." National Breast Cancer Foundation, 2015.

Part Three

Risk Factors, Symptoms, and Prevention of Breast Cancer

Chapter 17

Breast Cancer Risk Factors and Symptoms

Overview

Some women develop breast cancer and others do not, and the risk factors for the disease vary. Breast cancer may affect younger women, but three-fourths of all breast cancers occur in women between the ages of 45 to 85.

In Situ and Invasive Breast Cancer

Researchers often talk about breast cancer in two ways: *in situ* and invasive. *In situ* refers to cancer that has not spread beyond its site of origin. Invasive applies to cancer that has spread to the tissue around it.

This chart shows what the approximate chances are of a woman getting invasive breast cancer in her lifetime.

Risk Factors

Risk factors are conditions or agents that increase a person's chances of getting a disease. Here are the most common risk factors for breast cancer.

This chapter includes text excerpted from "Breast Cancer," NIHSeniorHealth, National Institute on Aging (NIA), April 2015.

Table 17.1. Lifetime Chances of Getting Invasive Breast Cancer

Ages	Chances
30 to 40	Chances are 1 out of 227
40 to 50	Chances are 1 out of 68
50 to 60	Chances are 1 out of 41
60 to 70	Chances are 1 out of 27
70 to 80	Chances are 1 out of 25

- **Older age.** The risk of breast cancer in a 70 year old woman is about 10 times that of a 30 year old woman, but risk decreases after age 85.

- **Personal and family history.** A personal history of breast cancer or breast cancer among one or more of your close relatives, such as a sister, mother, or daughter.

- **Estrogen levels in the body.** High estrogen levels over a long time may increase the risk of breast cancer. Estrogen levels are highest during the years a woman is menstruating.

- **Never being pregnant** or having your first child in your mid-30s or later.

- **Early menstruation.** Having your first menstrual period before age 12.

- **Breast density.** Women with very dense breasts have a higher risk of breast cancer than women with low or normal breast density.

- **Combination hormone replacement therapy/Hormone therapy.** Estrogen, progestin, or both may be given to replace the estrogen no longer made by the ovaries in postmenopausal women or women who have had their ovaries removed. This is called hormone replacement therapy. (HRT) or hormone therapy (HT). Combination HRT/HT is estrogen combined with progestin. This type of HRT/HT can increase the risk of breast cancer.

- **Exposure to radiation.** Radiation therapy to the chest for the treatment of cancer can increase the risk of breast cancer, starting 10 years after treatment. Radiation therapy to treat cancer in one breast does not appear to increase the risk of cancer in the other breast.

- **Obesity.** Obesity increases the risk of breast cancer, especially in postmenopausal women who have not used hormone replacement therapy.

- **Alcohol.** Drinking alcohol increases the risk of breast cancer. The level of risk rises as the amount of alcohol consumed rises.

- **Gaining weight after menopause,** especially after natural menopause and/or after age 60.

- **Race.** White women are at greater risk than black women. However, black women diagnosed with breast cancer are more likely to die of the disease.

- **Inherited gene changes.** Women who have inherited certain changes in the genes named BRCA1 and BRCA2 have a higher risk of breast cancer, ovarian cancer and maybe colon cancer. The risk of breast cancer caused by inherited gene changes depends on the type of gene mutation, family history of cancer, and other factors. Men who have inherited certain changes in the BRCA2 gene have a higher risk of breast, prostate and pancreatic cancers, and lymphoma.

Five percent to ten percent of all breast cancers are thought to be inherited.

Warning Signs

When breast cancer first develops, there may be no symptoms at all. But as the cancer grows, it can cause changes that women should watch for. You can help safeguard your health by learning the following warning signs of breast cancer.

- a lump or thickening in or near the breast or in the underarm area.

- a change in the size or shape of the breast.

- nipple discharge or tenderness, or the nipple is pulled back or inverted into the breast.

- ridges or pitting of the breast. The skin looks like the skin of an orange.

- a change in the way the skin of the breast, areola, or nipple looks or feels. For example, the skin may be warm, swollen, red, or scaly.

Don't Ignore Symptoms

You should see your doctor about any symptoms like these. Most often, they are not cancer, but it's important to check with the doctor so that any problems can be diagnosed and treated as early as possible.

Some women believe that as they age, health problems are due to "growing older." Because of this myth, many illnesses go undiagnosed and untreated. Don't ignore your symptoms because you think they are not important or because you believe they are normal for your age. Talk to your doctor.

Chapter 18

Age and Cancer Risk

Age

Advancing age is the most important risk factor for cancer overall, and for many individual cancer types. According to the most recent statistical data from National Cancer Institute's (NCI) Surveillance, Epidemiology, and End Results (SEER) program, the median age of a cancer diagnosis is 66 years. This means that half of cancer cases occur in people below this age and half in people above this age. One-quarter of new cancer cases are diagnosed in people aged 65 to 74.

A similar pattern is seen for many common cancer types. For example, the median age at diagnosis is 61 years for breast cancer, 68 years for colorectal cancer, 70 years for lung cancer, and 66 years for prostate cancer.

But the disease can occur at any age. For example, bone cancer is most frequently diagnosed among people under age 20, with more than one-fourth of cases occurring in this age group. And 10 percent of leukemias are diagnosed in children and adolescents under 20 years of age, whereas only 1 percent of cancer overall is diagnosed in that age group. Some types of cancer, such as neuroblastoma, are more common in children or adolescents than in adults.

This chapter contains text excerpted from the following sources: Text under the heading "Age" is excerpted from "Age," National Cancer Institute (NCI), April 29, 2015; Text under the heading "NIH Study Offers Insight into Why Cancer Incidence Increases with Age" is excerpted from "NIH Study Offers Insight into Why Cancer Incidence Increases with Age," National Institutes of Health (NIH), February 3, 2014.

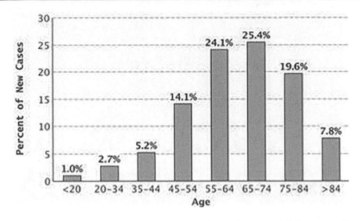

Figure 18.1. *Percent of New Cancers by Age Group: All Cancer Sites*

NIH Study Offers Insight into Why Cancer Incidence Increases with Age

The accumulation of age-associated changes in a biochemical process that helps control genes may be responsible for some of the increased risk of cancer seen in older people, according to a National Institutes of Health study.

Scientists have known for years that age is a leading risk factor for the development of many types of cancer, but why aging increases cancer risk remains unclear. Researchers suspect that DNA methylation, or the binding of chemical tags, called methyl groups, onto DNA, may be involved. Methyl groups activate or silence genes, by affecting interactions between DNA and the cell's protein-making machinery.

Zongli Xu, Ph.D., and Jack Taylor, M.D., Ph.D., researchers from the National Institute of Environmental Health Sciences (NIEHS), part of NIH, identified DNA methylation sites across the human genome that changed with age. They demonstrated that a subset of those sites—the ones that become increasingly methylated with advancing age—are also disproportionately methylated in a variety of human cancers. Their findings were published online in the journal Carcinogenesis.

"You can think of methylation as dust settling on an unused switch, which then prevents the cell from turning on certain genes," Taylor said. "If a cell can no longer turn on critical developmental programs, it might be easier for it to become a cancer cell."

Xu and Taylor made the discovery using blood samples from participants in the Sister Study, a nationwide research effort to find the environmental and genetic causes of breast cancer and other diseases.

110

More than 50,000 sisters of women who have had breast cancer are participating in the study.

The researchers analyzed blood samples from 1,000 women, using a microarray that contained 27,000 specific methylation sites. Nearly one-third of the sites showed increased DNA methylation in association with age. They then looked at three additional data sets from smaller studies that used the same microarray and found 749 methylation sites that behaved consistently across all four data sets. As an additional check, they consulted methylation data from normal tissues and seven different types of cancerous tumors in The Cancer Genome Atlas, a database funded by the National Cancer Institute and the National Human Genome Research Institute.

Taylor said that DNA methylation appears to be part of the normal aging process and occurs in genes involved in cell development. Cancer cells often have altered DNA methylation, but the researchers were surprised to find that 70-90 percent of the sites associated with age showed significantly increased methylation in all seven cancer types. Taylor suggests that age-related methylation may disable the expression of certain genes, making it easier for cells to transition to cancer.

The research also determined how fast these methylation events accumulate in cells. They occur at a rate of one per year, according to Xu.

"On your 50th birthday, you would have 50 of these sites [from the subset of 749] that have acquired methyl groups in each cell," Xu said. "The longer you live, the more methylation you will have."

For future work, Xu and Taylor want to examine more samples, using a newer microarray that will explore methylation at 450,000 genomic methylation sites. The additional samples and larger microarray, which will provide 16 times more genomic coverage, will allow them to address whether environmental exposures during adulthood or infancy affect methylation profiles. These additional studies will help scientists better understand why methylation happens as people march toward their retirement years.

DNA methylation is one of several epigenetic mechanisms that can control gene expression without changes in DNA sequence. This study is part of a broader research effort, funded by NIEHS, to understand how environmental and other factors affect epigenetic mechanisms in relation to health.

Chapter 19

Alcohol Consumption and Breast Cancer Risk

What Is Alcohol?

Alcohol is the common term for ethanol or ethyl alcohol, a chemical substance found in beer, wine, and liquor, as well as in some medicines, mouthwashes, household products, and essential oils (scented liquids taken from plants). Alcohol is produced by the fermentation of sugars and starches by yeast.

The main types of alcoholic drinks and their alcohol content are as follows:

- Beers and hard ciders: 3–7 percent alcohol

- Wines, including sake: 9–15 percent alcohol

- Wines fortified with liquors, such as port: 16–20 percent alcohol

- Liquor, or distilled spirits, such as gin, rum, vodka, and whiskey, which are produced by distilling the alcohol from fermented grains, fruits, or vegetables: usually 35–40 percent alcohol (70–80 proof), but can be higher

According to the National Institute on Alcohol Abuse and Alcoholism (NIAAA), a standard alcoholic drink in the United States contains

This chapter includes text excerpted from "Alcohol and Cancer Risk," National Cancer Institute (NCI), June 24, 2013.

14.0 grams (0.6 ounces) of pure alcohol. Generally, this amount of pure alcohol is found in

- 12 ounces of beer

- 8 ounces of malt liquor

- 5 ounces of wine

- 1.5 ounces or a "shot" of 80-proof liquor

The federal government's *Dietary Guidelines for Americans 2010* defines moderate alcohol drinking as up to one drink per day for women and up to two drinks per day for men. Heavy alcohol drinking is defined as having more than three drinks on any day or more than seven drinks per week for women and more than four drinks on any day or more than 14 drinks per week for men.

What Is the Evidence That Alcohol Drinking Is a Cause of Cancer?

Based on extensive reviews of research studies, there is a strong scientific consensus of an association between alcohol drinking and several types of cancer. In its Report on Carcinogens, the National Toxicology Program of the U.S. Department of Health and Human Services (HHS) lists consumption of alcoholic beverages as a known human carcinogen. The research evidence indicates that the more alcohol a person drinks—particularly the more alcohol a person drinks regularly over time—the higher his or her risk of developing an alcohol-associated cancer. Based on data from 2009, an estimated 3.5 percent of all cancer deaths in the United States (about 19,500 deaths) were alcohol related.

Breast Cancer

More than 100 epidemiologic studies have looked at the association between alcohol consumption and the risk of breast cancer in women. These studies have consistently found an increased risk of breast cancer associated with increasing alcohol intake. A meta-analysis of 53 of these studies (which included a total of 58,000 women with breast cancer) showed that women who drank more than 45 grams of alcohol per day (approximately three drinks) had 1.5 times the risk of developing breast cancer as nondrinkers (a modestly increased risk). The risk of breast cancer was higher across all levels of alcohol intake: for every 10 grams of alcohol consumed per day (slightly less than one drink), researchers observed a small (7 percent) increase in the risk of breast cancer.

The Million Women Study in the United Kingdom (which included more than 28,000 women with breast cancer) provided a more recent, and slightly higher, estimate of breast cancer risk at low to moderate levels of alcohol consumption: every 10 grams of alcohol consumed per day was associated with a 12 percent increase in the risk of breast cancer.

Research on Alcohol Consumption and Other Cancers

Numerous studies have examined the association between alcohol consumption and the risk of other cancers, including cancers of the pancreas, ovary, prostate, stomach, uterus, and bladder. For these cancers, either no association with alcohol use has been found or the evidence for an association is inconsistent.

However, for two cancers—renal cell (kidney) cancer and non-Hodgkin lymphoma (NHL)—multiple studies have shown that increased alcohol consumption is associated with a decreased risk of cancer. A meta-analysis of the NHL studies (which included 18,759 people with NHL) found a 15 percent lower risk of NHL among alcohol drinkers compared with nondrinkers. The mechanisms by which alcohol consumption would decrease the risks of either renal cell cancer or NHL are not understood.

How Does Alcohol Increase the Risk of Cancer?

Researchers have identified multiple ways that alcohol may increase the risk of cancer, including:

- metabolizing (breaking down) ethanol in alcoholic drinks to acetaldehyde, which is a toxic chemical and a probable human carcinogen; acetaldehyde can damage both DNA (the genetic material that makes up genes) and proteins

- generating reactive oxygen species (chemically reactive molecules that contain oxygen), which can damage DNA, proteins, and lipids (fats) through a process called oxidation

- impairing the body's ability to break down and absorb a variety of nutrients that may be associated with cancer risk, including vitamin A; nutrients in the vitamin B complex, such as folate; vitamin C; vitamin D; vitamin E; and carotenoids

- increasing blood levels of estrogen, a sex hormone linked to the risk of breast cancer

115

Alcoholic beverages may also contain a variety of carcinogenic contaminants that are introduced during fermentation and production, such as nitrosamines, asbestos fibers, phenols, and hydrocarbons.

How Does the Combination of Alcohol and Tobacco Affect Cancer Risk?

Epidemiologic research shows that people who use both alcohol and tobacco have much greater risks of developing cancers of the oral cavity, pharynx (throat), larynx, and esophagus than people who use either alcohol or tobacco alone. In fact, for oral and pharyngeal cancers, the risks associated with using both alcohol and tobacco are multiplicative; that is, they are greater than would be expected from adding the individual risks associated with alcohol and tobacco together.

Can a Person's Genes Affect Their Risk of Alcohol-Related Cancers?

A person's risk of alcohol-related cancers is influenced by their genes, specifically the genes that encode enzymes involved in metabolizing (breaking down) alcohol.

For example, one way the body metabolizes alcohol is through the activity of an enzyme called alcohol dehydrogenase, or ADH. Many individuals of Chinese, Korean, and especially Japanese descent carry a version of the gene for ADH that codes for a "superactive" form of the enzyme. This superactive ADH enzyme speeds the conversion of alcohol (ethanol) to toxic acetaldehyde. As a result, when people who have the superactive enzyme drink alcohol, acetaldehyde builds up. Among people of Japanese descent, those who have this superactive ADH have a higher risk of pancreatic cancer than those with the more common form of ADH.

Another enzyme, called aldehyde dehydrogenase 2 (ALDH2), metabolizes toxic acetaldehyde to non-toxic substances. Some people, particularly those of East Asian descent, carry a variant of the gene for ALDH2 that codes for a defective form of the enzyme. In people who have the defective enzyme, acetaldehyde builds up when they drink alcohol. The accumulation of acetaldehyde has such unpleasant effects (including facial flushing and heart palpitations) that most people who have inherited the ALDH2 variant are unable to consume large amounts of alcohol. Therefore, most people with the defective form of ALDH2 have a low risk of developing alcohol-related cancers.

116

However, some individuals with the defective form of ALDH2 can become tolerant to the unpleasant effects of acetaldehyde and consume large amounts of alcohol. Epidemiologic studies have shown that such individuals have a higher risk of alcohol-related esophageal cancer, as well as of head and neck cancers, than individuals with the fully active enzyme who drink comparable amounts of alcohol. These increased risks are seen only among people who carry the ALDH2 variant and drink alcohol—they are not observed in people who carry the variant but do not drink alcohol.

Can Drinking Red Wine Help Prevent Cancer?

Researchers conducting studies using purified proteins, human cells, and laboratory animals have found that certain substances in red wine, such as resveratrol, have anticancer properties. Grapes, raspberries, peanuts, and some other plants also contain resveratrol. However, clinical trials in humans have not provided evidence that resveratrol is effective in preventing or treating cancer. Few epidemiologic studies have looked specifically at the association between red wine consumption and cancer risk in humans.

What Happens to Cancer Risk after a Person Stops Drinking Alcohol?

Most of the studies that have examined whether cancer risk declines after a person stops drinking alcohol have focused on head and neck cancers and on esophageal cancer. In general, these studies have found that stopping alcohol consumption is not associated with immediate reductions in cancer risk; instead, it may take years for the risks of cancer to return to those of never drinkers.

For example, a pooled analysis of 13 case-control studies of cancer of the oral cavity and pharynx combined found that alcohol-associated cancer risk did not begin to decrease until at least 10 years after stopping alcohol drinking. Even 16 years after they stopped drinking alcohol, the risk of cancer was still higher for ex-drinkers than for never drinkers.

In several studies, the risk of esophageal cancer was also found to decrease slowly with increasing time since stopping alcohol drinking. A pooled analysis of five case-control studies found that the risk of esophageal cancer did not approach that of never drinkers for at least 15 years after stopping alcohol drinking.

117

Is It Safe for Someone to Drink Alcohol While Undergoing Cancer Chemotherapy?

As with most questions related to a specific individual's cancer treatment, it is best for a patient to check with their healthcare team about whether or not it is safe to drink alcohol during or immediately following chemotherapy treatment. The doctors and nurses administering the treatment will be able to give specific advice about whether drinking alcohol is safe with particular chemotherapy drugs and/or other medications prescribed along with chemotherapy.

Chapter 20

Diethylstilbestrol (DES) and Breast Cancer Risk

What Is DES?

Diethylstilbestrol (DES) is a synthetic form of the female hormone estrogen. It was prescribed to pregnant women between 1940 and 1971 to prevent miscarriage, premature labor, and related complications of pregnancy. The use of DES declined after studies in the 1950s showed that it was not effective in preventing these problems.

In 1971, researchers linked prenatal (before birth) DES exposure to a type of cancer of the cervix and vagina called clear cell adenocarcinoma in a small group of women. Soon after, the U.S. Food and Drug Administration (FDA) notified physicians throughout the country that DES should not be prescribed to pregnant women. The drug continued to be prescribed to pregnant women in Europe until 1978.

DES is now known to be an endocrine-disrupting chemical, one of a number of substances that interfere with the endocrine system to cause cancer, birth defects, and other developmental abnormalities. The effects of endocrine-disrupting chemicals are most severe when exposure occurs during fetal development.

This chapter includes text excerpted from "Diethylstilbestrol (DES) and Cancer," National Cancer Institute (NCI), October 5, 2011. Reviewed April 2016.

What Is the Cancer Risk of Women Who Were Exposed to DES before Birth?

The daughters of women who used DES while pregnant—commonly called DES daughters—have about 40 times the risk of developing clear cell adenocarcinoma of the lower genital tract than unexposed women. However, this type of cancer is still rare; approximately 1 in 1,000 DES daughters develops it.

The first DES daughters who were diagnosed with clear cell adenocarcinoma were very young at the time of their diagnoses. Subsequent research has shown that the risk of developing this disease remains elevated as women age into their 40s.

DES daughters have an increased risk of developing abnormal cells in the cervix and the vagina that are precursors of cancer (dysplasia, cervical intraepithelial neoplasia, and squamous intraepithelial lesions). These abnormal cells resemble cancer cells, but they do not invade nearby healthy tissue and are not cancer. They may develop into cancer, however, if left untreated. Scientists estimated that DES-exposed daughters were 2.2 times more likely to have these abnormal cell changes in the cervix than unexposed women. Approximately 4 percent of DES daughters developed these conditions because of their exposure. It has been recommended that DES daughters have a yearly Pap test and pelvic exam to check for abnormal cells.

DES daughters may also have a slightly increased risk of breast cancer after age 40. A 2006 study from the United States suggested that, overall, breast cancer risk is not increased in DES daughters, but that, after age 40, DES daughters have approximately twice the risk of breast cancer as unexposed women of the same age and with similar risk factors. However, a 2010 study from Europe found no difference in breast cancer risk between DES daughters and unexposed women and no difference in overall cancer risk. A 2011 study found that about 2 percent of a large cohort of DES daughters has developed breast cancer due to their exposure.

DES daughters should be aware of these health risks, share their medical history with their doctors, and get regular physical examinations.

What Health Problems Might Women Who Took DES during Pregnancy Have?

Women who used DES themselves have a slightly increased risk of breast cancer—approximately 30 percent higher than that of women who did not take DES. Women who used DES also have a 30 percent higher risk of death from breast cancer than unexposed women. This risk has been found to be stable over time—that is, it does not increase as the mothers become older. No evidence exists to suggest that women who took DES are at higher risk for any other type of cancer.

How Can People Find out If They Took DES during Pregnancy or Were Exposed to DES in Utero?

It is estimated that 5 to 10 million Americans—pregnant women and the children born to them—were exposed to DES between 1940 and 1971. DES was given widely to pregnant women between 1940 and 1971 to prevent complications during pregnancy. DES was provided under many different product names and also in various forms, such as pills, creams, and vaginal suppositories.

Women who think they used DES during pregnancy, or people who think that their mother used DES during pregnancy, can try contacting the physician or institution where they received their care to request a review of their medical records. If any pills were taken during pregnancy, obstetrical records could be checked to determine the name of the drug.

However, finding medical records after a long period of time can be difficult. If the doctor has retired or died, another doctor may have taken over the practice as well as the records. The county medical society or health department may know where the records have been stored. Some pharmacies keep records for a long time and can be contacted regarding prescription dispensing information. Military medical records are kept for 25 years. In most cases, however, it may be impossible to determine whether DES was used.

What Should DES-Exposed Daughters Do?

Women who know or believe they were exposed to DES before birth should be aware of the health effects of DES and inform their doctor about their possible exposure. It has been recommended that exposed women have an annual medical examination to check for the adverse health effects of DES. A thorough examination may include the following:

- Pelvic examination

- Pap test and colposcopy—A routine cervical Pap test is not adequate for DES daughters. The Pap test must gather cells from the cervix and the vagina. It is also good for a clinician to see the cervix and vaginal walls. They may use a colposcope to follow-up if there are any abnormal findings.

- Biopsy

- Breast examinations—It is recommended that DES daughters continue to rigorously follow the routine breast cancer screening recommendations for their age group

What Should DES-Exposed Mothers Do?

A woman who took DES while pregnant or who suspects she may have taken it should inform her doctor. She should try to learn the dosage, when the medication was started, and how it was used. She also should inform her children who were exposed before birth so that this information can be included in their medical records.

It is recommended that DES-exposed mothers have regular breast cancer screenings and yearly medical checkups that include a pelvic examination and a Pap test.

What Should DES-Exposed Sons Do?

Men whose mothers took DES while pregnant should inform their physician of their exposure and be examined periodically. Although the risk of developing testicular cancer among DES-exposed sons is unclear, males with undescended or unusually small testicles have an increased risk of testicular cancer whether or not they were exposed to DES.

Chapter 21

Environmental Factors and Breast Cancer Risk

Environmental Carcinogens and Cancer Risk

Does Any Exposure to a Known Carcinogen Always Result in Cancer?

Any substance that causes cancer is known as a carcinogen. But simply because a substance has been designated as a carcinogen does not mean that the substance will necessarily cause cancer. Many factors influence whether a person exposed to a carcinogen will develop cancer, including the amount and duration of the exposure and the individual's genetic background. Cancers caused by involuntary exposures to environmental carcinogens are most likely to occur in subgroups of the population, such as workers in certain industries who may be exposed to carcinogens on the job.

This chapter contains text excerpted from the following sources: Text beginning with the heading "Environmental Carcinogens and Cancer Risk" is excerpted from "Environmental Carcinogens and Cancer Risk," National Cancer Institute (NCI), March 20, 2015; Text under the heading "Cancer-Causing Substances in the Environment" is excerpted from "Cancer-Causing Substances in the Environment," National Cancer Institute (NCI), March 18, 2015; Text beginning with the heading "Environmental Influences on Breast Cancer Risk—the Evidence Mounts" is excerpted from "Environmental Influences on Breast Cancer Risk—the Evidence Mounts," National Institute of Environmental Health Sciences (NIEHS), March 18, 2015.

How Can Exposures to Carcinogens Be Limited?

In the United States, regulations have been put in place to reduce exposures to known carcinogens in the workplace. Outside of the workplace, people can also take steps to limit their exposure to known carcinogens, such as testing their basement for radon, quitting smoking, limiting sun exposure, or maintaining a healthy weight.

How Many Cancers Are Caused by Involuntary Exposure to Carcinogens in the Environment?

This question cannot be answered with certainty because the precise causes of most cancers are not known. Some researchers have suggested that, in most populations, environmental exposures are responsible for a relatively small proportion of total cancers (less than 4 percent), whereas other researchers attribute a higher proportion (19 percent) to environmental exposures.

Who Decides Which Environmental Exposures Cause Cancer in Humans?

Two organizations—the National Toxicology Program (NTP), an interagency program of the U.S. Department of Health and Human Services (HHS), and the International Agency for Research on Cancer (IARC), the cancer agency of the World Health Organization—have developed lists of substances that, based on the available scientific evidence, are known or are reasonably anticipated to be human carcinogens.

Specifically, the NTP publishes the Report on Carcinogens every few years. This congressionally mandated publication identifies agents, substances, mixtures, or exposures (collectively called "substances") in the environment that may cause cancer in humans. The 2014 edition lists 56 known human carcinogens and includes descriptions of the process for preparing the science-based report and the criteria used to list a substance as a carcinogen.

IARC also produces science-based reports on substances that can increase the risk of cancer in humans. Since 1971, the agency has evaluated more than 900 agents, including chemicals, complex mixtures, occupational exposures, physical agents, biological agents, and lifestyle factors. Of these, more than 400 have been identified as carcinogenic, probably carcinogenic, or possibly carcinogenic to humans.

IARC convenes expert scientists to evaluate the evidence that an agent can increase the risk of cancer. The agency describes the principles, procedures, and scientific criteria that guide the evaluations. For instance, agents are selected for review based on two main criteria: (a) there is evidence of human exposure and (b) there is some evidence or suspicion of carcinogenicity.

How Does the NTP Decide Whether to Include a Substance on Its List of Known Human Carcinogens?

As new potential carcinogens are identified, they are evaluated scientifically by the NTP's Board of Scientific Counselors and the NTP Director. Next, a draft Report on Carcinogens monograph is prepared, which is reviewed by other scientific experts as needed, the public, and other federal agencies. The draft monograph is then revised as necessary and released for additional public comment and peer review by a dedicated panel of experts. Lastly, a finalized monograph and recommendation for listing is sent to the HHS Secretary for approval.

Cancer-Causing Substances in the Environment

Cancer is caused by changes to certain genes that alter the way our cells function. Some of these genetic changes occur naturally when DNA is replicated during the process of cell division. But others are the result of environmental exposures that damage DNA. These exposures may include substances, such as the chemicals in tobacco smoke, or radiation, such as ultraviolet rays from the sun.

People can avoid some cancer-causing exposures, such as tobacco smoke and the sun's rays. But others are harder to avoid, especially if they are in the air we breathe, the water we drink, the food we eat, or the materials we use to do our jobs. Scientists are studying which exposures may cause or contribute to the development of cancer. Understanding which exposures are harmful, and where they are found, may help people to avoid them.

The substances listed below are among the most likely carcinogens to affect human health. Simply because a substance has been designated as a carcinogen, however, does not mean that the substance will necessarily cause cancer. Many factors influence whether a person exposed to a carcinogen will develop cancer, including the amount and duration of the exposure and the individual's genetic background.

- Aflatoxins
- Aristolochic Acids

- Arsenic

- Asbestos

- Benzene

- Benzidine

- Beryllium

- 1,3-Butadiene

- Cadmium

- Coal Tar and Coal-Tar Pitch

- Coke-Oven Emissions

- Crystalline Silica (respirable size)

- Erionite

- Ethylene Oxide

- Formaldehyde

- Hexavalent Chromium Compounds

- Indoor Emissions from the Household Combustion of Coal

- Mineral Oils: Untreated and Mildly Treated

- Nickel Compounds

- Radon

- Secondhand Tobacco Smoke (Environmental Tobacco Smoke)

- Soot

- Strong Inorganic Acid Mists Containing Sulfuric Acid

- Thorium

- Vinyl Chloride

- Wood Dust

Environmental Influences on Breast Cancer Risk—the Evidence Mounts

As a kid growing up on a farm in Wisconsin, Sue Fenton was fascinated by dairy cows. "I always wondered how they could produce milk nearly year-round, for year after year," she said.

Now a Ph.D. and a reproductive endocrinologist with the National Toxicology Program (NTP) at NIEHS, Fenton highlighted the cutting edge of mammary gland research, guest editing "Environmental Impact on Breast Development and Disease," a July 2015 special issue of the journal Reproductive Toxicology.

The extent of the problem was spelled out in a summary article co-authored by Linda Birnbaum, Ph.D., director of NIEHS and NTP, and Gwen Collman, Ph.D., NIEHS Director of Division of Extramural Research and Training.

"Despite decades of research, the number of women diagnosed with breast cancer continues to rise," they wrote. "In 2014, an estimated 233,000 women and 2400 men in the United States were diagnosed with breast cancer, and approximately 40,000 women died from it."

It's Complicated

According to Fenton, the breast's susceptibility to cancer is exceptional among the reproductive organs. "Other tissues such as the ovary, testis, and uterus are also critical for reproduction; yet, they do not display the high degree of carcinogenicity in humans as seen in the breast," she wrote in her editorial.

The reason, she explained, is the complexity of the tissue, which makes it difficult to get a handle on the reasons for its carcinogenicity.

"There are many cell types in the mammary gland, plus its own fat, which means it has its own hormones from fat. And the breast actually receives signals from about ten different organs," she said. "This is one of the reasons why more people don't do this kind of work. You can't just take the epithelial cells out of their tissue, use them in culture, and expect them to behave as they would in the body, as you can do with many other tissues."

Timing Matters

To better understand how endocrine disrupting chemicals (EDCs) cause cancer, the scientists in the special issue relied on animal studies and on associations found in cohorts of children.

"We looked at early exposure to a chemical, as opposed to at the time of diagnosis, and we're finding some strong risk factors associated with that," Fenton said. "Fetal exposure, or in utero exposure, or prenatal—one of those words is used in almost every one of these studies. I didn't ask for such papers. It's just that people are recognizing the importance of it, and they are setting their experiments up that way."

127

Birnbaum and her co-authors reinforced the importance of timing in their summary. "There are windows of susceptibility during the life course," they wrote. "To understand the role of the environment in the etiology of breast cancer, we must understand life stages when the breast is most susceptible to environmental insults."

A Sense of Urgency

The evidence for the role of chemical exposure shows up in outcomes such as early puberty and accelerated breast development, which Fenton said is rampant across the globe. "It's happening much faster than gene change, it's not genetic," she said. "It's definitely the environment playing a role."

Over the years, with growing evidence for the environmental contributions to cancer, Fenton has acquired a sense of urgency. "It's one of the most often diagnosed cancers in women, and we know so much less than we know about other cancers."

Chapter 22

Hormone Replacement Therapy and Breast Cancer Risk

What Are Hormones?

A hormone is a chemical substance made by an organ like the thyroid gland or ovary. Hormones control different body functions. Examples of hormones are estrogen, progesterone, testosterone, and thyroid hormone. In a woman's body during the menopause transition, the months or years right before menopause (her final menstrual period), levels of several hormones, including estrogen and progesterone, go up and down irregularly. This happens as the ovaries begin working less and less well.

Menopause is a normal part of aging. It is not a disease or disorder. Women who have symptoms like hot flashes and night sweats may decide to use hormones like estrogen because of the benefits, but there are also side effects and risks to consider.

What about Hormones?

Symptoms such as hot flashes might result from the changing hormone levels during the menopause transition. After a woman's last

This chapter includes text excerpted from "Hormones and Menopause," National Institute on Aging (NIA), August 2012. Reviewed April 2016.

menstrual period, when her ovaries make much less estrogen and progesterone, some symptoms of menopause might disappear, but others may continue or get worse.

To help relieve these symptoms, some women use hormones. This is called menopausal hormone therapy (MHT). This approach used to be called hormone replacement therapy or HRT. MHT is a more current, umbrella term that describes several different hormone combinations available in a variety of forms and doses.

How Would I Use Menopausal Hormone Therapy?

Estrogen is a hormone used to relieve the symptoms of menopause. A woman whose uterus has been removed can use estrogen only (E). But a woman who still has a uterus must add progesterone or a progestin (synthetic progesterone) along with the estrogen (E+P). This combination lowers the chance of an unwanted thickening of the lining of the uterus and reduces the risk of cancer of the uterus, an uncommon, but possible result of using estrogen alone.

Estrogen comes in many forms. You can use a skin patch, vaginal tablet, or cream; take a pill; or get an implant, shot, or vaginal ring insert. You could even apply a gel or spray. There are also different types of estrogen (such as estradiol and conjugated estrogens). Estradiol is the most important type of estrogen in a woman's body before menopause. Other hormones, progesterone or progestin, can be taken as a pill, sometimes in the same pill as the estrogen, as well as a patch (combined with estrogen), shot, IUD (intrauterine device), gel, or vaginal suppository.

The form of MHT your doctor suggests may depend on your symptoms. For example, an estrogen patch (also called transdermal estrogen) or pill (oral estrogen) can relieve hot flashes, night sweats (hot flashes that bother you at night), and vaginal dryness. Other forms—vaginal creams, tablets, or rings—are used mostly for vaginal dryness alone. The vaginal ring insert might also help some urinary tract symptoms.

The dose can also vary, as can the timing of those doses. Some doctors suggest that estrogen be used every day, but that the progesterone or progestin be used cyclically—for 10 to 14 straight days every 4 weeks. A cyclic schedule is thought to mimic how the body makes estrogen and progesterone before menopause. This approach can cause some spotting or bleeding, like a light period, which might get lighter or go away in time. Alternatively, some women take estrogen and progesterone or progestin continuously—every day of the month.

Is There a Downside to Taking Hormones?

Research has found that, for some women, there are serious risks, including an increased chance of heart disease, stroke, blood clots, and breast cancer, when using MHT. The Women's Health Initiative also found an increased risk of possible dementia in women who started MHT after age 65. These concerns are why every woman needs to think a lot before deciding to use menopausal hormone therapy.

Also, some women develop noticeable side effects from using hormones:

- Breast tenderness

- Spotting or a return of monthly periods

- Cramping

- Bloating

By changing the type or amount of the hormones, the way they are taken, or the timing of the doses, your doctor may be able to help control these side effects. Or, over time, they may go away on their own.

What More Should I Know about the Benefits and Risks of Hormones?

Over the years, research findings have led to a variety of positive, negative, and sometimes conflicting reports about menopausal hormone therapy. Some of these findings came from randomized clinical trials, the most convincing type of research. Historically, clinical trials often used one type of estrogen called conjugated estrogens. Several other types of estrogen, as well as progesterone and progestins, have also been tested in small trials to see if they have an effect on heart disease, breast cancer, or dementia.

Let's look more closely at what we have learned from these small studies.

Hot flashes and night sweats. Estrogen will relieve most women's hot flashes and night sweats. If you stop using estrogen, you may again start having hot flashes. Lifestyle changes and certain prescription medicines also might help some women with hot flashes. For most women, hot flashes and night sweats go away in time.

Vaginal dryness. Estrogen improves vaginal dryness, probably for as long as you continue to use it. If vaginal dryness is your only symptom, your doctor might prescribe a vaginal estrogen. A water-based lubricant, but not petroleum jelly, may also relieve vaginal discomfort.

Cholesterol levels. Estrogen improves cholesterol levels, lowering LDLs (the "bad" kind of cholesterol) and raising HDLs (the "good" kind of cholesterol). The pill form of estrogen can cause the level of triglycerides (a type of fat in the blood) to go up. The estrogen patch does not seem to have this effect, but it also does not improve cholesterol to the same degree as the pill form. But, improving cholesterol levels is not a reason to take estrogen. Other medicines and lifestyle changes will improve cholesterol levels more effectively.

What Is the Women's Health Initiative? What Have We Learned from It?

Before menopause, women generally have a lower risk of heart disease than men. This led experts to wonder whether giving women estrogen after menopause might help prevent heart disease. In 1992, the National Institutes of Health (NIH), the nation's premier medical research agency, began the Women's Health Initiative (WHI) to explore ways postmenopausal women might prevent heart disease, as well as osteoporosis and cancer. One part of the WHI, the Hormone Trial, looked at oral conjugated estrogens used alone (E therapy or ET) or with a particular progestin (EPT) to see if, in postmenopausal women, estrogen could prevent heart disease without increasing the chance of breast cancer.

In July 2002, the EPT part of the WHI Hormone Trial was stopped early because it became clear to the researchers that the overall risk of taking E+P outweighed the benefits:

Benefits

- Fewer fractures
- Less chance of cancer in the colon and/or rectum

Risks

- More strokes
- More serious blood clots
- More heart attacks
- More breast cancers

In April 2004, the rest of the Hormone Trial, the E alone or ET trial, was also halted because using estrogen alone increased the risk of stroke, and it was not likely that there would be a positive effect on heart attacks. Unlike using estrogen plus progestin, using estrogen alone did not increase the risk of heart attacks or breast cancer, but like the EPT trial, there were fewer fractures.

During the first 3 years after stopping the WHI EPT trial, women were no longer at greater risk of heart disease, stroke, or serious blood clots than women who had not used MHT. On the other hand, they also no longer had greater protection from fractures. The women still had an increased risk of breast cancer, but their risk was smaller than it was while they were using hormones. During the first 4 years after stopping the WHI ET trial, the increased risk of stroke disappeared, there was no effect on risk of heart attack, but the slightly lower risk of breast cancer continued.

It appears from the WHI that women **should** not begin using MHT to protect their health—it does not appear to prevent heart disease or dementia when started several years after menopause. In fact, older women in the study using MHT were at increased risk of certain diseases. Women who were less than age 60 did not appear to be at increased risk of heart disease but were at increased risk of stroke. For these women, the overall risks and benefits appeared to be balanced, but there is no strong evidence to support women under age 60 using MHT to prevent chronic diseases of aging, such as heart disease and dementia.

It is important to remember that the WHI findings are based on the specific oral form (rather than patch, gel, etc.), dose, and type of estrogen and progestin studied in the WHI. Which hormones and dose you use and the way you take them might change these benefits and risks. We don't know how the WHI findings apply to these other types, forms, and doses of estrogen and progesterone or progestin, or what the effects of other treatment options are.

What Are Some Other Options?

Women now have more options than when the WHI study was first planned. More types of estrogens are available, and some of them come in a variety of forms. For example, synthetic estradiol, now available in several forms (pill, patch, cream, gel, etc.), is chemically identical to the estrogen most active in women's bodies before menopause. If it is not taken by mouth, but rather applied to the skin or taken as a shot, estradiol appears to work the same way as estradiol made in the body. Lower doses of estrogen are available. Investigators are now studying a low-dose estradiol patch (transdermal estradiol) compared to a low-dose conjugated-estrogens pill to see whether one or both slow hardening of the arteries in women around the age of menopause and whether the estradiol patch is as effective and, perhaps, safer than the conjugated estrogens pill. These alternatives are creating more choices for women seeking relief from their menopausal symptoms, as well as a variety of new opportunities for research.

Besides a pill, some estrogens come in different and sometimes new forms—skin patch, gel, emulsion, spray, and vaginal ring, cream, and tablet. These forms work in the body somewhat differently than a pill by entering your body directly through the skin or walls of the vagina. Oral estrogen (a pill) is chemically changed in the liver before reaching your tissues. Some studies suggest that if estrogen enters through the skin and bypasses the liver, the risk of serious blood clots might be lower. Others suggest a lower risk of gallbladder disease. This may also allow a change in dosage—further testing may show that the same benefits might come from lower doses than are needed with a pill.

What Questions Remain Unanswered?

Experts now know more about menopause and have a better understanding of what the WHI results mean. But, they have new questions also.

- The average age of women participating in the trial was 63, more than 10 years older than the average age of menopause, and the WHI was looking at reducing the risk of chronic diseases of growing older like heart disease and osteoporosis. Do the WHI results apply to younger women choosing MHT to relieve symptoms around the time of menopause or to women who have early surgical menopause (surgery to remove both ovaries or the uterus)?

- Other studies show that lower doses of estrogen than were studied in the WHI provide relief from symptoms of menopause for some women and still help women maintain bone density. What are the long-term benefits and risks of lower doses of estrogen?

- In the WHI, women using E alone did not seem to have a greater risk of heart disease than women not using hormones. Does this mean that healthy women in their 50s who start using estrogen alone are not at higher eventual risk for heart disease than women who don't use estrogen?

- Would using progesterone or a different progestin than the one used in the WHI be less risky to a woman's heart, blood vessels, and breasts?

- The combination menopausal hormone therapy used in the WHI makes it somewhat more likely that a woman could develop breast cancer, especially with long-term use. Is using a different type of estrogen, a smaller dose of estrogen or progesterone, or a different progestin (instead of medroxyprogesterone acetate) safer?

- Does using estrogen around the time of menopause increase the risk of possible dementia in later life, as starting it after age 65 did in the WHI Memory Study (WHIMS)? Or does it decrease the risk of dementia later in life?

The National Institute on Aging and other parts of the National Institutes of Health, along with other medical research centers, continue to explore questions such as these. They hope that in the future these studies will give women additional facts needed to make informed decisions about relieving menopausal symptoms.

What Are "Natural Hormones"?

The "natural hormones" used are estrogen and progesterone made from plants such as soy or yams. Some people also call them bioidentical hormones because they are supposed to be chemically the same as the hormones naturally made by a woman's body. These so-called natural hormones are put together (compounded) by a compounding pharmacist. This pharmacist follows a formula decided on by a doctor familiar with this approach. Compounded hormones are not regulated or approved by the FDA. So, we don't know much about how safe or effective they are or how the quality and quantity vary from batch to batch.

Some drug companies also make estrogens and progesterone from plants like soy and yams. Some of these are also chemically identical to the hormones made by your body. These other forms of MHT are available by prescription. Importantly, these estrogens and progesterone made by drug companies are regulated and approved by the FDA.

There are also "natural" treatments for the symptoms of menopause that are available over-the-counter, without a prescription. Black cohosh is one that women use, but a couple of clinical trials have shown that it did not relieve hot flashes in postmenopausal women or those approaching menopause. Because of rare reports of serious liver disease, scientists are concerned about the possible effects of black cohosh on the liver. Other "natural" treatments are made from soy or yams. None of these are regulated or approved by the FDA.

What's Right for Me?

There is no single answer for all women who are trying to decide whether to use MHT. You have to look at your own needs and weigh your own risks. Here are some questions you can ask yourself and talk to your doctor about:

- *Do menopausal symptoms such as hot flashes or vaginal dryness bother me a lot?* Like many women, your hot flashes or night sweats will likely go away over time, but vaginal dryness may not. MHT and other options can help with troubling symptoms.

- *Am I at risk for developing osteoporosis?* Estrogen might protect bone mass while you use it. However, there are other drugs that can protect your bones without MHT's risks. Talk to your doctor about the risks and benefits of those medicines for you.

- *Do I have a history of heart disease or risk factors such as high blood cholesterol?* If so, using estrogen and progestin can increase that risk even more.

- *Do I have a family history of breast cancer?* If you have a family history of breast cancer, check with your doctor about your risk.

- *I have high levels of triglycerides and a family history of gall-bladder disease. Can I use MHT?* The safety of any kind of MHT in women with high levels of triglycerides or a family history of gallbladder disease is not known. But some experts think that using a patch will not raise your triglyceride level or increase your chance of gallbladder problems. Using an oral estrogen pill might.

- *Do I have liver disease or a history of stroke or blood clots in my veins?* MHT, especially taken by mouth, might not be safe for you to use.

In all cases, talk to your doctor about how best to treat or prevent your menopause symptoms or diseases for which you are at risk.

If you are already using menopausal hormone therapy and think you would like to stop, first ask your doctor how to do that. Some doctors suggest tapering off slowly.

Whatever decision you make now about using MHT is not final. You can start or end the treatment at any time, although, as we learned from the WHI, it appears that it is best not to start MHT many years after menopause. If you stop, some of your risks will lessen over time, but so will the benefits. Discuss your decision about menopausal hormone therapy with your doctor at your annual checkup.

MHT Is Not One Size Fits All

Each woman is different, and the decision for each one about menopausal hormone therapy will probably also be different.

Chapter 23

Oral Contraceptives and Breast Cancer Risk

What Causes Breast Cancer?

National Institute of Environmental Health Sciences (NIEHS) research has clearly shown that breast cancer is caused by a combination of genetic, hormonal, and environmental risk factors. Since environmental factors may be identified and modified, NIEHS scientists believe that prevention strategies are the best way to stop breast cancer before it starts.

Several environmental factors have been consistently associated with increased breast cancer risk:

- Use of combination hormone therapy products

- Use of oral contraceptives

- Exposure to ionizing radiation

- Being overweight or obese, especially after menopause

- Alcohol

This chapter contains text excerpted from the following sources: Text under the heading "What Causes Breast Cancer?" is excerpted from "Breast Cancer," National Institute of Environmental Health Sciences (NIEHS), January 7, 2016; Text beginning with the heading "What Types of Oral Contraceptives Are Available in the United States?" is excerpted from "Oral Contraceptives and Cancer Risk," National Cancer Institute (NCI), March 21, 2012. Reviewed April 2016.

- Diethylstilbestrol (DES), a synthetic estrogen given to pregnant women in the 1940s to 1971 to prevent miscarriages or premature deliveries

Research also shows that more physical activity is linked to decreased breast cancer risk.

What Types of Oral Contraceptives Are Available in the United States?

Two types of oral contraceptives (birth control pills) are currently available in the United States. The most commonly prescribed type of oral contraceptive contains man-made versions of the natural female hormones estrogen and progesterone. This type of birth control pill is often called a "combined oral contraceptive." The second type is called the minipill. It contains only progestin, which is the man-made version of progesterone that is used in oral contraceptives.

How Could Oral Contraceptives Influence Cancer Risk?

Naturally occurring estrogen and progesterone have been found to influence the development and growth of some cancers. Because birth control pills contain female hormones, researchers have been interested in determining whether there is any link between these widely used contraceptives and cancer risk.

The results of population studies to examine associations between oral contraceptive use and cancer risk have not always been consistent. Overall, however, the risks of endometrial and ovarian cancer appear to be reduced with the use of oral contraceptives, whereas the risks of breast, cervical, and liver cancer appear to be increased.

How Do Oral Contraceptives Affect Breast Cancer Risk?

A woman's risk of developing breast cancer depends on several factors, some of which are related to her natural hormones. Hormonal and reproductive history factors that increase the risk of breast cancer include factors that may allow breast tissue to be exposed to high levels of hormones for longer periods of time, such as the following:

- Beginning menstruation at an early age
- Experiencing menopause at a late age

- Later age at first pregnancy
- Not having children at all

A 1996 analysis of epidemiologic data from more than 50 studies worldwide by the Collaborative Group on Hormonal Factors in Breast Cancer found that women who were current or recent users of birth control pills had a slightly higher risk of developing breast cancer than women who had never used the pill. The risk was highest for women who started using oral contraceptives as teenagers. However, 10 or more years after women stopped using oral contraceptives, their risk of developing breast cancer had returned to the same level as if they had never used birth control pills, regardless of family history of breast cancer, reproductive history, geographic area of residence, ethnic background, differences in study design, dose and type of hormone(s) used, or duration of use. In addition, breast cancers diagnosed in women who had stopped using oral contraceptives for 10 or more years were less advanced than breast cancers diagnosed in women who had never used oral contraceptives.

A recent analysis of data from the Nurses' Health Study, which has been following more than 116,000 female nurses who were 24 to 43 years old when they enrolled in the study in 1989, found that the participants who used oral contraceptives had a slight increase in breast cancer risk. However, nearly all of the increased risk was seen among women who took a specific type of oral contraceptive, a "triphasic" pill, in which the dose of hormones is changed in three stages over the course of a woman's monthly cycle.

141

Chapter 24

Overweight, Obesity, and Cancer Risk

Obesity

People who are obese may have an increased risk of several types of cancer, including cancers of the breast (in women who have been through menopause), colon, rectum, endometrium (lining of the uterus), esophagus, kidney, pancreas, and gallbladder.

Conversely, eating a healthy diet, being physically active, and keeping a healthy weight may help reduce risk of some cancers. These healthy behaviors are also important to lessen the risk of other illnesses, such as heart disease, type II diabetes, and high blood pressure.

How Common Is Overweight or Obesity?

Results from the 2007-2008 National Health and Nutrition Examination Survey (NHANES) show that 68 percent of U.S. adults age

This chapter contains text excerpted from the following sources: Text under the heading "Obesity" is excerpted from "Obesity," National Cancer Institute (NCI), April 29, 2015; Text beginning with the heading "How Common Is Overweight or Obesity?" is excerpted from "Obesity and Cancer Risk," National Cancer Institute (NCI), January 3, 2012. Reviewed April 2016; Text under the heading "Health Effects of Overweight and Obesity" is excerpted from "The Health Effects of Overweight and Obesity," Centers for Disease Control and Prevention (CDC), June 5, 2015.

20 years and older are overweight or obese. In 1988–1994, by contrast, only 56 percent of adults age 20 and older were overweight or obese.

In addition, the percentage of children who are overweight or obese has also increased. Among children and teens ages 2 to 19, 17 percent are estimated to be obese, based on the 2007–2008 survey. In 1988–1994, that figure was only 10 percent.

What Is Known about the Relationship between Obesity and Cancer?

Obesity is associated with increased risks of the following cancer types, and possibly others as well:

- Esophagus
- Pancreas
- Colon and rectum
- Breast (after menopause)
- Endometrium (lining of the uterus)
- Kidney
- Thyroid
- Gallbladder

One study, using NCI Surveillance, Epidemiology, and End Results (SEER) data, estimated that in 2007 in the United States, about 34,000 new cases of cancer in men (4 percent) and 50,500 in women (7 percent) were due to obesity. The percentage of cases attributed to obesity varied widely for different cancer types but was as high as 40 percent for some cancers, particularly endometrial cancer and esophageal adenocarcinoma.

A projection of the future health and economic burden of obesity in 2030 estimated that continuation of existing trends in obesity will lead to about 500,000 additional cases of cancer in the United States by 2030. This analysis also found that if every adult reduced their BMI by 1 percent, which would be equivalent to a weight loss of roughly 1 kg (or 2.2 lbs) for an adult of average weight, this would prevent the increase in the number of cancer cases and actually result in the avoidance of about 100,000 new cases of cancer.

Several possible mechanisms have been suggested to explain the association of obesity with increased risk of certain cancers:

- Fat tissue produces excess amounts of estrogen, high levels of which have been associated with the risk of breast, endometrial, and some other cancers.

144

- Obese people often have increased levels of insulin and insulin-like growth factor-1 (IGF-1) in their blood (a condition known as hyperinsulinemia or insulin resistance), which may promote the development of certain tumors.

- Fat cells produce hormones, called adipokines, that may stimulate or inhibit cell growth. For example, leptin, which is more abundant in obese people, seems to promote cell proliferation, whereas adiponectin, which is less abundant in obese people, may have antiproliferative effects.

- Fat cells may also have direct and indirect effects on other tumor growth regulators, including mammalian target of rapamycin (mTOR) and AMP-activated protein kinase.

- Obese people often have chronic low-level, or "subacute," inflammation, which has been associated with increased cancer risk.

Other possible mechanisms include altered immune responses, effects on the nuclear factor kappa beta system, and oxidative stress.

What Is Known about the Relationship between Obesity and Breast Cancer?

Many studies have shown that overweight and obesity are associated with a modest increase in risk of postmenopausal breast cancer. This higher risk is seen mainly in women who have never used menopausal hormone therapy (MHT) and for tumors that express both estrogen and progesterone receptors.

Overweight and obesity have, by contrast, been found to be associated with a reduced risk of premenopausal breast cancer in some studies.

The relationship between obesity and breast cancer may be affected by the stage of life in which a woman gains weight and becomes obese. Epidemiologists are actively working to address this question. Weight gain during adult life, most often from about age 18 to between the ages of 50 and 60, has been consistently associated with risk of breast cancer after menopause.

The increased risk of postmenopausal breast cancer is thought to be due to increased levels of estrogen in obese women. After menopause, when the ovaries stop producing hormones, fat tissue becomes the most important source of estrogen. Because obese women have more fat tissue, their estrogen levels are higher, potentially leading to more rapid growth of estrogen-responsive breast tumors.

The relationship between obesity and breast cancer risk may also vary by race and ethnicity. There is limited evidence that the risk associated with overweight and obesity may be less among African American and Hispanic women than among white women.

Health Effects of Overweight and Obesity

People who are obese, compared to those with a normal or healthy weight, are at increased risk for many serious diseases and health conditions, including the following:

- All-causes of death (mortality)
- High blood pressure (Hypertension)
- High LDL cholesterol, low HDL cholesterol, or high levels of triglycerides (Dyslipidemia)
- Type 2 diabetes
- Coronary heart disease
- Stroke
- Gallbladder disease
- Osteoarthritis (a breakdown of cartilage and bone within a joint)
- Sleep apnea and breathing problems
- Some cancers (endometrial, breast, colon, kidney, gallbladder, and liver)
- Low quality of life
- Mental illness such as clinical depression, anxiety, and other mental disorders
- Body pain and difficulty with physical functioning

Chapter 25

Reproductive History and Breast Cancer Risk

Is There a Relationship between Pregnancy and Breast Cancer Risk?

Studies have shown that a woman's risk of developing breast cancer is related to her exposure to hormones that are produced by her ovaries (endogenous estrogen and progesterone). Reproductive factors that increase the duration and/or levels of exposure to ovarian hormones, which stimulate cell growth, have been associated with an increase in breast cancer risk. These factors include early onset of menstruation, late onset of menopause, later age at first pregnancy, and never having given birth.

Pregnancy and breastfeeding both reduce a woman's lifetime number of menstrual cycles, and thus her cumulative exposure to endogenous hormones. In addition, pregnancy and breastfeeding have direct effects on breast cells, causing them to differentiate, or mature, so they can produce milk. Some researchers hypothesize that these differentiated cells are more resistant to becoming transformed into cancer cells than cells that have not undergone differentiation.

This chapter includes text excerpted from "Reproductive History and Breast Cancer Risk," National Cancer Institute (NCI), May 10, 2011. Reviewed April 2016.

Are Any Pregnancy-Related Factors Associated with a Lower Risk of Breast Cancer?

Some pregnancy-related factors have been associated with a reduced risk of developing breast cancer later in life. These factors include the following:

- **Early age at first full-term pregnancy:** Women who have their first full-term pregnancy at an early age have a decreased risk of developing breast cancer later in life. For example, in women who have a first full-term pregnancy before age 20, the risk of developing breast cancer is about half that of women whose first full-term pregnancy occurs after the age of 30. This risk reduction is limited to hormone receptor-positive breast cancer; age at first full-term pregnancy does not appear to affect the risk of hormone receptor-negative breast cancer.

- **Increasing number of births:** The risk of breast cancer declines with the number of children born. Women who have given birth to five or more children have half the risk of women who have not given birth. Some evidence indicates that the reduced risk associated with an increased number of births may be limited to hormone receptor-positive breast cancer.

- **History of preeclampsia:** Women who have had preeclampsia may have a decreased risk of developing breast cancer. Preeclampsia is a complication of pregnancy in which a woman develops high blood pressure and excess amounts of protein in her urine. Scientists are studying whether certain hormones and proteins associated with preeclampsia may affect breast cancer risk.

- **Longer duration of breastfeeding**: Breastfeeding for an extended period (at least a year) is associated with a decreased risk of both hormone receptor-positive and hormone receptor-negative breast cancer.

Are Any Pregnancy-Related Factors Associated with an Increase in Breast Cancer Risk?

Some factors related to pregnancy may increase the risk of breast cancer. These factors include the following:

- **Older age at birth of first child**: The older a woman is when she has her first full-term pregnancy, the higher her risk of breast cancer. Women who are older than 30 when they give birth to their first child have a higher risk of breast cancer than women who have never given birth.

- **Recent childbirth**: Women who have recently given birth have a short-term increase in risk that declines after about 10 years. The reason for this temporary increase is not known, but some researchers believe that it may be due to the effect of high levels of hormones on microscopic cancers or to the rapid growth of breast cells during pregnancy.

- **Taking diethylstilbestrol (DES) during pregnancy**: Women who took DES during pregnancy have a slightly higher risk of developing breast cancer than women who did not take DES during pregnancy. Daughters of women who took DES during pregnancy may also have a slightly higher risk of developing breast cancer after age 40 than women who were not exposed to DES while in the womb. DES is a synthetic form of estrogen that was used between the early 1940s and 1971 to prevent miscarriages and other pregnancy problems.

Is Abortion Linked to Breast Cancer Risk?

A few retrospective (case-control) studies reported in the mid-1990s suggested that induced abortion (the deliberate ending of a pregnancy) was associated with an increased risk of breast cancer. However, these studies had important design limitations that could have affected the results. A key limitation was their reliance on self-reporting of medical history information by the study participants, which can introduce bias. Prospective studies, which are more rigorous in design and unaffected by such bias, have consistently shown no association between induced abortion and breast cancer risk. Moreover, in 2009, the Committee on Gynecologic Practice of the American College of Obstetricians and Gynecologists concluded that "more rigorous recent studies demonstrate no causal relationship between induced abortion and a subsequent increase in breast cancer risk." Major findings from these recent studies include the following:

- Women who have had an induced abortion have the same risk of breast cancer as other women.

- Women who have had a spontaneous abortion (miscarriage) have the same risk of breast cancer as other women.

- Cancers other than breast cancer also appear to be unrelated to a history of induced or spontaneous abortion.

149

Does Pregnancy Affect the Risk of Other Cancers?

Research has shown the following with regard to pregnancy and the risk of other cancers:

- Women who have had a full-term pregnancy have reduced risks of ovarian and endometrial cancer. Furthermore, the risks of these cancers decline with each additional full-term pregnancy.

- Pregnancy also plays a role in an extremely rare type of tumor called a gestational trophoblastic tumor. In this type of tumor, which starts in the uterus, cancer cells grow in the tissues that are formed following conception.

- There is some evidence that pregnancy-related factors may affect the risk of other cancer types, but these relationships have not been as well studied as those for breast and gynecologic cancers. The associations require further study to clarify the exact relationships.

As in the development of breast cancer, exposures to hormones are thought to explain the role of pregnancy in the development of ovarian, endometrial, and other cancers. Changes in the levels of hormones during pregnancy may contribute to the variation in risk of these tumors after pregnancy.

Chapter 26

Personal Care Products and the Risk of Breast Cancer

Are There Safety Concerns Related to the Use of Parabens in Cosmetics?

Parabens are preservatives that prevent the growth of potentially harmful bacteria that could live in some cosmetics products. Safety questions about the use of parabens in cosmetics center around parabens' potential to act like estrogen, a hormone that can be associated with the development of breast cancer. Studies have shown, however, that parabens have significantly less estrogenic activity than the body's naturally occurring estrogen. Parabens have not been shown to be harmful as used in cosmetics, where they are present only in very small amounts.

This chapter contains text excerpted from the following sources: Text under the heading "Are There Safety Concerns Related to the Use of Parabens in Cosmetics?" is excerpted from "Cosmetics Safety Q and A: Parabens," U.S. Food and Drug Administration (FDA), December 9, 2015; Text beginning with the heading "Paired Serum and Urine Concentrations of Biomarkers of Diethyl Phthalate, Methyl Paraben, and Triclosan in Rats" is excerpted from "Paired Serum and Urine Concentrations of Biomarkers of Diethyl Phthalate, Methyl Paraben, and Triclosan in Rats," National Institute of Environmental Health Sciences (NIEHS), January 2016.

Paired Serum and Urine Concentrations of Biomarkers of Diethyl Phthalate, Methyl Paraben, and Triclosan in Rats

Effects of Phthalates and Phenols

Exposure to environmental chemicals, including phthalates and phenols such as parabens and triclosan, is ubiquitous within the U.S. general population. There is growing interest in the possible adverse human health outcomes associated with exposure to these chemicals.

Phthalates are used in a wide range of consumer goods. Low molecular weight phthalates [e.g., diethyl phthalate (DEP)] are often found in personal care products (e.g., fragrances, shampoo, cosmetics). In rats, DEP is hydrolyzed to its monoester metabolite, monoethyl phthalate (MEP); DEP metabolism is assumed to be similar in humans. Elimination half-lives of DEP and MEP in mammals have not been experimentally defined but are believed to be a few hours. Therefore, MEP has been used as a biomarker of recent exposure to DEP. Several health effects have been associated with elevated urinary concentrations of MEP, including adverse male reproductive outcomes, altered neonatal behavior and neurobehavioral development, and increased breast cancer risk.

Parabens are commonly used as preservatives in personal care products, cosmetics, pharmaceuticals, and even in the processing of foods and beverages. Most Americans are exposed to various parabens, including methylparaben (MPB). Because of their potential estrogenic activity, parabens have been suggested to play a role in breast cancer, albeit orders of magnitude lower than that of endogenous estrogens; however, strong epidemiologic evidence is lacking. Parabens are hydrolyzed to p-hydroxybenzoic acid, which can be conjugated and excreted in urine. p-Hydroxybenzoic acid and its conjugates are nonspecific metabolites of all parabens. However, the concentrations of total (free plus conjugated) urinary species of the parent parabens are considered valid biomarkers of paraben exposure in humans and have been used as measures of environmental exposure to these chemicals in epidemiologic studies.

Triclosan is a commonly used antimicrobial in personal care and household products ranging from toothpaste, deodorant, and hand soap to cutting boards and textiles. Public interest has been steadily increasing in the ubiquitous sources of exposure to this chemical. The hormonal activity of triclosan has not been clearly established owing to conflicting results from different investigations, including evidence of weak estrogenic and androgenic activity, estrogen receptor antagonism, and anti-androgenic properties. The excretion half-life of triclosan has been estimated as 11 hours for urine and 21 hours for plasma. When excreted in urine, triclosan is mainly in its conjugated form, whereas the percentage of free triclosan is higher in plasma. Urinary concentrations of triclosan (conjugated plus free species) can be used as a biomarker of exposure.

Given the variability in the bioactivities of these chemicals, understanding the dose—response relationship is fundamental and essential for studying their potential biologic or health effects. Furthermore, the dose—response relationship may depart from linearity at low doses, making dose extrapolation difficult and potentially unreliable. Thus, to evaluate risks or investigate the biological effects of environmental chemicals, it is critical to employ doses in animal experiments that are comparable to the human experience. However, the dose ranges used for DEP, MPB, and triclosan in animal studies have been wide and often orders of magnitude higher than humans are likely to encounter. On the basis of increasing evidence suggesting low-dose health effects of these chemicals, there is an urgent need for studies that utilize doses in the range of typical human exposure.

The objective of this study was to investigate the relationship between oral doses of three widely used personal care product ingredients (DEP, MPB, and triclosan) in rats and the resulting urinary and serum biomarker concentrations. We used a traditional rat model, which is commonly employed in toxicology and risk assessment research. The rat has been used extensively for research in developmental and reproductive physiology and endocrinology and has been more thoroughly characterized in these research fields than other species, likewise for identifying likely human carcinogens. Although these experiments are part of a larger study examining personal care product ingredients and breast cancer risk, the results of our study will provide a foundation for future rodent-based health risk assessment studies for human exposure to these chemicals.

The results of this study indicate that oral exposure to three commonly used environmental chemicals, that is, DEP, MPB, and triclosan, has a strong linear relationship with the urinary concentrations of their corresponding biomarkers, but this relationship is not as uniformly strong in serum. The relatively weak association between administered oral gavage dose of DEP and MPB and the serum concentrations of their biomarkers exemplifies why there is growing concern about the use of the proper biologic matrix for exposure assessment. The timing of urine and serum collection was the same, that

153

is, 24 hours after completing treatment; however, urine was collected over a 24-hr period, and blood was collected as a spot sample. The half-lives of the investigated chemicals are relatively short, such that the interval between exposure and biomarker measurement may influence the findings if half-lives differ according to biologic matrix. Moreover, in general, the concentrations of MEP, MPB, and triclosan were much lower in serum than in urine, which is in accord with results obtained in human studies. Taken together, the positive linear association of oral dose with urinary biomarkers, the higher percentages of urinary biomarkers detected compared with serum biomarkers, and the relatively low concentration of biomarkers in serum all support the use of urine as the appropriate biologic matrix for assessing exposure to these non-persistent chemicals.

Conclusion of the Study

In this study, we identified a range of oral doses of three common environmental chemicals that result in urinary biomarker concentrations in a rat model that are consistent with the biomarker concentrations measured in the U.S. female population. Although endemic environmental exposure to the parent chemicals may have contributed to the biomarker concentrations measured in the rodents' urine, the results of this study highlight the importance of carefully considering the oral dose used in animal experiments and provide useful information for selecting doses of DEP, MPB, and triclosan in future studies that evaluate their biological effects in experimental settings.

Chapter 27

Understanding Your Risk: Genetic Counseling for Cancer

What Is Genetic Testing?

Genetic testing looks for specific inherited changes (mutations) in a person's chromosomes, genes, or proteins. Genetic mutations can have harmful, beneficial, neutral (no effect), or uncertain effects on health. Mutations that are harmful may increase a person's chance, or risk, of developing a disease such as cancer. Overall, inherited mutations are thought to play a role in about 5 to 10 percent of all cancers.

Cancer can sometimes appear to "run in families" even if it is not caused by an inherited mutation. For example, a shared environment or lifestyle, such as tobacco use, can cause similar cancers to develop among family members. However, certain patterns—such as the types of cancer that develop, other non-cancer conditions that are seen, and the ages at which cancer typically develops—may suggest the presence of a hereditary cancer syndrome.

The genetic mutations that cause many of the known hereditary cancer syndromes have been identified, and genetic testing can confirm whether a condition is, indeed, the result of an inherited syndrome.

This chapter includes text excerpted from "Genetic Testing for Hereditary Cancer Syndromes," National Cancer Institute (NCI), April 11, 2013.

Genetic testing is also done to determine whether family members without obvious illness have inherited the same mutation as a family member who is known to carry a cancer-associated mutation.

Inherited genetic mutations can increase a person's risk of developing cancer through a variety of mechanisms, depending on the function of the gene. Mutations in genes that control cell growth and the repair of damaged DNA are particularly likely to be associated with increased cancer risk.

Genetic testing of tumor samples can also be performed, but this Fact Sheet does not cover such testing.

Does Someone Who Inherits a Cancer-Predisposing Mutation Always Get Cancer?

No. Even if a cancer-predisposing mutation is present in a family, it does not necessarily mean that everyone who inherits the mutation will develop cancer. Several factors influence the outcome in a given person with the mutation.

One factor is the pattern of inheritance of the cancer syndrome. To understand how hereditary cancer syndromes may be inherited, it is helpful to keep in mind that every person has two copies of most genes, with one copy inherited from each parent. Most mutations involved in hereditary cancer syndromes are inherited in one of two main patterns: autosomal dominant and autosomal recessive.

With autosomal dominant inheritance, a single altered copy of the gene is enough to increase a person's chances of developing cancer. In this case, the parent from whom the mutation was inherited may also show the effects of the gene mutation. The parent may also be referred to as a carrier.

With autosomal recessive inheritance, a person has an increased risk of cancer only if he or she inherits a mutant (altered) copy of the gene from each parent. The parents, who each carry one copy of the altered gene along with a normal (unaltered) copy, do not usually have an increased risk of cancer themselves. However, because they can pass the altered gene to their children, they are called carriers.

A third form of inheritance of cancer-predisposing mutations is X-linked recessive inheritance. Males have a single X chromosome, which they inherit from their mothers, and females have two X chromosomes (one from each parent). A female with a recessive cancer-predisposing mutation on one of her X chromosomes and a normal copy of the gene on her other X chromosome is a carrier but will not have an increased risk of cancer. Her sons, however, will have only the altered copy of the gene and will therefore have an increased risk of cancer.

Even when people have one copy of a dominant cancer-predisposing mutation, two copies of a recessive mutation, or, for males, one copy of an X-linked recessive mutation, they may not develop cancer. Some mutations are "incompletely penetrant," which means that only some people will show the effects of these mutations. Mutations can also "vary in their expressivity," which means that the severity of the symptoms may vary from person to person.

What Genetic Tests Are Available for Cancer Risk?

More than 50 hereditary cancer syndromes have been described. The majority of these are caused by highly penetrant mutations that are inherited in a dominant fashion. The list below includes some of the more common inherited cancer syndromes for which genetic testing is available, the gene(s) that are mutated in each syndrome, and the cancer types most often associated with these syndromes.

Hereditary breast cancer and ovarian cancer syndrome

- Genes: BRCA1, BRCA2

- Related cancer types: Female breast, ovarian, and other cancers, including prostate, pancreatic, and male breast cancer

Li-Fraumeni syndrome

- Gene: *TP53*

- Related cancer types: Breast cancer, soft tissue sarcoma, osteosarcoma (bone cancer), leukemia, brain tumors, adrenocortical carcinoma (cancer of the adrenal glands), and other cancers

Cowden syndrome (*PTEN* hamartoma tumor syndrome)

- Gene: *PTEN*

- Related cancer types: Breast, thyroid, endometrial (uterine lining), and other cancers

Lynch syndrome (hereditary nonpolyposis colorectal cancer)

- Genes: *MSh2, MLH1, MSH6, PMS2, EPCAM*

- Related cancer types: Colorectal, endometrial, ovarian, renal pelvis, pancreatic, small intestine, liver and biliary tract, stomach, brain, and breast cancers

Familial adenomatous polyposis

- Gene: *APC*
- Related cancer types: Colorectal cancer, multiple non-malignant colon polyps, and both non-cancerous (benign) and cancerous tumors in the small intestine, brain, stomach, bone, skin, and other tissues

Retinoblastoma

- Gene: *RB1*
- Related cancer types: Eye cancer (cancer of the retina), pineal-oma (cancer of the pineal gland), osteosarcoma, melanoma, and soft tissue sarcoma

Multiple endocrine neoplasia type 1 (Wermer syndrome)

- Gene: *MEN1*
- Related cancer types: Pancreatic endocrine tumors and (usually benign) parathyroid and pituitary gland tumors

Multiple endocrine neoplasia type 2

- Gene: *RET*
- Related cancer types: Medullary thyroid cancer and pheochro-mocytoma (benign adrenal gland tumor)

Von Hippel-Lindau syndrome

- Gene: *VHL*
- Related cancer types: Kidney cancer and multiple noncancerous tumors, including pheochromocytoma

Who Should Consider Genetic Testing for Cancer Risk?

Many experts recommend that genetic testing for cancer risk should be strongly considered when all three of the following criteria are met:

- The person being tested has a personal or family history that suggests an inherited cancer risk condition
- The test results can be adequately interpreted (that is, they can clearly tell whether a specific genetic change is present or absent)
- The results provide information that will help guide a person's future medical care

The features of a person's personal or family medical history that, particularly in combination, may suggest a hereditary cancer syndrome include:

- Cancer that was diagnosed at an unusually young age

- Several different types of cancer that have occurred independently in the same person

- Cancer that has developed in both organs in a set of paired organs, such as both kidneys or both breasts

- Several close blood relatives that have the same type of cancer (for example, a mother, daughter, and sisters with breast cancer)

- Unusual cases of a specific cancer type (for example, breast cancer in a man)

- The presence of birth defects, such as certain noncancerous (benign) skin growths or skeletal abnormalities, that are known to be associated with inherited cancer syndromes

- Being a member of a racial/ethnic group that is known to have an increased chance of having a certain hereditary cancer syndrome and having one or more of the above features as well

It is strongly recommended that a person who is considering genetic testing speak with a professional trained in genetics before deciding whether to be tested. These professionals can include doctors, genetic counselors, and other health care providers (such as nurses, psychologists, or social workers). Genetic counseling can help people consider the risks, benefits, and limitations of genetic testing in their particular situation. Sometimes the genetic professional finds that testing is not needed.

Genetic counseling includes a detailed review of the individual's personal and family medical history related to possible cancer risk. Counseling also includes discussions about such issues as:

- Whether genetic testing is appropriate, which specific test(s) might be used, and the technical accuracy of the test(s)

- The medical implications of a positive or a negative test result

- The possibility that a test result might not be informative—that is, that the information may not be useful in making health care decisions

- The psychological risks and benefits of learning one's genetic test results

- The risk of passing a genetic mutation (if one is present in a parent) to children

Learning about these issues is a key part of the informed consent process. Written informed consent is strongly recommended before a genetic test is ordered. People give their consent by signing a form saying that they have been told about, and understand, the purpose of the test, its medical implications, the risks and benefits of the test, possible alternatives to the test, and their privacy rights.

Unlike most other medical tests, genetic tests can reveal information not only about the person being tested but also about that person's relatives. The presence of a harmful genetic mutation in one family member makes it more likely that other blood relatives may also carry the same mutation. Family relationships can be affected when one member of a family discloses genetic test results that may have implications for other family members. Family members may have very different opinions about how useful it is to learn whether they do or do not have a disease-related genetic mutation.

Health discussions may get complicated when some family members know their genetic status while other family members do not choose to know their test results. A conversation with genetics professionals may help family members better understand the complicated choices they may face.

How Is Genetic Testing Done?

Genetic tests are usually requested by a person's doctor or other health care provider. Although it may be possible to obtain some genetic tests without a health care provider's order, this approach is not recommended because it does not give the patient the valuable opportunity to discuss this complicated decision with a knowledgeable professional.

Testing is done on a small sample of body fluid or tissue—usually blood, but sometimes saliva, cells from inside the cheek, skin cells, or amniotic fluid (the fluid surrounding a developing fetus).

The sample is then sent to a laboratory that specializes in genetic testing. The laboratory returns the test results to the doctor or genetic counselor who requested the test. In some cases, the laboratory may send the results to the patient directly. It usually takes several weeks or longer to get the test results. Genetic counseling is recommended both before and after genetic testing to make sure that patients have accurate information about what a particular genetic test means for their health and care.

What Do the Results of Genetic Testing Mean?

Genetic testing can have several possible results: positive, negative, true negative, uninformative negative, false negative, variant of unknown significance, or benign polymorphism. These results are described below.

A **"positive test result"** means that the laboratory found a specific genetic alteration (or mutation) that is associated with a hereditary cancer syndrome. A positive result may:

- Confirm the diagnosis of a hereditary cancer syndrome

- Indicate an increased risk of developing certain cancer(s) in the future

- Show that someone carries a particular genetic change that does not increase their own risk of cancer but that may increase the risk in their children if they also inherit an altered copy from their other parent (that is, if the child inherits two copies of the abnormal gene, one from their mother and one from their father).

- Suggest a need for further testing

- Provide important information that can help other family members make decisions about their own health care

Also, people who have a positive test result that indicates that they have an increased risk of developing cancer in the future may be able to take steps to lower their risk of developing cancer or to find cancer earlier, including:

- Being checked at a younger age or more often for signs of cancer

- Reducing their cancer risk by taking medications or having surgery to remove "at-risk" tissue (These approaches to risk reduction are options for only a few inherited cancer syndromes.)

- Changing personal behaviors (like quitting smoking, getting more exercise, and eating a healthier diet) to reduce the risk of certain cancers

A positive result on a prenatal genetic test for cancer risk may influence a decision about whether to continue a pregnancy. The results of pre-implantation testing (performed on embryos created by in vitro fertilization) can guide a doctor in deciding which embryo (or embryos) to implant in a woman's uterus.

Finally, in patients who have already been diagnosed with cancer, a positive result for a mutation associated with certain hereditary cancer syndromes can influence how the cancer is treated. For example, some hereditary cancer disorders interfere with the body's ability to repair damage that occurs to cellular DNA. If someone with one of these conditions receives a standard dose of radiation or chemotherapy to treat their cancer, they may experience severe, potentially life-threatening treatment side effects. Knowing about the genetic disorder before treatment begins allows doctors to modify the treatment and reduce the severity of the side effects.

A **"negative test result"** means that the laboratory did not find the specific alteration that the test was designed to detect. This result is most useful when working with a family in which the specific, disease-causing genetic alteration is already known to be present. In such a case, a negative result can show that the tested family member has not inherited the mutation that is present in their family and that this person therefore does not have the inherited cancer syndrome tested for, does not have an increased genetic risk of developing cancer, or is not a carrier of a mutation that increases cancer risk. Such a test result is called a **"true negative."** A true negative result does not mean that there is no cancer risk, but rather that the risk is probably the same as the cancer risk in the general population.

When a person has a strong family history of cancer but the family has not been found to have a known mutation associated with a hereditary cancer syndrome, a negative test result is classified as an **"uninformative negative"** (that is, does not provide useful information). It is not possible to tell whether someone has a harmful gene mutation that was not detected by the particular test used (a **"false negative"**) or whether the person truly has no cancer-predisposing genetic alterations in that gene. It is also possible for a person to have a mutation in a gene other than the gene that was tested.

If genetic testing shows a change that has not been previously associated with cancer in other people, the person's test result may report **"variant of unknown significance,"** or VUS. This result may be interpreted as "ambiguous" (uncertain), which is to say that the information does not help in making health care decisions.

If the test reveals a genetic change that is common in the general population among people without cancer, the change is called a **polymorphism**. Everyone has commonly occurring genetic variations (polymorphisms) that are not associated with any increased risk of disease.

Who Can Help People Understand Their Test Results?

A genetic counselor, doctor, or other health care professional trained in genetics can help an individual or family understand their test results. Such counseling may include discussing recommendations for preventive care and screening with the patient, referring the patient to support groups and other information resources, and providing emotional support to the person receiving the results.

In some cases, a genetic counselor or doctor may recommend that other family members consider being tested for specific gene changes that indicate an increased risk of cancer. The decision to test other family members is complicated. It requires a careful evaluation of family history and other factors as well as advice from a genetic counselor or other professional trained in genetics. In general, physicians rely on the family member who has been tested to share the genetic information with their relatives so that family members will know that a genetic condition has been identified in their family. Then, each family member will need to make their own decision regarding whether or not to be tested themselves.

Who Has Access to a Person's Genetic Test Results?

Medical test results are normally included in a person's medical records, particularly if a doctor or other health care provider has ordered the test or has been consulted about the test results. Therefore, people considering genetic testing must understand that their results may become known to other people or organizations that have legitimate, legal access to their medical records, such as their insurance company or employer, if their employer provides the patient's health insurance as a benefit.

However, legal protections are in place to prevent genetic discrimination, which would occur if insurance companies or employers were to treat people differently because they have a gene mutation that increases their risk of a disease such as cancer or because they have a strong family history of a disease such as cancer.

In 2008, the Genetic Information Nondiscrimination Act (GINA) became federal law for all U.S. residents. GINA prohibits discrimination based on genetic information in determining health insurance eligibility or rates and suitability for employment. However, GINA does not cover members of the military, and it does not apply to life insurance, disability insurance, or long-term care insurance. Some states have additional genetic nondiscrimination legislation that addresses the possibility of discrimination in those contexts.

In addition, because a person's genetic information is considered one kind of health information, it is covered by the Privacy Rule of the Health Information Portability and Accountability Act (HIPAA) of 1996. The Privacy Rule requires that health care providers and others with medical record access protect the privacy of health information, sets limits on the use and release of health records, and empowers people to control certain uses and sharing of their health-related information. Many states also have laws to protect patient privacy and limit the release of genetic and other health information. The National Human Genome Research Institute Genetic Discrimination page includes links to more information about GINA, HIPAA, and other legislation related to genetic discrimination in insurance or employment.

What Are At-Home or Direct-to-Consumer Genetic Tests?

Some companies offer at-home genetic testing, also known as direct-to-consumer (DTC) genetic testing. People collect a tissue sample themselves and submit the sample through the mail. They learn about the test results online, by mail, or over the phone. DTC genetic testing is often done without a doctor's order or guidance from a doctor or genetic counselor before the test. Some states in the United States do not allow DTC genetic testing.

Whereas the genetic testing for cancer that is typically ordered by a doctor involves testing for rare major hereditary cancer syndromes, most DTC genetic testing for cancer risk involves the analysis of common inherited genetic variants, called single-nucleotide polymorphisms, that have been shown to be statistically associated with a particular type of cancer. Each individual variant is generally associated with only a minor increase in risk, and even when added together all the known variants for a particular cancer type account for only a small portion of a person's risk of that cancer. Although the identification and study of such variants is an active area of research, genetic tests based on these variants have not yet been found to help patients and their care providers make health care decisions and, therefore, they are not a part of recommended clinical practice.

Even when people have DTC genetic tests for known mutations in genes associated with hereditary cancer syndrome, there are potential risks and drawbacks to the use of DTC testing. In particular, without guidance about genetic test results from an informed, genetically knowledgeable health care provider, people may experience unneeded anxiety or false reassurance, or they may make important decisions about medical treatment or care based on incomplete information.

Also, although some people may view DTC genetic testing as a way to ensure the privacy of their genetic test results, companies that offer DTC genetic testing do not always tell the consumer the details of their privacy policies. In addition, if people consult their doctor or other health care provider about the test results obtained from a DTC testing vendor, the results may become part of the patient's medical record anyway. Also, companies that provide DTC testing may not be subject to current state and federal privacy laws and regulations. It is generally recommended that people considering DTC genetic testing make sure that they have chosen a reputable company.

The U.S. Federal Trade Commission (FTC) has a fact sheet about at-home genetic tests which offers advice for people who are considering such a test. As part of its mission, the FTC investigates complaints about false or misleading health claims in advertisements.

The American Society of Human Genetics, a membership organization of genetics professionals, has issued a statement about DTC genetic tests that recommends transparency in such testing, provider education about the testing, and the development of appropriate regulations to ensure test and laboratory quality.

How Are Genetic Tests Regulated?

U.S. laboratories that perform health-related testing, including genetic testing, are regulated under the Clinical Laboratory Improvement Amendments (CLIA) program. Laboratories that are certified under CLIA are required to meet federal standards for quality, accuracy, and reliability of tests. All laboratories that do genetic testing and share results must be CLIA certified. However, CLIA certification only indicates that appropriate laboratory quality control standards are being followed; it does not guarantee that a genetic test being done by a laboratory is medically useful.

The Centers for Medicare and Medicaid Services has more information about CLIA programs. The National Library of Medicine also has information about how genetic testing is regulated and how to judge the quality of a genetic test. This information is available in the Genetics Home Reference.

What Research Is Being Done to Improve Genetic Testing for Cancer?

Research to find newer and better ways of detecting, treating, and preventing cancer in people who carry genetic mutations that increase the risk of certain cancers is ongoing. Scientists are also doing studies to find additional genetic changes that can increase a person's risk of cancer.

NCI's Cancer Genetic Markers of Susceptibility project, launched in 2005, is identifying common inherited genetic variations that are associated with an increased risk of breast cancer, prostate cancer, and other cancer types. This research may lead to new ways to prevent, diagnose, and treat cancer. However, none of the genetic variants identified through that type of research has yet proven useful for clinical management, so this remains a research effort.

NCI also funds the Cancer Genetics Network. This network is a resource for researchers studying inherited cancer risk, the integration of this information into medical practice, and behavioral, ethical, and public health issues associated with human genetics.

Additional NCI research is focused on improving genetic counseling methods and outcomes, the risks and benefits of at-home genetic testing, and the effects of advertising of these tests on patients, providers, and the health care system. Researchers are also working to improve the laboratory methods available for genetic testing.

Chapter 28

Breast Cancer Genetic Testing: Understanding BRCA1 and BRCA2

What Are BRCA1 and BRCA2?

BRCA1 and BRCA2 are human genes that produce tumor suppressor proteins. These proteins help repair damaged DNA and, therefore, play a role in ensuring the stability of the cell's genetic material. When either of these genes is mutated, or altered, such that its protein product either is not made or does not function correctly, DNA damage may not be repaired properly. As a result, cells are more likely to develop additional genetic alterations that can lead to cancer.

Specific inherited mutations in BRCA1 and BRCA2 increase the risk of female breast and ovarian cancers, and they have been associated with increased risks of several additional types of cancer. Together, BRCA1 and BRCA2 mutations account for about 20 to 25 percent of *hereditary* breast cancers and about 5 to 10 percent of all breast cancers. In addition, mutations in BRCA1 and BRCA2 account for around 15 percent of ovarian cancers overall. Breast and ovarian cancers associated with BRCA1 and BRCA2 mutations tend to develop at younger ages than their nonhereditary counterparts.

This chapter includes text excerpted from "BRCA1 and BRCA2: Cancer Risk and Genetic Testing," National Cancer Institute (NCI), April 1, 2015.

A harmful BRCA1 or BRCA2 mutation can be inherited from a person's mother or father. Each child of a parent who carries a mutation in one of these genes has a 50 percent chance (or 1 chance in 2) of inheriting the mutation. The effects of mutations in BRCA1 and BRCA2 are seen even when a person's second copy of the gene is normal.

How Much Does Having a BRCA1 or BRCA2 Gene Mutation Increase a Woman's Risk of Breast and Ovarian Cancer?

A woman's lifetime risk of developing breast and/or ovarian cancer is greatly increased if she inherits a harmful mutation in BRCA1 or BRCA2.

Breast cancer: About 12 percent of women in the general population will develop breast cancer sometime during their lives. By contrast, according to the most recent estimates, 55 to 65 percent of women who inherit a harmful BRCA1 mutation and around 45 percent of women who inherit a harmful BRCA2 mutation will develop breast cancer by age 70 years.

Ovarian cancer: About 1.3 percent of women in the general population will develop ovarian cancer sometime during their lives. By contrast, according to the most recent estimates, 39 percent of women who inherit a harmful BRCA1 mutation and 11 to 17 percent of women who inherit a harmful BRCA2 mutation will develop ovarian cancer by age 70 years.

It is important to note that these estimated percentages of lifetime risk are different from those available previously; the estimates have changed as more information has become available, and they may change again with additional research. No long-term general population studies have directly compared cancer risk in women who have and do not have a harmful BRCA1 or BRCA2 mutation.

It is also important to note that other characteristics of a particular woman can make her cancer risk higher or lower than the average risks. These characteristics include her family history of breast, ovarian, and, possibly, other cancers; the specific mutation(s) she has inherited; and other risk factors, such as her reproductive history. However, at this time, based on current data, none of these other factors seems to be as strong as the effect of carrying a harmful BRCA1 or BRCA2 mutation.

What Other Cancers Have Been Linked to Mutations in BRCA1 and BRCA2?

Harmful mutations in BRCA1 and BRCA2 increase the risk of several cancers in addition to breast and ovarian cancer. BRCA1 mutations may increase a woman's risk of developing fallopian tube cancer and peritoneal cancer. Men with BRCA2 mutations, and to a lesser extent BRCA1 mutations, are also at increased risk of breast cancer. Men with harmful BRCA1 or BRCA2 mutations have a higher risk of prostate cancer. Men and women with BRCA1 or BRCA2 mutations may be at increased risk of pancreatic cancer. Mutations in BRCA2 (also known as FANCD1), if they are inherited from both parents, can cause a Fanconi anemia subtype (FA-D1), a syndrome that is associated with childhood solid tumors and development of acute myeloid leukemia. Likewise, mutations in BRCA1 (also known as FANCS), if they are inherited from both parents, can cause another Fanconi anemia subtype.

Are Mutations in BRCA1 and BRCA2 More Common in Certain Racial/Ethnic Populations than Others?

Yes. For example, people of Ashkenazi Jewish descent have a higher prevalence of harmful BRCA1 and BRCA2 mutations than people in the general U.S. population. Other ethnic and geographic populations around the world, such as the Norwegian, Dutch, and Icelandic peoples, also have a higher prevalence of specific harmful BRCA1 and BRCA2 mutations.

In addition, limited data indicate that the prevalence of specific harmful BRCA1 and BRCA2 mutations may vary among individual racial and ethnic groups in the United States, including African Americans, Hispanics, Asian Americans, and non-Hispanic whites.

Are Genetic Tests Available to Detect BRCA1 and BRCA2 Mutations?

Yes. Several different tests are available, including tests that look for a known mutation in one of the genes (i.e., a mutation that has already been identified in another family member) and tests that check for all possible mutations in both genes. DNA (from a blood or saliva sample) is needed for mutation testing. The sample is sent to a laboratory for analysis. It usually takes about a month to get the test results.

Who Should Consider Genetic Testing for BRCA1 and BRCA2 Mutations?

Because harmful BRCA1 and BRCA2 gene mutations are relatively rare in the general population, most experts agree that mutation testing of individuals who do not have cancer should be performed only when the person's individual or family history suggests the possible presence of a harmful mutation in BRCA1 or BRCA2.

In December 2013, the United States Preventive Services Task Force recommended that women who have family members with breast, ovarian, fallopian tube, or peritoneal cancer be evaluated to see if they have a family history that is associated with an increased risk of a harmful mutation in one of these genes.

Several screening tools are now available to help health care providers with this evaluation. These tools assess family history factors that are associated with an increased likelihood of having a harmful mutation in BRCA1 or BRCA2, including:

- Breast cancer diagnosed before age 50 years
- Cancer in both breasts in the same woman
- Both breast and ovarian cancers in either the same woman or the same family
- Multiple breast cancers
- Two or more primary types of BRCA1- or BRCA2-related cancers in a single family member
- Cases of male breast cancer
- Ashkenazi Jewish ethnicity

When an individual has a family history that is suggestive of the presence of a BRCA1 or BRCA2 mutation, it may be most informative to first test a family member who has cancer if that person is still alive and willing to be tested. If that person is found to have a harmful BRCA1 or BRCA2 mutation, then other family members may want to consider genetic counseling to learn more about their potential risks and whether genetic testing for mutations in BRCA1 and BRCA2 might be appropriate for them.

If it is not possible to confirm the presence of a harmful BRCA1 or BRCA2 mutation in a family member who has cancer, it is appropriate for both men and women who do not have cancer but have a family medical history that suggests the presence of such a mutation to have genetic counseling for possible testing.

Some individuals—for example, those who were adopted at birth—may not know their family history. In cases where a woman with an unknown family history has an early-onset breast cancer or ovarian cancer or a man with an unknown family history is diagnosed with breast cancer, it may be reasonable for that individual to consider genetic testing for a BRCA1 or BRCA2 mutation. Individuals with an unknown family history who do not have an early-onset cancer or male breast cancer are at very low risk of having a harmful BRCA1 or BRCA2 mutation and are unlikely to benefit from routine genetic testing.

Professional societies do not recommend that children, even those with a family history suggestive of a harmful BRCA1 or BRCA2 mutation, undergo genetic testing for BRCA1 or BRCA2. This is because no risk-reduction strategies exist for children, and children's risks of developing a cancer type associated with a BRCA1 or BRCA2 mutation are extremely low. After children with a family history suggestive of a harmful BRCA1 or BRCA2 mutation become adults, however, they may want to obtain genetic counseling about whether or not to undergoing genetic testing.

Should People Considering Genetic Testing for BRCA1 and BRCA2 Mutations Talk with a Genetic Counselor?

Genetic counseling is generally recommended before and after any genetic test for an inherited cancer syndrome. This counseling should be performed by a health care professional who is experienced in cancer genetics. Genetic counseling usually covers many aspects of the testing process, including:

- A hereditary cancer risk assessment based on an individual's personal and family medical history

- Discussion of:

- The appropriateness of genetic testing

- The medical implications of a positive or a negative test result

- The possibility that a test result might not be informative

- The psychological risks and benefits of genetic test results

- The risk of passing a mutation to children

- Explanation of the specific test(s) that might be used and the technical accuracy of the test(s)

How Much Does BRCA1 and BRCA2 Mutation Testing Cost?

The Affordable Care Act considers genetic counseling and BRCA1 and BRCA2 mutation testing for individuals at high risk a covered preventive service. People considering BRCA1 and BRCA2 mutation testing may want to confirm their insurance coverage for genetic tests before having the test.

Some of the genetic testing companies that offer testing for BRCA1 and BRCA2 mutations may offer testing at no charge to patients who lack insurance and meet specific financial and medical criteria.

What Does a Positive BRCA1 or BRCA2 Genetic Test Result Mean?

BRCA1 and BRCA2 gene mutation testing can give several possible results: a positive result, a negative result, or an ambiguous or uncertain result.

A positive test result indicates that a person has inherited a known harmful mutation in BRCA1 or BRCA2 and, therefore, has an increased risk of developing certain cancers. However, a positive test result cannot tell whether or when an individual will actually develop cancer. For example, some women who inherit a harmful BRCA1 or BRCA2 mutation will never develop breast or ovarian cancer.

A positive genetic test result may also have important health and social implications for family members, including future generations. Unlike most other medical tests, genetic tests can reveal information not only about the person being tested but also about that person's relatives:

- Both men and women who inherit a harmful BRCA1 or BRCA2 mutation, whether or not they develop cancer themselves, may pass the mutation on to their sons and daughters. Each child has a 50 percent chance of inheriting a parent's mutation.

- If a person learns that he or she has inherited a harmful BRCA1 or BRCA2 mutation, this will mean that each of his or her full siblings has a 50 percent chance of having inherited the mutation as well.

What Does a Negative BRCA1 or BRCA2 Test Result Mean?

A negative test result can be more difficult to understand than a positive result because what the result means depends in part on an individual's family history of cancer and whether a BRCA1 or BRCA2 mutation has been identified in a blood relative.

If a close (first- or second-degree) relative of the tested person is known to carry a harmful BRCA1 or BRCA2 mutation, a negative test result is clear: it means that person does not carry the harmful mutation that is responsible for the familial cancer, and thus cannot pass it on to their children. Such a test result is called a *true negative*. A person with such a test result is currently thought to have the same risk of cancer as someone in the general population.

If the tested person has a family history that suggests the possibility of having a harmful mutation in BRCA1 or BRCA2 but complete gene testing identifies no such mutation in the family, a negative result is less clear. The likelihood that genetic testing will miss a known harmful BRCA1 or BRCA2 mutation is very low, but it could happen. Moreover, scientists continue to discover new BRCA1 and BRCA2 mutations and have not yet identified all potentially harmful ones. Therefore, it is possible that a person in this scenario with a "negative" test result actually has an as-yet unknown harmful BRCA1 or BRCA2 mutation that has not been identified.

It is also possible for people to have a mutation in a gene other than BRCA1 or BRCA2 that increases their cancer risk but is not detectable by the test used. People considering genetic testing for BRCA1 and BRCA2 mutations may want to discuss these potential uncertainties with a genetic counselor before undergoing testing.

What Does an Ambiguous or Uncertain BRCA1 or BRCA2 Test Result Mean?

Sometimes, a genetic test finds a change in BRCA1 or BRCA2 that has not been previously associated with cancer. This type of test result may be described as "ambiguous" (often referred to as "a genetic variant of uncertain significance") because it isn't known whether this specific gene change affects a person's risk of developing cancer. One study found that 10 percent of women who underwent BRCA1 and BRCA2 mutation testing had this type of ambiguous result.

As more research is conducted and more people are tested for BRCA1 and BRCA2 mutations, scientists will learn more about these changes and cancer risk. Genetic counseling can help a person understand what an ambiguous change in BRCA1 or BRCA2 may mean in terms of cancer risk. Over time, additional studies of variants of uncertain significance may result in a specific mutation being re-classified as either harmful or clearly not harmful.

173

How Can a Person Who Has a Positive Test Result Manage Their Risk of Cancer?

Several options are available for managing cancer risk in individuals who have a known harmful BRCA1 or BRCA2 mutation. These include enhanced screening, prophylactic (risk-reducing) surgery, and chemoprevention.

Enhanced Screening. Some women who test positive for BRCA1 and BRCA2 mutations may choose to start cancer screening at younger ages than the general population or to have more frequent screening. For example, some experts recommend that women who carry a harmful BRCA1 or BRCA2 mutation undergo clinical breast examinations beginning at age 25 to 35 years. And some expert groups recommend that women who carry such a mutation have a mammogram every year, beginning at age 25 to 35 years.

Enhanced screening may increase the chance of detecting breast cancer at an early stage, when it may have a better chance of being treated successfully. Women who have a positive test result should ask their health care provider about the possible harms of diagnostic tests that involve radiation (mammograms or X-rays).

Recent studies have shown that MRI may be more sensitive than mammography for women at high risk of breast cancer. However, mammography can also identify some breast cancers that are not identified by MRI, and MRI may be less specific (i.e., lead to more false-positive results) than mammography. Several organizations, such as the American Cancer Society and the National Comprehensive Cancer Network, now recommend annual screening with mammography and MRI for women who have a high risk of breast cancer.

No effective ovarian cancer screening methods currently exist. Some groups recommend transvaginal ultrasound, blood tests for the antigen CA-125, and clinical examinations for ovarian cancer screening in women with harmful BRCA1 or BRCA2 mutations, but none of these methods appears to detect ovarian tumors at an early enough stage to reduce the risk of dying from ovarian cancer. For a screening method to be considered effective, it must have demonstrated reduced mortality from the disease of interest. This standard has not yet been met for ovarian cancer screening.

The benefits of screening for breast and other cancers in men who carry harmful mutations in BRCA1 or BRCA2 is also not known, but some expert groups recommend that men who are known to carry a harmful mutation undergo regular mammography as well as testing for prostate cancer. The value of these screening strategies remains unproven at present.

Prophylactic (Risk-reducing) Surgery. Prophylactic surgery involves removing as much of the "at-risk" tissue as possible. Women may choose to have both breasts removed (bilateral prophylactic mastectomy) to reduce their risk of breast cancer. Surgery to remove a woman's ovaries and fallopian tubes (bilateral prophylactic salpingo-oophorectomy) can help reduce her risk of ovarian cancer. Removing the ovaries also reduces the risk of breast cancer in premenopausal women by eliminating a source of hormones that can fuel the growth of some types of breast cancer.

No evidence is available regarding the effectiveness of bilateral prophylactic mastectomy in reducing breast cancer risk in men with a harmful BRCA1 or BRCA2 mutation or a family history of breast cancer. Therefore, bilateral prophylactic mastectomy for men at high risk of breast cancer is considered an experimental procedure, and insurance companies will not normally cover it.

Prophylactic surgery does not completely guarantee that cancer will not develop because not all at-risk tissue can be removed by these procedures. Some women have developed breast cancer, ovarian cancer, or primary peritoneal carcinomatosis (a type of cancer similar to ovarian cancer) even after prophylactic surgery. Nevertheless, the mortality reduction associated with this surgery is substantial: Research demonstrates that women who underwent bilateral prophylactic salpingo-oophorectomy had a nearly 80 percent reduction in risk of dying from ovarian cancer, a 56 percent reduction in risk of dying from breast cancer, and a 77 percent reduction in risk of dying from any cause.

Emerging evidence suggests that the amount of protection that removing the ovaries and fallopian tubes provides against the development of breast and ovarian cancer may be similar for carriers of BRCA1 and BRCA2 mutations, in contrast to earlier studies.

Chemoprevention. Chemoprevention is the use of drugs, vitamins, or other agents to try to reduce the risk of, or delay the recurrence of, cancer. Although two chemopreventive drugs (tamoxifen and raloxifene) have been approved by the U.S. Food and Drug Administration (FDA) to reduce the risk of breast cancer in women at increased risk, the role of these drugs in women with harmful BRCA1 or BRCA2 mutations is not yet clear.

Data from three studies suggest that tamoxifen may be able to help lower the risk of breast cancer in BRCA1 and BRCA2 mutation carriers, including the risk of cancer in the opposite breast among women previously diagnosed with breast cancer. Studies have not examined the effectiveness of raloxifene in BRCA1 and BRCA2 mutation carriers specifically.

Oral contraceptives (birth control pills) are thought to reduce the risk of ovarian cancer by about 50 percent both in the general population and in women with harmful BRCA1 or BRCA2 mutations.

What Are Some of the Benefits of Genetic Testing for Breast and Ovarian Cancer Risk?

There can be benefits to genetic testing, regardless of whether a person receives a positive or a negative result.

The potential benefits of a *true negative* result include a sense of relief regarding the future risk of cancer, learning that one's children are not at risk of inheriting the family's cancer susceptibility, and the possibility that special checkups, tests, or preventive surgeries may not be needed.

A positive test result may bring relief by resolving uncertainty regarding future cancer risk and may allow people to make informed decisions about their future, including taking steps to reduce their cancer risk. In addition, people who have a positive test result may choose to participate in medical research that could, in the long run, help reduce deaths from hereditary breast and ovarian cancer.

What Are Some of the Possible Harms of Genetic Testing for Breast and Ovarian Cancer Risk?

The direct medical harms of genetic testing are minimal, but knowledge of test results may have harmful effects on a person's emotions, social relationships, finances, and medical choices.

People who receive a positive test result may feel anxious, depressed, or angry. They may have difficulty making choices about whether to have preventive surgery or about which surgery to have.

People who receive a negative test result may experience "survivor guilt," caused by the knowledge that they likely do not have an increased risk of developing a disease that affects one or more loved ones.

Because genetic testing can reveal information about more than one family member, the emotions caused by test results can create tension within families. Test results can also affect personal life choices, such as decisions about career, marriage, and childbearing.

Violations of privacy and of the confidentiality of genetic test results are additional potential risks. However, the federal Health Insurance Portability and Accountability Act and various state laws protect the privacy of a person's genetic information. Moreover, the federal Genetic Information Nondiscrimination Act, along with many state laws, prohibits discrimination based on genetic information in relation to health insurance and employment, although it does not cover life insurance, disability insurance, or long-term care insurance.

Finally, there is a small chance that test results may not be accurate, leading people to make decisions based on incorrect information. Although inaccurate results are unlikely, people with these concerns should address them during genetic counseling.

What Are the Implications of Having a Harmful BRCA1 or BRCA2 Mutation for Breast and Ovarian Cancer Prognosis and Treatment?

A number of studies have investigated possible clinical differences between breast and ovarian cancers that are associated with harmful BRCA1 or BRCA2 mutations and cancers that are not associated with these mutations.

There is some evidence that, over the long term, women who carry these mutations are more likely to develop a second cancer in either the same (ipsilateral) breast or the opposite (contralateral) breast than women who do not carry these mutations. Thus, some women with a harmful BRCA1 or BRCA2 mutation who develop breast cancer in one breast opt for a bilateral mastectomy, even if they would otherwise be candidates for breast-conserving surgery. In fact, because of the increased risk of a second breast cancer among BRCA1 and BRCA2 mutation carriers, some doctors recommend that women with early-onset breast cancer and those whose family history is consistent with a mutation in one of these genes have genetic testing when breast cancer is diagnosed.

Breast cancers in women with a harmful BRCA1 mutation are also more likely to be "triple-negative cancers" (i.e., the breast cancer cells do not have estrogen receptors, progesterone receptors, or large amounts of HER2/neu protein), which generally have poorer prognosis than other breast cancers.

Because the products of the BRCA1 and BRCA2 genes are involved in DNA repair, some investigators have suggested that cancer cells with a harmful mutation in either of these genes may be more sensitive

177

to anticancer agents that act by damaging DNA, such as cisplatin. In preclinical studies, drugs called PARP inhibitors, which block the repair of DNA damage, have been found to arrest the growth of cancer cells that have BRCA1 or BRCA2 mutations. These drugs have also shown some activity in cancer patients who carry BRCA1 or BRCA2 mutations, and researchers are continuing to develop and test these drugs.

What Research Is Currently Being Done to Help Individuals with Harmful BRCA1 or BRCA2 Mutations?

Research studies are being conducted to find new and better ways of detecting, treating, and preventing cancer in people who carry mutations in BRCA1 and BRCA2. Additional studies are focused on improving genetic counseling methods and outcomes. Our knowledge in these areas is evolving rapidly.

Information about active clinical trials (research studies with people) for individuals with BRCA1 or BRCA2 mutations is available on NCI's website. The following links will retrieve lists of clinical trials open to individuals with BRCA1 or BRCA2 mutations.

- BRCA1 mutation carriers
- BRCA2 mutation carriers

NCI's Cancer Information Service (CIS) can also provide information about clinical trials and help with clinical trial searches.

Do Inherited Mutations in Other Genes Increase the Risk of Breast and/or Ovarian Tumors?

Yes. Although harmful mutations in BRCA1 and BRCA2 are responsible for the disease in nearly half of families with multiple cases of breast cancer and up to 90 percent of families with both breast and ovarian cancer, mutations in a number of other genes have been associated with increased risks of breast and/or ovarian cancers. These other genes include several that are associated with the inherited disorders Cowden syndrome, Peutz-Jeghers syndrome, Li-Fraumeni syndrome, and Fanconi anemia, which increase the risk of many cancer types.

Most mutations in these other genes are associated with smaller increases in breast cancer risk than are seen with mutations in BRCA1 and BRCA2. However, researchers recently reported that inherited mutations in the *PALB2* gene are associated with a risk of breast cancer nearly as high as that associated with inherited BRCA1 and BRCA2 mutation. They estimated that 33 percent of women who inherit a harmful mutation in *PALB2* will develop breast cancer by age 70 years. The estimated risk of breast cancer associated with a harmful *PALB2* mutation is even higher for women who have a family history of breast cancer: 58 percent of those women will develop breast cancer by age 70 years.

PALB2, like BRCA1 and BRCA2, is a tumor suppressor gene. The *PALB2* gene produces a protein that interacts with the proteins produced by the BRCA1 and BRCA2 genes to help repair breaks in DNA. Harmful mutations in *PALB2* (also known as FANCN) are associated with increased risks of ovarian, pancreatic, and prostate cancers in addition to an increased risk of breast cancer. Mutations in *PALB2*, when inherited from each parent, can cause a Fanconi anemia subtype, FA-N, that is associated with childhood solid tumors.

Although genetic testing for *PALB2* mutations is available, expert groups have not yet developed specific guidelines for who should be tested for, or the management of breast cancer risk in individuals with *PALB2* mutations.

Chapter 29

Preventing Breast Cancer in People Who Are Susceptible

Chapter Contents

Section 29.1

Overview of Protective Factors and Interventions

This section contains text excerpted from the following sources:
Text beginning with the heading "Breast Cancer Prevention"
is excerpted from "Breast Cancer Prevention–Patient
Version (PDQ®)," National Cancer Institute (NCI), October 22,
2015; Text beginning with the heading "Risk Reduction" is excerpted
from "Breast Cancer," NIHSeniorHealth, National
Institute on Aging (NIA), April 2015.

Breast Cancer Prevention

Avoiding Risk Factors and Increasing Protective Factors May Help Prevent Cancer

Avoiding cancer risk factors may help prevent certain cancers. Risk factors include smoking, being overweight, and not getting enough exercise. Increasing protective factors such as quitting smoking, eating a healthy diet, and exercising may also help prevent some cancers. Talk to your doctor or other health care professional about how you might lower your risk of cancer.

NCI's Breast Cancer Risk Assessment Tool uses a woman's risk factors to estimate her risk for breast cancer during the next five years and up to age 90. This online tool is meant to be used by a health care provider. For more information on breast cancer risk, call 1-800-4-CANCER.

The following are risk factors for breast cancer:

Older Age

Older age is the main risk factor for most cancers. The chance of getting cancer increases as you get older.

A Personal History of Breast Cancer or Benign (Noncancer) Breast Disease

Women with any of the following have an increased risk of breast cancer:

- A personal history of invasive breast cancer, ductal carcinoma in situ (DCIS), or lobular carcinoma in situ (LCIS).

- A personal history of benign (noncancer) breast disease.

A Family History of Breast Cancer

Women with a family history of breast cancer in a first-degree relative (mother, sister, or daughter) have an increased risk of breast cancer.

Inherited Gene Changes

Women who have inherited changes in the BRCA1 and BRCA2 genes or in certain other genes have a higher risk of breast cancer, ovarian cancer, and maybe colon cancer. The risk of breast cancer caused by inherited gene changes depends on the type of gene mutation, family history of cancer, and other factors.

Men who have inherited certain changes in the BRCA2 gene have a higher risk of breast, prostate, and pancreatic cancers, and lymphoma.

Dense Breasts

Having breast tissue that is dense on a mammogram is a factor in breast cancer risk. The level of risk depends on how dense the breast tissue is. Women with very dense breasts have a higher risk of breast cancer than women with low breast density.

Increased breast density is often an inherited trait, but it may also occur in women who have not had children, have a first pregnancy late in life, take postmenopausal hormones, or drink alcohol.

Exposure of Breast Tissue to Estrogen Made in the Body

Estrogen is a hormone made by the body. It helps the body develop and maintain female sex characteristics. Being exposed to estrogen over a long time may increase the risk of breast cancer. Estrogen levels are highest during the years a woman is menstruating.

A woman's exposure to estrogen is increased in the following ways:

- **Early menstruation:** Beginning to have menstrual periods at age 11 or younger increases the number of years the breast tissue is exposed to estrogen.

- **Starting menopause at a later age:** The more years a woman menstruates, the longer her breast tissue is exposed to estrogen.

- **Older age at first birth or never having given birth:**
  Because estrogen levels are lower during pregnancy, breast tissue is exposed to more estrogen in women who become pregnant for the first time after age 35 or who never become pregnant.

Taking Hormone Therapy for Symptoms of Menopause

Hormones, such as estrogen and progesterone, can be made into a pill form in a laboratory. Estrogen, progestin, or both may be given to replace the estrogen no longer made by the ovaries in postmenopausal women or women who have had their ovaries removed. This is called hormone replacement therapy (HRT) or hormone therapy (HT). Combination HRT/HT is estrogen combined with progestin. This type of HRT/HT increases the risk of breast cancer. Studies show that when women stop taking estrogen combined with progestin, the risk of breast cancer decreases.

Radiation Therapy to the Breast or Chest

Radiation therapy to the chest for the treatment of cancer increases the risk of breast cancer, starting 10 years after treatment. The risk of breast cancer depends on the dose of radiation and the age at which it is given. The risk is highest if radiation treatment was used during puberty, when breasts are forming.

Radiation therapy to treat cancer in one breast does not appear to increase the risk of cancer in the other breast.

For women who have inherited changes in the BRCA1 and BRCA2 genes, exposure to radiation, such as that from chest X-rays, may further increase the risk of breast cancer, especially in women who were X-rayed before 20 years of age.

Obesity

Obesity increases the risk of breast cancer, especially in postmenopausal women who have not used hormone replacement therapy.

Drinking Alcohol

Drinking alcohol increases the risk of breast cancer. The level of risk rises as the amount of alcohol consumed rises.

Being White

White women have an increased risk of breast cancer.

The following are protective factors for breast cancer:

Less Exposure of Breast Tissue to Estrogen Made by the Body

Decreasing the length of time a woman's breast tissue is exposed to estrogen may help prevent breast cancer. Exposure to estrogen is reduced in the following ways:

- **Early pregnancy:** Estrogen levels are lower during pregnancy. Women who have a full-term pregnancy before age 20 have a lower risk of breast cancer than women who have not had children or who give birth to their first child after age 35.

- **Breast-feeding:** Estrogen levels may remain lower while a woman is breast-feeding. Women who breastfed have a lower risk of breast cancer than women who have had children but did not breastfeed.

Taking Estrogen-Only Hormone Therapy after Hysterectomy, Selective Estrogen Receptor Modulators, or Aromatase Inhibitors and Inactivators

Estrogen-Only Hormone Therapy after Hysterectomy

Hormone therapy with estrogen only may be given to women who have had a hysterectomy. In these women, estrogen-only therapy after menopause may decrease the risk of breast cancer. There is an increased risk of stroke and heart and blood vessel disease in post-menopausal women who take estrogen after a hysterectomy.

Selective Estrogen Receptor Modulators

Tamoxifen and raloxifene belong to the family of drugs called selective estrogen receptor modulators (SERMs). SERMs act like estrogen on some tissues in the body, but block the effect of estrogen on other tissues.

Treatment with tamoxifen lowers the risk of estrogen receptor-positive (ER-positive) breast cancer and ductal carcinoma in situ in premenopausal and postmenopausal women at high risk. Treatment with raloxifene also lowers the risk of breast cancer in postmenopausal women. With either drug, the reduced risk lasts for several years or longer after treatment is stopped. Lower rates of broken bones have been noted in patients taking raloxifene.

Taking tamoxifen increases the risk of hot flashes, endometrial cancer, stroke, cataracts, and blood clots (especially in the lungs and legs). The risk of having these problems increases with age. Women younger than 50 years who have a high risk of breast cancer may benefit the most from taking tamoxifen. The risk of having these problems decreases after tamoxifen is stopped. Talk with your doctor about the risks and benefits of taking this drug.

Taking raloxifene increases the risk of blood clots in the lungs and legs, but does not appear to increase the risk of endometrial cancer. In postmenopausal women with osteoporosis (decreased bone density), raloxifene lowers the risk of breast cancer for women who have a high or low risk of breast cancer. It is not known if raloxifene would have the same effect in women who do not have osteoporosis. Talk with your doctor about the risks and benefits of taking this drug.

Other SERMs are being studied in clinical trials.

Aromatase Inhibitors and Inactivators

Aromatase inhibitors (anastrozole, letrozole) and inactivators (exemestane) lower the risk of a new breast cancer in women who have a history of breast cancer. Aromatase inhibitors also decrease the risk of breast cancer in women with the following conditions:

- Postmenopausal women with a personal history of breast cancer.

- Women with no personal history of breast cancer who are 60 years and older, have a history of ductal carcinoma in situ with mastectomy, or have a high risk of breast cancer based on the Gail model tool (a tool used to estimate the risk of breast cancer).

In women with an increased risk of breast cancer, taking aromatase inhibitors decreases the amount of estrogen made by the body. Before menopause, estrogen is made by the ovaries and other tissues in a woman's body, including the brain, fat tissue, and skin. After menopause, the ovaries stop making estrogen, but the other tissues do not. Aromatase inhibitors block the action of an enzyme called aromatase, which is used to make all of the body's estrogen. Aromatase inactivators stop the enzyme from working.

Possible harms from taking aromatase inhibitors include muscle and joint pain, osteoporosis, hot flashes, and feeling very tired.

Risk-Reducing Mastectomy

Some women who have a high risk of breast cancer may choose to have a risk-reducing mastectomy (the removal of both breasts when there are no signs of cancer). The risk of breast cancer is much lower in these women and most feel less anxious about their risk of breast cancer. However, it is very important to have a cancer risk assessment and counseling about the different ways to prevent breast cancer before making this decision.

Ovarian Ablation

The ovaries make most of the estrogen that is made by the body. Treatments that stop or lower the amount of estrogen made by the ovaries include surgery to remove the ovaries, radiation therapy, or taking certain drugs. This is called ovarian ablation.

Premenopausal women who have a high risk of breast cancer due to certain changes in the BRCA1 and BRCA2 genes may choose to have a risk-reducing oophorectomy (the removal of both ovaries when there are no signs of cancer). This decreases the amount of estrogen made by the body and lowers the risk of breast cancer. Risk-reducing oophorectomy also lowers the risk of breast cancer in normal premenopausal women and in women with an increased risk of breast cancer due to radiation to the chest. However, it is very important to have a cancer risk assessment and counseling before making this decision. The sudden drop in estrogen levels may cause the symptoms of menopause to begin. These include hot flashes, trouble sleeping, anxiety, and depression. Long-term effects include decreased sex drive, vaginal dryness, and decreased bone density.

Getting Enough Exercise

Women who exercise four or more hours a week have a lower risk of breast cancer. The effect of exercise on breast cancer risk may be greatest in premenopausal women who have normal or low body weight.

It Is Not Clear Whether the following Affect the Risk of Breast Cancer:

Oral Contraceptives

Certain oral contraceptives contain estrogen. Some studies have shown that taking oral contraceptives ("the pill") may slightly increase the risk of breast cancer in current users. This risk decreases over time. Other studies have not shown an increased risk of breast cancer in women who take oral contraceptives.

Progestin-only contraceptives that are injected or implanted do not appear to increase the risk of breast cancer. More studies are needed to know whether progestin-only oral contraceptives increase the risk of breast cancer.

Environment

Studies have not proven that being exposed to certain substances in the environment, such as chemicals, increases the risk of breast cancer.

The following Do Not Affect the Risk of Breast Cancer

The following do not affect the risk of breast cancer:

- Having an abortion.
- Making diet changes such as eating less fat or more fruits and vegetables.
- Taking vitamins, including fenretinide (a type of vitamin A).
- Cigarette smoking, both active and passive (inhaling second-hand smoke).
- Using underarm deodorant or antiperspirant.
- Taking statins (cholesterol-lowering drugs).
- Taking bisphosphonates (drugs used to treat osteoporosis and hypercalcemia) by mouth or by intravenous infusion.

Cancer Prevention Clinical Trials Are Used to Study Ways to Prevent Cancer

Cancer prevention clinical trials are used to study ways to lower the risk of developing certain types of cancer. Some cancer prevention trials are conducted with healthy people who have not had cancer but who have an increased risk for cancer. Other prevention trials are conducted with people who have had cancer and are trying to prevent another cancer of the same type or to lower their chance of developing a new type of cancer. Other trials are done with healthy volunteers who are not known to have any risk factors for cancer.

The purpose of some cancer prevention clinical trials is to find out whether actions people take can prevent cancer. These may include exercising more or quitting smoking or taking certain medicines, vitamins, minerals, or food supplements.

New Ways to Prevent Breast Cancer Are Being Studied in Clinical Trials

Clinical trials are taking place in many parts of the country. Information about clinical trials can be found in the Clinical Trials section of the NCI website. Check NCI's list of cancer clinical trials for breast cancer prevention trials that are now accepting patients.

Risk Reduction

What Is Cancer Prevention?

Cancer prevention is action taken to lower the chance of getting cancer. By preventing cancer, the number of new cases of cancer in a group or population is lowered. Hopefully, this will lower the number of deaths caused by cancer.

When studying ways to prevent cancer, scientists look at risk factors and protective factors. Anything that increases your chance of developing cancer is called a cancer risk factor. Anything that decreases your chance of developing cancer is called a cancer protective factor.

Risk Factors

Some risk factors for cancer can be avoided, but many cannot. For example, both smoking and inheriting certain genes are risk factors for some types of cancer, but only smoking can be avoided. Regular exercise and a healthy diet may be protective factors for some types of cancer. Avoiding risk factors and increasing protective factors may lower your risk but it does not mean that you will not get cancer.

Different ways to prevent cancer are being studied, including

- changing lifestyle or eating habits
- avoiding things known to cause cancer
- taking medicine to treat a precancerous condition or to keep cancer from starting

Here are protective factors for breast cancer.

Less Exposure to Estrogen

Decreasing the length of time a woman's breast tissue is exposed to estrogen may help lower her risk of developing breast cancer. Exposure to estrogen is reduced in the following ways.

- **Early pregnancy.** Estrogen levels are lower during pregnancy. Women who have a full-term pregnancy before age 20 have a lower risk of breast cancer than women who have not had children or who give birth to their first child after age 35.

- **Breast-feeding.** Estrogen levels may remain lower while a woman is breast-feeding. Women who breastfed have a lower risk of breast cancer than women who have had children but did not breastfeed.

- **Surgical removal of the ovaries.** The ovaries make estrogen. The amount of estrogen made by the body can be greatly reduced by removing one or both ovaries. Also, drugs may be taken to lower the amount of estrogen made by the ovaries.

- **Late menstruation.** Menstrual periods that start at age 14 or older decreases the number of years the breast tissue is exposed to estrogen.

- **Early menopause.** The fewer years a woman menstruates, the shorter the time her breast tissue is exposed to estrogen.

Exercise

Women who exercise four or more hours a week have a lower risk of breast cancer. The effect of exercise on breast cancer risk may be greatest in premenopausal women who have normal or low body weight.

Estrogen-only Hormone Therapy after Hysterectomy

Hormone therapy with estrogen only may be given to women who have had a hysterectomy. In these women, estrogen-only therapy after menopause may decrease the risk of breast cancer. There is an increased risk of stroke and heart and blood vessel disease in post-menopausal women who take estrogen after a hysterectomy.

Selective Estrogen Receptor Modulators (SERMs)

Tamoxifen and raloxifene belong to the family of drugs called selective estrogen receptor modulators (SERMs). SERMs act like estrogen on some tissues in the body, but block the effect of estrogen on other tissues.

Treatment with tamoxifen or raloxifene lowers the risk of breast cancer in postmenopausal women. Tamoxifen also lowers the risk of breast cancer in high-risk premenopausal women. With either drug, the reduced risk lasts for several years after treatment is stopped. Lower rates of broken bones have been noted in patients taking raloxifene.

Prophylactic Mastectomy

Some women who have a high risk of breast cancer may choose to have a prophylactic mastectomy (the removal of both breasts when there are no signs of cancer). The risk of breast cancer is much lower in these women and most feel less anxious about their risk of breast cancer. However, it is very important to have cancer risk assessment and counseling about the different ways to prevent breast cancer before making this decision.

Prophylactic Oophorectomy

Premenopausal women who have a high risk of breast cancer due to certain changes in the BRCA1 and BRCA2 genes may choose to have a prophylactic oophorectomy (the removal of both ovaries when there are no signs of cancer). This decreases the amount of estrogen made by the body and lowers the risk of breast cancer. Prophylactic oophorectomy also lowers the risk of breast cancer in normal premenopausal women and in women with an increased risk of breast cancer due to radiation to the chest. However, it is very important to have cancer risk assessment and counseling before making this decision. The sudden drop in estrogen levels may cause the symptoms of menopause to begin. These include hot flashes, trouble sleeping, anxiety, and depression. Long-term effects include decreased sex drive, vaginal dryness, and decreased bone density.

Unclear as Risk Factors

It is not clear whether the following affect the risk of breast cancer.

- **Oral contraceptives.** Taking oral contraceptives ("the pill") may slightly increase the risk of breast cancer in current users. This risk decreases over time. Some oral contraceptives contain estrogen. Progestin-only contraceptives that are injected or implanted do not appear to increase the risk of breast cancer.

- **Environment.** Studies have not proven that being exposed to certain substances in the environment, such as chemicals, increases the risk of breast cancer.

191

Section 29.2

Surgery to Reduce the Risk of Breast Cancer

This section includes text excerpted from "Surgery to
Reduce the Risk of Breast Cancer," National
Cancer Institute (NCI), August 12, 2013.

What Kinds of Surgery Can Reduce the Risk of Breast Cancer?

Two kinds of surgery can be performed to reduce the risk of breast
cancer in a woman who has never been diagnosed with breast cancer
but is known to be at very high risk of the disease.

A woman can be at very high risk of developing breast cancer if she
has a strong family history of breast and/or ovarian cancer, a deleterious (disease-causing) mutation in the BRCA1 gene or the BRCA2 gene,
or a high-penetrance mutation in one of several other genes associated
with breast cancer risk, such as *TP53* or *PTEN*.

The most common risk-reducing surgery is bilateral prophylactic
mastectomy (also called bilateral risk-reducing mastectomy). Bilateral prophylactic mastectomy may involve complete removal of both
breasts, including the nipples (total mastectomy), or it may involve
removal of as much breast tissue as possible while leaving the nipples
intact (subcutaneous or nipple-sparing mastectomy). Subcutaneous
mastectomies preserve the nipple and allow for more natural-looking
breasts if a woman chooses to have breast reconstruction surgery
afterward. However, total mastectomy provides the greatest breast
cancer risk reduction because more breast tissue is removed in this
procedure than in a subcutaneous mastectomy.

Even with total mastectomy, not all breast tissue that may be at
risk of becoming cancerous in the future can be removed. The chest
wall, which is not typically removed during a mastectomy, may contain
some breast tissue, and breast tissue can sometimes be found in the
armpit, above the collarbone, and as far down as the abdomen—and
it is impossible for a surgeon to remove all of this tissue.

The other kind of risk-reducing surgery is bilateral prophylactic salpingo-oophorectomy, which is sometimes called prophylactic oophorectomy. This surgery involves removal of the ovaries and fallopian tubes and may be done alone or along with bilateral prophylactic mastectomy in premenopausal women who are at very high risk of breast cancer. Removing the ovaries in premenopausal women reduces the amount of estrogen that is produced by the body. Because estrogen promotes the growth of some breast cancers, reducing the amount of this hormone in the body by removing the ovaries may slow the growth of those breast cancers.

How Effective Are Risk-Reducing Surgeries?

Bilateral prophylactic mastectomy has been shown to reduce the risk of breast cancer by at least 95 percent in women who have a deleterious (disease-causing) mutation in the BRCA1 gene or the BRCA2 gene and by up to 90 percent in women who have a strong family history of breast cancer.

Bilateral prophylactic salpingo-oophorectomy has been shown to reduce the risk of ovarian cancer by approximately 90 percent and the risk of breast cancer by approximately 50 percent in women at very high risk of developing these diseases.

Which Women Might Consider Having Surgery to Reduce Their Risk of Breast Cancer?

Women who inherit a deleterious mutation in the BRCA1 gene or the BRCA2 gene or mutations in certain other genes that greatly increase the risk of developing breast cancer may consider having bilateral prophylactic mastectomy and/or bilateral prophylactic salpingo-oophorectomy to reduce this risk.

In two studies, the estimated risks of developing breast cancer by age 70 years were 55 to 65 percent for women who carry a deleterious mutation in the BRCA1 gene and 45 to 47 percent for women who carry a deleterious mutation in the BRCA2 gene. Estimates of the lifetime risk of breast cancer for women with Cowden syndrome, which is caused by certain mutations in the *PTEN* gene, range from 25 to 50 percent or higher, and for women with Li-Fraumeni syndrome, which is caused by certain mutations in the *TP53* gene, from 49 to 60 percent. (By contrast, the lifetime risk of breast cancer for the average American woman is about 12 percent.)

Other women who are at very high risk of breast cancer may also consider bilateral prophylactic mastectomy, including:

- those with a strong family history of breast cancer (such as having a mother, sister, and/or daughter who was diagnosed with bilateral breast cancer or with breast cancer before age 50 years or having multiple family members with breast or ovarian cancer)

- those with lobular carcinoma in situ (LCIS) plus a family history of breast cancer (LCIS is a condition in which abnormal cells are found in the lobules of the breast. It is not cancer, but women with LCIS have an increased risk of developing invasive breast cancer in either breast. Many breast surgeons consider prophylactic mastectomy to be an overly aggressive approach for women with LCIS who do not have a strong family history or other risk factors.)

- those who have had radiation therapy to the chest (including the breasts) before the age of 30 years—for example, if they were treated with radiation therapy for Hodgkin lymphoma [Such women are at high risk of developing breast cancer throughout their lives.]

Can a Woman Have Risk-Reducing Surgery If She Has Already Been Diagnosed with Breast Cancer?

Yes. Some women who have been diagnosed with cancer in one breast, particularly those who are known to be at very high risk, may consider having the other breast (called the contralateral breast) removed as well, even if there is no sign of cancer in that breast. Prophylactic surgery to remove a contralateral breast during breast cancer surgery (known as contralateral prophylactic mastectomy) reduces the risk of breast cancer in that breast, although it is not yet known whether this risk reduction translates into longer survival for the patient.

However, doctors often discourage contralateral prophylactic mastectomy for women with cancer in one breast who do not meet the criteria of being at very high risk of developing a contralateral breast cancer. For such women, the risk of developing another breast cancer, either in the same or the contralateral breast, is very small, especially if they receive adjuvant chemotherapy or hormone therapy as part of their cancer treatment.

Given that most women with breast cancer have a low risk of developing the disease in their contralateral breast, women who are not known to be at very high risk but who remain concerned about cancer development in their other breast may want to consider options other than surgery to further reduce their risk of a contralateral breast cancer.

What Are the Potential Harms of Risk-Reducing Surgeries?

As with any other major surgery, bilateral prophylactic mastectomy and bilateral prophylactic salpingo-oophorectomy have potential complications or harms, such as bleeding or infection. Also, both surgeries are irreversible.

Bilateral prophylactic mastectomy can also affect a woman's psychological well-being due to a change in body image and the loss of normal breast functions. Although most women who choose to have this surgery are satisfied with their decision, they can still experience anxiety and concerns about body image. The most common psychological side effects include difficulties with body appearance, with feelings of femininity, and with sexual relationships. Women who undergo total mastectomies lose nipple sensation, which may hinder sexual arousal.

Bilateral prophylactic salpingo-oophorectomy causes a sudden drop in estrogen production, which will induce early menopause in a premenopausal woman (this is also called surgical menopause). Surgical menopause can cause an abrupt onset of menopausal symptoms, including hot flashes, insomnia, anxiety, and depression, and some of these symptoms can be severe. The long-term effects of surgical menopause include decreased sex drive, vaginal dryness, and decreased bone density.

Women who have severe menopausal symptoms after undergoing bilateral prophylactic salpingo-oophorectomy may consider using short-term menopausal hormone therapy after surgery to alleviate these symptoms. [The increase in breast cancer risk associated with certain types of menopausal hormone therapy is much less than the decrease in breast cancer risk associated with bilateral prophylactic salpingo-oophorectomy.]

What Are the Cancer Risk Reduction Options for Women Who Are at Increased Risk of Breast Cancer but Not at the Highest Risk?

Risk-reducing surgery is not considered an appropriate cancer prevention option for women who are not at the highest risk of breast cancer (that is, for those who do not carry a high-penetrance gene mutation that is associated with breast cancer or who do not have a clinical or medical history that puts them at very high risk). However, some women who are not at very high risk of breast cancer but are, nonetheless, considered as being at increased risk of the disease may choose to use drugs to reduce their risk.

Health care providers use several types of tools, called risk assessment models, to estimate the risk of breast cancer for women who do not have a deleterious mutation in BRCA1, BRCA2, or another gene associated with breast cancer risk. One widely used tool is the Breast Cancer Risk Assessment Tool (BRCAT), a computer model that takes a number of factors into account in estimating the risks of breast cancer over the next 5 years and up to age 90 years (lifetime risk). Women who have an estimated 5-year risk of 1.67 percent or higher are classified as "high-risk," which means that they have a higher than average risk of developing breast cancer. This high-risk cutoff (that is, an estimated 5-year risk of 1.67 percent or higher) is widely used in research studies and in clinical counseling.

Two drugs, tamoxifen and raloxifene, are approved by the U.S. Food and Drug Administration (FDA) to reduce the risk of breast cancer in women who have a 5-year risk of developing breast cancer of 1.67 percent or more. Tamoxifen is approved for risk reduction in both premenopausal and postmenopausal women, and raloxifene is approved for risk reduction in postmenopausal women only. In large randomized clinical trials, tamoxifen, taken for 5 years, reduced the risk of invasive breast cancer by about 50 percent in high-risk postmenopausal women; raloxifene, taken for 5 years, reduced breast cancer risk by about 38 percent in high-risk postmenopausal women. Both drugs block the activity of estrogen, thereby inhibiting the growth of some breast cancers. The U.S. Preventive Services Task Force (USPSTF) recommends that women at increased risk of breast cancer talk with their health care professional about the potential benefits and harms of taking tamoxifen or raloxifene to reduce their risk.

Another drug, exemestane, was recently shown to reduce the incidence of breast cancer in postmenopausal women who are at increased risk of the disease by 65 percent. Exemestane belongs to a class of drugs called aromatase inhibitors, which block the production of estrogen by the body. It is not known, however, whether any of these drugs reduces the very high risk of breast cancer for women who carry a known mutation that is strongly associated with an increased risk of breast cancer, such as deleterious mutations in BRCA1 and BRCA2.

Some women who have undergone breast cancer surgery, regardless of their risk of recurrence, may be given drugs to reduce the likelihood that their breast cancer will recur. (This additional treatment is called adjuvant therapy.) Such treatment also reduces the already low risks of contralateral and second primary breast cancers. Drugs that are used as adjuvant therapy to reduce the risk of breast cancer after breast cancer surgery include tamoxifen, aromatase inhibitors, traditional chemotherapy agents, and trastuzumab.

What Can Women at Very High Risk Do If They Do Not Want to Undergo Risk-Reducing Surgery?

Some women who are at very high risk of breast cancer (or of contralateral breast cancer) may undergo more frequent breast cancer screening (also called enhanced screening). For example, they may have yearly mammograms and yearly magnetic resonance imaging (MRI) screening—with these tests staggered so that the breasts are imaged every 6 months—as well as clinical breast examinations performed regularly by a health care professional. Enhanced screening may increase the chance of detecting breast cancer at an early stage, when it may have a better chance of being treated successfully.

Women who carry mutations in some genes that increase their risk of breast cancer may be more likely to develop radiation-associated breast cancer than the general population because those genes are involved in the repair of DNA breaks, which can be caused by exposure to radiation. Women who are at high risk of breast cancer should ask their health care provider about the risks of diagnostic tests that involve radiation (mammograms or X-rays). Ongoing clinical trials are examining various aspects of enhanced screening for women who are at high risk of breast cancer.

Chemoprevention (the use of drugs or other agents to reduce cancer risk or delay its development) may be an option for some women who wish to avoid surgery. Tamoxifen and raloxifene have both been approved by the FDA to reduce the risk of breast cancer in women at increased risk. Whether these drugs can be used to prevent breast cancer in women at much higher risk, such as women with harmful mutations in BRCA1 or BRCA2 or other breast cancer susceptibility genes, is not yet clear, although tamoxifen may be able to help lower the risk of contralateral breast cancer among BRCA1 and BRCA2 mutation carriers previously diagnosed with breast cancer.

Does Health Insurance Cover the Cost of Risk-Reducing Surgeries?

Many health insurance companies have official policies about whether and under what conditions they will pay for prophylactic mastectomy (bilateral or contralateral) and bilateral prophylactic salpingo-oophorectomy for breast and ovarian cancer risk reduction. However, the criteria used for considering these procedures as medically necessary may vary among insurance companies. Some insurance companies may require a second opinion or a letter of medical necessity from the health care provider before they will approve coverage of any surgical procedure. A woman who is considering prophylactic surgery to reduce her risk of breast and/or ovarian cancer should discuss insurance coverage issues with her doctor and insurance company before choosing to have the surgery.

The Women's Health and Cancer Rights Act (WHCRA), enacted in 1999, requires most health plans that offer mastectomy coverage to also pay for breast reconstruction surgery after mastectomy. More information about WHCRA can be found through the Department of Labor.

Who Should a Woman Talk to When Considering Surgery to Reduce Her Risk of Breast Cancer?

The decision to have any surgery to reduce the risk of breast cancer is a major one. A woman who is at high risk of breast cancer may wish to get a second opinion on risk-reducing surgery as well as on alternatives to surgery.

A woman who is considering prophylactic mastectomy may also want to talk with a surgeon who specializes in breast reconstruction. Other health care professionals, including a breast health specialist, medical social worker, or cancer clinical psychologist or psychiatrist, can also help a woman consider her options for reducing her risk of breast cancer.

Many factors beyond the risk of disease itself may influence a woman's decision about whether to undergo risk-reducing surgery. For example, for women who have been diagnosed with cancer in one breast, these factors can include distress about the possibility of having to go through cancer treatment a second time and the worry and inconvenience associated with long-term breast surveillance. For this reason, women who are considering risk-reducing surgery may want to talk with other women who have considered or had the procedure. Support groups can help connect women with others who have had similar cancer experiences.

Finally, if a woman has a strong family history of breast cancer, ovarian cancer, or both, she and other members of her family may want to obtain genetic counseling services. A genetic counselor or other healthcare provider trained in genetics can review the family's risks of disease and help family members obtain genetic testing for mutations in cancer-predisposing genes, if appropriate.

Section 29.3

Medications for Breast Cancer Risk Reduction

This section contains text excerpted from the following sources: Text beginning with the heading "Medications for Risk Reduction of Primary Breast Cancer in Women: U.S. Preventive Services Task Force Recommendation Statement" is excerpted from "Guideline Summary," Agency for Healthcare Research and Quality (AHRQ), U.S. Department of Health and Human Services (HHS), November 19, 2013; Text beginning with the heading "Areas of Agreement" is excerpted from "Pharmacologic Interventions for Breast Cancer Risk Reduction in Women," Agency for Healthcare Research and Quality (AHRQ), U.S. Department of Health and Human Services (HHS), May 2014.

Medications for Risk Reduction of Primary Breast Cancer in Women

Major Recommendations

The U.S. Preventive Services Task Force (USPSTF) grades its recommendations (A, B, C, D, or I) and identifies the Levels of Certainty regarding Net Benefit (High, Moderate, and Low). The definitions of these grades can be found at the end of the "Major Recommendations" field.

Summary of Recommendations and Evidence

The USPSTF recommends that clinicians engage in shared, informed decision making with women who are at increased risk for breast cancer about medications to reduce their risk. For women who are at increased risk for breast cancer and at low risk for adverse medication effects, clinicians should offer to prescribe risk-reducing medications, such as tamoxifen or raloxifene. (**B recommendation**)

The USPSTF recommends against the routine use of medications, such as tamoxifen or raloxifene, for risk reduction of primary breast cancer in women who are not at increased risk for breast cancer. (**D recommendation**)

Clinical Considerations

Patient Population under Consideration

This recommendation applies to asymptomatic women aged 35 years or older without a prior diagnosis of breast cancer, ductal carcinoma in situ (DCIS), or lobular carcinoma in situ (LCIS). Neither tamoxifen nor raloxifene should be used in women who have a history of thromboembolic events (deep venous thrombosis, pulmonary embolus, stroke, or transient ischemic attack). The USPSTF has issued separate recommendations for women with BRCA gene mutations.

Assessment of Breast Cancer Risk

If a family history of breast cancer or a personal history of breast biopsy is found during the usual patient assessment, clinicians may consider further evaluation using a breast cancer risk assessment tool. Risk assessment tools specifically for family history of breast cancer are available elsewhere.

The National Cancer Institute has developed a Breast Cancer Risk Assessment Tool that is based on the Gail model and estimates the 5-year incidence of invasive breast cancer in women on the basis of characteristics entered into a risk calculator. This tool helps identify women who may be at increased risk for the disease. Other risk assessment models have been developed by the Breast Cancer Surveillance Consortium (BCSC), Rosner and Colditz, Chlebowski, Tyrer and Cuzick, and others.

Examples of risk factors elicited by risk assessment tools include patient age, race or ethnicity, age at menarche, age at first live childbirth, personal history of DCIS or LCIS, number of first-degree relatives with breast cancer, personal history of breast biopsy, body mass index, menopause status or age, breast density, estrogen and progestin use, smoking, alcohol use, physical activity, and diet.

These models are not recommended for use in women with a personal history of breast cancer, a history of radiation treatment to the chest, or a possible family history of mutations in the BRCA1 or BRCA2 genes. Only a small fraction of women are at increased risk for breast cancer. Most who are at increased risk will not develop the disease, and most cases will arise in women who are not identified as being at increased risk. Risk assessment should be repeated when there is a significant change in breast cancer risk factors.

There is no single cutoff for defining increased risk. Most clinical trials defined increased risk as a 5-year risk for invasive breast cancer of 1.66% or greater, as determined by the BCPT (Breast Cancer Prevention Trial). At this cutoff, however, many women would not have a net benefit from risk-reducing medications. Freedman and colleagues developed risk tables that incorporate the BCPT estimate of a woman's breast cancer risk as well as her age, race or ethnicity, and presence of uterus.

On the basis of the Freedman risk–benefit tables for women aged 50 years or older, the USPSTF concludes that many women with an estimated 5-year breast cancer risk of 3% or greater are likely to have more benefit than harm from using tamoxifen or raloxifene, although the balance depends on age, race or ethnicity, the medication used, and whether the patient has a uterus.

Assessment of Risk for Adverse Effects

In general, women receiving medications for breast cancer risk reduction are less likely to have venous thromboembolic events (VTEs) if they are younger and have no other predisposition to thromboembolic events. Women with a personal or family history of venous thromboembolism are at higher risk for these adverse effects.

Women without a uterus are not at risk for tamoxifen-related endometrial cancer. Women with a uterus should have a baseline gynecologic examination before treatment with tamoxifen is started, with regular follow-up after the end of treatment.

Medications for Breast Cancer Risk Reduction

Selective estrogen receptor modulators (tamoxifen and raloxifene) have been shown to reduce the incidence of invasive breast cancer in several randomized, controlled trials. Tamoxifen has been approved for this use in women aged 35 years or older, and raloxifene has been approved for this use in postmenopausal women.

The usual daily doses for tamoxifen and raloxifene are 20 mg and 60 mg, respectively, for 5 years. Aromatase inhibitors (exemestane) have not been approved by the U.S. Food and Drug Administration (FDA) for this indication and are, therefore, beyond the scope of this recommendation.

Tamoxifen is not recommended for use in combination with hormone therapy or hormonal contraception or in women who are pregnant, may become pregnant, or are breastfeeding.

Other Approaches to Prevention

The USPSTF recommendation on risk assessment, genetic counseling, and genetic testing for BRCA-related cancer can be found at www.uspreventiveservicestaskforce.org. Clinical trials of tamoxifen and raloxifene have not been conducted specifically in women who are BRCA mutation carriers.

Potential Benefits of Medications for Breast Cancer Risk Reduction

- The U.S. Preventive Services Task Force (USPSTF) found adequate evidence that treatment with tamoxifen or raloxifene can significantly reduce the relative risk (RR) for invasive estrogen receptor (ER)-positive breast cancer in postmenopausal women who are at increased risk for breast cancer.

- A systematic review of clinical trials found that tamoxifen and raloxifene reduced the incidence of invasive breast cancer by 7 to 9 events per 1000 women over 5 years and that tamoxifen reduced breast cancer incidence more than raloxifene. Tamoxifen also reduces the incidence of invasive breast cancer in premenopausal women who are at increased risk for the disease.

- Women who are at increased risk for breast cancer are more likely to benefit from risk-reducing medications. In general, women with an estimated 5-year risk of 3% or greater are, on the basis of model estimates, more likely to benefit from tamoxifen or raloxifene. The USPSTF found that the benefits of tamoxifen and raloxifene for breast cancer risk reduction are no greater than small in women who are not at increased risk for the disease.

- In addition to breast cancer risk reduction, the USPSTF found adequate evidence that tamoxifen and raloxifene reduce the risk for nonvertebral and vertebral fractures, respectively, in postmenopausal women.

Potential Harms of Medications for Breast Cancer Risk Reduction

- The U.S. Preventive Services Task Force (USPSTF) found adequate evidence that tamoxifen and raloxifene increase risk for venous thromboembolic events (VTEs) by 4 to 7 events per 1000 women over 5 years and that tamoxifen increases risk more than raloxifene (refer to Appendix Table 3 in the original guideline document). The USPSTF found that potential harms from thromboembolic events are small to moderate, with increased potential for harms in older women.

- The USPSTF also found adequate evidence that tamoxifen but not raloxifene increases risk for endometrial cancer (4 more cases per 1000 women). Potential harms from tamoxifen-related endometrial cancer are small to moderate and depend on hysterectomy status and age. The potential risks for tamoxifen-related harms are higher in women older than 50 years and in women with a uterus. Tamoxifen may also increase the incidence of cataracts.

- Vasomotor symptoms (hot flashes), a common adverse effect of both medications that is not typically classified as serious, may affect a patient's quality of life and willingness to use or adhere to these medications.

Areas of Agreement

Selective Estrogen Receptor Modulators (SERMs)

The groups agree that the option to use tamoxifen and raloxifene to reduce the risk of estrogen receptor-positive breast cancer should be discussed between physicians and their eligible female patients as part of a shared, informed decision-making process. Eligibility criteria outlined by the groups are similar, with the developers agreeing that use of these SERMs for risk-reduction purposes is only appropriate for women aged 35 years or older **who are at increased risk of breast cancer**, who have never been diagnosed with breast cancer, including

DCIS, and who—in the event that raloxifene is being considered—are postmenopausal (tamoxifen is approved for this use in both pre- and postmenopausal women).

The groups agree that tamoxifen is not recommended for use in combination with hormone therapy or in women who are pregnant, may become pregnant, or are breastfeeding. There is further agreement that neither tamoxifen nor raloxifene is recommended for use in women with a history of thromboembolic events (deep vein thrombosis, pulmonary embolus, stroke, or transient ischemic attack); ASCO also cites prolonged immobilization as a contraindication.

USPSTF emphasizes that the use of breast cancer risk-reducing medications is not appropriate in women at high risk of adverse events. The groups agree that the usual daily doses for tamoxifen and raloxifene are 20 mg and 60 mg, respectively, for 5 years. ASCO states that raloxifene may be used longer than 5 years in women with osteoporosis, in whom breast cancer risk reduction is a secondary benefit.

Aromatase Inhibitors

ASCO examined the evidence for the aromatase inhibitors exemestane and anastrozole. The developer provides a recommendation for exemestane, but found insufficient evidence to make a recommendation for anastrozole. ASCO recommends that exemestane be discussed as an alternative to tamoxifen and/or raloxifene to reduce the risk of invasive breast cancer, specifically ER-positive breast cancer, in postmenopausal women age ≥35 years with a 5-year projected breast cancer absolute risk ≥1.66%, according to the National Cancer Institute (NCI) Breast Cancer Risk Assessment Tool (or equivalent measures), or with LCIS or atypical hyperplasia.

While exemestane is approved by the U.S. FDA for the adjuvant treatment of early breast cancer and the treatment of advanced breast cancer, no aromatase inhibitors are currently approved for breast cancer risk reduction. Citing the lack of approval for this indication, USPSTF notes that aromatase inhibitors were beyond the scope of its recommendation statement. The developer does, however, address exemestane and anastrozole in the context of research needs and gaps, stating that clinical trials that provide more information about the safety and effectiveness of other medications for breast cancer risk reduction, such as aromatase inhibitors and tibolone, are needed. According to the USPSTF, exemestane reduced the incidence of invasive breast cancer in postmenopausal women who were at moderately increased risk for the disease and did not significantly increase the incidence of morbidity or mortality. However, USPSTF adds, these findings were reported from a randomized, clinical trial with a median follow-up of 3 years and will require long-term assessment. With regard to anastrozole, USPSTF states that the IBIS-II (International Breast Cancer Intervention Study II), an ongoing British study, is comparing the aromatase inhibitor with placebo in women who are at increased risk for breast cancer.

Benefits

Appropriate management of women at increased risk of breast cancer.

Potential Benefits of Medications for Breast Cancer Risk Reduction

- The USPSTF found adequate evidence that treatment with tamoxifen or raloxifene can significantly reduce the relative risk (RR) for invasive estrogen receptor (ER)-positive breast cancer in postmenopausal women who are at increased risk for breast cancer.

- A systematic review of clinical trials found that tamoxifen and raloxifene reduced the incidence of invasive breast cancer by 7 to 9 events per 1000 women over 5 years and that tamoxifen reduced breast cancer incidence more than raloxifene. Tamoxifen also reduces the incidence of invasive breast cancer in premenopausal women who are at increased risk for the disease.

- Women who are at increased risk for breast cancer are more likely to benefit from risk-reducing medications. In general, women with an estimated 5-year risk of 3% or greater are, on the basis of model estimates, more likely to benefit from tamoxifen or raloxifene. The USPSTF found that the benefits of tamoxifen and raloxifene for breast cancer risk reduction are no greater than small in women who are not at increased risk for the disease.

- In addition to breast cancer risk reduction, the USPSTF found adequate evidence that tamoxifen and raloxifene reduce the risk for nonvertebral and vertebral fractures, respectively, in post-menopausal women.

Harms

Tamoxifen

Serious adverse events associated with tamoxifen use include endometrial cancer, stroke, transient ischemic attack, venous thromboembolism, deep vein thrombosis, and pulmonary embolism. Two studies have also identified specific subgroups of women at increased risk of developing venous thromboembolism while on tamoxifen: women who are immobilized in the prior 3 months and/or women who have body mass index (BMI) >25 kg/m2.

Raloxifene

Raloxifene is associated with a more favorable adverse effect profile compared with tamoxifen including a significantly lower risk of thromboembolic disease (statistically significant only for deep vein thrombosis) and uterine cancer and lower incidence of benign uterine hyperplasia, cataracts, and cataract surgery.

Exemestane

Overall, more adverse events occurred in the exemestane group compared with the placebo group of the MAP.3 trial. There were no statistically significant differences in the incidence of serious adverse events including cardiovascular events, skeletal fractures, other cancers, or treatment-related deaths. Statistically significant differences were observed for endocrine-related adverse events (i.e., hot flashes, fatigue, sweating, insomnia), constitutional and gastrointestinal (GI) events (i.e., diarrhea and nausea), and joint and muscle pain.

Results from a post hoc nested substudy of the MAP.3 trial demonstrated a statistically significant reduction in bone mineral density and cortical thickness at the distal tibia and distal radius, lumbar spine, total hip, and femoral neck. Compared with placebo, 2 years of treatment with exemestane worsened age-related bone loss in postmenopausal women, despite calcium and vitamin D supplementation.

Minimal differences in quality-of-life outcomes were observed between the exemestane and placebo groups. There was a statistically significant increase in the incidence of vasomotor symptoms, bodily pain, and sexual problems in women who took exemestane compared with women in the placebo group.

Potential Harms of Medications for Breast Cancer Risk Reduction

The USPSTF found adequate evidence that tamoxifen and raloxifene increase risk for venous thromboembolic events (VTEs) by 4 to 7 events per 1000 women over 5 years and that tamoxifen increases risk more than raloxifene. The USPSTF found that potential harms from thromboembolic events are small to moderate, with increased potential for harms in older women.

The USPSTF also found adequate evidence that tamoxifen but not raloxifene increases risk for endometrial cancer (4 more cases per 1000 women). Potential harms from tamoxifen-related endometrial cancer are small to moderate and depend on hysterectomy status and age. The potential risks for tamoxifen-related harms are higher in women older than 50 years and in women with a uterus. Tamoxifen may also increase the incidence of cataracts.

Vasomotor symptoms (hot flashes), a common adverse effect of both medications that is not typically classified as serious, may affect a patient's quality of life and willingness to use or adhere to these medications.

Contraindications

- Neither tamoxifen nor raloxifene is recommended for use in women with a personal history of deep vein thrombosis, pulmonary embolus, stroke, transient ischemic attack, or during prolonged immobilization, because of the increased risk of adverse events in these women.

- Tamoxifen is not recommended for use in women who are, or may become, pregnant, or nursing mothers.

- Neither raloxifene nor exemestane is recommended for use in premenopausal women.

Part Four

Screening, Diagnosis, and Stages of Breast Cancer

Chapter 30

Breast Cancer Screening and Exams

Chapter Contents

Section 30.1

Overview of Breast Cancer Screening

This section includes text excerpted from "Breast Cancer
Screening–Patient Version (PDQ®)," National
Cancer Institute (NCI), January 22, 2016.

What Is Screening?

Screening is looking for cancer before a person has any symptoms.
This can help find cancer at an early stage. When abnormal tissue or
cancer is found early, it may be easier to treat. By the time symptoms
appear, cancer may have begun to spread.

Scientists are trying to better understand which people are more
likely to get certain types of cancer. They also study the things we do
and the things around us to see if they cause cancer. This information
helps doctors recommend who should be screened for cancer, which
screening tests should be used, and how often the tests should be done.

It is important to remember that your doctor does not necessarily
think you have cancer if he or she suggests a screening test. Screening
tests are given when you have no cancer symptoms.

If a screening test result is abnormal, you may need to have more
tests done to find out if you have cancer. These are called diagnostic
tests.

Breast Cancer Screening

Tests Are Used to Screen for Different Types of Cancer

Some screening tests are used because they have been shown to
be helpful both in finding cancers early and in decreasing the chance
of dying from these cancers. Other tests are used because they have
been shown to find cancer in some people; however, it has not been
proven in clinical trials that use of these tests will decrease the risk
of dying from cancer.

Scientists study screening tests to find those with the fewest risks
and most benefits. Cancer screening trials also are meant to show
whether early detection (finding cancer before it causes symptoms)

decreases a person's chance of dying from the disease. For some types of cancer, the chance of recovery is better if the disease is found and treated at an early stage.

Clinical trials that study cancer screening methods are taking place in many parts of the country.

Three Tests Are Used by HealthCare Providers to Screen for Breast Cancer

Mammogram

Mammography is the most common screening test for breast cancer. A mammogram is an X-ray of the breast. This test may find tumors that are too small to feel. A mammogram may also find ductal carcinoma in situ (DCIS). In DCIS, there are abnormal cells in the lining of a breast duct, which may become invasive cancer in some women.

Mammograms are less likely to find breast tumors in women younger than 50 years than in older women. This may be because younger women have denser breast tissue that appears white on a mammogram. Because tumors also appear white on a mammogram, they can be harder to find when there is dense breast tissue.

The following may affect whether a mammogram is able to detect (find) breast cancer:

- The size of the tumor.

- How dense the breast tissue is.

- The skill of the radiologist.

Women aged 40 to 74 years who have screening mammograms have a lower chance of dying from breast cancer than women who do not have screening mammograms.

Clinical Breast Exam (CBE)

A clinical breast exam is an exam of the breast by a doctor or other health professional. The doctor will carefully feel the breasts and under the arms for lumps or anything else that seems unusual. It is not known if having clinical breast exams decreases the chance of dying from breast cancer.

Breast self-exams may be done by women or men to check their breasts for lumps or other changes. It is important to know how your breasts usually look and feel. If you feel any lumps or notice any other changes, talk to your doctor. Doing breast self-exams has not been shown to decrease the chance of dying from breast cancer.

MRI (Magnetic Resonance Imaging) in Women with a High Risk of Breast Cancer

MRI is a procedure that uses a magnet, radio waves, and a computer to make a series of detailed pictures of areas inside the body. This procedure is also called nuclear magnetic resonance imaging (NMRI). MRI does not use any X-rays.

MRI is used as a screening test for women who have one or more of the following:

- Certain gene changes, such as in the BRCA1 or BRCA2 genes

- A family history (first degree relative, such as a mother, daughter or sister) with breast cancer

- Certain genetic syndromes, such as Li-Fraumeni or Cowden syndrome

MRIs find breast cancer more often than mammograms do, but it is common for MRI results to appear abnormal even when there isn't any cancer.

Other Screening Tests Are Being Studied in Clinical Trials

Thermography

Thermography is a procedure in which a special camera that senses heat is used to record the temperature of the skin that covers the breasts. A computer makes a map of the breast showing the changes in temperature. Tumors can cause temperature changes that may show up on the thermogram.

There have been no clinical trials of thermography to find out how well it detects breast cancer or if having the procedure decreases the risk of dying from breast cancer.

Tissue Sampling

Breast tissue sampling is taking cells from breast tissue to check under a microscope. Abnormal cells in breast fluid have been linked to an increased risk of breast cancer in some studies. Scientists are studying whether breast tissue sampling can be used to find breast cancer at an early stage or predict the risk of developing breast cancer. Three ways of taking tissue samples are being studied:

- **Fine-needle aspiration:** A thin needle is inserted into the breast tissue around the areola (darkened area around the nipple) to take out a sample of cells and fluid.

- **Nipple aspiration:** The use of gentle suction to collect fluid through the nipple. This is done with a device similar to the breast pumps used by women who are breast-feeding.

- **Ductal lavage:** A hair-size catheter (tube) is inserted into the nipple and a small amount of salt water is released into the duct. The water picks up breast cells and is removed.

Screening clinical trials are taking place in many parts of the country.

Section 30.2

Breast Self-Exam

"Breast Self-Exam," © 2016 Omnigraphics, Inc.
Reviewed April 2016.

Overview

Breast self-examination is a technique people can use to visually and manually check their own breast tissue for lumps or other changes. Many healthcare practitioners and cancer-prevention organizations recommend performing monthly breast self-examinations beginning at age 18 as a method of early detection for breast cancer. People who conduct regular self-exams become familiar with the normal appearance and feel of their breast tissue, which enables them to recognize changes and discover lumps that may require medical attention. Some of the changes that should be checked by a doctor include:

- new lumps or areas of thickness, which may or may not be painful

- discharge of fluid from the nipples

- dimpling, puckering, rashes, or other changes to the skin

- changes to the size or shape of the breast

Finding lumps or noticing changes should not be a cause for alarm, however. An estimated 80 percent of lumps found in self-examinations are not cancerous, and most breast problems are caused by something other than cancer. In fact, some experts do not recommend self-examinations by people over 40 with no increased risk of breast cancer. They argue that the potential benefits of early detection are outweighed by the risks of undergoing tests and treatments that are unnecessary. Instead, they recommend regular checkups at a doctor's office as well as annual mammograms.

Self-Examination Procedures

Ideally, breast self-examinations should be performed on a monthly basis. For women who are menstruating, the best time is usually toward the end of the monthly period, when the breasts are less likely to be tender. For those who no longer have periods, experts recommend choosing a certain day of the month. Performing self-examinations on a regular schedule makes it easier to compare the results and recognize changes in breast tissue.

Visual Examination

The first part of the process involves a visual examination of the breasts. This examination should be conducted while standing in front of a mirror in three different positions: with your arms hanging naturally at your sides; with your arms raised above your head; and with your hands on your hips and your upper body leaning forward from the waist. Be sure to look from the right and left sides as well as from the front. Check carefully for any changes to the following:

- Size and shape

Make sure your breasts appear to be their usual size and shape, and that no sudden changes have occurred. Although one breast may normally be larger than the other, you should not see any visible swelling or bulging.

- Skin and veins

Check the skin on your breasts for anything that appears unusual, such as puckering, dimpling, or distortion. Also look for areas of redness, soreness, rashes, or texture changes. Make sure that the veins beneath the skin appear as they usually do. You should not see a noticeable increase in the size or number of veins in one breast as compared to the other breast.

- Nipples

Check for any physical changes to the appearance or position of the nipples, such as a sudden inversion. Also check the skin for redness, itching, scaliness, or swelling. Look for any fluid discharge, which may appear watery, milky, sticky, or bloody.

Manual Examination

The second part of the process involves a manual examination of each breast using the fingers of the opposite hand. It should cover the entire surface area of each breast, from the collarbone down to the abdomen, and from the armpit across to the cleavage. This examination should be conducted while lying down, and then again while standing up. The main steps are as follows:

1. Lie down on your back and place a pillow beneath your right shoulder.

2. Place your right arm on top of your head.

3. Use the pads of the three middle fingers on your left hand to examine your right breast.

4. Move your fingers in small circles, about the size of a quarter.

5. Vary the amount of pressure you apply in order to feel all levels of your breast tissue. Use light pressure to feel just beneath the skin, and firm pressure to feel the deep tissue against the ribcage.

6. Begin under the armpit and work from top to bottom along the outer part of your breast.

7. After completing one vertical strip, move over one finger width and begin a new strip, working from bottom to top. Do not lift the fingers between rows.

8. Check the entire breast area in an up-and-down pattern, as if mowing a lawn.

9. Repeat the process by using the left hand to examine the right breast.

10. Examine both breasts again while standing. Many women find it convenient to perform this part of the self-examination in the shower, while the skin is wet and soapy.

If you discover a lump in one breast, check to see if the same kind of lump exists in the other breast. If so, the lumps are probably normal. Many women have fibrocystic lumps that occur throughout both breasts, which may make self-examination difficult. By performing regular self-examinations, women can become familiar with the normal appearance of their breast tissue and consult with medical professionals if they notice any changes.

References

1. "Breast Self-Examination." Healthwise, February 20, 2015.

2. "The Five Steps of a Breast Self-Exam." Breastcancer.org, 2016.

3. "How to Do a Breast Self-Exam." Maurer Foundation, March 26, 2016.

Section 30.3

Screening for Women with Dense Breasts

This section includes text excerpted from "ONE's Column: Breast Cancer Screening for Women with Dense Breasts: The Gray Zone (or Actually the White Zone)," National Cancer Institute (NCI), December 18, 2015.

Breast Cancer Screening for Women with Dense Breasts: The Gray Zone

"For women with dense breasts, mammograms can be less accurate so new tests offer better detection but more often more false alarms," so said a recent article in the Wall Street Journal. As the 'gold standard' for breast cancer screening, mammography is the screening tool of choice, yet for women with dense breasts, mammograms often are of limited benefit. We have long educated women that dense breasts are considered a risk factor for breast cancer because dense breast tissue may make it more difficult to find tumors on standard imaging test, such as mammography. So where does this leave women with dense breasts regarding screening mammograms?

First, what do we mean by dense breast? This is not about how the breast feels, but how the breasts look on a mammogram. The breast is made up of a mixture of fibrous and glandular tissue and fatty tissue. When the breasts are dense the fibrous and glandular tissue is more compact, much closer together. Young women often have denser breasts because the fat to fibrous-glandular tissue ratio is less. As women age, this ratio changes. Older women have more fatty tissue than fibrous-glandular tissue, meaning a low breast density.

Dense fibrous-glandular tissue is much less radiopaque than fatty tissue. Remember that a mammogram is an X-ray of the breast. X-ray passes much more easily and clearly through tissue that is less compact, radio-opaque, where dense tissue appears white on a mammogram making it harder to identify any abnormalities. Both dense tissue and tumors show up as solid white areas on X-ray images.

Recently some 21 states have passed a law where if breast density is noted on women's screening mammogram, they are sent a letter notifying them of this finding and informing them that they are at increased risk for breast cancer. The law was passed first in the state of Connecticut when a woman who hadn't been told that her mammogram showed dense breast tissue was later diagnosed with breast cancer. The law can vary among states, some requiring that physicians notify women with dense breasts of the finding and others stipulating that additional testing is offered.

Many cancers are first detect on mammograms even if one has dense breast tissue, but is there a better screening tool for women with dense breasts? Digital mammography appears to be more accurate than conventional film mammography in younger women with dense breasts. Yet, currently there is no clear consensus in the medical community about recommendations for women who have dense breasts. Some studies have shown that ultrasound and magnetic resonance imaging (MRI) can help find breast cancers in women with dense breasts that can't be seen on a mammogram. But both MRI and ultrasound can show more false negatives, findings that are not cancer. This can result in added anxiety, more testing and unnecessary biopsies. Also, the cost of ultrasound and MRI may not be covered by insurance.

Section 30.4

Breast Cancer Screening for Women with Disabilities

This section includes text excerpted from "Women with Disabilities and Breast Cancer Screening," Centers for Disease Control and Prevention (CDC), April 2, 2014.

Finding Breast Cancer Early Can Save Lives

Breast cancer is the most common type of cancer among women in the United States, and the second leading cause of cancer-related deaths. Thinking "breast cancer won't happen to me" is a risk no woman should take. Having a screening mammogram regularly is an important way to maintain good health. A mammogram, which is an X-ray picture of the breast, is the best way to find breast cancer early, when it is easiest to treat and before it is big enough to feel or cause symptoms.

- If breast cancer is found early, treatment can have a greater chance for success.

- Many women who are diagnosed with and treated for breast cancer live long and healthy lives.

Women with Disabilities Are Less Likely to Have Received a Mammogram during the past Two Years

Breast Cancer Screening Recommendations

If you are between the ages of 50-74 years, be sure to have a screening mammogram every two years. If you are between the ages of 40-49 years, talk to your doctor about when and how often you should have a screening mammogram.

Percentage of U.S. Adult Women 50-74 Years of Age Who Received a Mammogram during the past 2 Years, by Disability Status—2010 National Household Interview Survey (NHIS)

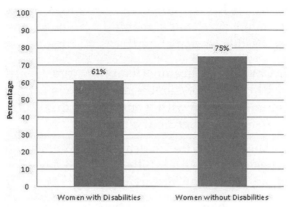

Figure 30.1. *Women with Disabilities versus Women without Disabilities*

CDC/NCHS. National Health Interview Survey Data, 2010.

CDC Is Working to Improve the Use of Mammography among Women with Disabilities

CDC-funded states are working to help more women with disabilities get screened for breast cancer. Here are a few examples:

The Florida Office on Disability and Health is increasing the number of train-the-trainer sessions on mammograms and women with disabilities.

The highlights of the program include:

- Educating women with disabilities on how to prepare for a mammogram, how to get regular breast cancer screening, and how to locate local disability accessible mammography facilities.

- Providing tips to health professionals on how to improve their mammography services for women with disabilities.

- Partnering with the Florida Board of Radiologic Technology in the Florida Department of Health to develop and promote radiology technology disability training.

The Rhode Island (R.I.) Disability and Health Program is ensuring that women with disabilities have access to mammograms.

The highlights of the program include:

- Collaborating with the R.I. Department of Health's Division of Community, Family Health and Equity to inform women with disabilities on locations of disability accessible mammography facilities with accessible mammography equipment.

- Working with the R.I. Department of Health's Cancer Screening Program to make sure that screening mammograms are available and accessible to women with disabilities.

The North Carolina Office on Disability and Health is working to educate healthcare professionals about the specific needs of and appropriate communication with women with disabilities.

The highlights of the program include:

- Supporting the Women Be Healthy health education curriculum, which teaches women with intellectual and developmental disabilities about breast cancer screening.

- Providing education and training about women with disabilities to North Carolina's Breast and Cervical Cancer Control Program, which offers free or low-cost breast and cervical cancer screenings.

Getting Screened: Tips for Women with Disabilities

If you are a woman living with a disability, you may face challenges that make it hard to get a mammogram. Here are some questions to ask when scheduling your mammogram that can help you prepare for your appointment:

- How should I dress?

- How do I prepare if I use a wheelchair or a scooter?

- Can the machine be adjusted so I can remain seated?

- How long is the appointment and can I have more time if I need it?

Let the scheduling staff, radiology technicians, or radiologist know if you can/cannot:

- Sit upright with or without assistance

- Lift and move your arms

- Transfer from your chair/scooter

- Undress/dress without assistance

When preparing for your mammogram, remember:

- Wear a blouse that opens in the front

- Wear a bra that you can remove easily

- Do not wear deodorant or body powder

- If you have any disability-related concerns, discuss them with your primary care physician, women's health specialist, radiologist, physician's assistant, or other healthcare professional.

Section 30.5

National Program for Early Detection of Breast Cancer

This section includes text excerpted from "National Breast and Cervical Cancer Early Detection Program (NBCCEDP)," Centers for Disease Control and Prevention (CDC), March 15, 2016.

National Breast and Cervical Cancer Early Detection Program (NBCCEDP)

About the Program

Through the National Breast and Cervical Cancer Early Detection Program (NBCCEDP), CDC provides low-income, uninsured, and underserved women access to timely breast and cervical cancer screening and diagnostic services.

To improve access to screening, Congress passed the Breast and Cervical Cancer Mortality Prevention Act of 1990 which directed CDC to create the NBCCEDP. Currently, the NBCCEDP funds all 50 states, the District of Columbia, 5 U.S. territories, and 11 American Indian/ Alaska Native tribes or tribal organizations to provide screening services for breast and cervical cancer. The program helps low-income, uninsured, and underinsured women gain access to breast and cervical cancer screening and diagnostic services. These services include—

- Clinical breast examinations
- Mammograms
- Pap tests
- Pelvic examinations
- Human papillomavirus (HPV) tests
- Diagnostic testing if results are abnormal
- Referrals to treatment

In 2000, Congress passed the Breast and Cervical Cancer Prevention and Treatment Act, which allowed states to offer women who are diagnosed with cancer in the NBCCEDP access to treatment through Medicaid. All 50 states and the District of Columbia approved this option. In 2001, with passage of the Native American Breast and Cervical Cancer Treatment Technical Amendment Act Congress explained that his option also applies to American Indians and Alaska Natives who are eligible for health services provided by the Indian Health Service or by a tribal organization.

Program Eligibility

Federal guidelines establish an eligibility baseline to direct services to uninsured and underinsured women at or below 250% of federal poverty level; ages 21 to 64 for cervical cancer screening; ages 40 to 64 for breast cancer screening.

Accomplishments

Since 1991, NBCCEDP-funded programs have served more than 4.8 million women, provided more than 12.2 million breast and cervical cancer screening examinations, and diagnosed more than 69,507 breast cancers, 3,771 invasive cervical cancers, and 173,582 premalignant cervical lesions, of which 40% were high-grade.

In calendar year 2014, the NBCCEDP—

- Screened 242,534 women for breast cancer with mammography and diagnosed 4,325 breast cancers.

- Screened 146,947 women for cervical cancer with the Pap test and diagnosed 194 cervical cancers and 6,491 premalignant cervical lesions, of which 39% were high-grade.

To reach underserved women, the NBCCEDP Conceptual Framework supports an array of strategies, including program management, screening and diagnostic services, data management, quality assurance and quality improvement, evaluation, partnerships, professional development, and recruitment. Providers in the program work collaboratively to provide breast and cervical cancer screening, diagnostic evaluation, and treatment referrals (where appropriate). The program's continued success depends in large part on the complementary efforts of a variety of national partner organizations, as well as on state and community partners.

Screening

Deaths from breast and cervical cancers could be avoided if cancer screening rates increased among women at risk. Deaths from these diseases occur disproportionately among women who are uninsured or underinsured. Mammography and Pap tests are underused by women who have no regular source of health care, women without health insurance, and women who immigrated to the United States within the past 10 years.

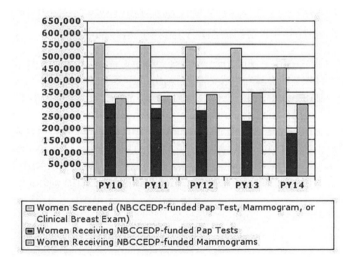

Figure 30.2. *Number of Women Screened through the NBCCEDP by Year*

Expanded Focus

Implementation of health care reform through the Affordable Care Act will increase access to breast and cervical cancer screening services for many low-income, underserved women through expanded insurance coverage and eliminating cost-sharing. But even with adequate health insurance, many women will still face substantial barriers to obtaining breast and cervical cancer screening such as geographic isolation, limited health literacy or self-efficacy, lack of provider recommendation, inconvenient times to access services, and language barriers.

CDC and other public health agencies now have an unprecedented opportunity to build on the existing capacity and the extensive clinical network of NBCCEDP by focusing on population-based approaches to ensure women overcome barriers to getting screened for breast and cervical cancer.

In addition to funding screening provision—reaching and serving NBCCEDP-eligible women—NBCCEDP supports planning and implementing activities to increase breast and cervical cancer screening rates among all women of appropriate screening age. This includes women who have—

- Health insurance, especially the newly insured.

- Publicly funded insurance, such as Medicare or Medicaid.

- Access to Indian Health Service or tribal health clinics.

- Coverage through other programs or services.

NBCCEDP-funded programs use population-based approaches to improve systems that increase high-quality breast and cervical cancer screening. Research suggests that social, organizational, and policy environments impact the ability or likelihood of individuals engaging in healthy behaviors, such as breast and cervical cancer screening. Behavior is difficult to change, especially in an environment that does not readily support change. Therefore, NBCCEDP has adopted the social ecological model, which not only focuses on the behavior choices of individuals, but also on organizational, community, and policy level factors that influence those choices.

Chapter 31

Mammograms

Chapter Contents

Section 31.1

Mammography—An Overview

Text beginning with the heading "What Is a Mammogram?"
is excerpted from "Mammograms," National Cancer
Institute (NCI), March 25, 2014; Text under the heading
"Mammograms: Questions for the Doctor" is excerpted
from "Mammograms: Questions for the Doctor,"
Office of Disease Prevention and Health
Promotion (ODPHP), November 23, 2015.

What Is a Mammogram?

A mammogram is an X-ray picture of the breast.

Mammograms can be used to check for breast cancer in women who have no signs or symptoms of the disease. This type of mammogram is called a screening mammogram. Screening mammograms usually involve two X-ray pictures, or images, of each breast. The X-ray images make it possible to detect tumors that cannot be felt. Screening mammograms can also find microcalcifications (tiny deposits of calcium) that sometimes indicate the presence of breast cancer.

Mammograms can also be used to check for breast cancer after a lump or other sign or symptom of the disease has been found. This type of mammogram is called a diagnostic mammogram. Besides a lump, signs of breast cancer can include breast pain, thickening of the skin of the breast, nipple discharge, or a change in breast size or shape; however, these signs may also be signs of benign conditions. A diagnostic mammogram can also be used to evaluate changes found during a screening mammogram or to view breast tissue when it is difficult to obtain a screening mammogram because of special circumstances, such as the presence of breast implants.

How Are Screening and Diagnostic Mammograms Different?

Diagnostic mammography takes longer than screening mammography because more X-rays are needed to obtain views of the breast from several angles. The technician may magnify a suspicious area to produce a detailed picture that can help the doctor make an accurate diagnosis.

What Are the Benefits and Potential Harms of Screening Mammograms?

Early detection of breast cancer with screening mammography means that treatment can be started earlier in the course of the disease, possibly before it has spread. Results from randomized clinical trials and other studies show that screening mammography can help reduce the number of deaths from breast cancer among women ages 40 to 74, especially for those over age 50. However, studies to date have not shown a benefit from regular screening mammography in women under age 40 or from baseline screening mammograms (mammograms used for comparison) taken before age 40.

The benefits need to be balanced against the harms, including:

False-positive results. False-positive results occur when radiologists decide mammograms are abnormal but no cancer is actually present. All abnormal mammograms should be followed up with additional testing (diagnostic mammograms, ultrasound, and/or biopsy) to determine whether cancer is present.

False-positive results are more common for younger women, women who have had previous breast biopsies, women with a family history of breast cancer, and women who are taking estrogen.

False-positive mammogram results can lead to anxiety and other forms of psychological distress in affected women. The additional testing required to rule out cancer can also be costly and time consuming and can cause physical discomfort.

Overdiagnosis and overtreatment. Screening mammograms can find cancers and cases of ductal carcinoma in situ (DCIS, a noninvasive tumor in which abnormal cells that may become cancerous build up in the lining of breast ducts) that need to be treated. However, they can also find cancers and cases of DCIS that will never cause symptoms or threaten a woman's life, leading to "overdiagnosis" of breast cancer. Treatment of these latter cancers and cases of DCIS is not needed and leads to "overtreatment." Overtreatment exposes women unnecessarily to the adverse effects associated with cancer therapy.

Because doctors often cannot distinguish cancers and cases of DCIS that need to be treated from those that do not, they are all treated.

False-negative results. False-negative results occur when mammograms appear normal even though breast cancer is present. Overall, screening mammograms miss about 20 percent of breast cancers that are present at the time of screening.

The main cause of false-negative results is high breast density. Breasts contain both dense tissue (i.e., glandular tissue and connective tissue, together known as fibroglandular tissue) and fatty tissue. Fatty tissue appears dark on a mammogram, whereas fibroglandular tissue appears as white areas. Because fibroglandular tissue and tumors have similar density, tumors can be harder to detect in women with denser breasts.

False-negative results occur more often among younger women than among older women because younger women are more likely to have dense breasts. As a woman ages, her breasts usually become more fatty, and false-negative results become less likely. False-negative results can lead to delays in treatment and a false sense of security for affected women.

Some of the cancers missed by screening mammograms can be detected by clinical breast exams (physical exams of the breast done by a health care provider).

Finding cancer early does not always reduce a woman's chance of dying from breast cancer. Even though mammograms can detect malignant tumors that cannot be felt, treating a small tumor does not always mean that the woman will not die from the cancer. A fast-growing or aggressive cancer may have already spread to other parts of the body before it is detected. Women with such tumors live a longer period of time knowing that they likely have a fatal disease.

In addition, screening mammograms may not help prolong the life of a woman who is suffering from other, more life-threatening health conditions.

Radiation exposure. Mammograms require very small doses of radiation. The risk of harm from this radiation exposure is extremely low, but repeated X-rays have the potential to cause cancer. The benefits of mammography, however, nearly always outweigh the potential harm from the radiation exposure. Nevertheless, women should talk with their healthcare providers about the need for each X-ray. In addition, they should always let their health care provider and the X-ray technician know if there is any possibility that they are pregnant, because radiation can harm a growing fetus.

Where Can I Find Current Recommendations for Screening Mammography?

Many organizations and professional societies, including the United States Preventive Services Task Force (which is convened by the Agency for Healthcare Research and Quality, a federal agency), have developed guidelines for mammography screening. All recommend that women should talk with their doctor about the benefits and harms of mammography, when to start screening, and how often to be screened.

Although NCI does not issue guidelines for cancer screening, it conducts and facilitates basic and translational research that informs standard clinical practice and medical decision making that other organizations may use to develop their guidelines.

What Is the Best Method of Detecting Breast Cancer as Early as Possible?

Getting a high-quality screening mammogram and having a clinical breast exam on a regular basis are the most effective ways to detect breast cancer early.

Checking one's own breasts for lumps or other unusual changes is called a breast self-exam, or BSE. This type of exam cannot replace regular screening mammograms or clinical breast exams. In clinical trials, BSE alone was not found to help reduce the number of deaths from breast cancer.

Although regular BSE is not specifically recommended for breast cancer screening, many women choose to examine their own breasts. Women who do so should remember that breast changes can occur because of pregnancy, aging, or menopause; during menstrual cycles; or when taking birth control pills or other hormones. It is normal for breasts to feel a little lumpy and uneven. Also, it is common for breasts to be swollen and tender right before or during a menstrual period. If a woman notices any unusual changes in her breasts, she should contact her healthcare provider.

What Is the Breast Imaging Reporting and Database System (BI-RADS®)?

The American College of Radiology (ACR) has established a uniform way for radiologists to describe mammogram findings. The system, called BI-RADS, includes seven standardized categories, or levels. Each BI-RADS category has a follow-up plan associated with it to help radiologists and other physicians appropriately manage a patient's care.

Breast Imaging Reporting and Database System (BI-RADS)

Table 31.1. Assessment and Follow-Up Based on BI-RADS

Category	Assessment	Follow-up
0	Need additional imaging evaluation	Additional imaging needed before a category can be assigned
1	Negative	Continue regular screening mammograms (for women over age 40)
2	Benign (noncancerous) finding	Continue regular screening mammograms (for women over age 40)
3	Probably benign	Receive a 6-month follow-up mammogram
4	Suspicious abnormality	May require biopsy
5	Highly suggestive of malignancy (cancer)	Requires biopsy
6	Known biopsy-proven malignancy (cancer)	Biopsy confirms presence of cancer before treatment begins

How Much Does a Mammogram Cost?

For most women with private insurance, the cost of screening mammograms is covered without copayments or deductibles, but women should contact their mammography facility or health insurance company for confirmation of the cost and coverage.

Medicare pays for annual screening mammograms for all female Medicare beneficiaries who are age 40 or older. Medicare will also pay for one baseline mammogram for female beneficiaries between the ages of 35 and 39. There is no deductible requirement for this benefit. Information about coverage is available on the Medicare website or through the Medicare Hotline at 1–800–MEDICARE (1–800–633–4227). For the hearing impaired, the telephone number is 1–877–486–2048.

How Can Uninsured or Low-Income Women Obtain a Free or Low-Cost Screening Mammography?

Some state and local health programs and employers provide mammograms free or at low cost. For example, the Centers for Disease Control and Prevention (CDC) coordinates the National Breast and Cervical Cancer Early Detection Program. This program provides screening services, including clinical breast exams and mammograms, to low-income, uninsured women throughout the United States and in several U.S. territories. Contact information for local programs is available on the CDC website or by calling 1–800–CDC–INFO (1–800–232–4636).

Information about free or low-cost mammography screening programs is also available from NCI's Cancer Information Service at 1–800–4–CANCER (1–800–422–6237) and from local hospitals, health departments, women's centers, or other community groups.

Where Can Women Get High-Quality Mammograms?

Women can get high-quality mammograms in breast clinics, hospital radiology departments, mobile vans, private radiology offices, and doctor's' offices.

The Mammography Quality Standards Act (MQSA) is a Federal law that requires mammography facilities across the nation to meet uniform quality standards. Under the law, all mammography facilities must: 1) be accredited by an FDA-approved accreditation body; 2) be certified by the FDA, or an agency of a state that has been approved by the FDA, as meeting the standards; 3) undergo an annual MQSA inspection; and 4) prominently display the certificate issued by the agency.

Women can ask their doctors or staff at a local mammography facility about FDA certification before making an appointment. Women should look for the MQSA certificate at the mammography facility and check its expiration date. MQSA regulations also require that mammography facilities give patients an easy-to-read report of their mammogram results.

Information about local FDA-certified mammography facilities is available through NCI's Cancer Information Service at 1–800–4–CAN-CER (1–800–422–6237).

What Should Women with Breast Implants Do about Screening Mammograms?

Women with breast implants should continue to have mammograms. (A woman who had an implant following a mastectomy should ask her doctor whether a mammogram of the reconstructed breast is necessary.) It is important to let the mammography facility know about breast implants when scheduling a mammogram. The technician and radiologist must be experienced in performing mammography on women who have breast implants. Implants can hide some breast tissue, making it more difficult for the radiologist to detect an abnormality on the mammogram. If the technician performing the procedure is aware that a woman has breast implants, steps can be taken to make sure that as much breast tissue as possible can be seen on the mammogram. A special technique called implant displacement views may be used.

Mammograms: Questions for the Doctor

- If you are age 40 through 49, talk with your doctor about when to start getting mammograms and how often to get them.

- If you are age 50 to 74, get mammograms every 2 years. You may also choose to get them more often.

Together, you and your doctor can decide what's best for you.

Mammograms for women over age 40 are covered under the Affordable Care Act. Depending on your insurance plan, you may be able to get mammograms at no cost to you. Talk to your insurance provider.

Like all medical tests, mammograms have pros and cons. These pros and cons depend on your age and your risk for breast cancer. Use the questions below to start a conversation with your doctor about mammograms.

What Do I Ask the Doctor?

It helps to have questions for the doctor written down ahead of time. Print this list of questions, and take it to your next appointment. You may want to ask a family member or close friend to go with you to take notes.

- Do I have risk factors for breast cancer?
  - I am under age 50:
    - Based on my risk factors, what are my chances of getting breast cancer?
    - Should I start getting regular mammograms? If so, how often?
    - What are the pros and cons of getting mammograms before age 50?
  - I am between ages 50 and 74:
    - Based on my risk factors, what are my chances of getting breast cancer?
    - How often should I get mammograms?
    - What are the pros and cons of getting mammograms every 2 years instead of every year?

- What will happen when I go to get mammograms?

- How long will it take to get the results of my mammograms?

- If I don't hear back about the results of my mammograms, does that mean everything is okay?

Section 31.2

Types of Mammography

This section contains text excerpted from the following sources:
Text under the heading "What Is Digital Mammography?" is
excerpted from "Frequently Asked Questions about Digital
Mammography," U.S. Food and Drug Administration (FDA),
June 2, 2015; Text beginning with the heading "How Is Digital
Mammography Different from Conventional (Film) Mammography?"
is excerpted from "Mammograms," National Cancer Institute (NCI),
March 25, 2014; Text beginning with the heading "What Is 3D
Mammography?" is excerpted from "Mammograms," National
Cancer Institute (NCI), March 25, 2014.

What Is Digital Mammography?

Full field digital mammography (FFDM, also known simply as "digital mammography") is a mammography system where the X-ray film used in screen-film mammography is replaced by solid-state detectors, similar to those found in digital cameras, which convert X-rays into electrical signals. The electrical signals are used to produce images of the breast that can be seen on a computer screen, or printed on special films to look like screen-film mammograms. Types of digital mammography include direct radiography (the most common type, which captures the image directly onto a flat-panel detector), computed radiography (which involves the use of a cassette that contains an imaging plate), or digital breast tomosynthesis (DBT).

Digital and conventional mammography both use X-rays to produce an image of the breast; however, in conventional mammography, the image is stored directly on film, whereas, in digital mammography, an electronic image of the breast is stored as a computer file. This digital information can be enhanced, magnified, or manipulated for further evaluation more easily than information stored on film.

Because digital mammography allows a radiologist to adjust, store, and retrieve digital images electronically, digital mammography may offer the following advantages over conventional mammography:

- Health care providers can share image files electronically, making long-distance consultations between radiologists and breast surgeons easier.

- Subtle differences between normal and abnormal tissues may be more easily noted.

- Fewer follow-up procedures may be needed.

- Fewer repeat images may be needed, reducing the exposure to radiation.

To date, there is no evidence that digital mammography helps to reduce a woman's risk of dying from breast cancer compared with film mammography. Results from a large NCI-sponsored clinical trial that compared digital mammography with film mammography found no difference between digital and film mammograms in detecting breast cancer in the general population of women in the trial; however, digital mammography appeared to be more accurate than conventional film mammography in younger women with dense breasts. A subsequent analysis of women aged 40 through 79 who were undergoing screening in U.S. community-based imaging facilities also found that digital and film mammography had similar accuracy in most women. Digital screening had higher sensitivity in women with dense breasts.

Some healthcare providers recommend that women who have a very high risk of breast cancer, such as those with a known mutation in either the BRCA1 or BRCA2 gene or extremely dense breasts, have digital mammograms instead of conventional mammograms; however, no studies have shown that digital mammograms are superior to conventional mammograms in reducing the risk of death for these women.

Digital mammography can be done only in facilities that are certified to practice conventional mammography and have received FDA approval to offer digital mammography. The procedure for having a mammogram with a digital system is the same as with conventional mammography.

How Is Digital Mammography Different from Conventional (Film) Mammography?

Digital and conventional mammography both use X-rays to produce an image of the breast; however, in conventional mammography, the image is stored directly on film, whereas, in digital mammography, an electronic image of the breast is stored as a computer file. This digital information can be enhanced, magnified, or manipulated for further evaluation more easily than information stored on film.

Because digital mammography allows a radiologist to adjust, store, and retrieve digital images electronically, digital mammography may offer the following advantages over conventional mammography:

- Health care providers can share image files electronically, making long-distance consultations between radiologists and breast surgeons easier.

- Subtle differences between normal and abnormal tissues may be more easily noted.

- Fewer follow-up procedures may be needed.

- Fewer repeat images may be needed, reducing the exposure to radiation.

To date, there is no evidence that digital mammography helps to reduce a woman's risk of dying from breast cancer compared with film mammography. Results from a large NCI-sponsored clinical trial that compared digital mammography with film mammography found no difference between digital and film mammograms in detecting breast cancer in the general population of women in the trial; however, digital mammography appeared to be more accurate than conventional film mammography in younger women with dense breasts. A subsequent analysis of women aged 40 through 79 who were undergoing screening in U.S. community-based imaging facilities also found that digital and film mammography had similar accuracy in most women. Digital screening had higher sensitivity in women with dense breasts.

Some healthcare providers recommend that women who have a very high risk of breast cancer, such as those with a known mutation in either the BRCA1 or BRCA2 gene or extremely dense breasts, have digital mammograms instead of conventional mammograms; however, no studies have shown that digital mammograms are superior to conventional mammograms in reducing the risk of death for these women.

Digital mammography can be done only in facilities that are certified to practice conventional mammography and have received FDA approval to offer digital mammography. The procedure for having a mammogram with a digital system is the same as with conventional mammography.

What Is DBT?

Digital breast tomosynthesis is a relatively new technology. In DBT, the X-ray tube moves in an arc around the breast and takes multiple images from different angles. Similar to computed tomography (CT scan), these images are then reconstructed into parallel "slices" through the breast. This allows interpreting physicians to see through layers of overlapping tissue.

What Is 3D Mammography?

Three-dimensional (3D) mammography, also known as breast tomosynthesis, is a type of digital mammography in which X-ray machines are used to take pictures of thin slices of the breast from different angles and computer software is used to reconstruct an image. This process is similar to how a computed tomography (CT) scanner produces images of structures inside of the body. 3D mammography uses very low dose X-rays, but, because it is generally performed at the same time as standard two-dimensional (2D) digital mammography, the radiation dose is slightly higher than that of standard mammography. The accuracy of 3D mammography has not been compared with that of 2D mammography in randomized studies. Therefore, researchers do not know whether 3D mammography is better or worse than standard mammography at avoiding false-positive results and identifying early cancers.

What Other Technologies Are Being Developed for Breast Cancer Screening?

NCI is supporting the development of several new technologies to detect breast tumors. This research ranges from methods being developed in research labs to those that are being studied in clinical trials. Efforts to improve conventional mammography include digital mammography, magnetic resonance imaging (MRI), positron emission tomography (PET) scanning, and diffuse optical tomography, which uses light instead of X-rays to create pictures of the breast.

Section 31.3

Mammograms and Health Insurance

This section includes text excerpted from
"Bottom Line: Mammograms Are Still Covered," Office on
Women's Health (OWH), U.S. Department of Health and
Human Services (HHS), January 12, 2016.

Mammograms Are Still Covered under Insurance

Recently, several organizations have updated breast cancer screening recommendations, including the U.S. Preventive Services Task Force (USPSTF). The various screening recommendations may cause confusion among women about whether or not a mammogram is covered by their health insurance.

The various screening recommendations may cause confusion among women about whether or not a mammogram is covered by their health insurance. It should be made clear that coverage requirements for mammograms have not changed.

The Affordable Care Act improved access to health care, including preventive services, for millions of Americans. Today, most health insurance plans are required to cover many preventive services at no out-of-pocket cost to the consumer, including breast cancer screening. Coverage of preventive services improves access to affordable, quality health care, prevents serious health conditions before they start, and empowers women to obtain better care for their health. Specifically, coverage of preventive services without copays increases the likelihood that low-income and minority women receive these important health care services, such as mammography.

Now, without worry about whether they can afford it, American women can make informed decisions about mammography based on science. The updated USPSTF recommendations emphasize the benefits of mammography screening for all women between the ages of 50–74 years; screening can also be beneficial for women in their 40s, but there may be downsides that they should consider. The USPSTF encourages women ages 40–49 to discuss with their doctors the risks and benefits of mammography screening and then make informed decisions that take into account their own values and situations. As with all USPSTF recommendations, the breast cancer screening recommendations will be reevaluated as more science becomes available to better determine the risks and benefits of screening.

This USPSTF recommendation won't impact coverage requirements. Here's why:

In December 2015, the President signed a bill that ensures that women's coverage for mammography will remain the same through 2017. Women 40 years and older enrolled in most health insurance plans will continue to be covered for screening mammography every 1–2 years without copays, coinsurance, or deductibles—just as they are today. If a woman 40 years and older and her doctor determine that a mammogram is appropriate, she will not have to pay out of pocket.

Chapter 32

Other Breast Cancer Screening Procedures

Chapter Contents

Section 32.1

Breast Magnetic Resonance Imaging (MRI)

"Breast Magnetic Resonance Imaging (MRI),"
© 2016 Omnigraphics, Inc. Reviewed April 2016.

What Is a Breast Magnetic Resonance Imaging (MRI)

Magnetic resonance imaging (MRI) is a noninvasive diagnostic test that generates a series of detailed images of internal organs and body structures using a magnetic field and radio waves. These images are combined by a computer and examined by a radiologist to aid in detection of cancer and other abnormalities. MRI of the breast is often performed following a diagnosis of breast cancer to gather additional information about the extent of the disease. Breast MRI is also used as a screening tool along with mammograms in women at high risk for developing breast cancer.

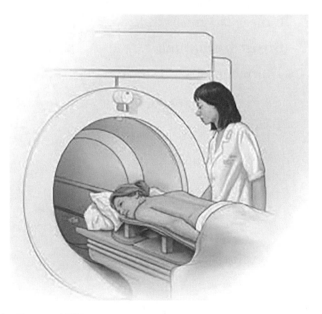

Figure 32.1. *Breast MRI*

The Breast MRI Procedure

While undergoing a breast MRI, the patient typically lies face down on a table with her breasts positioned through special openings. In most cases, a contrast dye is injected into a vein in her arm either before or during the procedure. The dye helps create clearer images to make any abnormalities easier to detect. The table then slides into a large, cylindrical machine that looks like a tunnel.

With a technician operating the MRI machine from a separate room, it creates a strong magnetic field around the patient and then sends pulses of radio waves from a scanner. Although this process is completely painless, the magnetic field and radio waves change the alignment of hydrogen atoms in the patient's body. The activity of the hydrogen atoms is analyzed by a computer, which converts the information into a detailed image of the breast. This image appears on a viewing monitor.

Advantages of Breast MRI

Breast MRI offers a number of advantages in screening and diagnosis of breast cancer and other breast abnormalities. Since MRIs do not use radiation, they are less dangerous for younger women or for women at high risk for breast cancer who must undergo multiple screenings per year. In addition, research has shown that breast MRI is capable of finding some small breast legions that might be missed by mammography or other screening methods. Because it is highly sensitive, breast MRI can also help detect breast cancer in women with dense breast tissue or breast implants.

Breast MRI is often used as a screening tool to find early breast cancers in women at high risk, including those with a strong family history of the disease, a BRCA gene mutation, precancerous breast changes such as lobular carcinoma in situ (LCIS), or a history of receiving radiation to the chest area. Breast MRI also may be used to further evaluate abnormalities or assess the extent of breast cancer detected through other means. Some of the common uses of breast MRI include:

- Detecting small lesions or abnormalities not visible using mammography or ultrasound

- Evaluating the size and location of breast cancer that may have spread to more than one area of the breast

- Determining whether breast cancer may have spread into the chest wall

243

- Evaluating the opposite breast for changes in women who have been recently diagnosed with cancer in one breast

- Determining the best surgical treatment options for removing breast cancer

- Checking for recurrence of breast cancer in women with lumpectomy scars that may produce inaccurate mammogram results

- Assessing whether a silicone gel breast implant may have leaked or ruptured

Risks of Breast MRI

Although it offers many advantages, breast MRI also has some limitations. Since it can miss some breast cancers that will usually be detected by mammography, it should not be considered a substitute or replacement for mammograms. In addition, a breast MRI may produce false-positive results by identifying areas as suspicious that turn out to be benign. This may lead to unwarranted anxiety and unnecessary testing for the patient.

While breast MRI is generally considered safe and painless, it does involve a few potential risks, such as:

- Allergic reaction to the contrast dye, which can also cause complications for patients with kidney problems

- Danger related to exposure to a strong magnet for patients with implanted medical devices, such as pacemakers or cochlear implants, or internal metal objects, such as plates, screws, clips, or wire mesh

- Anxiety attacks for patients with severe claustrophobia

- Potential harm to a fetus during the first trimester, which may make MRI testing inadvisable for women who are pregnant

References

1. "Breast Magnetic Resonance Imaging (MRI)." Johns Hopkins Medical, n.d.

2. "Breast MRI for the Early Detection of Breast Cancer." Cancer.net, March 2014.

3. "Tests and Procedures: Breast MRI." Mayo Clinic, August 22, 2013.

Section 32.2

3D Technologies Changing Breast Cancer Diagnosis

This section includes text excerpted from "3D Technologies Poised to Change How Doctors Diagnose Cancers," U.S. Food and Drug Administration (FDA), September 30, 2014.

3D Technologies to Diagnose Cancers

Scientists at the U.S. Food and Drug Administration (FDA) are studying the next generation of screening and diagnostic devices, some of which borrow from the world of entertainment. Soon, three-dimensional (3D) images in actual 3D might help your doctor find hidden tumors and better diagnose cancers, thanks to the regulatory work being done by a team at FDA's Division of Imaging, Diagnostics, and Software Reliability.

The team is led by Division Director Kyle Myers, a physicist with a Ph.D. in optical sciences. It includes Aldo Badano, Ph.D., a world-renowned expert in display evaluation technology, and Brian Garra, M.D., a diagnostic radiologist doing research in regulatory science at FDA.

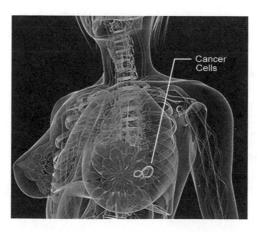

Figure 32.2. *Breast Cancer Diagnoised Using 3D Technology*

245

They are studying how clinicians receive visual information and analyze it to diagnose a disease. At the center of their research are breast cancer screening devices, which are making the leap from traditional two-dimensional (2D) screening such as mammography to 3D breast tomosynthesis, 3D ultrasound and breast computerized tomography (CT). This technology is very exploratory and years away from becoming standard in your doctor's office.

New Era in Breast Cancer Detection

There are many new technologies being developed for breast cancer screening, especially 3D alternatives that may eventually replace today's 2D mammography. FDA has already approved two of these state-of-the-art devices: The Selenia Dimensions 3D System, which provides 3D breast tomosynthesis images of the breast for breast cancer diagnosis; and the GE Healthcare's SenoClaire, which uses a combination of 2D mammogram images and 3D breast tomosynthesis images.

The technologies under development include 3D breast tomosynthesis, which artificially creates 3D images of the breast from a limited set of 2D images. Tomosynthesis reveals sections of the breast that can be hidden by overlapping tissue in a standard mammogram.

"The problem of overlapping shadows has confounded breast cancer screening because mammograms don't show cancers that are hidden by overlapping tissue," Myers says. And compounding the problem is overlapping tissue that can look like cancer but isn't. "The new technologies we're studying overcome these barriers," she adds.

Another benefit of 3D breast tomosynthesis: It's more accurate than mammography in pinpointing the size and location of cancer tumors in dense breast tissue, Myers says. With 3D breast tomosynthesis, doctors can detect abnormalities earlier and better see small tumors because the images are clearer and have greater contrast.

"Clinical studies have shown that 3D breast tomosynthesis can increase the cancer detection rate, reduce the number of women sent for biopsy who don't have cancer, or achieve some balance of these two goals of this new screening technology," she adds.

There's also a lot of research and development in 3D ultrasound, which automatically scans the breast and generates 3D data that can be sliced and examined from any direction. Garra, who is a leader in this field, says 3D ultrasound improves breast cancer detection in women with dense breast tissue.

"Both 3D breast tomosynthesis and 3D ultrasound detect breast cancer. But for radiologists and other doctors, there are many more images to examine, and that can reduce the speed at which studies can be interpreted," he says.

Another promising technology—the dedicated breast CT system—creates a full 3D representation of the breast. The scan is taken while the patient lies face down on a bed with her breast suspended through a cup and the X-ray machine rotates around it. For patients, the procedure is more comfortable than regular mammography because the breast isn't compressed. Also, there's less radiation exposure than during a CT exam of the entire chest because only the breast is exposed to X-rays.

Health care practitioners using this technology have to learn how to read and interpret hundreds of high-resolution images produced by the scanner. But what makes the task easier is that the images have less distortion than mammography, and the system is optimized to differentiate between the breast's soft tissue and cancer tissue.

"These images will be very different from 2D mammograms. They're truly 3D images of the breast from any orientation. You can scroll through the slices—up and down, left and right—and get a unique view of the breast like never before," Myers says. "It gives doctors tremendous freedom in how they look at the interior of the breast and evaluate its structures. It's almost like seeing the anatomy itself."

New Era in How We See

How can radiologists look at these images and convert them into three dimensions? That's where Badano's work comes in. His research lab is exploring various display device technologies to improve how radiologists review 3D images. The studied technologies include devices supported by mobile technologies and special-purpose 3D displays developed specifically for 3D imaging systems.

"These are no longer conventional images, so you need to examine them in the 3D space," he says. "Using a 2D display might no longer be ideal." Device manufacturers are building on technologies developed primarily for other markets, including the gaming industry, to show 3D images in actual 3D. But the work is painstaking and far from ready for a medical use.

"As people have experienced in movie theaters and when playing video games, 3D displays have problems, including the image resolution and added noise. When wearing 3D glasses, our brain needs to separate the images from the left eye and the right eye and reconstruct a 3D object," Badano says. "In the lab, we're doing experiments to see how different technologies handle these tradeoffs."

One of the challenges is that 3D displays for medical imaging require better resolution. For a medical use, the specifications are high—"and so are the stakes," he adds.

Section 32.3

Breast Ultrasound

This section includes text excerpted from "Ultrasound," National Institute of Biomedical Imaging and Bioengineering (NIBIB), July 27, 2013.

What Is Medical Ultrasound?

Diagnostic ultrasound (also known as sonography or ultrasonography) is a non-invasive diagnostic technique used to image inside the body. Diagnostic ultrasound probes, called transducers, produce sound waves that have frequencies above the threshold of human hearing (above 20 KHz), but most transducers in current use operate at much higher frequencies (in the megahertz (MHz) range).

Diagnostic ultrasound can be further sub-divided into anatomical and functional ultrasound. Anatomical Ultrasound produces images of the internal organs or other structures. Functional ultrasound combines information such as the movement and velocity of tissue or blood, softness or hardness of tissue, and other physical characteristics with anatomical images to create "information maps". These maps help doctors visualize changes/differences in function within a structure or organ.

Therapeutic ultrasound also uses sound waves above the range of human hearing but does not produce images. Its purpose is to interact with tissues in the body such that they are either modified or destroyed. Among the modifications possible are: moving or pushing tissue, heating tissue, dissolving blood clots, or delivering drugs to specific locations in the body. These destructive, or ablative, functions are made possible by use of very high-intensity beams that can destroy diseased or abnormal tissues such as tumors. The advantage of using ultrasound therapies is that, in most cases, they are non-invasive. No incisions or cuts need to be made to the skin, leaving no wounds or scars.

How Does It Work?

Ultrasound waves are produced by a **transducer** (a hand-held probe), which can both emit ultrasound waves, as well as detect the ultrasound echoes reflected back. In most cases, the active elements in ultrasound transducers are made of special ceramic crystal materials called piezoelectrics. These materials are able to produce sound waves when an electric current passes through them, but can also work in reverse, producing electricity when a sound wave hits them. When used in an ultrasound scanner, the transducer sends out a directed beam of sound waves into the body, and the sound waves are reflected back to the transducer from the tissues and organs in the path of the beam. When these echoes hit the transducer, they generate electrical signals that the ultrasound scanner converts into images of the tissues and organs.

Many other types of materials are currently being investigated for use as transducers. New materials are being developed that will make it easier to build single transducers or arrays of transducers.

What Is Ultrasound Used For?

Diagnostic ultrasound. Diagnostic ultrasound is able to noninvasively image internal organs within the body. However, it is not good for imaging bones or any tissues that contain air, like the lungs. Under some conditions, ultrasound can image bones (such as in a fetus or in small babies) or the lungs, when they are filled or partially filled with fluid. One of the most common uses of ultrasound is during pregnancy, to monitor the growth and development of the fetus, but there are many other uses, including imaging the heart, blood vessels, eyes, thyroid, brain, breast, abdominal organs, skin, and muscles. Ultrasound Images are displayed in either 2D, 3D, or 4D (which is 3D in motion).

Functional ultrasound applications include Doppler and color Doppler ultrasound for measuring and visualizing blood flow in vessels within the body or in the heart as well as the speed of the blood flow and direction of movement. This is done using color-coded maps called color Doppler imaging or by producing a graphical display of the actual velocity measurements of blood at specific locations in a blood vessel.

Another functional form of ultrasound is elastography, a method for measuring and displaying the relative stiffness of tissues which can be used to differentiate tumors from healthy tissue. This information can be displayed as either color-coded maps of the relative stiffness; black-and white maps that display high-contrast images of tumors compared with anatomical images; or color-coded maps that are over-layed on the anatomical image.

Ultrasound is also an important method for imaging interventions in the body. For example, ultrasound-guided needle biopsy helps physicians see the position of a needle while it is being guided to a selected target, such as a mass or a tumor in the breast. Also, ultrasound is used for real-time imaging of the location of the tip of a catheter as it is inserted in a blood vessel and guided along the length of the vessel. It can also be used for minimally invasive surgery to guide the surgeon with real-time images of the inside of the body.

Therapeutic or interventional ultrasound. Therapeutic ultrasound produces high or very high levels of acoustic output that can be focused on specific targets for the purpose of heating, ablating, or breaking up tissue. Most uses of therapeutic ultrasound are still in the research stage, although at least one application—the ablation of uterine fibroids—has been approved by the FDA and is currently in clinical use. One type of therapeutic ultrasound uses high-intensity beams of sound that are highly focused, and is called High Intensity Focused Ultrasound (HIFU).

HIFU is being investigated as a non-invasive method for modifying or destroying diseased or abnormal tissues inside the body (e.g. tumors) and could become a substitute for invasive surgery. It can be used to destroy a diseased or abnormal growth or lesion inside the body without having to open or tear the skin or cause damage to the surrounding tissue. This technique is also being investigated as a way to close wounds and stop bleeding as well as break up clots in blood vessels.

Are There Risks?

Diagnostic ultrasound is generally safe and does not produce ionizing radiation like that produced by X-rays. Still, ultrasound is capable of producing some biological effects in the body under specific settings and conditions. For this reason, the FDA requires that diagnostic ultrasound devices operate within acceptable limits. The FDA, as well as many professional societies, discourage the casual use of ultrasound (e.g. for keepsake videos) and recommend that it be used only when there is a true medical need.

Section 32.4

Thermography versus Mammography

This section includes text excerpted from "Thermogram No Substitute for Mammogram," U.S. Food and Drug Administration (FDA), June 2, 2011. Reviewed April 2016.

Thermogram No Substitute for Mammogram

Despite widely publicized claims to the contrary, thermography should not be used in place of mammography for breast cancer screening or diagnosis.

The U.S. Food and Drug Administration (FDA) says mammography—an X-ray of the breast—is still the most effective way of detecting breast cancer in its earliest, most treatable stages. Thermography produces an infrared image that shows the patterns of heat and blood flow on or near the surface of the body.

The agency has sent several warning letters to health care providers and a thermography manufacturer who claim that the thermal imaging can take the place of mammography.

Web sites have been touting thermography as a replacement for mammography and claim that thermography can find breast cancer years before it would be detected by mammography.

The problem is that FDA has no evidence to support these claims.

"Mammography is still the most effective screening method for detecting breast cancer in its early, most treatable stages" said Helen Barr, M.D., director of the Division of Mammography Quality and Radiation Programs in the FDA's Center for Devices and Radiological Health. "Women should not rely solely on thermography for the screening or diagnosis of breast cancer."

"While there is plenty of evidence that mammography is effective in breast cancer detection, there is simply no evidence that thermography can take its place," said Barr.

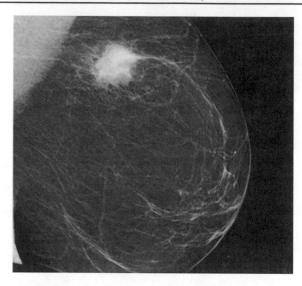

Figure 32.3. *Mammogram Showing Cancer Cells*

Thermography devices have been cleared by the FDA for use as an adjunct, or additional, tool for detecting breast cancer. Toni Stifano, a consumer safety officer in FDA's Center for Devices and Radiological Health, explains that this means thermography should not be used by itself to screen for or to diagnose breast cancer.

The National Cancer Institute (NCI), part of the National Institutes of Health (NIH), estimates that about 1 in 8 women will be diagnosed with breast cancer sometime in her life.

The greatest danger, says Stifano, a breast cancer survivor herself, is that patients who substitute thermography for mammography may miss the chance to detect cancer at its earliest stage. There has been a steady decline in breast cancer deaths and one of the reasons is early detection through mammography, says FDA.

As for concerns about exposure to radiation from a mammogram, evidence shows that the benefits outweigh the risks of harm, especially when compared to the danger of breast cancer.

FDA is advising patients to continue to have regular mammograms according to screening guidelines or as recommended by their health care professional.

Patients are also advised to follow their health care professional's recommendations for additional diagnostic procedures, such as other mammographic views, clinical breast exam, breast ultrasound, MRI or biopsy. Additional procedures could include thermography.

FDA's position on thermography is shared by prominent organizations active in the fight against breast cancer, including the Susan G. Komen for the Cure, a nonprofit that has raised billions of dollars for education and research, and the American Cancer Society.

Chapter 33

Breast Biopsy

Screening for Breast Cancer

Screening for breast cancer increases the chance of surviving breast cancer. Screening tests can find cancers before they cause symptoms and when they are most treatable. Two common tests are used to screen for breast cancer.

Mammogram

A mammogram is a breast X-ray. It looks for suspicious changes in breast tissue. It can detect cancers even when they are too small to be felt. A mammogram is the best screening test for breast cancer.

Breast Exam by Your Doctor or Nurse

This is usually part of a woman's yearly exam. But if you find a breast lump or another change that worries you, don't wait. Make an appointment with your doctor or nurse to have it checked.

Follow-Up Tests

When a suspicious area on a mammogram or a lump is found, your doctor will probably send you for more tests. Your doctor might send

This chapter includes text excerpted from "Having a Breast Biopsy: A Guide for Women and Their Families," Agency for Healthcare Research and Quality (AHRQ), U.S. Department of Health and Human Services (HHS), April 2010. Reviewed April 2016.

you for another mammogram or a breast ultrasound. These tests tell your doctor if you need a biopsy. Most women who have further tests do not need a biopsy.

Biopsy

If the test results are still suspicious, your doctor will recommend a biopsy.

What Is a Breast Biopsy?

A biopsy is the only test that can tell for sure if a suspicious area is cancer. During a breast biopsy, the doctor removes a small amount of tissue from the breast.

There are two main kinds of breast biopsies. One is called surgical biopsy. The other is called core-needle biopsy.

The kind of breast biopsy a doctor recommends may depend on what the suspicious area looks like. It also might depend on the size and where it is located in the breast.

After the biopsy, the tissue is sent to a doctor who will look at the tissue under a microscope. This doctor, called a pathologist, looks for tissue changes. The pathology report tells if there is cancer or not. It takes about a week to get the report.

Types of Breast Biopsy

Surgical Biopsy

A surgical biopsy is usually done using local anesthesia. Local anesthesia means that the breast will be numbed. You will have an IV and may have medicine to make you drowsy.

The surgeon makes a 1- to 2-inch cut on the breast and removes part or all of the suspicious tissue. Some of the tissue around it also may be taken out.

A radiologist is a doctor who specializes in medical imaging (like X-rays and mammograms). If the suspicious area can be seen on mammogram or ultrasound but can't be felt, a radiologist usually inserts a thin wire to mark the spot for the surgeon before the biopsy.

Core-Needle Biopsy

A core-needle biopsy is done using local anesthesia. The doctor inserts a hollow needle into the breast and removes a small amount of suspicious tissue. The doctor may place a tiny marker inside the breast. It marks the spot where the biopsy was done.

Ultrasound-guided core-needle biopsy uses ultrasound to guide the needle to the suspicious area. Ultrasound uses sound waves to create a picture of the inside of the breast. It is like what is used to look at the baby when a woman is pregnant. You will lie on your back or side for this procedure. The doctor will hold the ultrasound device against your breast to guide the needle.

Stereotactic-guided core-needle biopsy uses X-ray equipment and a computer to guide the needle. Usually for this kind of biopsy, you lie on your stomach on a special table. The table will have an opening for your breast. Your breast will be compressed like it is for a mammogram.

Freehand core-needle biopsy does not use ultrasound or X-ray equipment. It is used less often and only for lumps that can be felt through the skin.

It is not unusual to feel anxious about having a biopsy. Ask your doctor or nurse what to expect. It may help to talk to your family and friends. You also might want someone to come to your appointment with you.

Research about Breast Biopsy

Accuracy

Surgical biopsies and core-needle biopsies both work well for finding breast cancer. But biopsies are not 100-percent accurate. In a few cases, a biopsy can miss breast cancer.

Surgical biopsies and ultrasound or stereotactic-guided core-needle biopsies have about the same accuracy. Freehand core-needle biopsies are less accurate.

Out of every 100 women who have breast cancer:

- Surgical biopsies will find 98 to 99 of those breast cancers.
- Ultrasound or stereotactic-guided biopsies will find 97 to 99 of those breast cancers.
- Freehand biopsies will find about 86 of those breast cancers.

Side Effects

Bleeding, bruising, and infection can happen after a biopsy. Core-needle biopsies have a much lower risk of these problems than surgical biopsies.

Side effects are rare with any kind of core-needle biopsy.

- Less than 1 out of 100 women who have a core-needle biopsy have a problem like severe bruising, bleeding, or infection.

Side effects happen more often with surgical biopsy.

- Up to 10 out of 100 women who have surgical biopsy get severe bruising.

- About 5 out of 100 women who have surgical biopsy get an infection.

Some medicines, including aspirin, increase the risk of bleeding and bruising. Your doctor will ask you about the medicines you take. You may need to stop some medicines a few days before the biopsy.

Pain

Women who have a surgical biopsy sometimes need prescription pain medicine to control pain after the procedure. Women who have a core-needle biopsy rarely need prescription pain medicine.

Biopsy Results

After the biopsy, the pathologist who looked at the tissue will send the pathology report to your doctor. It will tell if the suspicious area is cancer or not. Your doctor will go over the report with you. Waiting for these results can be difficult. It can take about a week to get the results.

If No Cancer Is Found

If no cancer is found, the biopsy result is called benign. Benign means it is not cancer. Some benign results need follow-up or treatment. Talk to your doctor or nurse about what they recommend.

If Cancer Is Found

If cancer is found, the report will tell you the kind of cancer. It will help you and your doctor talk about the next steps. Usually, you will be referred to a breast cancer specialist. You may need more imaging tests or surgery. All this information will help you and your doctor think through your treatment options.

Take time to think. Most women with breast cancer have time to consider their options.

Make sure to ask your doctor if you don't understand your test results. After going over the results with your doctor, ask for a copy of the pathology report for your records.

Questions for Your Doctor or Nurse

Deciding on a Biopsy

- What kind of biopsy are you recommending?
- Why are you recommending this kind of biopsy?
- Are there any other options?
- What are the possible side effects from my biopsy?
- How long will it take?

Preparing for a Biopsy

- How many days before my biopsy should I stop taking aspirin?
- Are there other medicines to avoid?
- Can I have someone in the room with me?
- Do I need someone to drive me home?
- Who will give me the results?
- When will I get the results?

When My Biopsy Is Benign

- What kind of follow-up do I need?
- When should I have my next mammogram?

When My Biopsy Finds Cancer

- What are the next steps?
- What are my options for treatment?
- Can you tell me about support groups for breast cancer?

Chapter 34

Understanding Laboratory Tests and Pathology Reports

Laboratory Tests

What Are Laboratory Tests?

A laboratory test is a procedure in which a sample of blood, urine, other bodily fluid, or tissue is examined to get information about a person's health. Some laboratory tests provide precise and reliable information about specific health problems. Other tests provide more general information that helps doctors identify or rule out possible health problems. Doctors often use other types of tests, such as imaging tests, in addition to laboratory tests to learn more about a person's health.

How Are Laboratory Tests Used in Cancer Medicine?

Laboratory tests are used in cancer medicine in many ways:

- To screen for cancer or precancerous conditions before a person has any symptoms of disease

- To help diagnose cancer

This chapter contains text excerpted from the following sources: Text beginning with the heading "What Are Laboratory Tests?" is excerpted from "Understanding Laboratory Tests," National Cancer Institute (NCI), December 11, 2013; Text beginning with the heading "Pathology Reports" is excerpted from "Pathology Reports," National Cancer Institute (NCI), September 23, 2010. Reviewed April 2016.

- To provide information about the stage of a cancer (that is, its severity); for malignant tumors, this includes the size and/or extent (reach) of the original (primary) tumor and whether or not the tumor has spread (metastasized) to other parts of the body

- To plan treatment

- To monitor a patient's general health during treatment and to check for potential side effects of the treatment

- To determine whether a cancer is responding to treatment

- To find out whether a cancer has recurred (come back)

Which Laboratory Tests Are Used in Cancer Medicine?

Categories of some common laboratory tests used in cancer medicine are listed below in alphabetical order.

- **Blood chemistry test**

  What it measures: The amounts of certain substances that are released into the blood by the organs and tissues of the body, such as metabolites, electrolytes, fats, and proteins, including enzymes. Blood chemistry tests usually include tests for blood urea nitrogen (BUN) and creatinine.

  How it is used: Diagnosis and monitoring of patients during and after treatment. High or low levels of some substances can be signs of disease or side effects of treatment.

- **Cancer gene mutation testing**

  What it measures: The presence or absence of specific inherited mutations in genes that are known to play a role in cancer development. Examples include tests to look for BRCA1 and BRCA2 gene mutations, which play a role in development of breast, ovarian, and other cancers.

  How it is used: Assessment of cancer risk

- **Complete blood count (CBC)**

  What it measures: Numbers of the different types of blood cells, including red blood cells, white blood cells, and platelets, in a sample of blood. This test also measures the amount of hemoglobin (the protein that carries oxygen) in the blood, the percentage of the total blood volume that is taken up by red blood cells (hematocrit), the size of the red blood cells, and the amount of hemoglobin in red blood cells.

How it is used: Diagnosis, particularly in leukemias, and monitoring during and after treatment

- **Cytogenetic analysis**

  What it measures: Changes in the number and/or structure of chromosomes in a patient's white blood cells or bone marrow cells

  How it is used: Diagnosis, deciding on appropriate treatment

- **Immunophenotyping**

  What it measures: Identifies cells based on the types of antigens present on the cell surface

  How it is used: Diagnosis, staging, and monitoring of cancers of the blood system and other hematologic disorders, including leukemias, lymphomas, myelodysplastic syndromes, and myeloproliferative disorders. It is most often done on blood or bone marrow samples, but it may also be done on other bodily fluids or biopsy tissue samples.

- **Sputum cytology (also called sputum culture)**

  What it measures: The presence of abnormal cells in sputum (mucus and other matter brought up from the lungs by coughing)

  How it is used: Diagnosis of lung cancer

- **Tumor marker tests**

  What they measure: Some measure the presence, levels, or activity of specific proteins or genes in tissue, blood, or other bodily fluids that may be signs of cancer or certain benign (noncancerous) conditions. A tumor that has a greater than normal level of a tumor marker may respond to treatment with a drug that targets that marker. For example, cancer cells that have high levels of the HER2/neu gene or protein may respond to treatment with a drug that targets the HER2/neu protein.

Some tumor marker tests analyze DNA to look for specific gene mutations that may be present in cancers but not normal tissues. Examples include EGFR gene mutation analysis to help determine treatment and assess prognosis in non-small cell lung cancer and BRAF gene mutation analysis to predict response to targeted therapies in melanoma and colorectal cancer.

Still other tumor marker tests, called multigene tests (or multiparameter gene expression tests), analyze the expression of a specific group of genes in tumor samples. These tests are used for prognosis and treatment planning. For example, the 21-gene signature can help patients with lymph node–negative, estrogen receptor–positive breast cancer decide if there may be benefit to treating with chemotherapy in addition to hormone therapy, or not.

How they are used: Diagnosis, deciding on appropriate treatment, assessing response to treatment, and monitoring for cancer recurrence

- **Urinalysis**

  What it measures: The color of urine and its contents, such as sugar, protein, red blood cells, and white blood cells.

  How it is used: Detection and diagnosis of kidney cancer and urothelial cancers

- **Urine cytology**

  What it measures: The presence of abnormal cells shed from the urinary tract into urine to detect disease.

  How it is used: Detection and diagnosis of bladder cancer and other urothelial cancers, monitoring patients for cancer recurrence

How Do I Interpret My Test Results?

With some laboratory tests, the results obtained for healthy people can vary somewhat from person to person. Factors that can cause person-to-person variation in laboratory test results include a person's age, sex, race, medical history, and general health. In fact, the results obtained from a single person given the same test on different days can also vary. For these tests, therefore, the results are considered normal if they fall between certain lower and upper limits or values. This range of normal values is known as the "normal range," the "reference range," and the "reference interval." When healthy people take such tests, it is expected that their results will fall within the normal range 95 percent of the time. (Five percent of the time, the results from healthy people will fall outside the normal range and will be marked as "abnormal.") Reference ranges are based on test results from large numbers of people who have been tested in the past.

Some test results can be affected by certain foods and medications. For this reason, people may be asked to not eat or drink for several hours before a laboratory test or to delay taking medications until after the test.

For many tests, it is possible for someone with cancer to have results that fall within the normal range. Likewise, it is possible for someone who doesn't have cancer to have test results that fall outside the normal range. This is one reason that many laboratory tests alone cannot provide a definitive diagnosis of cancer or other diseases.

In general, laboratory test results must be interpreted in the context of the overall health of the patient and are considered along with the results of other examinations, tests, and procedures. A doctor who is familiar with a patient's medical history and current situation is the best person to explain test results and what they mean.

What If a Laboratory Test Result Is Unclear or Inconclusive?

If a test result is unclear or inconclusive, the doctor will likely repeat the test to be certain of the result and may order additional tests. The doctor may also compare the latest test result to previous results, if available, to get a better idea of what is normal for that person.

What Are Some Questions to Ask the Doctor about Laboratory Tests?

It can be helpful to take a list of questions to the doctor's office. Questions about laboratory test might include:

- What will this test measure?
- Why is this test being ordered?
- Does this test have any risks or side effects?
- How should I prepare for the test?
- When will the test results be available?
- How will the results be given (a letter, a phone call, online)?
- Will this test need to be done more than once?

How Reliable Are Laboratory Tests and Their Results?

The results of laboratory tests affect many of the decisions a doctor makes about a person's health care, including whether additional tests are necessary, developing a treatment plan, or monitoring a person's response to treatment. It is very important, therefore, that the laboratory tests themselves are trustworthy and that the laboratory that performs the tests meets rigorous state and federal regulatory standards.

The U.S. Food and Drug Administration (FDA) regulates the development and marketing of all laboratory tests that use test kits and equipment that are commercially manufactured in the United States. After the FDA approves a laboratory test, other federal and state agencies make sure that the test materials and equipment meet strict standards while they are being manufactured and then used in a medical or clinical laboratory.

All laboratory testing that is performed on humans in the United States (except testing done in clinical trials and other types of human research) is regulated through the Clinical Laboratory Improvement Amendments (CLIA), which were passed by Congress in 1988. The CLIA laboratory certification program is administered by the Centers for Medicare and Medicaid Services (CMS) in conjunction with the FDA and the Centers for Disease Control and Prevention. CLIA ensures that laboratory staff are appropriately trained and supervised and that testing laboratories have quality control programs in place so that test results are accurate and reliable.

To enroll in the CLIA program, laboratories must complete a certification process that is based on the level of complexity of tests that the laboratory will perform. The more complicated the test, the more demanding the requirements for certification. Laboratories must demonstrate that they can perform tests as accurately and as precisely as the manufacturer did to gain FDA approval of the test. Laboratories must also evaluate the tests regularly to make sure that they continue to meet the manufacturer's specifications. Laboratories undergo regular unannounced on-site inspections to ensure they are following the requirements outlined in CLIA to receive and maintain certification.

Some states have additional requirements that are equal to or more stringent than those outlined in CLIA. CMS has determined that Washington and New York have state licensure programs that are exempt from CLIA program requirements. Therefore, licensing authorities in Washington and New York have primary responsibility for oversight of their state's laboratory practices.

What New Laboratory Tests for Cancer Medicine Are on the Horizon?

Tests that measure the number of cancer cells in a sample of blood (circulating tumors cells) or examine the DNA of such cells are of great interest in cancer medicine because research suggests that levels of these cells might be useful for evaluating response to treatment and detecting cancer recurrence. One circulating tumor cell test has been approved by the U.S. Food and Drug Administration (FDA) to monitor patients with breast, colorectal, or prostate cancer. However, such tests are still being studied in clinical trials and are not routinely used in clinical practice.

Tests that determine the sequences of a large number of genes at one time using next generation DNA sequencing methods are being developed to provide gene mutation profiles of solid tumors (e.g., lung cancer). Some of these tests are being used to help choose the best treatment, but none are FDA approved.

Pathology Reports

What Is a Pathology Report?

A pathology report is a document that contains the diagnosis determined by examining cells and tissues under a microscope. The report may also contain information about the size, shape, and appearance of a specimen as it looks to the naked eye. This information is known as the gross description.

A pathologist is a doctor who does this examination and writes the pathology report. Pathology reports play an important role in cancer diagnosis and staging (describing the extent of cancer within the body, especially whether it has spread), which helps determine treatment options.

How Is Tissue Obtained for Examination by the Pathologist?

In most cases, a doctor needs to do a biopsy or surgery to remove cells or tissues for examination under a microscope.

Some common ways a biopsy can be done are as follows:

- A needle is used to withdraw tissue or fluid.

- An endoscope (a thin, lighted tube) is used to look at areas inside the body and remove cells or tissues.

- Surgery is used to remove part of the tumor or the entire tumor. If the entire tumor is removed, typically some normal tissue around the tumor is also removed.

Tissue removed during a biopsy is sent to a pathology laboratory, where it is sliced into thin sections for viewing under a microscope. This is known as histologic (tissue) examination and is usually the best way to tell if cancer is present. The pathologist may also examine cytologic (cell) material. Cytologic material is present in urine, cerebrospinal fluid (the fluid around the brain and spinal cord), sputum (mucus from the lungs), peritoneal (abdominal cavity) fluid, pleural (chest cavity) fluid, cervical/vaginal smears, and in fluid removed during a biopsy.

How Is Tissue Processed after a Biopsy or Surgery? What Is a Frozen Section?

The tissue removed during a biopsy or surgery must be cut into thin sections, placed on slides, and stained with dyes before it can be examined under a microscope. Two methods are used to make the tissue firm enough to cut into thin sections: frozen sections and paraffin-embedded (permanent) sections. All tissue samples are prepared as permanent sections, but sometimes frozen sections are also prepared.

Permanent sections are prepared by placing the tissue in fixative (usually formalin) to preserve the tissue, processing it through additional solutions, and then placing it in paraffin wax. After the wax has hardened, the tissue is cut into very thin slices, which are placed on slides and stained. The process normally takes several days. A permanent section provides the best quality for examination by the pathologist and produces more accurate results than a frozen section.

Frozen sections are prepared by freezing and slicing the tissue sample. They can be done in about 15 to 20 minutes while the patient is in the operating room. Frozen sections are done when an immediate answer is needed; for example, to determine whether the tissue is cancerous so as to guide the surgeon during the course of an operation.

How Long after the Tissue Sample Is Taken Will the Pathology Report Be Ready?

The pathologist sends a pathology report to the doctor within 10 days after the biopsy or surgery is performed. Pathology reports are written in technical medical language. Patients may want to ask their doctors to give them a copy of the pathology report and to explain the report to them. Patients also may wish to keep a copy of their pathology report in their own records.

What Information Does a Pathology Report Usually Include?

The pathology report may include the following information:

- Patient information: Name, birth date, biopsy date

- Gross description: Color, weight, and size of tissue as seen by the naked eye

- Microscopic description: How the sample looks under the microscope and how it compares with normal cells

- Diagnosis: Type of tumor/cancer and grade (how abnormal the cells look under the microscope and how quickly the tumor is likely to grow and spread)

- Tumor size: Measured in centimeters

- Tumor margins: There are three possible findings when the biopsy sample is the entire tumor:

  1. Positive margins mean that cancer cells are found at the edge of the material removed

  2. Negative, not involved, clear, or free margins mean that no cancer cells are found at the outer edge

  3. Close margins are neither negative nor positive

- Other information: Usually notes about samples that have been sent for other tests or a second opinion

- Pathologist's signature and name and address of the laboratory

What Might the Pathology Report Say about the Physical and Chemical Characteristics of the Tissue?

After identifying the tissue as cancerous, the pathologist may perform additional tests to get more information about the tumor that cannot be determined by looking at the tissue with routine stains, such as hematoxylin and eosin (also known as H&E), under a microscope. The pathology report will include the results of these tests. For example, the pathology report may include information obtained from immunochemical stains (IHC). IHC uses antibodies to identify specific antigens on the surface of cancer cells. IHC can often be used to:

- Determine where the cancer started

- Distinguish among different cancer types, such as carcinoma, melanoma, and lymphoma

- Help diagnose and classify leukemias and lymphomas

The pathology report may also include the results of flow cytometry. Flow cytometry is a method of measuring properties of cells in a sample, including the number of cells, percentage of live cells, cell size and shape, and presence of tumor markers on the cell surface. Tumor markers are substances produced by tumor cells or by other cells in the body in response to cancer or certain noncancerous conditions.) Flow cytometry can be used in the diagnosis, classification, and management of cancers such as acute leukemia, chronic lymphoproliferative disorders, and non-Hodgkin lymphoma.

Finally, the pathology report may include the results of molecular diagnostic and cytogenetic studies. Such studies investigate the presence or absence of malignant cells, and genetic or molecular abnormalities in specimens.

What Information about the Genetics of the Cells Might Be Included in the Pathology Report?

Cytogenetics uses tissue culture and specialized techniques to provide genetic information about cells, particularly genetic alterations. Some genetic alterations are markers or indicators of a specific cancer. For example, the Philadelphia chromosome is associated with chronic myelogenous leukemia (CML). Some alterations can provide information about prognosis, which helps the doctor make treatment recommendations. Some tests that might be performed on a tissue sample include:

- Fluorescence in situ hybridization (FISH): Determines the positions of particular genes. It can be used to identify chromosomal abnormalities and to map genes.

- Polymerase chain reaction (PCR): A method of making many copies of particular DNA sequences of relevance to the diagnosis.

- Real-time PCR or quantitative PCR: A method of measuring how many copies of a particular DNA sequence are present.

- Reverse-transcriptase polymerase chain reaction (RT-PCR): A method of making many copies of a specific RNA sequence.

- Southern blot hybridization: Detects specific DNA fragments.

- Western blot hybridization: Identifies and analyzes proteins or peptides.

Can Individuals Get a Second Opinion about Their Pathology Results?

Although most cancers can be easily diagnosed, sometimes patients or their doctors may want to get a second opinion about the pathology results. Patients interested in getting a second opinion should talk with their doctor. They will need to obtain the slides and/or paraffin block from the pathologist who examined the sample or from the hospital where the biopsy or surgery was done.

Many institutions provide second opinions on pathology specimens. NCI-designated cancer centers or academic institutions are reasonable places to consider. Patients should contact the facility in advance to determine if this service is available, the cost, and shipping instructions.

What Research Is Being Done to Improve the Diagnosis of Cancer?

NCI, a component of the National Institutes of Health, is sponsoring clinical trials that are designed to improve the accuracy and specificity of cancer diagnoses. Before any new method can be recommended for general use, doctors conduct clinical trials to find out whether it is safe and effective.

People interested in taking part in a clinical trial should talk with their doctor.

Chapter 35

Breast Cancer Staging

Overview

After breast cancer has been diagnosed, tests are done to find out if cancer cells have spread within the breast or to other parts of the body.

The process used to find out whether the cancer has spread within the breast or to other parts of the body is called staging. The information gathered from the staging process determines the stage of the disease. It is important to know the stage in order to plan treatment. The results of some of the tests used to diagnose breast cancer are also used to stage the disease.

The following tests and procedures also may be used in the staging process:

- **Sentinel lymph node biopsy:** The removal of the sentinel lymph node during surgery. The sentinel lymph node is the first lymph node to receive lymphatic drainage from a tumor. It is the first lymph node the cancer is likely to spread to from the tumor. A radioactive substance and/or blue dye is injected near the tumor. The substance or dye flows through the lymph ducts to the lymph nodes. The first lymph node to receive the substance or dye is removed. A pathologist views the tissue under a microscope to look for cancer cells. If cancer cells are not found, it may not be necessary to remove more lymph nodes.

This chapter includes text excerpted from "Breast Cancer Treatment–Patient Version (PDQ®)," National Cancer Institute (NCI), March 11, 2016.

- **Chest X-ray:** An X-ray of the organs and bones inside the chest. An X-ray is a type of energy beam that can go through the body and onto film, making a picture of areas inside the body.

- **CT scan (CAT scan):** A procedure that makes a series of detailed pictures of areas inside the body, taken from different angles. The pictures are made by a computer linked to an X-ray machine. A dye may be injected into a vein or swallowed to help the organs or tissues show up more clearly. This procedure is also called computed tomography, computerized tomography, or computerized axial tomography.

- **Bone scan:** A procedure to check if there are rapidly dividing cells, such as cancer cells, in the bone. A very small amount of radioactive material is injected into a vein and travels through the bloodstream. The radioactive material collects in the bones and is detected by a scanner.

- **PET scan (positron emission tomography scan):** A procedure to find malignant tumor cells in the body. A small amount of radioactive glucose (sugar) is injected into a vein. The PET scanner rotates around the body and makes a picture of where glucose is being used in the body. Malignant tumor cells show up brighter in the picture because they are more active and take up more glucose than normal cells do.

There Are Three Ways That Cancer Spreads in the Body

Cancer can spread through tissue, the lymph system, and the blood:

1. **Tissue.** The cancer spreads from where it began by growing into nearby areas.

2. **Lymph system.** The cancer spreads from where it began by getting into the lymph system. The cancer travels through the lymph vessels to other parts of the body.

3. **Blood.** The cancer spreads from where it began by getting into the blood. The cancer travels through the blood vessels to other parts of the body.

Cancer May Spread from Where It Began to Other Parts of the Body

When cancer spreads to another part of the body, it is called metastasis. Cancer cells break away from where they began (the primary tumor) and travel through the lymph system or blood.

- **Lymph system.** The cancer gets into the lymph system, travels through the lymph vessels, and forms a tumor (metastatic tumor) in another part of the body.

- **Blood.** The cancer gets into the blood, travels through the blood vessels, and forms a tumor (metastatic tumor) in another part of the body.

The metastatic tumor is the same type of cancer as the primary tumor. For example, if breast cancer spreads to the bone, the cancer cells in the bone are actually breast cancer cells. The disease is metastatic breast cancer, not bone cancer.

The following Stages Are Used for Breast Cancer

This section describes the stages of breast cancer. The breast cancer stage is based on the results of tests that are done on the tumor and lymph nodes removed during surgery and on other tests.

Stage 0 (Carcinoma in Situ)

There are 3 types of breast carcinoma in situ:

1. Ductal carcinoma in situ (DCIS) is a noninvasive condition in which abnormal cells are found in the lining of a breast duct. The abnormal cells have not spread outside the duct to other tissues in the breast. In some cases, DCIS may become invasive cancer and spread to other tissues. At this time, there is no way to know which lesions could become invasive.

2. Lobular carcinoma in situ (LCIS) is a condition in which abnormal cells are found in the lobules of the breast. This condition seldom becomes invasive cancer. Information about LCIS is not included in this summary.

3. Paget disease of the nipple is a condition in which abnormal cells are found in the nipple only.

Stage I

In stage I, cancer has formed. Stage I is divided into stages IA and IB.

- In stage IA, the tumor is 2 centimeters or smaller. Cancer has not spread outside the breast.

- In stage IB, small clusters of breast cancer cells (larger than 0.2 millimeter but not larger than 2 millimeters) are found in the lymph nodes and either:
  - no tumor is found in the breast; or
  - the tumor is 2 centimeters or smaller.

Stage II

Stage II is divided into stages IIA and IIB.

- In stage IIA:
  - no tumor is found in the breast or the tumor is 2 centimeters or smaller. Cancer (larger than 2 millimeters) is found in 1 to 3 axillary lymph nodes or in the lymph nodes near the breastbone (found during a sentinel lymph node biopsy); or
  - the tumor is larger than 2 centimeters but not larger than 5 centimeters. Cancer has not spread to the lymph nodes.
- In stage IIB, the tumor is:
  - larger than 2 centimeters but not larger than 5 centimeters. Small clusters of breast cancer cells (larger than 0.2 millimeter but not larger than 2 millimeters) are found in the lymph nodes; or
  - larger than 2 centimeters but not larger than 5 centimeters. Cancer has spread to 1 to 3 axillary lymph nodes or to the lymph nodes near the breastbone (found during a sentinel lymph node biopsy); or
  - larger than 5 centimeters. Cancer has not spread to the lymph nodes.

Stage IIIA

In stage IIIA:

- no tumor is found in the breast or the tumor may be any size. Cancer is found in 4 to 9 axillary lymph nodes or in the lymph nodes near the breastbone (found during imaging tests or a physical exam); or
- the tumor is larger than 5 centimeters. Small clusters of breast cancer cells (larger than 0.2 millimeter but not larger than 2 millimeters) are found in the lymph nodes; or

- the tumor is larger than 5 centimeters. Cancer has spread to 1 to 3 axillary lymph nodes or to the lymph nodes near the breastbone (found during a sentinel lymph node biopsy).

Stage IIIB

In stage IIIB, the tumor may be any size and cancer has spread to the chest wall and/or to the skin of the breast and caused swelling or an ulcer. Also, cancer may have spread to:

- up to 9 axillary lymph nodes; or

- the lymph nodes near the breastbone.

Cancer that has spread to the skin of the breast may also be inflammatory breast cancer.

Stage IIIC

In stage IIIC, no tumor is found in the breast or the tumor may be any size. Cancer may have spread to the skin of the breast and caused swelling or an ulcer and/or has spread to the chest wall. Also, cancer has spread to:

- 10 or more axillary lymph nodes; or

- lymph nodes above or below the collarbone; or

- axillary lymph nodes and lymph nodes near the breastbone.

Cancer that has spread to the skin of the breast may also be inflammatory breast cancer.

Stage IV

In stage IV, cancer has spread to other organs of the body, most often the bones, lungs, liver, or brain.

Chapter 36

Breast Cancer Diagnosis: Questions to Ask Your Doctor and Other FAQs

Questions to Ask Your Doctor about Your Diagnosis

Learning that you have cancer can be a shock and you may feel overwhelmed at first. When you meet with your doctor, you will hear a lot of information. These questions may help you learn more about your cancer and what you can expect next.

- What type of cancer do I have?
- What is the stage of my cancer?
- Has it spread to other areas of my body?
- Will I need more tests before treatment begins? Which ones?
- Will I need a specialist(s) for my cancer treatment?
- Will you help me find a doctor to give me another opinion on the best treatment plan for me?

This chapter contains text excerpted from the following sources: Text under the heading "Questions to Ask Your Doctor about Your Diagnosis" is excerpted from "Questions to Ask Your Doctor about Your Diagnosis," National Cancer Institute (NCI), April 2, 2015; Text beginning with the heading "Other Frequently Asked Questions" is excerpted from "Frequently Asked Questions," NIHSeniorHealth, National Institute on Aging (NIA), April 2015.

- How serious is my cancer?

- What are my chances of survival?

Other Frequently Asked Questions

Should I Perform Regular Breast Self-Exams?

The U.S. Preventive Services Task Force (USPSTF) recommends against teaching breast self-examination (BSE).

What Is a Prophylactic Mastectomy?

Some women who have a high risk of breast cancer may choose to have a prophylactic mastectomy (the removal of both breasts when there are no signs of cancer). The risk of breast cancer is much lower in these women and most feel less anxious about their risk of breast cancer. However, it is very important to have cancer risk assessment and counseling about the different ways to reduce the risk of breast cancer before making this decision.

What Is a Prophylactic Oophorectomy?

Premenopausal women who have a high risk of breast cancer due to certain changes in the BRCA1 and BRCA2 genes may choose to have a prophylactic oophorectomy (the removal of both ovaries when there are no signs of cancer). This decreases the amount of estrogen made by the body and lowers the risk of breast cancer. Prophylactic oophorectomy also lowers the risk of breast cancer in normal premenopausal women and in women with an increased risk of breast cancer due to radiation to the chest.

However, it is very important to have a cancer risk assessment and counseling before making this decision. The sudden drop in estrogen levels may cause the symptoms of menopause to begin. These include hot flashes, trouble sleeping, anxiety, and depression. Long-term effects include decreased sex drive, vaginal dryness, and decreased bone density.

What Role Do Gene Mutations Play in Breast Cancer?

Many clinical trials now include gene profiles of cancer patients as a way to tell how cancer may progress or be diagnosed. Gene profiles are even used to monitor how cancer genes are affected by targeted therapies. The knowledge from this new study will be used to bring earlier and better treatments to cancer patients.

A full analysis of all of the genes that determine cancer outcomes remains a difficult challenge. However, recent results from The Cancer Genome Atlas, an NIH study that included analyses of gene mutations in breast cancer, provide a list of mutations for other scientists to study and explore.

What Are the Symptoms of Breast Cancer?

When breast cancer first develops, there may be no symptoms at all. But as the cancer grows, it can cause changes that women should watch for. You can help safeguard your health by learning the following warning signs of breast cancer.

- a lump or thickening in or near the breast or in the underarm area

- a change in the size or shape of the breast

- ridges or pitting of the breast; the skin looks like the skin of an orange

- a change in the way the skin of the breast, areola, or nipple looks or feels; for example, it may be warm, swollen, red, or scaly

- nipple discharge or tenderness, or the nipple is pulled back or inverted into the breast.

You should see your doctor about any symptoms like these. Most often, they are not cancer, but it's important to check with the doctor so that any problems can be diagnosed and treated as early as possible.

What Happens during a Clinical Breast Exam?

During a clinical breast exam, a doctor or other health care professional checks the breasts and underarms for lumps or other changes that could be a sign of breast cancer. The doctor can tell a lot about a lump by carefully feeling it and the tissue around it. Benign lumps often feel different from cancerous ones.

It is important for women to report lumps or other significant changes that they note in their breasts to their health care provider.

What Happens during a Mammogram?

Mammography is a simple procedure. A registered technologist takes an X-ray of each breast with a machine that is used only for breast X-rays. It is different from X-ray machines that are used to take X-rays of the bones or other parts of the body. The standard mammogram exam includes two views of each breast, one from above and one angled from the side.

The technologist places the breast between two flat plastic plates. The two plates are then pressed together. The idea is to flatten the breast as much as possible. Spreading the tissue out makes any abnormal details easier to spot with a minimum of radiation. The technologist takes the X-ray, and then repeats the procedure for the next view. The pressure from the plates may be uncomfortable, or even slightly painful, but each X-ray takes less than one minute.

How Often Should I Have a Mammogram?

The U.S. Preventive Services Task Force (USPSTF) recommends a screening mammography for women 50-74 years every two years.

The USPSTF concludes that the current evidence is insufficient to assess the benefits and harms of screening mammography in women 75 years and older.

What Are Some of the Possible Benefits of a Mammogram?

A mammogram can often detect breast changes in women who have no signs of breast cancer. Often, it can find a breast lump before it can be felt. If the results indicate that cancer might be present, your doctor will advise you to have a follow-up test called a biopsy.

Are There Any Risks in Having a Mammogram?

The risks of breast cancer screening tests include the following.

- **Finding breast cancer may not improve health or help a woman live longer.** Screening may not help you if you have fast-growing breast cancer or if it has already spread to other places in your body. Also, some breast cancers found on a screening mammogram may never cause symptoms or become life-threatening. Finding these cancers is called overdiagnosis.

- **False-negative test results can occur.** Screening test results may appear to be normal even though breast cancer is present. A woman who receives a false-negative test result (one that shows there is no cancer when there really is) may delay seeking medical care even if she has symptoms.

- **False-positive test results can occur.** Screening test results may appear to be abnormal even though no cancer is present. A false-positive test result (one that shows there is cancer when there really isn't) is usually followed by more tests (such as biopsy), which also have risks.

- **Anxiety from additional testing may result from false positive results.** In one study, women who had a false-positive screening mammogram followed by more testing reported feeling anxiety 3 months later, even though cancer was not diagnosed. However, several studies show that women who feel anxiety after false-positive test results are more likely to schedule regular breast screening exams in the future.

- **Mammograms expose the breast to radiation.** Being exposed to radiation is a risk factor for breast cancer. The risk of breast cancer from radiation exposure is higher in women who received radiation before age 30 and at high doses. For women older than 40 years, the benefits of an annual screening mammogram may be greater than the risks from radiation exposure.

- **There may be pain or discomfort during a mammogram.** During a mammogram, the breast is placed between 2 plates that are pressed together. Pressing the breast helps to get a better X-ray of the breast. Some women have pain or discomfort during a mammogram.

Some women worry about radiation exposure, but the risk of any harm from a mammogram is actually quite small. The doses of radiation used are very low and considered safe. The exact amount of radiation used during a mammogram will depend on several factors. For instance, breasts that are large or dense will require higher doses to get a clear image.

If a Breast Exam or Mammogram Does Indicate the Possibility of Cancer, What Happens Next?

If the results of a clinical breast exam or a mammogram indicate that cancer might be present, the doctor will order a follow-up test. The most common follow-up test is called a biopsy. This is a procedure where a doctor removes a small amount of fluid or tissue from the breast to make a definitive diagnosis. A doctor might perform fine needle aspiration, a needle or "core" biopsy, or a surgical biopsy.

Part Five

Breast Cancer Treatments

Chapter 37

How to Find a Doctor or Treatment Facility If You Have Cancer?

Finding Health Care Services

If you have been diagnosed with cancer, finding a doctor and treatment facility for your cancer care is an important step to getting the best treatment possible.

You will have many factors to consider when choosing a doctor. It's important for you to feel comfortable with the specialist that you choose because you will be working closely with that person to make decisions about your cancer treatment.

Choosing a Doctor

To find a doctor that specializes in cancer care, ask your primary care doctor for a referral. (If you don't have a primary care doctor, call the National Cancer Institute (NCI) at 1-800-4-CANCER for help.) Depending on your health insurance plan, your choices may be limited to doctors who participate in your plan. You also have the option of seeing a doctor outside your health insurance plan and paying the

---

This chapter includes text excerpted from "Finding Health Care Services," National Cancer Institute (NCI), March 10, 2015.

costs yourself. If you have the option to change health insurance plans, first you may want to decide which doctor or doctors you would like to use, and then choose the plan that includes your chosen physician(s).

Some specialists that treat cancer are:

Oncologist: specializes in treating cancer

Hematologist: focuses on diseases of the blood and related tissues, including the bone marrow, spleen, and lymph nodes

Radiation oncologist: uses X-rays and other forms of radiation to diagnose and treat disease

Surgeon: performs operations on almost any area of the body and may specialize in a certain type of surgery

If you are using a federal or state health insurance program such as Medicare or Medicaid, you will want to ask if the doctor you would like to see is accepting patients who use these programs.

To help make your decision, when you meet with each person, think about if the doctor:

- Listens to you and treats you with respect

- Explains things clearly

- Encourages you to ask questions

- Has office hours that meet your needs

- Has someone who provides care if the doctor is unavailable

- Is easy to get an appointment with

It's important for you to feel good about the doctor you choose. You will be working with this person closely as you make decisions about your cancer treatment. Trust your own feelings and observations as you make your choice.

Getting a Second Opinion from Another Doctor

After you talk to a doctor about the diagnosis and treatment plan for your cancer, you may want to get a second opinion from another doctor before you begin treatment. You want to be as informed as possible when making your treatment choices. Some patients worry that doctors will be offended if they ask for a second opinion. Usually the opposite is true. Most doctors welcome a second opinion. And many health insurance companies pay for them or even require them.

If you get a second opinion, the doctor may agree with your first doctor's treatment plan. Or he or she may suggest another approach or modify the first one. Either way, you will have more information and perhaps a greater sense of control. You can feel more confident about the decisions you make, knowing that you've looked at all of your options.

If your doctor can't recommend another specialist for a second opinion, call the National Cancer Institute at 1-800-4-CANCER for help.

Choosing a Treatment Facility

If you have already found a doctor for your cancer treatment, you may need to choose a treatment facility based on where your doctor practices. However, you may be limited to facilities that take part in your health insurance plan. If you are thinking about paying for treatment yourself, you will want to discuss the possible costs with your doctor beforehand. Nurses and social workers may also be able to give you more information about coverage, eligibility, and insurance issues.

NCI-Designated Cancer Centers may be another source for cancer treatment. The centers are institutions dedicated to providing more effective approaches to prevent, diagnose, and treat cancer. Most of the centers include clinical programs that offer patients the latest forms of treatment for a wide range of cancers, as well as access to clinical trials.

Finding Health Insurance

The Affordable Care Act changes how health insurance works in the United States, with implications for the prevention, screening, and treatment of cancer. Under this health care law, most Americans are required to have health insurance.

If you do not have health insurance or want to look at new options, the online Health Insurance Marketplace lets you compare plans in your state based on price, benefits, quality, and other needs you may have.

Home Care Services

Sometimes patients want to be cared for at home so they can be in familiar surroundings with family and friends. Home care services can help patients stay at home by using a team approach with doctors, nurses, social workers, physical therapists, and others.

If the patient qualifies for home care services, such services may include:

- Managing symptoms and monitoring care

- Delivery of medications

- Physical therapy

- Emotional and spiritual care

- Help with preparing meals and personal hygiene

- Providing medical equipment

For many patients and families, home care can be both rewarding and demanding. It can change relationships and require families to cope with all aspects of patient care. New issues may also arise that families need to address such as the logistics of having home care providers coming into the home at regular intervals. To prepare for these changes, patients and caregivers should ask questions and get as much information as possible from the home care team or organization. A doctor, nurse, or social worker can provide information about a patient's specific needs, the availability of services, and the local home care agencies.

Getting Financial Assistance for Home Care

Help with paying for home care services may be available from public or private sources. Private health insurance may cover some home care services, but benefits vary from plan to plan.

Some public resources to help pay for home care are:

- **Centers for Medicare and Medicaid Services (CMS):** A government agency responsible for the administration of several key federal healthcare programs. Two of these are

  - **Medicare:** A government health insurance program for the elderly or disabled. For information, visit their website or call 1-800-MEDICARE (1-800-633-4227).

  - **Medicaid:** A joint federal and state health insurance program for those who need help with medical expenses. Coverage varies by state.

Both Medicare and Medicaid may cover home care services for patients who qualify, but some rules apply. Talk to a social worker and other members of the health care team to find out more about home care providers and agencies. For more information contact the CMS online or call 1-877-267-2323.

- **Eldercare Locator:** Run by the U.S. Administration on Aging, it provides information about local Area Agencies on Aging and other assistance for older people. These agencies may provide funds for home care. Eldercare Locator can be reached at 1-800-677-1116 for more information.

- **Department of Veterans Affairs (VA):** Veterans who are disabled as a result of military service can receive home care services from the U.S. Department of Veteran's Affairs (VA). However, only home care services provided by VA hospitals may be used. More information about these benefits can be found on their website or by calling 1–877–222–VETS (1–877–222–8387)

For other resources for home care, call the NCI Cancer Information Service at 1-800-4-CANCER (1-800-422-6237) or visit cancer.gov.

Chapter 38

Making Breast Cancer Treatment Decisions

Understanding Cancer Prognosis

If you have cancer, you may have questions about how serious your cancer is and your chances of survival. The estimate of how the disease will go for you is called prognosis. It can be hard to understand what prognosis means and also hard to talk about, even for doctors.

Many Factors Can Affect Your Prognosis

Some of the factors that affect prognosis include:

- The type of cancer and where it is in your body

- The stage of the cancer, which refers to the size of the cancer and if it has spread to other parts of your body

- The cancer's grade, which refers to how abnormal the cancer cells look under a microscope. Grade provides clues about how quickly the cancer is likely to grow and spread.

This chapter contains text excerpted from the following sources: Text beginning with the heading "Understanding Cancer Prognosis" is excerpted from "Understanding Cancer Prognosis," National Cancer Institute (NCI), November 24, 2014; Text beginning with the heading "How to Get a Second Opinion?" is excerpted from "How to Find a Doctor or Treatment Facility If You Have Cancer," National Cancer Institute (NCI), June 5, 2013.

293

- Certain traits of the cancer cells

- Your age and how healthy you were before cancer

- How you respond to treatment

Seeking Information about Your Prognosis Is a Personal Decision

When you have cancer, you and your loved ones face many unknowns. Understanding your cancer and knowing what to expect can help you and your loved ones make decisions. Some of the decisions you may face include:

- Which treatment is best for you

- If you want treatment

- How to best take care of yourself and manage treatment side effects

- How to deal with financial and legal matters.

Many people want to know their prognosis. They find it easier to cope when they know more about their cancer. You may ask your doctor about survival statistics or search for this information on your own. Or, you may find statistics confusing and frightening, and think they are too impersonal to be of value to you. It is up to you to decide how much information you want.

If you do decide you want to know more, the doctor who knows the most about your situation is in the best position to discuss your prognosis and explain what the statistics may mean.

Understanding Statistics about Survival

Doctors estimate prognosis by using statistics that researchers have collected over many years about people with the same type of cancer. Several types of statistics may be used to estimate prognosis. The most commonly used statistics include:

Cancer-specific survival

This is the percentage of patients with a specific type and stage of cancer who have not died from their cancer during a certain period of time after diagnosis. The period of time may be 1 year, 2 years, 5 years, etc., with 5 years being the time period most often used.

Cancer-specific survival is also called disease-specific survival. In most cases, cancer-specific survival is based on causes of death listed in medical records.

Relative survival

This statistic is another method used to estimate cancer-specific survival that does not use information about the cause of death. It is the percentage of cancer patients who have survived for a certain period of time after diagnosis compared to people who do not have cancer.

Overall survival

This is the percentage of people with a specific type and stage of cancer who have not died from any cause during a certain period of time after diagnosis.

Disease-free survival

This statistic is the percentage of patients who have no signs of cancer during a certain period of time after treatment. Other names for this statistic are recurrence-free or progression-free survival.

Because statistics are based on large groups of people, they cannot be used to predict exactly what will happen to you. Everyone is different. Treatments and how people respond to treatment can differ greatly. Also, it takes years to see the benefit of new treatments and ways of finding cancer. So, the statistics your doctor uses to make a prognosis may not be based on treatments being used today.

Still, your doctor may tell you that you have a good prognosis if statistics suggest that your cancer is likely to respond well to treatment. Or, he may tell you that you have a poor prognosis if the cancer is harder to control. Whatever your doctor tells you, keep in mind that a prognosis is an educated guess. Your doctor cannot be certain how it will go for you.

If You Decide Not to Have Treatment

If you decide not to have treatment, the doctor who knows your situation best is in the best position to discuss your prognosis.

Survival statistics most often come from studies that compare treatments with each other, rather than treatment with no treatment. So, it may not be easy for your doctor to give you an accurate prognosis.

Understanding the Difference between Cure and Remission

Cure means that there are no traces of your cancer after treatment and the cancer will never come back.

Remission means that the signs and symptoms of your cancer are reduced. Remission can be partial or complete. In a complete remission, all signs and symptoms of cancer have disappeared.

If you remain in complete remission for 5 years or more, some doctors may say that you are cured. Still, some cancer cells can remain in your body for many years after treatment. These cells may cause the cancer to come back one day. For cancers that return, most do so within the first 5 years after treatment. But, there is a chance that cancer will come back later. For this reason, doctors cannot say for sure that you are cured. The most they can say is that there are no signs of cancer at this time.

Because of the chance that cancer can come back, your doctor will monitor you for many years and do tests to look for signs of cancer's return. They will also look for signs of late side effects from the cancer treatments you received.

How to Get a Second Opinion?

How Can I Get Another Doctor's Opinion about the Diagnosis and Treatment Plan?

After your doctor gives you advice about the diagnosis and treatment plan, you may want to get another doctor's opinion before you begin treatment. This is known as getting a second opinion. You can do this by asking another specialist to review all of the materials related to your case. The doctor who gives the second opinion can confirm or suggest modifications to your doctor's proposed treatment plan, provide reassurance that you have explored all of your options, and answer any questions you may have.

Getting a second opinion is done frequently, and most physicians welcome another doctor's views. In fact, your doctor may be able to recommend a specialist for this consultation. However, some people find it uncomfortable to request a second opinion. When discussing this issue with your doctor, it may be helpful to express satisfaction with your doctor's decision and care and to mention that you want your decision about treatment to be as thoroughly informed as possible. You may also wish to bring a family member along for support when asking for a second opinion. It is best to involve your doctor in the process of getting a second opinion, because your doctor will need to make your medical records (such as your test results and X-rays) available to the specialist who is giving the second opinion.

Some health care plans require a second opinion, particularly if a doctor recommends surgery. Other health care plans will pay for a second opinion if the patient requests it. If your plan does not cover a second opinion, you can still obtain one if you are willing to cover the cost.

If your doctor is unable to recommend a specialist for a second opinion, or if you prefer to choose one on your own, the following resources can help:

- Many of the resources listed above for finding a doctor can also help you find a specialist for a consultation.

- The NIH Clinical Center in Bethesda, Maryland, is the research hospital for the NIH, including NCI. Several branches of the NCI provide second opinion services. The NCI fact sheet Cancer Clinical Trials at the NIH Clinical Center describes these NCI branches and their services.

- The R. A. Bloch Cancer Foundation, Inc., can refer cancer patients to institutions that are willing to provide multidisciplinary second opinions. A list of these institutions is available on the organization's website Exit Disclaimer. You can also contact the R. A. Bloch Cancer Foundation, Inc., by telephone at 816–854–5050 or 1–800–433–0464.

How Can U.S. Residents Find Treatment Facilities?

Choosing a treatment facility is another important consideration for getting the best medical care possible. Although you may not be able to choose which hospital treats you in an emergency, you can choose a facility for scheduled and ongoing care. If you have already found a doctor for your cancer treatment, you may need to choose a facility based on where your doctor practices. Your doctor may be able to recommend a facility that provides quality care to meet your needs. You may wish to ask the following questions when considering a treatment facility:

- Has the facility had experience and success in treating my condition?

- Has the facility been rated by state, consumer, or other groups for its quality of care?

- How does the facility check on and work to improve its quality of care?

- Has the facility been approved by a nationally recognized accrediting body, such as the ACS Commission on Cancer and/or The Joint Commission?

- Does the facility explain patients' rights and responsibilities? Are copies of this information available to patients?

- Does the treatment facility offer support services, such as social workers and resources, to help me find financial assistance if I need it?

- Is the facility conveniently located?

If you are a member of a health insurance plan, your choice of treatment facilities may be limited to those that participate in your plan. Your insurance company can provide you with a list of approved facilities. Although the costs of cancer treatment can be very high, you do have the option of paying out-of-pocket if you want to use a treatment facility that is not covered by your insurance plan. If you are considering paying for treatment yourself, you may wish to discuss the possible costs with your doctor beforehand. You may also want to speak with the person who does the billing for the treatment facility. Nurses and social workers may also be able to provide you with more information about coverage, eligibility, and insurance issues.

The following resources may help you find a hospital or treatment facility for your care:

- The NCI-Designated Cancer Centers Find a Cancer Center page provides contact information for NCI-designated cancer centers located throughout the country.

- The ACS's Commission on Cancer (CoC) accredits cancer programs at hospitals and other treatment facilities. More than 1,430 programs in the United States have been designated by the CoC as Approved Cancer Programs. The ACS website offers a searchable database of these programs. The CoC can be contacted by telephone at 312–202–5085 or by e-mail at CoC@facs.org.

- The Joint Commission is an independent not-for-profit organization that evaluates and accredits health care organizations and programs in the United States. It also offers information for the general public about choosing a treatment facility. The Joint Commission can be contacted by telephone at 630–792–5000.

How Can People Who Live outside the United States Find Treatment Facilities in or near Their Countries?

If you live outside the United States, facilities that offer cancer treatment may be located in or near your country. Cancer information services are available in many countries to provide information and answer questions about cancer; they may also be able to help you find a cancer treatment facility close to where you live. A list of these cancer information services is available on the website of the International Cancer Information Service Group, an independent international organization of cancer information services. A list may also be requested by writing to the NCI Public Inquiries Office at:

Cancer Information Service
BG 9609 MSC 9760
9609 Medical Center Drive
Bethesda, MD 20892-9760

The Union for International Cancer Control (UICC) is another resource for people living outside the United States who want to find a cancer treatment facility. The UICC consists of international cancer-related organizations devoted to the worldwide fight against cancer. UICC membership includes research facilities and treatment centers and, in some countries, ministries of health. Other members include volunteer cancer leagues, associations, and societies. These organizations serve as resources for the public and may have helpful information about cancer and treatment facilities. To find a resource in or near your country, contact the UICC at:

Union for International Cancer Control (UICC)
62 route de Frontenex
1207 Geneva
Switzerland
+41-22-809-1811
http://www.uicc.org

How Can People Who Live outside the United States Get a Second Opinion or Have Cancer Treatment in the United States?

Some people living outside the United States may wish to obtain a second opinion or have their cancer treatment in this country. Many facilities in the United States offer these services to international cancer patients. These facilities may also provide support services, such as language interpretation, assistance with travel, and guidance in finding accommodations near the treatment facility for patients and their families.

If you live outside the United States and would like to obtain cancer treatment in this country, you should contact cancer treatment facilities directly to find out whether they have an international patient office. The NCI-Designated Cancer Centers Find a Cancer Center page offers contact information for NCI-designated cancer centers throughout the United States.

Citizens of other countries who are planning to travel to the United States for cancer treatment generally must first obtain a nonimmigrant visa for medical treatment from the U.S. Embassy or Consulate in their home country. Visa applicants must demonstrate that the purpose of their trip is to enter the United States for medical treatment; that they plan to remain for a specific, limited period; that they have funds to cover expenses in the United States; that they have a residence and social and economic ties outside the United States; and that they intend to return to their home country.

To determine the specific fees and documentation required for the nonimmigrant visa and to learn more about the application process, contact the U.S. Embassy or Consulate in your home country. A list of links to the websites of U.S. Embassies and Consulates worldwide can be found on the U.S. Department of State's website.

Chapter 39

Adjuvant and Neoadjuvant Therapy for Breast Cancer

Treatment Option Overview

There Are Different Types of Treatment for Patients with Breast Cancer

Different types of treatment are available for patients with breast cancer. Some treatments are standard (the currently used treatment), and some are being tested in clinical trials. A treatment clinical trial is a research study meant to help improve current treatments or obtain information on new treatments for patients with cancer. When clinical trials show that a new treatment is better than the standard treatment, the new treatment may become the standard treatment. Patients may want to think about taking part in a clinical trial. Some clinical trials are open only to patients who have not started treatment.

Five Types of Standard Treatment Are Used

Surgery

Most patients with breast cancer have surgery to remove the cancer.

This chapter includes text excerpted from "Breast Cancer Treatment–Patient Version (PDQ®)," National Cancer Institute (NCI), February 25, 2016.

Sentinel lymph node biopsy is the removal of the sentinel lymph node during surgery. The sentinel lymph node is the first lymph node to receive lymphatic drainage from a tumor. It is the first lymph node where the cancer is likely to spread. A radioactive substance and/or blue dye is injected near the tumor. The substance or dye flows through the lymph ducts to the lymph nodes. The first lymph node to receive the substance or dye is removed. A pathologist views the tissue under a microscope to look for cancer cells. After the sentinel lymph node biopsy, the surgeon removes the tumor using breast-conserving surgery or mastectomy. If cancer cells are not found, it may not be necessary to remove more lymph nodes. If cancer cells are found, more lymph nodes will be removed through a separate incision. This is called a lymph node dissection.

Types of surgery include the following:

- **Breast-conserving surgery** is an operation to remove the cancer and some normal tissue around it, but not the breast itself. Part of the chest wall lining may also be removed if the cancer is near it. This type of surgery may also be called lumpectomy, partial mastectomy, segmental mastectomy, quadrantectomy, or breast-sparing surgery.

- **Total mastectomy:** Surgery to remove the whole breast that has cancer. This procedure is also called a simple mastectomy. Some of the lymph nodes under the arm may be removed and checked for cancer. This may be done at the same time as the breast surgery or after. This is done through a separate incision.

- **Modified radical mastectomy:** Surgery to remove the whole breast that has cancer, many of the lymph nodes under the arm, the lining over the chest muscles, and sometimes, part of the chest wall muscles.

Chemotherapy may be given before surgery to remove the tumor. When given before surgery, chemotherapy will shrink the tumor and reduce the amount of tissue that needs to be removed during surgery. Treatment given before surgery is called preoperative therapy or neo-adjuvant therapy.

Even if the doctor removes all the cancer that can be seen at the time of the surgery, some patients may be given radiation therapy, chemotherapy, or hormone therapy after surgery, to kill any cancer cells that are left. Treatment given after the surgery, to lower the risk that the cancer will come back, is called postoperative therapy or adjuvant therapy.

If a patient is going to have a mastectomy, breast reconstruction (surgery to rebuild a breast's shape after a mastectomy) may be considered. Breast reconstruction may be done at the time of the mastectomy or at some time after. The reconstructed breast may be made with the patient's own (non-breast) tissue or by using implants filled with saline or silicone gel. Before the decision to get an implant is made, patients can call the U.S. Food and Drug Administration's (FDA) Center for Devices and Radiological Health at 1-888-INFO-FDA (1-888-463-6332) or visit the FDA website for more information on breast implants.

Radiation Therapy

Radiation therapy is a cancer treatment that uses high-energy X-rays or other types of radiation to kill cancer cells or keep them from growing. There are two types of radiation therapy. External radiation therapy uses a machine outside the body to send radiation toward the cancer. Internal radiation therapy uses a radioactive substance sealed in needles, seeds, wires, or catheters that are placed directly into or near the cancer.

External radiation therapy is used to treat breast cancer. Internal radiation therapy with strontium-89 (a radionuclide) is used to relieve bone pain caused by breast cancer that has spread to the bones. Strontium-89 is injected into a vein and travels to the surface of the bones. Radiation is released and kills cancer cells in the bones.

The way the radiation therapy is given depends on the type and stage of the cancer being treated. External radiation therapy is used to treat breast cancer.

Chemotherapy

Chemotherapy is a cancer treatment that uses drugs to stop the growth of cancer cells, either by killing the cells or by stopping them from dividing. When chemotherapy is taken by mouth or injected into a vein or muscle, the drugs enter the bloodstream and can reach cancer cells throughout the body (systemic chemotherapy). When chemotherapy is placed directly into the cerebrospinal fluid, an organ, or a body cavity such as the abdomen, the drugs mainly affect cancer cells in those areas (regional chemotherapy).

The way the chemotherapy is given depends on the type and stage of the cancer being treated. Systemic chemotherapy is used in the treatment of breast cancer.

Hormone Therapy

Hormone therapy is a cancer treatment that removes hormones or blocks their action and stops cancer cells from growing. Hormones are substances made by glands in the body and circulated in the bloodstream. Some hormones can cause certain cancers to grow. If tests show that the cancer cells have places where hormones can attach (receptors), drugs, surgery, or radiation therapy is used to reduce the production of hormones or block them from working. The hormone estrogen, which makes some breast cancers grow, is made mainly by the ovaries. Treatment to stop the ovaries from making estrogen is called ovarian ablation.

Hormone therapy with tamoxifen is often given to patients with early localized breast cancer that can be removed by surgery and those with metastatic breast cancer (cancer that has spread to other parts of the body). Hormone therapy with tamoxifen or estrogens can act on cells all over the body and may increase the chance of developing endometrial cancer. Women taking tamoxifen should have a pelvic exam every year to look for any signs of cancer. Any vaginal bleeding, other than menstrual bleeding, should be reported to a doctor as soon as possible.

Hormone therapy with a luteinizing hormone-releasing hormone (LHRH) agonist is given to some premenopausal women who have just been diagnosed with hormone receptor positive breast cancer. LHRH agonists decrease the body's estrogen and progesterone. Buserelin is an LHRH agonist.

Hormone therapy with an aromatase inhibitor is given to some postmenopausal women who have hormone receptor–positive breast cancer. Aromatase inhibitors decrease the body's estrogen by blocking an enzyme called aromatase from turning androgen into estrogen. Anastrozole, and letrozole are two types of aromatase inhibitors.

For the treatment of early localized breast cancer that can be removed by surgery, certain aromatase inhibitors may be used as adjuvant therapy instead of tamoxifen or after 2 to 3 years of tamoxifen use. For the treatment of metastatic breast cancer, aromatase inhibitors are being tested in clinical trials to compare them to hormone therapy with tamoxifen.

Other types of hormone therapy include megestrol acetate or anti-estrogen therapy such as fulvestrant.

Targeted Therapy

Targeted therapy is a type of treatment that uses drugs or other substances to identify and attack specific cancer cells without harming normal cells. Monoclonal antibodies, tyrosine kinase inhibitors, and cyclin-dependent kinase inhibitors, are types of targeted therapies used in the treatment of breast cancer.

Monoclonal antibody therapy is a cancer treatment that uses antibodies made in the laboratory, from a single type of immune system cell. These antibodies can identify substances on cancer cells or normal substances that may help cancer cells grow. The antibodies attach to the substances and kill the cancer cells, block their growth, or keep them from spreading. Monoclonal antibodies are given by infusion. They may be used alone or to carry drugs, toxins, or radioactive material directly to cancer cells. Monoclonal antibodies may be used in combination with chemotherapy as adjuvant therapy.

Types of monoclonal antibody therapy include the following:

- **Trastuzumab** is a monoclonal antibody that blocks the effects of the growth factor protein HER2, which sends growth signals to breast cancer cells. About one-fourth of patients with breast cancer have tumors that may be treated with trastuzumab combined with chemotherapy.

- **Pertuzumab** is a monoclonal antibody that may be combined with trastuzumab and chemotherapy to treat breast cancer. It may be used to treat certain patients with HER2 positive breast cancer that has metastasized (spread to other parts of the body). It may also be used as neoadjuvant therapy in certain patients with early stage HER2 positive breast cancer.

- **Ado-trastuzumab emtansine** is a monoclonal antibody linked to an anticancer drug. This is called an antibody-drug conjugate. It is used to treat HER2 positive breast cancer that has spread to other parts of the body or recurred (come back).

Tyrosine kinase inhibitors are targeted therapy drugs that block signals needed for tumors to grow. Tyrosine kinase inhibitors may be used with other anticancer drugs as adjuvant therapy. Tyrosine kinase inhibitors include the following:

- **Lapatinib** is a tyrosine kinase inhibitor that blocks the effects of the HER2 protein and other proteins inside tumor cells. It may be used with other drugs to treat patients with HER2 positive breast cancer that has progressed after treatment with trastuzumab.

Cyclin-dependent kinase inhibitors are targeted therapy drugs that block proteins called cyclin-dependent kinases, which cause the growth of cancer cells. Cyclin-dependent kinase inhibitors include the following:

- **Palbociclib** is a cyclin-dependent kinase inhibitor used with the drug letrozole to treat breast cancer that is estrogen receptor positive and HER2 negative and has spread to other parts of the body. It is used in postmenopausal women whose cancer has not been treated with hormone therapy.

Mammalian target of rapamycin (mTOR) inhibitors block a protein called mTOR, which may keep cancer cells from growing and prevent the growth of new blood vessels that tumors need to grow. mTOR inhibitors include the following:

- **Everolimus** is an mTOR inhibitor used in postmenopausal women with advanced hormone receptor positive breast cancer that is also HER2 negative and has not gotten better with other treatment.

PARP inhibitors are a type of targeted therapy that block DNA repair and may cause cancer cells to die. PARP inhibitor therapy is being studied for the treatment of patients with triple negative breast cancer or tumors with BRCA1 or BRCA2 mutations.

Some Treatments for Breast Cancer May Cause Side Effects Months or Years after Treatment Has Ended

Some treatments for breast cancer may cause side effects that continue or appear months or years after treatment has ended. These are called late effects.

Late effects of radiation therapy are not common, but may include:

- Inflammation of the lung after radiation therapy to the breast, especially when chemotherapy is given at the same time.

- Arm lymphedema, especially when radiation therapy is given after lymph node dissection.

- In women younger than 45 years who receive radiation therapy to the chest wall after mastectomy, there may be a higher risk of developing breast cancer in the other breast.

Late effects of chemotherapy depend on the drugs used, but may include:

- Heart failure.

- Blood clots.

- Premature menopause.

- Second cancer, such as leukemia.

Late effects of targeted therapy with trastuzumab may include:

- Heart problems such as heart failure.

New Types of Treatment Are Being Tested in Clinical Trials

This summary section describes treatments that are being studied in clinical trials. It may not mention every new treatment being studied.

High-Dose Chemotherapy with Stem Cell Transplant

High-dose chemotherapy with stem cell transplant is a way of giving high doses of chemotherapy and replacing blood-forming cells destroyed by the cancer treatment. Stem cells (immature blood cells) are removed from the blood or bone marrow of the patient or a donor and are frozen and stored. After the chemotherapy is completed, the stored stem cells are thawed and given back to the patient through an infusion. These reinfused stem cells grow into (and restore) the body's blood cells.

Studies have shown that high-dose chemotherapy followed by stem cell transplant does not work better than standard chemotherapy in the treatment of breast cancer. Doctors have decided that, for now, high-dose chemotherapy should be tested only in clinical trials. Before taking part in such a trial, women should talk with their doctors about the serious side effects, including death, that may be caused by high-dose chemotherapy.

Patients May Want to Think about Taking Part in a Clinical Trial

For some patients, taking part in a clinical trial may be the best treatment choice. Clinical trials are part of the cancer research process. Clinical trials are done to find out if new cancer treatments are safe and effective or better than the standard treatment.

Many of today's standard treatments for cancer are based on earlier clinical trials. Patients who take part in a clinical trial may receive the standard treatment or be among the first to receive a new treatment.

Patients who take part in clinical trials also help improve the way cancer will be treated in the future. Even when clinical trials do not lead to effective new treatments, they often answer important questions and help move research forward.

Patients Can Enter Clinical Trials before, during, or after Starting Their Cancer Treatment

Some clinical trials only include patients who have not yet received treatment. Other trials test treatments for patients whose cancer has not gotten better. There are also clinical trials that test new ways to stop cancer from recurring (coming back) or reduce the side effects of cancer treatment.

Clinical trials are taking place in many parts of the country. See the Treatment Options section that follows for links to current treatment clinical trials. These have been retrieved from NCI's listing of clinical trials.

Follow-Up Tests May Be Needed

Some of the tests that were done to diagnose the cancer or to find out the stage of the cancer may be repeated. Some tests will be repeated in order to see how well the treatment is working. Decisions about whether to continue, change, or stop treatment may be based on the results of these tests. Some of the tests will continue to be done from time to time after treatment has ended. The results of these tests can show if your condition has changed or if the cancer has recurred (come back). These tests are sometimes called follow-up tests or check-ups.

Chapter 40

Surgical Treatments for Breast Cancer

Chapter Contents

Section 40.1

Overview of Surgeries for Early-Stage Breast Cancer

This section includes text excerpted from "Surgery Choices
for Women with DCIS or Breast Cancer," National
Cancer Institute (NCI), January 19, 2015.

Surgery Choices for Women with DCIS or Breast Cancer

Are You Facing a Decision about Surgery for DCIS or Breast Cancer?

Do you have ductal carcinoma in situ (DCIS) or breast cancer
that can be removed with surgery? If so, you may be able to choose
which type of breast surgery to have. Often, your choice is between
breast-sparing surgery (surgery that takes out the cancer and leaves
most of the breast) and a mastectomy (surgery that removes the whole
breast).

Once you are diagnosed, treatment will usually not begin right
away. There should be enough time for you to meet with breast cancer
surgeons, learn the facts about your surgery choices, and think about
what is important to you. Learning all you can will help you make a
choice you can feel good about.

Talk with Your Doctor

Talk with a breast cancer surgeon about your choices. Find out:

- what happens during surgery

- the types of problems that sometimes occur

- any treatment you might need after surgery

Be sure to ask a lot of questions and learn as much as you can. You
may also wish to talk with family members, friends, or others who
have had surgery.

Get a Second Opinion

After talking with a surgeon, think about getting a second opinion. A second opinion means getting the advice of another surgeon. This surgeon might tell you about other treatment options. Or, he or she may agree with the advice you got from the first doctor.

Some people worry about hurting their surgeon's feelings if they get a second opinion. But, it is very common and good surgeons don't mind. Also, some insurance companies require it. It is better to get a second opinion than worry that you made the wrong choice.

If you think you might have a mastectomy, this is also a good time to learn about breast reconstruction. Think about meeting with a reconstructive plastic surgeon to learn about this surgery and if it seems like a good option for you.

Check with Your Insurance Company

Each insurance plan is different. Knowing how much your plan will pay for each type of surgery, including reconstruction, special bras, prostheses, and other needed treatments can help you decide which surgery is best for you.

Learn about the Types of Surgery

Most women with DCIS or breast cancer that can be treated with surgery have three surgery choices.

Breast-Sparing Surgery

Breast-sparing surgery means the surgeon removes only the DCIS or cancer and some normal tissue around it. If you have cancer, the surgeon will also remove one or more lymph nodes from under your arm. Breast-sparing surgery usually keeps your breast looking much like it did before surgery. Other words for breast-sparing surgery include:

- Lumpectomy
- Partial mastectomy
- Breast-conserving surgery
- Segmental mastectomy

After breast-sparing surgery, most women also receive radiation therapy. The main goal of this treatment is to keep cancer from coming

311

back in the same breast. Some women will also need chemotherapy, hormone therapy, and/or targeted therapy.

Mastectomy

In a mastectomy, the surgeon removes the whole breast that contains the DCIS or cancer. There are two main types of mastectomy. They are:

- Total (simple) mastectomy. The surgeon removes your whole breast. Sometimes, the surgeon also takes out one or more of the lymph nodes under your arm.

- Modified radical mastectomy. The surgeon removes your whole breast, many of the lymph nodes under your arm, and the lining over your chest muscles.

Some women will also need radiation therapy, chemotherapy, hormone therapy, and/or targeted therapy.

If you have a mastectomy, you may choose to wear a prosthesis (breast-like form) in your bra or have breast reconstruction surgery.

Mastectomy with Breast Reconstruction Surgery

You can have breast reconstruction at the same time as the mastectomy, or anytime after. This type of surgery is done by a plastic surgeon with experience in reconstruction surgery. The surgeon uses an implant or tissue from another part of your body to create a breast-like shape that replaces the breast that was removed. The surgeon may also make the form of a nipple and add a tattoo that looks like the areola (the dark area around your nipple).

There are two main types of breast reconstruction surgery:

1. Breast Implant

Breast reconstruction with an implant is often done in steps. The first step is called tissue expansion. This is when the plastic surgeon places a balloon expander under the chest muscle. Over many weeks, saline (salt water) will be added to the expander to stretch the chest muscle and the skin on top of it. This process makes a pocket for the implant.

Once the pocket is the correct size, the surgeon will remove the expander and place an implant (filled with saline or silicone gel) into the pocket. This creates a new breast-like shape. Although this shape looks like a breast, you will not have the same feeling in it because nerves were cut during your mastectomy.

Breast implants do not last a lifetime. If you choose to have an implant, chances are you will need more surgery later on to remove or replace it. Implants can cause problems such as breast hardness, pain, and infection. The implant may also break, move, or shift. These problems can happen soon after surgery or years later.

2. Tissue Flap

In tissue flap surgery, a reconstructive plastic surgeon builds a new breast-like shape from muscle, fat, and skin taken from other parts of your body (usually your belly, back, or buttock). This new breast-like shape should last the rest of your life. Women who are very thin or obese, smoke, or have serious health problems often cannot have tissue flap surgery.

Healing after tissue flap surgery often takes longer than healing after breast implant surgery. You may have other problems, as well. For example, if you have a muscle removed, you might lose strength in the area from which it was taken. Or, you may get an infection or have trouble healing. Tissue flap surgery is best done by a reconstructive plastic surgeon who has special training in this type of surgery and has done it many times before.

Compare the Types of Surgery

The charts in this section can help you compare the different surgeries with each other. See how the surgeries are alike and how they are different.

Before Surgery

Is This Surgery Right for Me?

Breast-Sparing Surgery	Most women with DCIS or breast cancer can choose to have breast-sparing surgery, usually followed by radiation therapy.
Mastectomy	Most women with DCIS or breast cancer can choose to have a mastectomy. A mastectomy may be a better choice for you if: • You have small breasts and a large area of DCIS or cancer. • You have DCIS or cancer in more than one part of your breast. • The DCIS or cancer is under the nipple. • You are not able to receive radiation therapy.

Mastectomy with Reconstruction	If you have a mastectomy, you might also want breast reconstruction surgery.
	You can choose to have reconstruction surgery at the same time as your mastectomy or wait and have it later.

Recovering from Surgery

Will I Have Pain?

Most people have some pain after surgery.

Talk with your doctor or nurse before surgery about ways to control pain after surgery. Also, tell them if your pain control is not working.

How Long Before I Can Return to Normal Activities?

Breast-Sparing Surgery	Most women are ready to return to most of their usual activities within 5 to 10 days.
Mastectomy	It may take 3 to 4 weeks to feel mostly normal after a mastectomy.
Mastectomy with Reconstruction	Your recovery will depend on the type of reconstruction you have. It can take 6 to 8 weeks or longer to fully recover from breast reconstruction.

What Other Problems Might I Have?

Breast-Sparing Surgery	You may feel very tired and have skin changes from radiation therapy.
Mastectomy	You may feel out of balance if you had large breasts and do not have reconstruction surgery. This may also lead to neck and shoulder pain.
Mastectomy with Reconstruction	You may not like how your breast-like shape looks. If you have an implant: • Your breast may harden and can become painful. • You will likely need more surgery if your implant breaks or leaks. If you have flap surgery, you may lose strength in the part of your body where a muscle was removed.

What Other Types of Treatment Might I Need?

If you chose to have breast sparing surgery, you will usually need radiation therapy. Radiation treatments are usually given 5 days a week for 5 to 8 weeks.

If you have a mastectomy, you may still need radiation therapy. No matter which surgery you choose, you might need:

- Chemotherapy

- Hormone therapy

- Targeted therapy

Life after Surgery

What Will My Breast Look Like?

Breast-Sparing Surgery	Your breast should look a lot like it did before surgery. But if your tumor is large, your breast may look different or smaller after breast-sparing surgery. You will have a small scar where the surgeon cut to remove the DCIS or cancer. The length of the scar will depend on how large an incision the surgeon needed to make.
Mastectomy	Your breast and nipple will be removed. You will have a flat chest on the side of your body where the breast was removed. You will have a scar over the place where your breast was removed. The length of the scar will depend on the size of your breast. If you have smaller breasts, your scar is likely to be smaller than if you have larger breasts.
Mastectomy with Reconstruction	You will have a breast-like shape, but your breast will not look or feel like it did before surgery. And, it will not look or feel like your other breast. You will have scars where the surgeon stitched skin together to make the new breast-like shape. If you have tissue flap reconstruction, you will have scars around the new breast, as well as the area where the surgeon removed the muscle, fat, and skin to make the new breast-like shape.

To get a better idea of what to expect, ask your surgeon if you can see before and after pictures of other women who have had different types of surgery.

315

Remember, even though surgery leaves scars where the surgeon cut the skin and stitched it back together, they tend to fade over time.

Will My Breast Have Feeling?

Breast-Sparing Surgery	Yes. You should still have feeling in your breast, nipple, and areola (the dark area around your nipple).
Mastectomy	Maybe. After surgery, the skin around where the surgeon cut and maybe the area under your arm will be numb (have no feeling). This numb feeling may improve over 1 to 2 years, but it will never feel like it once did. Also, the skin where your breast was may feel tight.
Mastectomy with Reconstruction	No. The area around your breast will not have feeling.

Will I Need More Surgery?

Breast-Sparing Surgery	If the surgeon does not remove all the DCIS or cancer the first time, you may need more surgery.
Mastectomy	If you have problems after your mastectomy, you may need more surgery.
Mastectomy with Reconstruction	You will need more than one surgery to build a new breast-like shape. The number of surgeries you need will depend on the type of reconstruction you have and if you choose to have a nipple or areola added. Some women may also decide to have surgery on the opposite breast to help it match the new breast-like shape better. If you have an implant, you are likely to need surgery many years later to remove or replace it.

With all three surgeries, you may need more surgery to remove lymph nodes from under your arm. Having your lymph nodes removed can cause lymphedema.

Will the Type of Surgery I Have Affect How Long I Live?

No. Research has shown that women who have breast-sparing surgery live as long as women who have a mastectomy. This does not change if you also have reconstruction.

316

What Are the Chances That My Cancer Will Return in the Same Area?

Breast-Sparing Surgery	There is a chance that your cancer will come back in the same breast. But if it does, it is not likely to affect how long you live. About 10% of women (1 out of every 10) who have breast-sparing surgery along with radiation therapy get cancer in the same breast within 12 years. If this happens, you can be effectively treated with a mastectomy.
Mastectomy	There is a smaller chance that your cancer will return in the same area than if you have breast-sparing surgery. About 5% of women (1 out of every 20) who have a mastectomy will get cancer on the same side of their chest within 12 years.
Mastectomy with Reconstruction	Your chances are the same as mastectomy, since breast reconstruction surgery does not affect the chances of the cancer returning.

Think about What Is Important to You

After you have talked with a breast cancer surgeon and learned the facts, you may also want to talk with your spouse or partner, family, friends, or other women who have had breast cancer surgery.

Then, think about what is important to you. Thinking about these questions and talking them over with others might help:

About Surgery Choices

- If I have breast-sparing surgery, am I willing and able to have radiation therapy 5 days a week for 5 to 8 weeks?

- If I have a mastectomy, do I also want breast reconstruction surgery?

- If I have breast reconstruction surgery, do I want it at the same time as my mastectomy?

- What treatment does my insurance cover? What do I have to pay for?

Life after Surgery

- How important is it to me how my breast looks after cancer surgery?

- How important is it to me how my breast feels after cancer surgery?

- If I have a mastectomy and do not have reconstruction, will my insurance cover my prostheses and special bras?

- Where can I find breast prostheses and special bras?

Learning More

- Do I want a second opinion?

- Is there someone else I should talk with about my surgery choices?

- What else do I want to learn or do before I make my choice about breast cancer surgery?

Section 40.2

Mastectomy and Lumpectomy

"Mastectomy and Lumpectomy,"
© 2016 Omnigraphics, Inc.
Reviewed April 2016.

What Are Mastectomy and Lumpectomy?

Mastectomy is a type of surgery that involves the complete removal of tissue from one breast (called a unilateral mastectomy) or both breasts (bilateral mastectomy). Mastectomy is usually performed as a form of treatment for breast cancer, although it may also be used as a method of preventing breast cancer in people who are at very high risk of developing it due to a strong family history or genetic mutations (known as preventative, prophylactic, or risk-reducing mastectomy).

Lumpectomy is a less-invasive form of surgery that involves removing only the cancerous or abnormal tissue from the breast. The surgery is usually followed by radiation therapy to eliminate any cancerous cells that may remain in the breast. Since only a portion of the breast is removed, lumpectomy is also known as breast-conserving surgery or excisional biopsy. Lumpectomy is also sometimes performed to help confirm or rule out a diagnosis of breast cancer.

Both mastectomy and lumpectomy are often presented as treatment options for women with early-stage breast cancer. Studies have shown that the long-term survival rates for mastectomy are the same as for lumpectomy plus radiation therapy. In addition, the risk of cancer spreading beyond the breast to other organs is the same for the two procedures. However, lumpectomy carries a slightly higher risk of recurrence of cancer in the same area.

The main benefit of lumpectomy is the preservation of breast tissue, although newer mastectomy and breast reconstruction techniques can preserve breast skin and provide a more natural appearance following surgery. A potential benefit of mastectomy is that the patient is less likely to require radiation therapy, which involves side effects and can be time consuming. The characteristics of the tumor, rather than the type of surgery, determines whether a patient requires chemotherapy or other types of drug therapies. Deciding between the two procedures can be difficult for many patients, and it requires a careful consideration of the advantages and disadvantages of each.

Advantages and Disadvantages of Mastectomy

One of the main reasons some women opt for mastectomy is that it offers peace of mind. Removing the entire breast eliminates the possibility of recurrence and also reduces the likelihood of radiation therapy. Some patients simply want to get rid of the cancer and be done with it. Mastectomy offers advantages over lumpectomy plus radiation in other situations, as well. It is often recommended for patients who:

- have multiple or widespread malignancies in separate areas of the breast

- have previously undergone lumpectomy but still have cancer cells on the margins of the surgical area

- have previously undergone radiation treatment but experienced a recurrence of breast cancer

- have a gene mutation that increases the chance of recurrence

- have a tumor that is large compared to the overall size of the breast, which reduces the likelihood that lumpectomy will produce acceptable cosmetic results

- cannot tolerate radiation due to pregnancy, connective tissue disease, or other health conditions

- live too far from a treatment facility to have radiation treatment for five to seven weeks

For many women, the main disadvantage of mastectomy is that it means a complete and permanent loss of the breast. The surgery is more invasive than lumpectomy, so it requires general anesthesia and an overnight hospital stay. It often involves more post-surgery side effects, and the recovery time tends to be longer. In addition, many patients who undergo mastectomy have further reconstructive surgery to restore the appearance of the breast.

Advantages and Disadvantages of Lumpectomy

Given the option, many women opt for lumpectomy because it preserves as much breast tissue as possible. Some patients feel strongly about keeping their breast and maintaining its normal appearance and sensation. Lumpectomy is also a less-invasive surgery than mastectomy, so the recovery time is likely to be shorter. It is often recommended for patients who have pre-cancerous breast abnormalities or malignancies that are small, localized, and at an early stage.

Lumpectomy also has a few potential disadvantages, however, including the following:

- Most patients require five to seven weeks of daily radiation therapy following surgery

- Additional surgeries may be required following the lumpectomy if the pathologist finds cancer cells in the margins around the tumor that was removed

- It involves a slightly higher risk of recurrence than mastectomy

- If there is a recurrence in the same breast, it will usually require a mastectomy because the breast tissue cannot tolerate additional radiation

Deciding between Mastectomy and Lumpectomy

Patients who are offered a choice between mastectomy and lumpectomy plus radiation must weigh the advantages and disadvantages of each procedure. Personal preferences play an important role in the decision. Some factors to consider include the patient's feelings about keeping her breast and ensuring that her breasts match in size and shape. In addition, the patient must decide whether she will worry about the recurrence of breast cancer if she has a lumpectomy.

The decision of whether to have a mastectomy or lumpectomy may also be influenced by where the patient lives. Research has shown that American women are more likely to have mastectomies than women in other countries. Within the United States, mastectomy is most common in the Midwest and South, while lumpectomy is more prevalent on the East Coast and West Coast. The distance a patient must drive to reach a radiation center may also affect her decision.

Finally, the doctor and hospital that provide the treatment may influence the patient's decision whether to have a lumpectomy or mastectomy. University-based hospitals tend to perform more lumpectomies, while community-based hospitals tend to perform more mastectomies. Likewise, older surgeons who were trained prior to 1980, when mastectomy was the standard treatment for all stages of breast cancer, are less likely to recommend lumpectomy. As a result, patients who feel strongly about one procedure or the other may wish to seek a second opinion to more fully understand their options.

References

1. "Deciding between Mastectomy or Lumpectomy." Susan G. Komen Foundation, July 24, 2015.

2. "Mastectomy vs. Lumpectomy." BreastCancer.org, 2016.

3. "Tests and Procedures: Lumpectomy." Mayo Clinic, October 23, 2014.

4. "Tests and Procedures: Mastectomy." Mayo Clinic, October 22, 2014.

Section 40.3

Breast Reconstruction Surgery

This section contains text excerpted from the following sources:
Text beginning with the heading "Breast Reconstruction with
Implants–Understanding the Procedure" is excerpted from "Breast
Reconstruction with Sientra Silicone Gel Breast Implants,"
U.S. Food and Drug Administration (FDA), February 15, 2012.
Reviewed April 2016; Text beginning with the heading "What
Factors Can Affect the Choice of Breast Reconstruction Method?"
is excerpted from "Breast Reconstruction After Mastectomy,"
National Cancer Institute (NCI), February 12, 2013.

Breast Reconstruction with Implants–Understanding the Procedure

The surgical procedure for breast reconstruction with implants consists of choices you and your surgical team (surgeon(s), nurses, anesthetist, etc.) will make as you plan your surgery. If you are continuing treatment for cancer (like chemotherapy or radiation), your surgeon(s) should consult with your oncologist. For breast reconstruction, the type of procedure that is available to you depends on your medical situation, breast shape and size, general health, lifestyle, and goals for the reconstruction. The outcome of a mastectomy will affect the amount of breast tissue left to cover a breast implant.

Breast Reconstruction with Implants–Staging the Procedures

Breast reconstruction is usually done in stages. It often takes more than one surgery. A primary (first) reconstruction after mastectomy is often started during the same surgery as your mastectomy, but you may need follow-up surgeries to finish and make the reconstructed breast match the other breast. The stages may include

- Putting in a soft tissue expander, an implanted silicone shell that can be filled with more and more saline solution to slowly stretch your skin enough to allow it to cover an implant (more information is provided below),

- Taking out the tissue expander and putting in a breast implant (silicone gel-filled or saline-filled),

- Surgery to adjust the shape and or size of the opposite breast so it matches the reconstructed breast, and

- Nipple reconstruction (if you have a mastectomy, the nipple is usually removed; usually a new nipple is created later, as an outpatient procedure after the initial reconstruction surgery is finished; a nipple may be created using skin taken from the opposite breast or another part of your body).

Use of Tissue Expander(s) in Breast Reconstruction Surgery

Placing a tissue expander may be one step in your breast reconstruction. If you are having a mastectomy, the surgeon will remove breast tissue and also some skin. Afterwards, your chest will be flatter and tighter. For many women (especially if you had small-to-medium-sized breasts before your mastectomy), there will not be enough skin and tissue to cover a breast implant comfortably; the breast "pocket" (space for an implant) will be too small.

Placing an implant in a breast pocket that is too small can cause complications such as drooping or sagging at an earlier age, implant extrusion, skin wrinkling, infection, and hematoma. You may also be able to feel folds on the implant created by the implant being squeezed tightly by the surrounding skin and other breast-area tissue.

Tissue expanders (also called soft-tissue expanders) are devices that are used when there is not enough skin or breast tissue to cover an implant. They are made of a silicone elastomer (stretchy, rubbery silicone) shell like a breast implant but are empty of filler when they are put in your breast. The tissue expander has a port (valve) that will lie under your skin after it is placed. Your surgeon can then gradually fill the tissue expander with sterile saline solution (salt water) over several weeks or months by injecting the saline into the device through the port under your skin. As the device expands, it will cause your breast skin and tissues to stretch like a woman's abdomen stretches during pregnancy. Eventually, the skin and breast tissue are stretched enough to create a space for your breast implant, as shown in Figure 41.1. below.

A tissue expander can be placed at the time of your mastectomy or months or years later. Your reconstruction surgeon can tell you whether tissue expansion may be necessary in your case.

The tissue expander is placed surgically, usually in an operating room under general anesthesia. You may be able to go home the same day or may stay overnight at the hospital. Most women can go back to their usual activities within 2 to 3 weeks after the expander is placed. If you have a tissue expander placed during the same surgery as your mastectomy, the breast tissues are usually numb from the mastectomy; you may not feel pain after the tissue expander surgery. You will probably feel tightness, pressure, or discomfort each time the tissue expander is filled with saline. This can last a week or more, but goes away as the skin and tissues stretch. Tissue expansion may take up to 4 to 6 months.

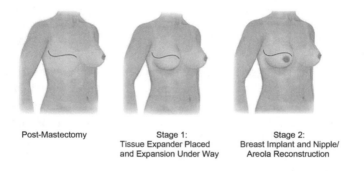

Post-Mastectomy

Stage 1:
Tissue Expander Placed
and Expansion Under Way

Stage 2:
Breast Implant and Nipple/
Areola Reconstruction

Figure 40.1. *Breast Reconstruction Using a Tissue Expander and Breast Implant*

Breast Reconstruction without Implants (Tissue Flap Reconstruction)

A tissue flap is skin, fat, and/or muscle taken from another part of your body, like your stomach, back, hip, or bottom. Two kinds of flaps are usually used for breast reconstruction surgeries: a flap from your stomach (called a "TRAM flap") or a flap from your back (called a "latissimus dorsi flap"). In each case, the flap is moved to the chest where it is shaped into a new breast. In some cases, a tissue flap is used just to provide more skin or tissue, for example, to cover an implant.

Breast reconstruction using only your own tissue flap is major surgery and you will likely have a longer recovery time than for breast reconstruction using just a breast implant. Some women who have a tissue flap reconstruction return to their normal activities after a few weeks. Others may take up to a full year to get back to their normal lifestyle.

An advantage of breast reconstruction using a tissue flap may be that usually no other procedures are needed to make the opposite (unaffected) breast match the reconstructed breast.

TRAM Flap

The TRAM flap (the transverse rectus abdominis musculocutaneous flap) is named for the section of the abdomen from which the tissue flap is taken—that consists of the transverse rectus abdominis muscle and some tissue (skin, fat, connective tissue, and vascular [blood vessels] tissue) surrounding it. As shown in Figure 40.2. below, during a TRAM flap procedure your doctor will take the TRAM flap from your abdomen and move it to your breast to replace the breast tissue that was lost during your cancer surgery.

The TRAM flap procedure is done in the hospital under general anesthesia. Your hospital stay may range from 2 to 5 days. The recovery time may be 6 to 8 weeks. You will have two incision site s (on your abdomen and on your breast) resulting in two wounds to heal after surgery and, therefore, two scars. Both TRAM flap methods can cause temporary or permanent muscle weakness in your tummy (because the muscles there have been cut).

If you are considering becoming pregnant after your reconstruction, discuss this with your doctors before surgery. You will have a large scar on your abdomen and scarring on your reconstructed breast(s) that may be affected as your skin stretches to accommodate a growing baby.

The TRAM flap procedure can be done two ways. In one method, the tissue flap is removed from your abdomen but the blood vessels are not cut. The TRAM flap is then moved through a tunnel made under your skin up to the breast area where it is sutured into place to create the new breast. This is called a "pedicle" TRAM flap procedure. It usually takes 3 to 6 hours in surgery to complete.

The other possibility is a "free" TRAM flap. In this case, the tissue is taken from your abdomen and the blood supply is cut. The flap is taken off completely from your tummy and then relocated and sutured in place to create the new breast. The doctor must reconnect blood vessels at the breast site. This is a very involved procedure: your surgeon will need to use a microscope to do it and it usually takes longer than a pedicle TRAM fl ap procedure. Your surgical team may ask a surgeon who specializes in surgery using a microscope to reconnect blood vessels to do that part of your procedure (a vascular surgeon). You may need to have a blood transfusion during or after a free TRAM flap procedure.

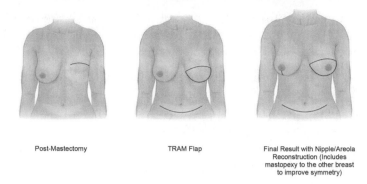

Post-Mastectomy   TRAM Flap   Final Result with Nipple/Areola
                                            Reconstruction (Includes
                                            mastopexy to the other breast
                                            to improve symmetry)

Figure 40.2. *Breast Reconstruction Using a Tram Flap*

Latissimus Dorsi Flap

Breast Reconstruction Using a Latissimus Dorsi Flap is illustrated below in Figure 40.3. During latissimus dorsi flap reconstruction, a section of tissue [skin, fat, connective tissue, and vascular (blood vessels) tissue] is taken from your back. A latissimus dorsi flap is usually smaller than a TRAM flap, so this procedure may be better for a woman with smaller breasts.

The latissimus dorsi flap procedure usually takes 2 to 4 hours of surgery. It is done in a hospital under general anesthesia. Most patients can resume their normal activities after 2 to 3 weeks.

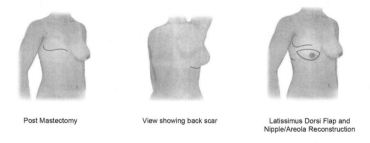

Post Mastectomy   View showing back scar   Latissimus Dorsi Flap and
                                                  Nipple/Areola Reconstruction

Figure 40.3. *Breast Reconstruction Using a Latissimus Dorsi Flap*

Complications Associated with Flap Reconstruction

Flap reconstruction is major surgery, especially TRAM flap reconstruction. It is more involved than a mastectomy and more involved than reconstruction with implants. Patients who choose this method of reconstruction should be in good general health and have strong emotional motivation. If you are very overweight, smoke cigarettes, have had other surgeries at the flap site, or have circulatory problems (problems with your heart or blood vessels), you may not be a good candidate for tissue flap reconstruction. If you are very thin, you may not be able to have tissue flap reconstruction because there may not be enough extra tissue on your abdomen or back to form a new breast. Complications of flap reconstruction procedures may include:

- Temporary or permanent muscle weakness in your abdominal muscles for TRAM flap and in your back or side for latissimus dorsi flap

- Distorted navel (belly button) and/or the need for the doctor to build a new belly button after the TRAM procedure

- Loss of feeling in the abdomen and/or reconstructed breast. You will probably not have normal sensation in that breast because nerves are cut during the surgery.

- A blood transfusion is sometimes necessary after a free TRAM flap procedure.

Choosing Breast Reconstruction with Breast Implants

Your doctor(s) can tell you whether you are a good candidate for breast reconstruction with implants, given your health and medical condition. Your surgeon may recommend some other procedures for the opposite (non-implanted) breast to make your breasts look more symmetrical after reconstruction. The other procedures may include:

- Having an implant in the other breast (contralateral augmentation mammoplasty),

- Having the other breast made smaller (contralateral reduction mammoplasty) by surgically removing breast tissue and skin, or

- Having a surgery to lift one or both breasts (Mastopexy) so they are at the same level on your chest. This is done by surgically removing a strip of skin from under your breast or around your nipple to lift and tighten the skin.

If you do not want to change your unaffected breast, discuss this with your surgeon well before the surgery so he or she can plan the procedure to give you the best result.

Choosing the Right Implant for You

Implants are available in several different shapes, profiles (the contour the implant provides to your body), and sizes to help each woman achieve the result that is best for her body. If you are having one breast reconstructed, but the other one is not affected, you and your doctor can choose the implant that will most closely match your unaffected breast.

When you and your doctor decide what you want your breasts to look like after reconstruction, your doctor can help you choose the right implant to get the effect you want. Your body type, height, and weight will be factors your surgeon considers to help you achieve the best result.

Table 40.1. Silicone Gel Breast Implant Designs

Silicone Gel Breast Implant Designs			
Implant Shell Texture	Implant Shape	Implant Profile	Volume Range
Smooth	Round	Moderate	80–700 cc
		High	95–695 cc
Textured	Round	Low	60–700 cc
		Moderate/High	95–695 cc
Textured	Shaped Superior Pole	Low	170–500 cc
		Moderate/High	170–700 cc
		High	180–550 cc
Textured	Shaped Superior Pole	Moderate	115–690 cc

Implant Size, Shape, and Surface

Your surgeon will examine your breast tissue and skin to figure out if you will have enough to cover the implant. This is especially important after mastectomy. It is possible that you will not have enough skin and/or breast tissue left to cover an implant. In this case, you may be offered several choices.

Breast implants that are too big for the amount of breast tissue or skin can cause problems. For example, your breasts may droop or sag earlier with implants that are too large. Implants that are too large can also cause implant extrusion, skin wrinkling, infection, and hematoma. You may be able to feel folds on the implant created by it being squeezed too tightly by the surrounding tissue and skin. If you do not have enough skin, and it is stretched too thin over the implant, you may be able to feel or see the edges of the implant under your skin surface after surgery.

What Factors Can Affect the Choice of Breast Reconstruction Method?

Most women can choose their type of breast reconstruction method based on what is important to them. However, some treatment issues are important to think about. For example, radiation therapy can damage a reconstructed breast, especially if it contains an implant. Therefore, if a woman knows she needs radiation therapy after mastectomy, that information may affect her decision.

Sometimes, a woman may not know whether she needs radiation therapy until after her mastectomy. This can make planning ahead for an immediate reconstruction difficult. In this case, it may be helpful for the woman to talk with a reconstructive surgeon in addition to her breast surgeon or oncologist before choosing the type of reconstructive surgery.

Other factors that can influence the type of reconstructive surgery a woman chooses include the size and shape of the breast that is being replaced, the woman's age and health, the availability of autologous tissue, and the location of the breast tumor.

Each type of reconstruction has factors that a woman should think about before making a decision. Some of the more common concerns are listed below.

Reconstruction with Implants

Surgery and recovery

- Enough skin and muscle must remain after mastectomy to cover the implant

- Shorter surgical procedure than for reconstruction with autologous tissue; little blood loss

- Recovery period may be shorter

- Many follow-up visits may be needed to inflate the expander and insert the implant

Possible complications

- Infection

- Pooling of blood (hematoma) within the reconstructed breast

- Extrusion of the implant (the implant breaks through the skin)

- Implant rupture (the implant breaks open and saline or silicone leaks into the surrounding tissue)

- Formation of hard scar tissue around the implant (known as a contracture)

Other considerations

- Can be damaged by radiation therapy

- May not be adequate for women with very large breasts

- Will not last a lifetime; the longer a woman has implants, the more likely she is to have complications and to need to have her implants removed or replaced

- Silicone implants may provide a more natural-looking breast shape than saline

- The U.S. Food and Drug Administration (FDA) recommends that women with silicone implants undergo periodic MRI screenings to detect possible "silent" rupture of the implants

Reconstruction with Autologous Tissue

Surgery and recovery

- Longer surgical procedure than for implants; more blood loss

- Recovery period may be longer

- Pedicled flap reconstruction is a shorter operation than free flap but requires more donor tissue

- Free flap reconstruction uses less donor tissue than pedicled flap reconstruction but is a longer, highly technical operation requiring a surgeon with experience re-attaching blood vessels

Possible complications

- Necrosis (death) of the transferred tissue

- Blood clots

- Pain and weakness at the site from which the donor tissue was taken

- Obesity, diabetes, and smoking may increase the rate of complications

Other considerations

• May provide a more natural breast shape than implants

• Less likely to be damaged by radiation therapy than implants

• Leaves a scar at the site from which the donor tissue was taken

Any type of breast reconstruction can fail if healing does not occur properly. In these cases, the implant or flap will have to be removed. If an implant reconstruction fails, a woman can sometimes have a second reconstruction using autologous tissue. If an autologous tissue reconstruction fails, a second flap cannot be moved to the breast area, and an implant cannot be used for another reconstruction attempt due to the lack of chest tissue available to cover the implant.

What Type of Follow-Up Care and Rehabilitation Is Needed after Breast Reconstruction?

Any type of reconstruction increases the number of side effects a woman may experience compared with those after a mastectomy alone. A woman's medical team will watch her closely after surgery for complications, some of which can occur months or even years later.

Women who have autologous tissue reconstruction may need physical therapy to help them make up for weakness experienced at the site from which the donor tissue was taken, such as abdominal weakness. A physical therapist can help a woman use exercises to regain strength, adjust to new physical limitations, and figure out the safest ways to perform everyday activities.

Will Health Insurance Pay for Breast Reconstruction?

Since 1999, the Women's Health and Cancer Rights Act (WHCRA) has required group health plans, insurance companies, and HMOs that offer mastectomy coverage to also pay for reconstructive surgery after mastectomy. This coverage must include reconstruction of the other breast to give a more balanced look, breast prostheses, and treatment of all physical complications of the mastectomy, including lymphedema.

WHCRA does not apply to Medicare and Medicaid recipients. Some health plans sponsored by religious organizations and some government health plans may also be exempt from WHCRA.

A woman considering breast reconstruction may want to discuss costs and health insurance coverage with her doctor and insurance company before choosing to have the surgery. Some insurance companies require a second opinion before they will agree to pay for a surgery.

Does Breast Reconstruction Affect the Ability to Check for Breast Cancer Recurrence?

Studies have shown that breast reconstruction does not increase the chances of breast cancer coming back or make it harder to check for recurrence with mammography.

Women who have one breast removed by mastectomy will still have mammograms of the other breast. Women who have had a skin-sparing mastectomy or who are at high risk of breast cancer recurrence may have mammograms of the reconstructed breast if it was reconstructed using autologous tissue. However, mammograms are generally not performed on breasts that are reconstructed with an implant after mastectomy.

A woman with a breast implant should tell the radiology technician about her implant before she has a mammogram. Special procedures may be necessary to improve the accuracy of the mammogram and to avoid damaging the implant.

Chapter 41

Radiation Therapy for Breast Cancer

Radiation Therapy

Radiation therapy (also called radiotherapy) is a cancer treatment that uses high doses of radiation to kill cancer cells and shrink tumors. At low doses, radiation is used in X-rays to see inside your body, as with X-rays of your teeth or broken bones.

How Radiation Therapy Works against Cancer

At high doses, radiation kills cancer cells or slows their growth. Radiation therapy is used to:

- **Treat cancer**

  Radiation can be used to cure cancer, to prevent it from returning, or to stop or slow its growth.

- **Ease cancer symptoms**

  Radiation may be used to shrink a tumor to treat pain and other problems caused by the tumor. Or, it can lessen problems that

---

This chapter includes text excerpted from "Radiation Therapy," National Cancer Institute (NCI), April 29, 2015.

may be caused by a growing tumor, such as trouble breathing or loss of bowel and bladder control.

Radiation therapy does not kill cancer cells right away. It takes days or weeks of treatment before cancer cells start to die. Then, cancer cells keep dying for weeks or months after radiation therapy ends.

Types of Radiation Therapy

There are two main types of radiation therapy, external beam and internal.

1. External Beam Radiation Therapy

External beam radiation therapy comes from a machine that aims radiation at your cancer. The machine is large and may be noisy. It does not touch you, but can move around you, sending radiation to a part of your body from many directions.

External beam radiation therapy treats a specific part of your body. For example, if you have cancer in your lung, you will have radiation only to your chest, not to your whole body.

2. Internal Radiation Therapy

Internal radiation therapy is a treatment in which a source of radiation is put inside your body. The radiation source can be solid or liquid.

Internal radiation therapy with a solid source is called brachytherapy. In this type of treatment, radiation in the form of seeds, ribbons, or capsules is placed in your body in or near the cancer.

You receive liquid radiation through an IV line. Liquid radiation travels throughout your body, seeking out and killing cancer cells.

Who Receives Radiation Therapy

External beam radiation therapy is used to treat many types of cancer. For some people, radiation may be the only treatment you need. But, most often, you will have radiation therapy and other cancer treatments, such as surgery and chemotherapy.

Brachytherapy is used to treat cancers of the head and neck, breast, cervix, prostate, and eye.

Liquid forms of internal radiation are most often used to treat thyroid cancer.

How Radiation Is Used with Other Cancer Treatments

Radiation may be given before, during, or after surgery. Doctors may use radiation:

- Before surgery, to shrink the size of the cancer.

- During surgery, so that it goes straight to the cancer without passing through the skin. Radiation therapy used this way is called intraoperative radiation.

- After surgery, to kill any cancer cells that may remain.

Radiation may also be given before, during, or after other cancer treatments to shrink the cancer or to kill any cancer cells that might remain.

Radiation Therapy Can Cause Side Effects

Radiation not only kills or slows the growth of cancer cells, it can also affect nearby healthy cells. Damage to healthy cells can cause side effects. External radiation and brachytherapy cause side effects only in the part of the body being treated.

The most common side effect of radiation therapy is fatigue, which is feeling exhausted and worn out. Fatigue can happen all at once or little by little. People feel fatigue in different ways. You may feel more or less fatigue than someone else who is also getting radiation therapy.

You can prepare for fatigue by:

- Asking someone to drive you to and from radiation therapy

- Planning time to rest

- Asking for help with meals and childcare

Healthy cells that are damaged during radiation treatment almost always recover after it is over. But sometimes people may have side effects that are severe or do not improve. Other side effects may show up months or years after radiation therapy is over. These are called late effects.

Doctors try to protect healthy cells during treatment by:

- **Using as low a dose of radiation as possible**

  The radiation dose is balanced between being high enough to kill cancer cells, yet low enough to limit damage to healthy cells.

- **Spreading out treatment over time**

  You may get radiation therapy once a day, or in smaller doses twice a day for several weeks. Spreading out the radiation dose allows normal cells to recover while cancer cells die.

- **Aiming radiation at a precise part of your body**

  With external radiation therapy, for example, your doctor is able to aim high doses of radiation at your cancer while reducing the amount of radiation that reaches nearby healthy tissue. These treatments use a computer to deliver precise radiation doses to a tumor or to specific areas within the tumor.

How Much Radiation Therapy Costs

Radiation therapy can be expensive. It uses complex machines and involves the services of many health care providers. The exact cost of your radiation therapy depends on the cost of health care where you live, what kind of radiation therapy you get, and how many treatments you need.

Talk with your health insurance company about what services it will pay for. Most insurance plans pay for radiation therapy. To learn more, talk with the business office at the clinic or hospital where you go for treatment. If you need financial assistance, there are organizations that may be able to help. To find such organizations, go to the National Cancer Institute database, Organizations that Offer Support Services and search for "financial assistance." Or call toll-free 1-800-4-CANCER (1-800-422-6237) to ask for information on organizations that may help.

What to Expect When Having External Beam Radiation Therapy

How Often Will You Have Treatment

Most people have external beam radiation therapy with the same dose of radiation once a day, 5 days a week, Monday through Friday. Treatment lasts up to 6 weeks, depending on the type of cancer you have and the treatment goal. This span of time is called a course of treatment.

Sometimes, the radiation dose or schedule is changed to reach the total dose of radiation more quickly. This can be done in one of these ways:

- Accelerated fractionation, which gives the half of the usual daily dose of radiation twice each day.

- Hyperfractionation, which is a smaller than usual daily dose of radiation given twice each day.

- Hypofractionation, which is a larger than usual daily dose of radiation given once a day for up to 3 weeks.

The doctor may prescribe one of these treatment schedules if he or she feels that it will work better for the type of cancer you have.

Where You Go for Treatment

Most of the time, you will get external beam radiation therapy as an outpatient. This means that you will have treatment at a clinic or radiation therapy center and will not stay the night in the hospital.

What Happens before Your First Treatment

You will have a 1- to 2-hour meeting with your doctor or nurse before you begin radiation therapy. At this time, you will have a physical exam, talk about your medical history, and maybe have imaging tests. Your doctor or nurse will discuss external beam radiation therapy, its benefits and side effects, and ways you can care for yourself during and after treatment. You can then choose whether to have external beam radiation therapy.

If you decide to have external beam radiation therapy, you will be scheduled for a treatment planning session called a simulation. At this time:

- A radiation oncologist (a doctor who specializes in using radiation to treat cancer) and radiation therapist will figure out your treatment area. You may also hear the treatment area referred to as the treatment port or treatment field. These terms refer to the places in your body that will get radiation. You will be asked to lie very still while X-rays or scans are taken.

- The radiation therapist will tattoo or draw small dots of colored ink on your skin to mark the treatment area. These dots will be needed throughout your course of radiation therapy. The radiation therapist will use them to make sure you are in exactly the same position for every treatment. The dots are about the size of a freckle. If the dots are tattooed, they will remain on your skin for the rest of your life. Ink markings will fade over time. Be careful not to remove them and tell the radiation therapist if they have faded or lost color.

- A body mold may be made of the part of the body that is being treated. This is a plastic or plaster form that keeps you from moving during treatment. It also helps make sure that you are in exactly the same position for each treatment

- If you are getting radiation to the head and neck area you may be fitted for a mask. The mask has many air holes. It attaches to the table where you will lie for your treatments. The mask helps keep your head from moving so that you are in exactly the same position for each treatment.

What to Wear for Your Treatments

Wear clothes that are comfortable and made of soft fabric, such as fleece or cotton. Choose clothes that are easy to take off, since you may need to expose the treatment area or change into a hospital gown. Do not wear clothes that are tight, such as close-fitting collars or waist-bands, near your treatment area. Also, do not wear jewelry, adhesive bandages, or powder in the treatment area.

What Happens during a Treatment Session

- You may be asked to change into a hospital gown or robe.

- You will go to the treatment room where you will receive radiation. The temperature in this room will be very cool.

- Depending on where your cancer is, you will either lie down on a treatment table or sit in a special chair. The radiation therapist will use the dots on your skin and body mold or face mask, if you have one, to help you get into the right position.

- You may see colored lights pointed at your skin marks. These lights are harmless and help the therapist position you for treatment.

- You will need to stay very still so the radiation goes to the exact same place each time. You will get radiation for 1 to 5 minutes. During this time, you can breathe normally.

The radiation therapist will leave the room just before your treatment begins. He or she will go to a nearby room to control the radiation machine. The therapist watches you on a TV screen or through a window and talks with you through a speaker in the treatment room. Make sure to tell the therapist if you feel sick or are uncomfortable.

He or she can stop the radiation machine at any time. You will hear the radiation machine and see it moving around, but you won't be able to feel, hear, see, or smell the radiation.

Most visits last from 30 minutes to an hour, with most of that time spent helping you get into the correct position.

How to Relax for Treatment Sessions

Keep yourself busy while you wait:

- Read a book or magazine.

- Work on crossword puzzles or needlework.

- Use headphones to listen to music or recorded books.

- Meditate, breathe deeply, pray, use imagery, or find other ways to relax.

External Beam Radiation Therapy Will Not Make You Radioactive

People often wonder if they will be radioactive when they are having treatment with radiation. External beam radiation therapy will not make you radioactive. You may safely be around other people, even pregnant women, babies, and young children.

What to Expect When Having Internal Radiation Therapy

What Happens before Your First Treatment

You will have a 1- to 2-hour meeting with your doctor or nurse to plan your treatment before you begin internal radiation therapy. At this time, you will have a physical exam, talk about your medical history, and maybe have imaging tests. Your doctor will discuss the type of internal radiation therapy that is best for you, its benefits and side effects, and ways you can care for yourself during and after treatment. You can then decide whether to have internal radiation therapy.

How Brachytherapy Is Put in Place

Most brachytherapy is put in place through a catheter, which is a small, stretchy tube. Sometimes, brachytherapy is put in place through a larger device called an applicator. The way the brachytherapy is put in place depends on your type of cancer. Your doctor will place the catheter or applicator into your body before you begin treatment.

Once the catheter or applicator is in place, the radiation source is placed inside it. The radiation source may be kept in place for a few minutes, for many days, or for the rest of your life. How long it remains in place depends on the type of radiation source, your type of cancer, where the cancer is in your body, your health, and other cancer treatments you have had.

Types of Brachytherapy

There are three types of brachytherapy:

- **Low-dose rate (LDR) implants**

  In this type of brachytherapy, the radiation source stays in place for 1 to 7 days. You are likely to be in the hospital during this time. Once your treatment is finished, your doctor will remove the radiation source and the catheter or applicator.

- **High-dose rate (HDR) implants**

  In this type of brachytherapy, the radiation source is left in place for just 10 to 20 minutes at a time and then taken out. You may have treatment twice a day for 2 to 5 days or once a week for 2 to 5 weeks. The schedule depends on your type of cancer. During the course of treatment, your catheter or applicator may stay in place, or it may be put in place before each treatment. You may be in the hospital during this time, or you may make daily trips to the hospital to have the radiation source put in place. As with LDR implants, your doctor will remove the catheter or applicator once you have finished treatment.

- **Permanent implants**

  After the radiation source is put in place, the catheter is removed. The implants remain in your body for the rest of your life, but the radiation gets weaker each day. As time goes on, almost all the radiation will go away. When the radiation is first put in place, you may need to limit your time around other people and take other safety measures. Be extra careful not to spend time with children or pregnant women.

Internal Radiation Therapy Makes You Give off Radiation

With liquid radiation, your body fluids (urine, sweat, and saliva) will give off radiation for a while. With brachytherapy, your body fluids will not give off radiation, but the radiation source in your body will.

If the radiation you receive is a very high dose, you may need to follow some safety measures. These measures may include:

- Staying in a private hospital room to protect others from radiation coming from your body

- Being treated quickly by nurses and other hospital staff. They will provide all the care you need, but may stand at a distance, talk with you from the doorway of your room, and wear protective clothing.

Your visitors will also need to follow safety measures, which may include:

- Not being allowed to visit when the radiation is first put in

- Needing to check with the hospital staff before they go to your room

- Standing by the doorway rather than going into your hospital room

- Keeping visits short (30 minutes or less each day). The length of visits depends on the type of radiation being used and the part of your body being treated.

- Not having visits from pregnant women and children younger than a year old

You may also need to follow safety measures once you leave the hospital, such as not spending much time with other people. Your doctor or nurse will talk with you about any safety measures you should follow when you go home.

What to Expect When the Catheter Is Removed

Once you finish treatment with LDR or HDR implants, the catheter will be removed. Here are some things to expect:

- You will get medicine for pain before the catheter or applicator is removed.

- The area where the catheter or applicator was might be tender for a few months.

- There is no radiation in your body after the catheter or applicator is removed. It is safe for people to be near you—even young children and pregnant women.

For a week or two, you may need to limit activities that take a lot of effort. Ask your doctor what kinds of activities are safe for you and which ones you should avoid.

Special Diet Needs

Radiation can cause side effects that make it hard to eat, such as nausea, mouth sores, and throat problems called esophagitis. Since your body uses a lot of energy to heal during radiation therapy, it is important that you eat enough calories and protein to maintain your weight during treatment.

If you are having trouble eating and maintaining your weight, talk to your doctor or nurse. You might also find it helpful to speak with a dietitian.

Working during Radiation Therapy

Some people are able to work full-time during radiation therapy. Others can work only part-time or not at all. How much you are able to work depends on how you feel. Ask your doctor or nurse what you may expect from the treatment you will have.

You are likely to feel well enough to work when you first start your radiation treatments. As time goes on, do not be surprised if you are more tired, have less energy, or feel weak. Once you have finished treatment, it may take just a few weeks for you to feel better—or it could take months.

You may get to a point during your radiation therapy when you feel too sick to work. Talk with your employer to find out if you can go on medical leave. Check that your health insurance will pay for treatment while you are on medical leave.

Chapter 42

Chemotherapy for Breast Cancer

Chemotherapy

Chemotherapy (also called chemo) is a type of cancer treatment that uses drugs to kill cancer cells.

How Chemotherapy Works against Cancer

Chemotherapy works by stopping or slowing the growth of cancer cells, which grow and divide quickly. Chemotherapy is used to:

- **Treat cancer**

  Chemotherapy can be used to cure cancer, lessen the chance it will return, or stop or slow its growth.

- **Ease cancer symptoms**

  Chemotherapy can be used to shrink tumors that are causing pain and other problems.

Who Receives Chemotherapy

Chemotherapy is used to treat many types of cancer. For some people, chemotherapy may be the only treatment you receive. But

This chapter includes text excerpted from "Chemotherapy," National Cancer Institute (NCI), April 29, 2015.

most often, you will have chemotherapy and other cancer treatments. The types of treatment that you need depends on the type of cancer you have, if it has spread and where, and if you have other health problems.

How Chemotherapy Is Used with Other Cancer Treatments?

When used with other treatments, chemotherapy can:

- Make a tumor smaller before surgery or radiation therapy. This is called neoadjuvant chemotherapy.
- Destroy cancer cells that may remain after treatment with surgery or radiation therapy. This is called adjuvant chemotherapy.
- Help other treatments work better.
- Kill cancer cells that have returned or spread to other parts of your body.

Chemotherapy Can Cause Side Effects

Chemotherapy not only kills fast-growing cancer cells, but also kills or slows the growth of healthy cells that grow and divide quickly. Examples are cells that line your mouth and intestines and those that cause your hair to grow. Damage to healthy cells may cause side effects, such as mouth sores, nausea, and hair loss. Side effects often get better or go away after you have finished chemotherapy.

The most common side effect is fatigue, which is feeling exhausted and worn out. You can prepare for fatigue by:

- Asking someone to drive you to and from chemotherapy
- Planning time to rest on the day of and day after chemotherapy
- Asking for help with meals and childcare on the day of and at least one day after chemotherapy

There are many ways you can help manage chemotherapy side effects.

How Much Chemotherapy Costs

The cost of chemotherapy depends on:

- The types and doses of chemotherapy used

- How long and how often chemotherapy is given

- Whether you get chemotherapy at home, in a clinic or office, or during a hospital stay

- The part of the country where you live

Talk with your health insurance company about what services it will pay for. Most insurance plans pay for chemotherapy. To learn more, talk with the business office where you go for treatment.

If you need financial assistance, there are organizations that may be able to help. To find such organizations, go to the National Cancer Institute database, Organizations that Offer Support Services and search for "financial assistance." Or call toll-free 1-800-4-CANCER (1-800-422-6237) to ask for information on organizations that may help.

What to Expect When Receiving Chemotherapy?

How Chemotherapy Is Given

Chemotherapy may be given in many ways. Some common ways include:

- **Oral**

  The chemotherapy comes in pills, capsules, or liquids that you swallow

- **Intravenous (IV)**

  The chemotherapy goes directly into a vein

- **Injection**

  The chemotherapy is given by a shot in a muscle in your arm, thigh, or hip, or right under the skin in the fatty part of your arm, leg, or belly

- **Intrathecal**

  The chemotherapy is injected into the space between the layers of tissue that cover the brain and spinal cord

- **Intraperitoneal (IP)**

  The chemotherapy goes directly into the peritoneal cavity, which is the area in your body that contains organs such as your intestines, stomach, and liver

- **Intra-arterial (IA)**

  The chemotherapy is injected directly into the artery that leads to the cancer

- **Topical**

  The chemotherapy comes in a cream that you rub onto your skin Chemotherapy is often given through a thin needle that is placed in a vein on your hand or lower arm. Your nurse will put the needle in at the start of each treatment and remove it when treatment is over. IV chemotherapy may also be given through catheters or ports, sometimes with the help of a pump.

- **Catheter**

  A catheter is a thin, soft tube. A doctor or nurse places one end of the catheter in a large vein, often in your chest area. The other end of the catheter stays outside your body. Most catheters stay in place until you have finished your chemotherapy treatments. Catheters can also be used to give you other drugs and to draw blood. Be sure to watch for signs of infection around your catheter.

- **Port**

  A port is a small, round disc that is placed under your skin during minor surgery. A surgeon puts it in place before you begin your course of treatment, and it remains there until you have finished. A catheter connects the port to a large vein, most often in your chest. Your nurse can insert a needle into your port to give you chemotherapy or draw blood. This needle can be left in place for chemotherapy treatments that are given for longer than one day. Be sure to watch for signs of infection around your port.

- **Pump**

  Pumps are often attached to catheters or ports. They control how much and how fast chemotherapy goes into a catheter or port, allowing you to receive your chemotherapy outside of the hospital. Pumps can be internal or external. External pumps remain outside your body. Internal pumps are placed under your skin during surgery.

How Your Doctor Decides Which Chemotherapy Drugs to Give You

There are many different chemotherapy drugs. Which ones are included in your treatment plan depends mostly on:

- The type of cancer you have and how advanced it is

- Whether you have had chemotherapy before

- Whether you have other health problems, such as diabetes or heart disease

Where You Go for Treatment

You may receive chemotherapy during a hospital stay, at home, or as an outpatient at a doctor's office, clinic, or hospital. Outpatient means you do not stay overnight. No matter where you go for chemotherapy, your doctor and nurse will watch for side effects and help you manage them.

How Often You Receive Chemotherapy

Treatment schedules for chemotherapy vary widely. How often and how long you get chemotherapy depends on:

- Your type of cancer and how advanced it is

- Whether chemotherapy is used to:

  - Cure your cancer

  - Control its growth

  - Ease symptoms

- The type of chemotherapy you are getting

- How your body responds to the chemotherapy

You may receive chemotherapy in cycles. A cycle is a period of chemotherapy treatment followed by a period of rest. For instance, you might receive chemotherapy every day for 1 week followed by 3 weeks with no chemotherapy. These 4 weeks make up one cycle. The rest period gives your body a chance to recover and build new healthy cells

Missing a Treatment

It is best not to skip a chemotherapy treatment. But, sometimes your doctor may change your chemotherapy schedule if you are having certain side effects. If this happens, your doctor or nurse will explain what to do and when to start treatment again.

How Chemotherapy May Affect You

Chemotherapy affects people in different ways. How you feel depends on:

- The type of chemotherapy you are getting
- The dose of chemotherapy you are getting
- Your type of cancer
- How advanced your cancer is
- How healthy you are before treatment

Since everyone is different and people respond to chemotherapy in different ways, your doctor and nurses cannot know for sure how you will feel during chemotherapy.

How Will I Know If My Chemotherapy Is Working?

You will see your doctor often. During these visits, she will ask you how you feel, do a physical exam, and order medical tests and scans. Tests might include blood tests. Scans might include MRI, CT, or PET scans.

You cannot tell if chemotherapy is working based on its side effects. Some people think that severe side effects mean that chemotherapy is working well, or that no side effects mean that chemotherapy is not working. The truth is that side effects have nothing to do with how well chemotherapy is fighting your cancer.

Special Diet Needs

Chemotherapy can damage the healthy cells that line your mouth and intestines and cause eating problems. Tell your doctor or nurse if you have trouble eating while you are receiving chemotherapy. You might also find it helpful to speak with a dietitian.

Working during Chemotherapy

Many people can work during chemotherapy, as long as they match their work schedule to how they feel. Whether or not you can work may depend on what kind of job you have. If your job allows, you may want to see if you can work part-time or from home on days you do not feel well.

Many employers are required by law to change your work schedule to meet your needs during cancer treatment. Talk with your employer about ways to adjust your work during chemotherapy. You can learn more about these laws by talking with a social worker.

Chapter 43

Hormone Therapy for Breast Cancer

Chapter Contents

Section 43.1

What Is Hormone Therapy?

This section includes text excerpted from
"Hormone Therapy for Breast Cancer," National Cancer
Institute (NCI), August 2, 2012. Reviewed April 2016.

What Are Hormones?

Hormones are substances that function as chemical messengers in the body. They affect the actions of cells and tissues at various locations in the body, often reaching their targets through the bloodstream.

The hormones estrogen and progesterone are produced by the ovaries in premenopausal women and by some other tissues, including fat and skin, in both premenopausal and postmenopausal women. Estrogen promotes the development and maintenance of female sex characteristics and the growth of long bones. Progesterone plays a role in the menstrual cycle and pregnancy.

Estrogen and progesterone can also promote the growth of some breast cancers, which are called hormone-sensitive (or hormone-dependent) breast cancers.

How Do Hormones Stimulate the Growth of Breast Cancer?

Hormone-sensitive breast cancer cells contain proteins known as hormone receptors that become activated when hormones bind to them. The activated receptors cause changes in the expression of specific genes, which can lead to the stimulation of cell growth.

To determine whether breast cancer cells contain hormone receptors, doctors test samples of tumor tissue that have been removed by surgery. If the tumor cells contain estrogen receptors, the cancer is called estrogen receptor-positive (ER-positive), estrogen-sensitive, or estrogen-responsive. Similarly, if the tumor cells contain progesterone receptors, the cancer is called progesterone receptor-positive (PR- or PgR-positive). Approximately 70 percent of breast cancers are ER-positive. Most ER-positive breast cancers are also PR-positive.

Breast cancers that lack estrogen receptors are called estrogen receptor-negative (ER-negative). These tumors are estrogen-insensitive, meaning that they do not use estrogen to grow. Breast tumors that lack progesterone receptors are called progesterone receptor-negative.

What Is Hormone Therapy?

Hormone therapy (also called hormonal therapy, hormone treatment, or endocrine therapy) slows or stops the growth of hormone-sensitive tumors by blocking the body's ability to produce hormones or by interfering with hormone action. Tumors that are hormone-insensitive do not respond to hormone therapy.

Hormone therapy for breast cancer is not the same as menopausal hormone therapy or female hormone replacement therapy, in which hormones are given to reduce the symptoms of menopause.

What Types of Hormone Therapy Are Used for Breast Cancer?

Several strategies have been developed to treat hormone-sensitive breast cancer, including the following:

Blocking ovarian function: Because the ovaries are the main source of estrogen in premenopausal women, estrogen levels in these women can be reduced by eliminating or suppressing ovarian function. Blocking ovarian function is called ovarian ablation.

Ovarian ablation can be done surgically in an operation to remove the ovaries (called oophorectomy) or by treatment with radiation. This type of ovarian ablation is usually permanent.

Alternatively, ovarian function can be suppressed temporarily by treatment with drugs called gonadotropin-releasing hormone (GnRH) agonists, which are also known as luteinizing hormone-releasing hormone (LH-RH) agonists. These medicines interfere with signals from the pituitary gland that stimulate the ovaries to produce estrogen.

Examples of ovarian suppression drugs that have been approved by the U.S. Food and Drug Administration (FDA) are goserelin (Zoladex®) and leuprolide (Lupron®).

Blocking estrogen production: Drugs called aromatase inhibitors can be used to block the activity of an enzyme called aromatase, which the body uses to make estrogen in the ovaries and in other tissues. Aromatase inhibitors are used primarily in postmenopausal women because the ovaries in premenopausal women produce too much aromatase for the inhibitors to block effectively. However, these drugs can be used in premenopausal women if they are given together with a drug that suppresses ovarian function.

Examples of aromatase inhibitors approved by the FDA are anastrozole (Arimidex®) and letrozole (Femara®), both of which temporarily inactivate aromatase, and exemestane (Aromasin®), which permanently inactivates the enzyme.

Blocking estrogen's effects: Several types of drugs interfere with estrogen's ability to stimulate the growth of breast cancer cells:

- **Selective estrogen receptor modulators (SERMs)** bind to estrogen receptors, preventing estrogen from binding. Examples of SERMs approved by the FDA are tamoxifen (Nolvadex®), raloxifene (Evista®), and toremifene (Fareston®). Tamoxifen has been used for more than 30 years to treat hormone receptor-positive breast cancer. Because SERMs bind to estrogen receptors, they can potentially not only block estrogen activity (i.e., serve as estrogen antagonists) but also mimic estrogen effects (i.e., serve as estrogen agonists). Most SERMs behave as estrogen antagonists in some tissues and as estrogen agonists in other tissues. For example, tamoxifen blocks the effects of estrogen in breast tissue but acts like estrogen in the uterus and bone.

- **Other antiestrogen drugs**, such as fulvestrant (Faslodex®), work in a somewhat different way to block estrogen's effects. Like SERMs, fulvestrant attaches to the estrogen receptor and functions as an estrogen antagonist. However, unlike SERMs, fulvestrant has no estrogen agonist effects. It is a pure antiestrogen. In addition, when fulvestrant binds to the estrogen receptor, the receptor is targeted for destruction.

How Is Hormone Therapy Used to Treat Breast Cancer?

There are three main ways that hormone therapy is used to treat hormone-sensitive breast cancer:

Adjuvant therapy for early-stage breast cancer: Research has shown that women treated for early-stage ER-positive breast cancer benefit from receiving at least 5 years of adjuvant hormone therapy. Adjuvant therapy is treatment given after the main treatment (surgery, in the case of early-stage breast cancer) to increase the likelihood of a cure.

Adjuvant therapy may include radiation therapy and some combination of chemotherapy, hormone therapy, and targeted therapy. Tamoxifen has been approved by the FDA for adjuvant hormone treatment of premenopausal and postmenopausal women (and men) with ER-positive early-stage breast cancer, and anastrozole and letrozole have been approved for this use in postmenopausal women.

A third aromatase inhibitor, exemestane, is approved for adjuvant treatment of early-stage breast cancer in postmenopausal women who have received tamoxifen previously.

Until recently, most women who received adjuvant hormone therapy to reduce the chance of a breast cancer recurrence took tamoxifen every day for 5 years. However, with the advent of newer hormone therapies, some of which have been compared with tamoxifen in clinical trials, additional approaches to hormone therapy have become common. For example, some women may take an aromatase inhibitor every day for 5 years, instead of tamoxifen. Other women may receive additional treatment with an aromatase inhibitor after 5 years of tamoxifen. Finally, some women may switch to an aromatase inhibitor after 2 or 3 years of tamoxifen, for a total of 5 or more years of hormone therapy.

Decisions about the type and duration of adjuvant hormone therapy must be made on an individual basis. This complicated decision-making process is best carried out by talking with an oncologist, a doctor who specializes in cancer treatment.

Treatment of metastatic breast cancer: Several types of hormone therapy are approved to treat hormone-sensitive breast cancer that is metastatic (has spread to other parts of the body).

Studies have shown that tamoxifen is effective in treating women and men with metastatic breast cancer. Toremifene is also approved for this use. The antiestrogen fulvestrant can be used in postmenopausal women with metastatic ER-positive breast cancer after treatment with other antiestrogens.

The aromatase inhibitors anastrozole and letrozole can be given to postmenopausal women as initial therapy for metastatic hormone-sensitive breast cancer. These two drugs, as well as the aromatase inhibitor exemestane, can also be used to treat postmenopausal women with advanced breast cancer whose disease has worsened after treatment with tamoxifen.

Neoadjuvant treatment of breast cancer: The use of hormone therapy to treat breast cancer before surgery (neoadjuvant therapy) has been studied in clinical trials. The goal of neoadjuvant therapy is to reduce the size of a breast tumor to allow breast-conserving surgery. Data from randomized controlled trials have shown that neoadjuvant hormone therapies—in particular, aromatase inhibitors—can be effective in reducing the size of breast tumors in postmenopausal women. The results in premenopausal women are less clear because only a few small trials involving relatively few premenopausal women have been conducted thus far.

No hormone therapy has yet been approved by the FDA for the neoadjuvant treatment of breast cancer.

Can Hormone Therapy Be Used to Prevent Breast Cancer?

Yes. Most early breast cancers are ER-positive, and clinical trials have studied whether hormone therapy can be used to prevent breast cancer in women who are at increased risk of getting the disease.

A large NCI-sponsored randomized clinical trial called the Breast Cancer Prevention Trial found that tamoxifen, taken for 5 years, reduced the risk of developing invasive breast cancer by about 50 percent in postmenopausal women who were at increased risk of getting the disease. A subsequent large randomized trial, the Study of Tamoxifen and Raloxifene, which was also sponsored by NCI, found that 5 years of raloxifene reduces breast cancer risk in such women by about 38 percent.

As a result of these trials, both tamoxifen and raloxifene have been approved by the FDA to reduce the risk of developing breast cancer in women at high risk of the disease. Tamoxifen is approved for use regardless of menopausal status. Raloxifene is approved for use only in postmenopausal women.

The aromatase inhibitor exemestane has also been found to reduce the risk of breast cancer in postmenopausal women at increased risk of the disease. After 3 years of follow-up in another randomized trial, women who took exemestane were 65 percent less likely than those who took a placebo to develop breast cancer. Longer follow-up studies will be necessary to determine whether the risk reduction with exemestane remains high over time, as well as to understand any risks of exemestane treatment. Although exemestane has been approved by the FDA for treatment of women with ER-positive breast cancer, it has not been approved for breast cancer prevention.

What Are the Side Effects of Hormone Therapy?

The side effects of hormone therapy depend largely on the specific drug or the type of treatment. The benefits and risks of taking hormone therapy should be carefully weighed for each woman.

Hot flashes, night sweats, and vaginal dryness are common side effects of hormone therapy. Hormone therapy also disrupts the menstrual cycle in premenopausal women.

Less common but serious side effects of hormone therapy drugs are listed below.

Tamoxifen

- Risk of blood clots, especially in the lungs and legs
- Stroke
- Cataracts
- Endometrial and uterine cancers
- Bone loss in premenopausal women
- Mood swings, depression, and loss of libido
- In men: headaches, nausea, vomiting, skin rash, impotence, and decreased sexual interest

Raloxifene

- Risk of blood clots, especially in the lungs and legs
- Stroke in certain subgroups

Ovarian suppression

- Bone loss
- Mood swings, depression, and loss of libido

Aromatase Inhibitors

- Risk of heart attack, angina, heart failure, and hypercholesterolemia
- Bone loss
- Joint pain
- Mood swings and depression

Fulvestrant

- Gastrointestinal symptoms
- Loss of strength
- Pain

A common switching strategy, in which patients take tamoxifen for 2 or 3 years, followed by an aromatase inhibitor for 2 or 3 years, may yield the best balance of benefits and harms of these two types of hormone therapy.

Can Other Drugs Interfere with Hormone Therapy?

Certain drugs, including several commonly prescribed antidepressants (those in the category called selective serotonin reuptake inhibitors, or SSRIs), inhibit an enzyme called CYP2D6. This enzyme plays a critical role in the use of tamoxifen by the body because it metabolizes, or breaks down, tamoxifen into molecules, or metabolites, that are much more active than tamoxifen itself.

The possibility that SSRIs might, by inhibiting CYP2D6, slow the metabolism of tamoxifen and reduce its potency is a concern given that as many as one-fourth of breast cancer patients experience clinical depression and may be treated with SSRIs. In addition, SSRIs are sometimes used to treat hot flashes caused by hormone therapy.

Researchers have found that women taking certain SSRIs together with tamoxifen have decreased blood levels of active tamoxifen metabolites. Because of this, many experts suggest that patients who are taking antidepressants along with tamoxifen should discuss treatment options with their doctors. For example, doctors may recommend switching from an SSRI that is a potent inhibitor of CYP2D6 (such as paroxetine) to one that is a weaker inhibitor (such as sertraline) or that has no inhibitory activity (such as venlafaxine or citalopram), or they may suggest that their postmenopausal patients take an aromatase inhibitor instead of tamoxifen.

Other medications that inhibit CYP2D6 include the following:

- Quinidine, which is used to treat abnormal heart rhythms
- Diphenhydramine, which is an antihistamine
- Cimetidine, which is used to reduce stomach acid

People who are prescribed tamoxifen should discuss the use of all other medications with their doctors.

Where Can Someone Find More Information about Drugs Used in Hormone Therapy for Breast Cancer?

NCI's Drug Information Summaries provide consumer-friendly information about certain drugs that are approved by the FDA to treat cancer or conditions related to cancer. For each drug, topics covered include background information, research results, possible side effects, FDA approval information, and ongoing clinical trials. The Drug Information Summaries include information about drugs that have been approved for breast cancer.

Section 43.2

Aromatase Inhibitors

This section includes text excerpted from "Aromatase Inhibitors," National Institutes of Health (NIH), February 6, 2013.

Overview

The aromatase inhibitors block estrogen synthesis and are used as therapy of estrogen receptor positive breast cancer, usually after resection and as a first line treatment or after failure of tamoxifen (another antiestrogen that acts by blocking the estrogen receptor). The aromatase inhibitors include anastrozole, letrozole and exemestane, some of which have been implicated in causing rare instances of clinically apparent liver injury.

Activities

Aromatase is the enzyme responsible for the conversion of testosterone to estrone (E1) and androstenedione to estradiol (E2). Highest levels of aromatase are found in the ovary and placenta, which are the major sources of estrogen in premenopausal women. However, aromatase is also found in other tissues, such as liver, kidney, adrenals, brain, muscle and subcutaneous fat where it is also active in producing estrogens, although at low levels. These tissues are the major source of estrogen after menopause or oophorectomy. Inhibitors of aromatase were developed to block the synthesis of estrogen in the peripheral tissues and, thus, as antiestrogen therapy of estrogen receptor positive breast cancer in postmenopausal women. initially developed as an anticonvulsant, but later found to inhibit adrenocortical steroid synthesis.

More specific aromatase inhibitors with anti estrogen effects only were subsequently developed, the current agents being considered third generation inhibitors. These inhibitors include anastrozole and letrozole which are nonsteroidal, and exemestane which is a steroidal aromatase inhibitor. These agents have little or no effect on adrenal glucocorticoid or mineralocorticoid synthesis. The commercial names and year of approval in the United States are: letrozole (Femara, 1995), anastrozole (Arimidex, 1997), and exemestane (Aromasin, 1999). All three agents are now available in generic forms as well. They are used largely as adjuvant therapy in postmenopausal women with estrogen sensitive breast cancer, generally given in daily oral doses of up to five years. All three agents are associated with a low rate of serum enzyme elevations during therapy. Exemestane and anastrozole have also been linked to rare instances of clinically apparent acute liver injury.

The three aromatase inhibitors are discussed separately, and references to their hepatotoxicity and safety are given in each section as well as together at the end of this overview section.

Drug Class: Antineoplastic Agents (Antiestrogens [includes Tamoxifen]): Aromatase Inhibitors

Drugs in the Subclass, Aromatase Inhibitors: Anastrozole, Exemestane, Letrozole

Table 43.1. Chemical Formulas and Structures of Drugs

Drug	CAS Registry Number	Molecular Formula	Structure
Anastrozole	120511-73-1	C17-H19-N5	Anastrozole Chemical Structure

358

Table 43.1. Continued

Drug	CAS Registry Number	Molecular Formula	Structure
Exemestane	107868-30-4	C20-H24-O2	 Exemestane Chemical Structure
Letrozole	112809-51-5	C17-H11-N5	 Letrozole Chemical Structure

Section 43.3

Tamoxifen

This section contains text excerpted from the following sources: Text in this section begins with excerpts from "Tamoxifen Citrate," National Cancer Institute (NCI), August 26, 2015; Text under the heading "Ten Years of Tamoxifen Reduces Breast Cancer Recurrences, Improves Survival" is excerpted from "Ten Years of Tamoxifen Reduces Breast Cancer Recurrences, Improves Survival," National Cancer Institute (NCI), March 20, 2013.

Tamoxifen citrate is approved to treat:

- Breast cancer in women and men.

Tamoxifen citrate is also approved to prevent:

- Breast cancer in women who are at high risk for the disease.

Tamoxifen citrate is also being studied in the treatment of other types of cancer.

Ten Years of Tamoxifen Reduces Breast Cancer Recurrences, Improves Survival

For some women with breast cancer, taking adjuvant tamoxifen (Nolvadex®) for 10 years after primary treatment leads to a greater reduction in breast cancer recurrences and deaths than taking the drug for only 5 years, according to the results of a large international clinical trial.

The findings from the ATLAS trial—presented at the San Antonio Breast Cancer Symposium (SABCS) and published in The Lancet on December 5, 2012—are likely to change clinical practice, several researchers said.

Nearly 7,000 women with early-stage, estrogen receptor-positive breast cancer were enrolled in the trial between 1996 and 2005. After taking tamoxifen for 5 years, participants were randomly assigned to continue taking tamoxifen for another 5 years or to stop taking it.

From 5 to 9 years after the women began tamoxifen therapy, there was little difference in outcomes between the two treatment groups. This finding is consistent with those from other trials of adjuvant tamoxifen therapy, which showed that 5 years of tamoxifen can substantially reduce the risk of the cancer returning and of cancer death in the next few years, what one of the trial investigators, Richard Gray, MSc, of Oxford University, UK, called a "carryover effect."

The improved outcomes with longer tamoxifen use emerged only after the 10-year mark, Gray explained during an SABCS press briefing. Among the women who took tamoxifen for 10 years, the risk of breast cancer returning between 10 and 14 years after starting tamoxifen was 25 percent lower than it was among women who took it for 5 years, and the risk of dying from breast cancer was nearly 30 percent lower.

Overall, from 5 to 14 years after participants began tamoxifen treatment, the risk of the cancer returning and the risk of dying from breast cancer were lower in women who took tamoxifen for 10 years, compared with those who took it for 5 years.

Tamoxifen can have side effects, including hot flashes, fatigue, and an increased risk of blood clots and endometrial cancer. But there was no substantial increase in serious side effects, including endometrial cancer incidence or death, in women who took tamoxifen for the longer period, Gray reported. The absolute increased risk of death from endometrial cancer in women who took tamoxifen for 10 years versus 5 years was 0.2 percent.

Table 43.2. Breast Cancer Recurrence and Death 5 to 14 Years after Beginning 5 or 10 Years of Adjuvant Tamoxifen

Risk	5 Years	10 Years
Recurrence	25.1 percent	21.4 percent
Death from Breast Cancer	15.0 percent	12.2 percent

The risk-benefit ratio of any treatment must always be seriously considered, he stressed. But, in the case of extended tamoxifen treatment, he argued, the "risks are far smaller than the benefits."

At least one other trial of extended tamoxifen therapy reached the opposite conclusion to the ATLAS trial. This much smaller trial (about 1,200 patients) conducted in the United States by the National Surgical Adjuvant Breast and Bowel Project (NSABP), ran from the early 1980s to the mid-1990s. It found that continuing adjuvant treatment with tamoxifen beyond 5 years did not decrease breast cancer recurrences or deaths.

Why the trials had different findings is unclear. However, with its larger size and longer follow-up, the ATLAS results are more definitive, noted several researchers.

The ATLAS results will have "a major, immediate impact on premenopausal women" with early-stage, estrogen receptor-positive breast cancer, said Peter Ravdin, M.D., Ph.D., of the University of Texas Health Sciences Center at San Antonio, who moderated the press briefing.

That patient population represents a substantial number of women diagnosed with breast cancer in the United States each year, approximately 30,000 to 35,000 women. Postmenopausal women with early-stage, estrogen receptor-positive breast cancer are often treated with aromatase inhibitors after tamoxifen. However, aromatase inhibitors are not effective in premenopausal women, Dr. Ravdin explained, so tamoxifen is the standard of care in these patients.

"We can now tell [premenopausal patients] that clinical evidence shows that 10 years [of tamoxifen] is superior to 5 years," Dr. Ravdin said. "And I'm going to be comfortable doing that."

But the decision to use tamoxifen for the extended period is by no means clear cut, he stressed.

Women with a higher risk of their cancer returning long after adjuvant therapy ends, such as those whose cancers had infiltrated their lymph nodes or who had larger tumors, "will definitely be strong candidates for continuation of [tamoxifen] therapy," he said. But a woman at low risk of recurrence at any point "may very well rationally decide she doesn't want to take tamoxifen beyond 5 years," he added.

The findings may have implications for postmenopausal women as well, said Claudine Isaacs, M.D., C.M., co-director of the breast cancer program at Georgetown Lombardi Comprehensive Cancer Center.

Postmenopausal women are often prescribed 5 years of adjuvant therapy with an aromatase inhibitor. (Some women, however, receive tamoxifen followed by an aromatase inhibitor over a 5-year period.) But, Dr. Isaacs noted, a fair number of women can't tolerate aromatase inhibitors because of their side effects, so the ATLAS results may lead some clinicians and their postmenopausal patients to consider whether an extended duration of adjuvant tamoxifen may be appropriate.

Chapter 44

Biological Therapies for Breast Cancer

What Is Biological Therapy?

Biological therapy involves the use of living organisms, substances derived from living organisms, or laboratory-produced versions of such substances to treat disease. Some biological therapies for cancer use vaccines or bacteria to stimulate the body's immune system to act against cancer cells. These types of biological therapy, which are sometimes referred to collectively as "immunotherapy" or "biological response modifier therapy," do not target cancer cells directly. Other biological therapies, such as antibodies or segments of genetic material (RNA or DNA), do target cancer cells directly. Biological therapies that interfere with specific molecules involved in tumor growth and progression are also referred to as targeted therapies.

For patients with cancer, biological therapies may be used to treat the cancer itself or the side effects of other cancer treatments. Although many forms of biological therapy have been approved by the U.S. Food and Drug Administration (FDA), others remain experimental and are available to cancer patients principally through participation in clinical trials (research studies involving people).

This chapter includes text excerpted from "Biological Therapies for Cancer," National Cancer Institute (NCI), June 12, 2013.

What Is the Immune System and What Role Does It Have in Biological Therapy for Cancer?

The Immune System Is a Complex Network of Organs, Tissues, and Specialized Cells. It Recognizes and Destroys Foreign Invaders, Such as Bacteria or Viruses, as Well as Some Damaged, Diseased, or Abnormal Cells in the Body, including Cancer Cells. An Immune Response Is Triggered When the Immune System Encounters a Substance, Called an Antigen, It Recognizes As "Foreign."

White Blood Cells Are the Primary Players in Immune System Responses. Some White Blood Cells, including Macrophages and Natural Killer Cells, Patrol the Body, Seeking out Foreign Invaders and Diseased, Damaged, or Dead Cells. These White Blood Cells Provide a General—or Nonspecific—Level of Immune Protection.

Other white blood cells, including cytotoxic T cells and B cells, act against specific targets. Cytotoxic T cells release chemicals that can directly destroy microbes or abnormal cells. B cells make antibodies that latch onto foreign intruders or abnormal cells and tag them for destruction by another component of the immune system. Still other white blood cells, including dendritic cells, play supporting roles to ensure that cytotoxic T cells and B cells do their jobs effectively.

It is generally believed that the immune system's natural capacity to detect and destroy abnormal cells prevents the development of many cancers. Nevertheless, some cancer cells are able to evade detection by using one or more strategies. For example, cancer cells can undergo genetic changes that lead to the loss of cancer-associated antigens, making them less "visible" to the immune system. They may also use several different mechanisms to suppress immune responses or to avoid being killed by cytotoxic T cells

The goal of immunotherapy for cancer is to overcome these barriers to an effective anticancer immune response. These biological therapies restore or increase the activities of specific immune-system components or counteract immunosuppressive signals produced by cancer cells.

What Are Monoclonal Antibodies, and How Are They Used in Cancer Treatment?

Monoclonal antibodies, or MAbs, are laboratory-produced antibodies that bind to specific antigens expressed by cells, such as a protein that is present on the surface of cancer cells but is absent from (or expressed at lower levels by) normal cells.

To create MAbs, researchers inject mice with an antigen from human cells. They then harvest the antibody-producing cells from the mice and individually fuse them with a myeloma cell (cancerous B cell) to produce a fusion cell known as a hybridoma. Each hybridoma then divides to produce identical daughter cells or clones—hence the term "monoclonal"—and antibodies secreted by different clones are tested to identify the antibodies that bind most strongly to the antigen. Large quantities of antibodies can be produced by these immortal hybridoma cells. Because mouse antibodies can themselves elicit an immune response in humans, which would reduce their effectiveness, mouse antibodies are often "humanized" by replacing as much of the mouse portion of the antibody as possible with human portions. This is done through genetic engineering.

Some MAbs stimulate an immune response that destroys cancer cells. Similar to the antibodies produced naturally by B cells, these MAbs "coat" the cancer cell surface, triggering its destruction by the immune system. FDA-approved MAbs of this type include rituximab, which targets the CD20 antigen found on non-Hodgkin lymphoma cells, and alemtuzumab, which targets the CD52 antigen found on B-cell chronic lymphocytic leukemia (CLL) cells. Rituximab may also trigger cell death (apoptosis) directly.

Another group of MAbs stimulates an anticancer immune response by binding to receptors on the surface of immune cells and inhibiting signals that prevent immune cells from attacking the body's own tissues, including cancer cells. One such MAb, ipilimumab, has been approved by the FDA for treatment of metastatic melanoma, and others are being investigated in clinical studies.

Other MAbs interfere with the action of proteins that are necessary for tumor growth. For example, bevacizumab targets vascular endothelial growth factor (VEGF), a protein secreted by tumor cells and other cells in the tumor's microenvironment that promotes the development of tumor blood vessels. When bound to bevacizumab, VEGF cannot interact with its cellular receptor, preventing the signaling that leads to the growth of new blood vessels.

Similarly, cetuximab and panitumumab target the epidermal growth factor receptor (EGFR), and trastuzumab targets the human epidermal growth factor receptor 2 (HER-2). MAbs that bind to cell surface growth factor receptors prevent the targeted receptors from sending their normal growth-promoting signals. They may also trigger apoptosis and activate the immune system to destroy tumor cells.

Another group of cancer therapeutic MAbs are the immunoconjugates. These MAbs, which are sometimes called immunotoxins or antibody-drug conjugates, consist of an antibody attached to a cell-killing substance, such as a plant or bacterial toxin, a chemotherapy drug, or a radioactive molecule. The antibody latches onto its specific antigen on the surface of a cancer cell, and the cell-killing substance is taken up by the cell. FDA-approved conjugated MAbs that work this way include 90Y-ibritumomab tiuxetan, which targets the CD20 antigen to deliver radioactive yttrium-90 to B-cell non-Hodgkin lymphoma cells, and ado-trastuzumab emtansine, which targets the HER-2 molecule to deliver the drug DM1, which inhibits cell proliferation, to HER-2 expressing metastatic breast cancer cells.

What Are Cytokines, and How Are They Used in Cancer Treatment?

Cytokines are signaling proteins that are produced by white blood cells. They help mediate and regulate immune responses, inflammation, and hematopoiesis (new blood cell formation). Two types of cytokines are used to treat patients with cancer: interferons (INFs) and interleukins (ILs). A third type, called hematopoietic growth factors, is used to counteract some of the side effects of certain chemotherapy regimens.

Researchers have found that one type of INF, INF-alfa, can enhance a patient's immune response to cancer cells by activating certain white blood cells, such as natural killer cells and dendritic cells. INF-alfa may also inhibit the growth of cancer cells or promote their death. INF-alfa has been approved for the treatment of melanoma, Kaposi sarcoma, and several hematologic cancers.

Like INFs, ILs play important roles in the body's normal immune response and in the immune system's ability to respond to cancer. Researchers have identified more than a dozen distinct ILs, including IL-2, which is also called T-cell growth factor. IL-2 is naturally produced by activated T cells. It increases the proliferation of white blood cells, including cytotoxic T cells and natural killer cells, leading to an enhanced anticancer immune response. IL-2 also facilitates the production of antibodies by B cells to further target cancer cells. Aldesleukin, IL-2 that is made in a laboratory, has been approved for the treatment of metastatic kidney cancer and metastatic melanoma. Researchers are currently investigating whether combining aldesleukin treatment with other types of biological therapies may enhance its anticancer effects.

Hematopoietic growth factors are a special class of naturally occurring cytokines. All blood cells arise from hematopoietic stem cells in the bone marrow. Because chemotherapy drugs target proliferating cells, including normal blood stem cells, chemotherapy depletes these stem cells and the blood cells that they produce. Loss of red blood cells, which transport oxygen and nutrients throughout the body, can cause anemia. A decrease in platelets, which are responsible for blood clotting, often leads to abnormal bleeding. Finally, lower white blood cell counts leave chemotherapy patients vulnerable to infections.

Several growth factors that promote the growth of these various blood cell populations have been approved for clinical use. Erythropoietin stimulates red blood cell formation, and IL-11 increases platelet production. Granulocyte-macrophage colony-stimulating factor (GM-CSF) and granulocyte colony-stimulating factor (G-CSF) both increase the number of white blood cells, reducing the risk of infections. Treatment with these factors allows patients to continue chemotherapy regimens that might otherwise be stopped temporarily or modified to reduce the drug doses because of low blood cell numbers.

G-CSF and GM-CSF can also enhance the immune system's specific anticancer responses by increasing the number of cancer-fighting T cells. Thus, GM-CSF and G-CSF are used in combination with other biological therapies to strengthen anticancer immune responses.

What Are Cancer Treatment Vaccines?

Cancer treatment vaccines are designed to treat cancers that have already developed rather than to prevent them in the first place. Cancer treatment vaccines contain cancer-associated antigens to enhance the immune system's response to a patient's tumor cells. The cancer-associated antigens can be proteins or another type of molecule found on the surface of or inside cancer cells that can stimulate B cells or killer T cells to attack them.

Some vaccines that are under development target antigens that are found on or in many types of cancer cells. These types of cancer vaccines are being tested in clinical trials in patients with a variety of cancers, including prostate, colorectal, lung, breast, and thyroid cancers. Other cancer vaccines target antigens that are unique to a specific cancer type. Still other vaccines are designed against an antigen specific to one patient's tumor and need to be customized for each patient. The one cancer treatment vaccine that has received FDA approval, sipuleucel-T, is this type of vaccine.

Because of the limited toxicity seen with cancer vaccines, they are also being tested in clinical trials in combination with other forms of therapy, such as hormonal therapy, chemotherapy, radiation therapy, and targeted therapies.

What Is Bacillus Calmette-Guérin Therapy?

Bacillus Calmette-Guérin (BCG) was the first biological therapy to be approved by the FDA. It is a weakened form of a live tuberculosis bacterium that does not cause disease in humans. It was first used medically as a vaccine against tuberculosis. When inserted directly into the bladder with a catheter, BCG stimulates a general immune response that is directed not only against the foreign bacterium itself but also against bladder cancer cells. How and why BCG exerts this anticancer effect is not well understood, but the efficacy of the treatment is well documented. Approximately 70 percent of patients with early-stage bladder cancer experience a remission after BCG therapy BCG is also being studied in the treatment of other types of cancer.

What Is Oncolytic Virus Therapy?

Oncolytic virus therapy is an experimental form of biological therapy that involves the direct destruction of cancer cells. Oncolytic viruses infect both cancer and normal cells, but they have little effect on normal cells. In contrast, they readily replicate, or reproduce, inside cancer cells and ultimately cause the cancer cells to die. Some viruses, such as reovirus, Newcastle disease virus, and mumps virus, are naturally oncolytic, whereas others, including measles virus, adenovirus, and vaccinia virus, can be adapted or modified to replicate efficiently only in cancer cells. In addition, oncolytic viruses can be genetically engineered to preferentially infect and replicate in cancer cells that produce a specific cancer-associated antigen, such as EGFR or HER-2.

One of the challenges in using oncolytic viruses is that they may themselves be destroyed by the patient's immune system before they have a chance to attack the cancer. Researchers have developed several strategies to overcome this challenge, such as administering a combination of immune-suppressing chemotherapy drugs like cyclophosphamide along with the virus or "cloaking" the virus within a protective envelope. But an immune reaction in the patient may actually have benefits: although it may hamper oncolytic virus therapy at the time of viral delivery, it may enhance cancer cell destruction after the virus has infected the tumor cells.

No oncolytic virus has been approved for use in the United States, although H101, a modified form of adenovirus, was approved in China in 2006 for the treatment of patients with head and neck cancer. Several oncolytic viruses are currently being tested in clinical trials. Researchers are also investigating whether oncolytic viruses can be combined with other types of cancer therapies or can be used to sensitize patients' tumors to additional therapy.

What Is Gene Therapy?

Still an experimental form of treatment, gene therapy attempts to introduce genetic material (DNA or RNA) into living cells. Gene therapy is being studied in clinical trials for many types of cancer.

In general, genetic material cannot be inserted directly into a person's cells. Instead, it is delivered to the cells using a carrier, or "vector." The vectors most commonly used in gene therapy are viruses, because they have the unique ability to recognize certain cells and insert genetic material into them. Scientists alter these viruses to make them more safe for humans (e.g., by inactivating genes that enable them to reproduce or cause disease) and/or to improve their ability to recognize and enter the target cell. A variety of liposomes (fatty particles) and nanoparticles are also being used as gene therapy vectors, and scientists are investigating methods of targeting these vectors to specific cell types.

Researchers are studying several methods for treating cancer with gene therapy. Some approaches target cancer cells, to destroy them or prevent their growth. Others target healthy cells to enhance their ability to fight cancer. In some cases, researchers remove cells from the patient, treat the cells with the vector in the laboratory, and return the cells to the patient. In others, the vector is given directly to the patient. Some gene therapy approaches being studied are described below.

- Replacing an altered tumor suppressor gene that produces a nonfunctional protein (or no protein) with a normal version of the gene. Because tumor suppressor genes (e.g., *TP53*) play a role in preventing cancer, restoring the normal function of these genes may inhibit cancer growth or promote cancer regression.

- Introducing genetic material to block the expression of an oncogene whose product promotes tumor growth. Short RNA or DNA molecules with sequences complementary to the gene's messenger RNA (mRNA) can be packaged into vectors or given to cells directly. These short molecules, called oligonucleotides, can bind to the target mRNA, preventing its translation into protein or even causing its degradation.

369

- Improving a patient's immune response to cancer. In one approach, gene therapy is used to introduce cytokine-producing genes into cancer cells to stimulate the immune response to the tumor.

- Inserting genes into cancer cells to make them more sensitive to chemotherapy, radiation therapy, or other treatments

- Inserting genes into healthy blood-forming stem cells to make them more resistant to the side effects of cancer treatments, such as high doses of anticancer drugs

- Introducing "suicide genes" into a patient's cancer cells. A suicide gene is a gene whose product is able to activate a "prodrug" (an inactive form of a toxic drug), causing the toxic drug to be produced only in cancer cells in patients given the pro-drug. Normal cells, which do not express the suicide genes, are not affected by the pro-drug.

- Inserting genes to prevent cancer cells from developing new blood vessels (angiogenesis)

Proposed gene therapy clinical trials, or protocols, must be approved by at least two review boards at the researcher's' institution before they can be conducted. Gene therapy protocols must also be approved by the FDA, which regulates all gene therapy products. In addition, gene therapy trials that are funded by the National Institutes of Health must be registered with the NIH Recombinant DNA Advisory Committee.

What Is Adoptive T-Cell Transfer Therapy?

Adoptive cell transfer is an experimental anticancer therapy that attempts to enhance the natural cancer-fighting ability of a patient's T cells. In one form of this therapy, researchers first harvest cytotoxic T cells that have invaded a patient's tumor. They then identify the cells with the greatest antitumor activity and grow large populations of those cells in a laboratory. The patients are then treated to deplete their immune cells, and the laboratory-grown T cells are infused into the patient's.

In another, more recently developed form of this therapy, which is also a kind of gene therapy, researchers isolate T cells from a small sample of the patient's blood. They genetically modify the cells by inserting the gene for a receptor that recognizes an antigen specific to the patient's cancer cells and grow large numbers of these modified cells in culture. The genetically modified cells are then infused into patients whose immune cells have been depleted. The receptor expressed by the modified T cells allows these cells to attach to antigens on the surface of the tumor cells, which activates the T cells to attack and kill the tumor cells.

Adoptive T-cell transfer was first studied for the treatment of metastatic melanoma because melanomas often cause a substantial immune response, with many tumor-invading cytotoxic T cells. Adoptive cell transfer with genetically modified T cells is also being investigated as a treatment for other solid tumors, as well as for hematologic cancers.

What Are the Side Effects of Biological Therapies?

The side effects associated with various biological therapies can differ by treatment type. However, pain, swelling, soreness, redness, itchiness, and rash at the site of infusion or injection are fairly common with these treatments.

Less common but more serious side effects tend to be more specific to one or a few types of biological therapy. For example, therapies intended to prompt an immune response against cancer can cause an array of flu-like symptoms, including fever, chills, weakness, dizziness, nausea or vomiting, muscle or joint aches, fatigue, headache, occasional breathing difficulties, and lowered or heightened blood pressure. Biological therapies that provoke an immune system response also pose a risk of severe or even fatal hypersensitivity (allergic) reactions.

Potential serious side effects of specific biological therapies are as follows:

Monoclonal Antibodies (mAbs)

- Flu-like symptoms

- Severe allergic reaction

- Lowered blood counts

- Changes in blood chemistry

- Organ damage (usually to heart, lungs, kidneys, liver or brain)

Cytokines (Interferons, Interleukins, Hematopoietic Growth Factors)

- Flu-like symptoms

371

- Severe allergic reaction
- Lowered blood counts
- Changes in blood chemistry
- Organ damage (usually to heart, lungs, kidneys, liver or brain)

Treatment vaccines

- Flu-like symptoms
- Severe allergic reaction

BCG

- Flu-like symptoms
- Severe allergic reaction
- Urinary side effects
  - Pain or burning sensation during urination
  - Increased urgency or frequency of urination
  - Blood in the urine

Oncolytic Viruses

- Flu-like symptoms
- Tumor lysis syndrome: severe, sometimes life-threatening alterations in blood chemistry following the release of materials formerly contained within cancer cells into the bloodstream

Gene Therapy

- Flu-like symptoms
- Secondary cancer: techniques that insert DNA into a host cell chromosome can cause cancer to develop if the insertion inhibits expression of a tumor suppressor gene or activates an oncogene; researchers are working to minimize this possibility
- Mistaken introduction of a gene into healthy cells, including reproductive cells
- Overexpression of the introduced gene may harm healthy tissues
- Virus vector transmission to other individuals or into the environment

How Can People Obtain Information about Clinical Trials of Biological Therapies for Cancer?

Both FDA-approved and experimental biological therapies for specific types of cancer are being studied in clinical trials. The names of the biological therapy types listed below are links to descriptions of ongoing clinical trials that are testing those types of biological therapies in cancer patients. These trial descriptions can also be accessed by searching NCI's list of cancer clinical trials on the NCI website. NCI's list of cancer clinical trials includes all NCI-funded clinical trials as well as studies conducted by investigators at hospitals and medical centers throughout the United States and around the world.

Chapter 45

Complementary and Alternative Medicine (CAM) Therapies Used in the Treatment of Breast Cancer

Chapter Contents

Section 45.1

Coenzyme Q10 and Cancer

This section includes text excerpted from "Coenzyme
Q10–Patient Version (PDQ®)," National Cancer
Institute (NCI), December 11, 2015.

Questions and Answers about Coenzyme Q10 (CoQ10) and Cancer

What Is CoQ10?

CoQ10 is a compound that is made naturally in the body. The Q and the 10 in coenzyme Q10 refer to the groups of chemicals that make up the coenzyme. CoQ10 is also known by these other names:

- Q10

- Vitamin Q10

- Ubiquinone

- Ubidecarenone

A coenzyme helps an enzyme do its job. An enzyme is a protein that speeds up the rate at which natural chemical reactions take place in cells of the body. The body's cells use CoQ10 to make energy needed for the cells to grow and stay healthy. The body also uses CoQ10 as an antioxidant. An antioxidant is a substance that protects cells from chemicals called free radicals. Free radicals can damage DNA (deoxyribonucleic acid). Genes, which are pieces of DNA, tell the cells how to work in the body and when to grow and divide. Damage to DNA has been linked to some kinds of cancer. By protecting cells against free radicals, antioxidants help protect the body against cancer.

CoQ10 is found in most body tissues. The highest amounts are found in the heart, liver, kidneys, and pancreas. The lowest amounts are found in the lungs. The amount of CoQ10 in tissues decreases as people get older.

What Is the History of the Discovery and Use of CoQ10 as a Complementary or Alternative Treatment for Cancer?

CoQ10 was first identified in 1957. Its chemical structure was determined in 1958. Interest in CoQ10 as a possible treatment for cancer began in 1961, when it was found that some cancer patients had a lower than normal amount of it in their blood. Low blood levels of CoQ10 have been found in patients with myeloma, lymphoma, and cancers of the breast, lung, prostate, pancreas, colon, kidney, and head and neck.

Research about how CoQ10 plays a key role in the way cells make energy was awarded the Nobel Prize in Chemistry in 1978.

Studies suggest that CoQ10 may help the immune system work better. Partly because of this, CoQ10 is used as adjuvant therapy for cancer. Adjuvant therapy is treatment given following the primary treatment to lower the risk that the cancer will come back.

What Is the Theory behind the Claim That CoQ10 Is Useful in Treating Cancer?

CoQ10 may be useful in treating cancer because it boosts the immune system. Also, studies suggest that CoQ10 analogs (drugs that are similar to CoQ10) may prevent the growth of cancer cells directly. As an antioxidant, CoQ10 may help prevent cancer from developing.

How Is CoQ10 Administered?

CoQ10 is usually taken by mouth as a pill (tablet or capsule). It may also be given by injection into a vein (IV). In animal studies, CoQ10 is given by injection.

Have Any Preclinical (Laboratory or Animal) Studies Been Conducted Using

A number of preclinical studies have been done with CoQ10. Research in a laboratory or using animals is done to find out if a drug, procedure, or treatment is likely to be useful in humans. These preclinical studies are done before any testing in humans is begun. Most laboratory studies of CoQ10 have looked at its chemical structure and how it works in the body. The following has been reported from preclinical studies of CoQ10 and cancer:

- Animal studies found that CoQ10 boosts the immune system and helps the body fight certain infections and types of cancer.

377

- CoQ10 helped to protect the hearts of study animals that were given the anticancer drug doxorubicin, an anthracycline that can cause damage to the heart muscle.

- Laboratory and animal studies have shown that analogs (drugs that are similar to CoQ10) may stop cancer cells from growing.

Have Any Clinical Trials (Research Studies with Humans) of CoQ10 Been Conducted?

There have been no well-designed clinical trials involving large numbers of patients to study the use of CoQ10 in cancer treatment. There have been some clinical trials with small numbers of people, but the way the studies were done and the amount of information reported made it unclear if benefits were caused by the CoQ10 or by something else. Most of the trials were not randomized or controlled. Randomized controlled trials give the highest level of evidence:

- In randomized trials, volunteers are assigned randomly (by chance) to one of 2 or more groups that compare different factors related to the treatment.

- In controlled trials, one group (called the control group) does not receive the new treatment being studied. The control group is then compared to the groups that receive the new treatment, to see if the new treatment makes a difference.

Some research studies are published in scientific journals. Most scientific journals have experts who review research reports before they are published, to make sure that the evidence and conclusions are sound. This is called peer review. Studies published in peer-reviewed scientific journals are considered better evidence. No randomized clinical trials of CoQ10 as a treatment for cancer have been published in a peer-reviewed scientific journal.

The following has been reported from studies of CoQ10 in humans:

Randomized Trials of CoQ10 and Doxorubicin

- A randomized trial of 20 children treated for acute lymphoblastic leukemia or non-Hodgkin lymphoma looked at whether CoQ10 would protect the heart from the damage caused by the anthracycline drug doxorubicin. The results of this trial and others have shown that CoQ10 decreases the harmful effects of doxorubicin on the heart.

- In a larger trial, 236 patients treated for breast cancer were randomized to receive oral supplements of either 300 mg CoQ10 or placebo, each combined with 300 IU vitamin E, for 24 weeks. The study found that levels of fatigue and quality of life were not improved in patients who received CoQ10 plus vitamin E compared to patients who received the placebo.

Studies of CoQ10 as an Adjuvant Therapy for Breast Cancer

Small studies have been done on the use of CoQ10 after standard treatment in patients with breast cancer:

- In a study of CoQ10 in 32 breast cancer patients, it was reported that some signs and symptoms of cancer went away in 6 patients. Details were given for only 3 of the 6 patients. The researchers also reported that all the patients in the study used less pain medicine, had improved quality of life, and did not lose weight during treatment.

- In another study led by the same researchers, 3 breast cancer patients were given high-dose CoQ10 and followed for 3 to 5 years. The study reported that one patient had complete remission of cancer that had spread to the liver, another had remission of cancer that had spread to the chest wall, and the third had no breast cancer found after surgery.

It is not clear, however, if the benefits reported in these studies were caused by CoQ10 therapy or something else. The studies had the following weaknesses:

- The studies were not randomized or controlled.

- The patients used other supplements in addition to CoQ10.

- The patients received standard treatments before or during the CoQ10 therapy.

- Details were not reported for all patients in the studies.

Anecdotal Reports of CoQ10

Anecdotal reports are incomplete descriptions of the medical and treatment history of one or more patients. There have been anecdotal reports that CoQ10 has helped some cancer patients live longer, including patients with cancers of the pancreas, lung, colon, rectum, and prostate. The patients described in these reports, however, also received treatments other than CoQ10, including chemotherapy, radiation therapy, and surgery.

In a follow-up study, two patients who had breast cancer remaining after surgery were treated with CoQ10 for 3 to 4 months. It was reported that after treatment with CoQ10, the cancer was completely gone in both patients.

Have Any Side Effects or Risks Been Reported from CoQ10?

No serious side effects have been reported from the use of CoQ10. The most common side effects include the following:

- Insomnia (being unable to fall sleep or stay asleep)
- Higher than normal levels of liver enzymes
- Rashes
- Nausea
- Pain in the upper part of the abdomen
- Dizziness
- Feeling sensitive to light
- Feeling irritable
- Headache
- Heartburn
- Feeling very tired

It is important to check with health care providers to find out if CoQ10 can be safely used along with other drugs. Certain drugs, such as those that are used to lower cholesterol, blood pressure, or blood sugar levels, may decrease the effects of CoQ10. CoQ10 may change way the body uses warfarin (a drug that prevents the blood from clotting) and insulin.

As noted before, the body uses CoQ10 as an antioxidant. Antioxidants protect cells from free radicals. Some conventional cancer therapies, such as anticancer drugs and radiation treatment, kill cancer cells in part by causing free radicals to form. Researchers are studying whether using CoQ10 along with conventional therapies has any effect, good or bad, on the way these conventional therapies work in the body.

Is CoQ10 Approved by the U.S. Food and Drug Administration (FDA) for Use as a Cancer Treatment in the United States?

CoQ10 is sold as a dietary supplement and is not approved by the FDA for use as a cancer treatment. Dietary supplements are products meant to be added to the diet. They are not drugs and are not meant to treat, prevent, or cure diseases. The manufacturer is responsible for ensuring that the product is safe and that the label claims are truthful and not misleading. The FDA does not approve dietary supplements as safe or effective before they are sold. Also, the way companies make CoQ10 is not regulated. Different batches and brands of CoQ10 supplements may be different from each other.

Section 45.2

Flaxseed and Breast Cancer

This section includes text excerpted from "Flaxseed and Flaxseed Oil," National Center for Complementary and Integrative Health (NCCIH), January 4, 2016.

Overview

This section provides basic information about flaxseed and flaxseed oil—common names, what the science says, potential side effects and cautions, and resources for more information.

Flaxseed is the seed of the flax plant, which is believed to have originated in Egypt. It grows throughout Canada and Northwestern United States. Flaxseed oil comes from flaxseeds. The most common folk or traditional use of flaxseed is as a laxative; it is also used for hot flashes and breast pain. Flaxseed oil has different folk or traditional uses, including arthritis. Both flaxseed and flaxseed oil have been used for high cholesterol levels and in an effort to prevent cancer.

Whole or crushed flaxseed can be mixed with water or juice and taken by mouth. Flaxseed is also available in powder form. Flaxseed oil is available in liquid and capsule forms. Flaxseed contains lignans

381

(phytoestrogens, or plant estrogens), while flaxseed oil preparations lack lignans.

What the Science Says

- Flaxseed contains soluble fiber, like that found in oat bran, and may have a laxative effect.

- Studies of flaxseed preparations to lower cholesterol levels report mixed results. A 2009 review of the clinical research found that cholesterol-lowering effects were more apparent in postmenopausal women and in people with high initial cholesterol concentrations.

- Some studies suggest that alpha-linolenic acid (a substance found in flaxseed and flaxseed oil) may benefit people with heart disease. But not enough reliable data are available to determine whether flaxseed is effective for heart conditions.

- Study results are mixed on whether flaxseed decreases hot flashes.

- Although some population studies suggest that flaxseed might reduce the risk of certain cancers, there is not enough research to support a recommendation for this use.

- NCCIH is funding studies on flaxseed. Recent studies are looking at its potential role in preventing or treating atherosclerosis (hardening of the arteries), breast cancer, and ovarian cysts.

Side Effects and Cautions

- Flaxseed and flaxseed oil supplements seem to be well tolerated. Few side effects have been reported.

- Flaxseed, like any supplemental fiber source, should be taken with plenty of water; otherwise, it could worsen constipation or, in rare cases, even cause intestinal blockage. Both flaxseed and flaxseed oil can cause diarrhea.

- The fiber in flaxseed may lower the body's ability to absorb medications that are taken by mouth. Flaxseed should not be taken at the same time as any conventional oral medications or other dietary supplements.

- Tell all your health care providers about any complementary health approaches you use. Give them a full picture of what you do to manage your health. This will help ensure coordinated and safe care.

Chapter 46

Treating Breast Cancer during Pregnancy

General Information about Breast Cancer and Pregnancy

Breast Cancer Is a Disease in Which Malignant (Cancer) Cells Form in the Tissues of the Breast

The breast is made up of lobes and ducts. Each breast has 15 to 20 sections called lobes. Each lobe has many smaller sections called lobules. Lobules end in dozens of tiny bulbs that can make milk. The lobes, lobules, and bulbs are linked by thin tubes called ducts.

Each breast also has blood vessels and lymph vessels. The lymph vessels carry an almost colorless fluid called lymph. Lymph vessels carry lymph between lymph nodes. Lymph nodes are small bean-shaped structures that are found throughout the body. They filter substances in lymph and help fight infection and disease. Clusters of lymph nodes are found near the breast in the axilla (under the arm), above the collarbone, and in the chest. Sometimes Breast Cancer Occurs in Women Who Are Pregnant or Have Just given Birth.

This chapter includes text excerpted from "Breast Cancer Treatment and Pregnancy–Patient Version (PDQ®)," National Cancer Institute (NCI), October 21, 2015.

Sometimes Breast Cancer Occurs in Women Who Are Pregnant or Have Just given Birth

Breast cancer occurs about once in every 3,000 pregnancies. It occurs most often between the ages of 32 and 38.

Signs of Breast Cancer Include a Lump or Change in the Breast

These and other signs may be caused by breast cancer or by other conditions. Check with your doctor if you have any of the following:

- A lump or thickening in or near the breast or in the underarm area.
- A change in the size or shape of the breast.
- A dimple or puckering in the skin of the breast.
- A nipple turned inward into the breast.
- Fluid, other than breast milk, from the nipple, especially if it's bloody.
- Scaly, red, or swollen skin on the breast, nipple, or areola (the dark area of skin around the nipple).
- Dimples in the breast that look like the skin of an orange, called peau d'orange.

It May Be Difficult to Detect (Find) Breast Cancer Early in Pregnant or Nursing Women

The breasts usually get larger, tender, or lumpy in women who are pregnant, nursing, or have just given birth. This occurs because of normal hormone changes that take place during pregnancy. These changes can make small lumps difficult to detect. The breasts may also become denser. It is more difficult to detect breast cancer in women with dense breasts using mammography. Because these breast changes can delay diagnosis, breast cancer is often found at a later stage in these women.

Breast Exams Should Be Part of Prenatal and Postnatal Care

To detect breast cancer, pregnant and nursing women should examine their breasts themselves. Women should also receive clinical breast exams during their regular prenatal and postnatal check-ups. Talk to your doctor if you notice any changes in your breasts that you do not expect or that worry you.

Tests That Examine the Breasts Are Used to Detect (Find) and Diagnose Breast Cancer

The following tests and procedures may be used:

- **Physical exam and history:** An exam of the body to check general signs of health, including checking for signs of disease, such as lumps or anything else that seems unusual. A history of the patient's health habits and past illnesses and treatments will also be taken.

- **Clinical breast exam (CBE):** An exam of the breast by a doctor or other health professional. The doctor will carefully feel the breasts and under the arms for lumps or anything else that seems unusual.

- **MRI (magnetic resonance imaging):** A procedure that uses a magnet, radio waves, and a computer to make a series of detailed pictures of both breasts. This procedure is also called nuclear magnetic resonance imaging (NMRI).

- **Ultrasound exam:** A procedure in which high-energy sound waves (ultrasound) are bounced off internal tissues or organs and make echoes. The echoes form a picture of body tissues called a sonogram. The picture can be printed to look at later.

- **Mammogram:** An X-ray of the breast. A mammogram can be done with little risk to the unborn baby. Mammograms in pregnant women may appear negative even though cancer is present.

- **Blood chemistry studies:** A procedure in which a blood sample is checked to measure the amounts of certain substances released into the blood by organs and tissues in the body. An unusual (higher or lower than normal) amount of a substance can be a sign of disease.

- **Biopsy:** The removal of cells or tissues so they can be viewed under a microscope by a pathologist to check for signs of cancer. If a lump in the breast is found, a biopsy may be done.

There are four types of breast biopsies:

1. **Excisional biopsy:** The removal of an entire lump of tissue.

2. **Incisional biopsy:** The removal of part of a lump or a sample of tissue.

3. **Core biopsy:** The removal of tissue using a wide needle.

4. **Fine-needle aspiration (FNA) biopsy:** The removal of tissue or fluid, using a thin needle.

If Cancer Is Found, Tests Are Done to Study the Cancer Cells

Decisions about the best treatment are based on the results of these tests and the age of the unborn baby. The tests give information about:

- How quickly the cancer may grow.

- How likely it is that the cancer will spread to other parts of the body.

- How well certain treatments might work.

- How likely the cancer is to recur (come back).

Tests may include the following:

- **Estrogen and progesterone receptor test:** A test to measure the amount of estrogen and progesterone (hormones) receptors in cancer tissue. If there are more estrogen and progesterone receptors than normal, the cancer is called estrogen and/or progesterone receptor positive. This type of breast cancer may grow more quickly. The test results show whether treatment to block estrogen and progesterone given after the baby is born may stop the cancer from growing.

- **Human epidermal growth factor type 2 receptor (HER2/neu) test:** A laboratory test to measure how many HER2/neu genes there are and how much HER2/neu protein is made in a sample of tissue. If there are more HER2/neu genes or higher levels of HER2/neu protein than normal, the cancer is called HER2/neu positive. This type of breast cancer may grow more quickly and is more likely to spread to other parts of the body. The cancer may be treated with drugs that target the HER2/neu protein, such as trastuzumab and pertuzumab, after the baby is born.

- **Multigene tests:** Tests in which samples of tissue are studied to look at the activity of many genes at the same time. These tests may help predict whether cancer will spread to other parts of the body or recur (come back).

- **Oncotype DX:** This test helps predict whether stage I or stage II breast cancer that is estrogen receptor positive and node-negative will spread to other parts of the body. If the risk of the cancer spreading is high, chemotherapy may be given to lower the risk.

- **MammaPrint:** This test helps predict whether stage I or stage II breast cancer that is node-negative will spread to other parts of the body. If the risk of the cancer spreading is high, chemotherapy may be given to lower the risk.

Certain Factors Affect Prognosis (Chance of Recovery) and Treatment Options

The prognosis (chance of recovery) and treatment options depend on the following:

- The stage of the cancer (the size of the tumor and whether it is in the breast only or has spread to other parts of the body).

- The type of breast cancer.

- The age of the unborn baby.

- Whether there are signs or symptoms.

- The patient's general health.

Chapter 47

Treating Male Breast Cancer

General Information about Male Breast Cancer

Male Breast Cancer Is a Disease in Which Malignant (Cancer) Cells Form in the Tissues of the Breast

Breast cancer may occur in men. Men at any age may develop breast cancer, but it is usually detected (found) in men between 60 and 70 years of age. Male breast cancer makes up less than 1% of all cases of breast cancer.

The following types of breast cancer are found in men:

- **Infiltrating ductal carcinoma:** Cancer that has spread beyond the cells lining ducts in the breast. Most men with breast cancer have this type of cancer.

- **Ductal carcinoma in situ:** Abnormal cells that are found in the lining of a duct; also called intraductal carcinoma.

- **Inflammatory breast cancer:** A type of cancer in which the breast looks red and swollen and feels warm.

- **Paget disease of the nipple:** A tumor that has grown from ducts beneath the nipple onto the surface of the nipple.

Lobular carcinoma in situ (abnormal cells found in one of the lobes or sections of the breast), which sometimes occurs in women, has not been seen in men.

This chapter includes text excerpted from "Male Breast Cancer Treatment–Patient Version (PDQ®)," National Cancer Institute (NCI), February 25, 2016.

Radiation Exposure, High Levels of Estrogen, and a Family History of Breast Cancer Can Increase a Man's Risk of Breast Cancer

Anything that increases your risk of getting a disease is called a risk factor. Having a risk factor does not mean that you will get cancer; not having risk factors doesn't mean that you will not get cancer. Talk with your doctor if you think you may be at risk. Risk factors for breast cancer in men may include the following:

- Being exposed to radiation.

- Having a disease linked to high levels of estrogen in the body, such as cirrhosis (liver disease) or Klinefelter syndrome (a genetic disorder.)

- Having several female relatives who have had breast cancer, especially relatives who have an alteration of the BRCA2 gene.

Male Breast Cancer Is Sometimes Caused by Inherited Gene Mutations (Changes)

The genes in cells carry the hereditary information that is received from a person's parents. Hereditary breast cancer makes up about 5% to 10% of all breast cancer. Some mutated genes related to breast cancer are more common in certain ethnic groups. Men who have a mutated gene related to breast cancer have an increased risk of this disease.

There are tests that can detect (find) mutated genes. These genetic tests are sometimes done for members of families with a high risk of cancer.

Men with Breast Cancer Usually Have Lumps That Can Be Felt

Lumps and other signs may be caused by male breast cancer or by other conditions. Check with your doctor if you notice a change in your breasts.

Tests That Examine the Breasts Are Used to Detect (Find) and Diagnose Breast Cancer in Men

The following tests and procedures may be used:

- **Physical exam and history:** An exam of the body to check general signs of health, including checking for signs of disease, such as lumps or anything else that seems unusual. A history of the patient's health habits and past illnesses and treatments will also be taken.

- **Clinical breast exam (CBE):** An exam of the breast by a doctor or other health professional. The doctor will carefully feel the breasts and under the arms for lumps or anything else that seems unusual.

- **Ultrasound exam:** A procedure in which high-energy sound waves (ultrasound) are bounced off internal tissues or organs and make echoes. The echoes form a picture of body tissues called a sonogram. The picture can be printed to be looked at later.

- **MRI (magnetic resonance imaging):** A procedure that uses a magnet, radio waves, and a computer to make a series of detailed pictures of areas inside the body. This procedure is also called nuclear magnetic resonance imaging (NMRI).

- **Blood chemistry studies:** A procedure in which a blood sample is checked to measure the amounts of certain substances released into the blood by organs and tissues in the body. An unusual (higher or lower than normal) amount of a substance can be a sign of disease.

- **Biopsy:** The removal of cells or tissues so they can be viewed under a microscope by a pathologist to check for signs of cancer. The following are different types of biopsies:

  - **Fine-needle aspiration (FNA) biopsy:** The removal of tissue or fluid using a thin needle.

  - **Core biopsy:** The removal of tissue using a wide needle.

  - **Excisional biopsy:** The removal of an entire lump of tissue.

If Cancer Is Found, Tests Are Done to Study the Cancer Cells

Decisions about the best treatment are based on the results of these tests. The tests give information about:

- How quickly the cancer may grow.
- How likely it is that the cancer will spread through the body.
- How well certain treatments might work.
- How likely the cancer is to recur (come back).

Tests include the following:

- **Estrogen and progesterone receptor test:** A test to measure the amount of estrogen and progesterone (hormones) receptors in cancer tissue. If cancer is found in the breast, tissue from the tumor is checked in the laboratory to find out whether estrogen and progesterone could affect the way cancer grows. The test results show whether hormone therapy may stop the cancer from growing.

- **HER2 test:** A test to measure the amount of HER2 in cancer tissue. HER2 is a growth factor protein that sends growth signals to cells. When cancer forms, the cells may make too much of the protein, causing more cancer cells to grow. If cancer is found in the breast, tissue from the tumor is checked in the laboratory to find out if there is too much HER2 in the cells. The test results show whether monoclonal antibody therapy may stop the cancer from growing.

Survival for Men with Breast Cancer Is Similar to Survival for Women with Breast Cancer

Survival for men with breast cancer is similar to that for women with breast cancer when their stage at diagnosis is the same. Breast cancer in men, however, is often diagnosed at a later stage. Cancer found at a later stage may be less likely to be cured.

Certain Factors Affect Prognosis (Chance of Recovery) and Treatment Options

The prognosis (chance of recovery) and treatment options depend on the following:

- The stage of the cancer (whether it is in the breast only or has spread to other places in the body).

- The type of breast cancer.

- Estrogen-receptor and progesterone-receptor levels in the tumor tissue.

- Whether the cancer is also found in the other breast.

- The patient's age and general health.

Treatment Option Overview

There Are Different Types of Treatment for Men with Breast Cancer

Different types of treatment are available for men with breast cancer. Some treatments are standard (the currently used treatment), and some are being tested in clinical trials. A treatment clinical trial is a research study meant to help improve current treatments or obtain information on new treatments for patients with cancer. When clinical trials show that a new treatment is better than the standard treatment, the new treatment may become the standard treatment.

For some patients, taking part in a clinical trial may be the best treatment choice. Many of today's standard treatments for cancer are based on earlier clinical trials. Patients who take part in a clinical trial may receive the standard treatment or be among the first to receive a new treatment.

Patients who take part in clinical trials also help improve the way cancer will be treated in the future. Even when clinical trials do not lead to effective new treatments, they often answer important questions and help move research forward.

Some clinical trials only include patients who have not yet received treatment. Other trials test treatments for patients whose cancer has not gotten better. There are also clinical trials that test new ways to stop cancer from recurring (coming back) or reduce the side effects of cancer treatment.

Clinical trials are taking place in many parts of the country. Information about clinical trials is available from the NCI website. Choosing the most appropriate cancer treatment is a decision that ideally involves the patient, family, and health care team.

Listed below Are the Five Types of Standard Treatment Used to Treat Men with Breast Cancer:

Surgery

Surgery for men with breast cancer is usually a modified radical mastectomy (removal of the breast, many of the lymph nodes under the arm, the lining over the chest muscles, and sometimes part of the chest wall muscles).

Breast-conserving surgery, an operation to remove the cancer but not the breast itself, is also used for some men with breast cancer.

A lumpectomy is done to remove the tumor (lump) and a small amount of normal tissue around it. Radiation therapy is given after surgery to kill any cancer cells that are left.

Chemotherapy

Chemotherapy is a cancer treatment that uses drugs to stop the growth of cancer cells, either by killing the cells or by stopping them from dividing. When chemotherapy is taken by mouth or injected into a vein or muscle, the drugs enter the bloodstream and can reach cancer cells throughout the body (systemic chemotherapy). When chemotherapy is placed directly into the cerebrospinal fluid, an organ, or a body cavity such as the abdomen, the drugs mainly affect cancer cells in those areas (regional chemotherapy). The way the chemotherapy is given depends on the type and stage of the cancer being treated.

Hormone Therapy

Hormone therapy is a cancer treatment that removes hormones or blocks their action and stops cancer cells from growing. Hormones are substances made by glands in the body and circulated in the bloodstream. Some hormones can cause certain cancers to grow. If tests show that the cancer cells have places where hormones can attach (receptors), drugs, surgery, or radiation therapy is used to reduce the production of hormones or block them from working.

Radiation Therapy

Radiation therapy is a cancer treatment that uses high-energy X-rays or other types of radiation to kill cancer cells or keep them from growing. There are two types of radiation therapy. External radiation therapy uses a machine outside the body to send radiation toward the cancer. Internal radiation therapy uses a radioactive substance sealed in needles, seeds, wires, or catheters that are placed directly into or near the cancer. The way the radiation therapy is given depends on the type and stage of the cancer being treated.

Targeted Therapy

Targeted therapy is a type of treatment that uses drugs or other substances to identify and attack specific cancer cells without harming normal cells. Monoclonal antibody (mAb) therapy is a type of targeted therapy used to treat men with breast cancer.

Monoclonal antibody therapy uses antibodies made in the laboratory from a single type of immune system cell. These antibodies can identify substances on cancer cells or normal substances that may help cancer cells grow. The antibodies attach to the substances and kill the cancer cells, block their growth, or keep them from spreading. Monoclonal antibodies are given by infusion. They may be used alone or to carry drugs, toxins, or radioactive material directly to cancer cells. Monoclonal antibodies are also used with chemotherapy as adjuvant therapy (treatment given after surgery to lower the risk that the cancer will come back).

Trastuzumab is a monoclonal antibody that blocks the effects of the growth factor protein HER2.

Chapter 48

Treating Advanced and Recurrent Breast Cancer

Chapter Contents

Section 48.1

Treating Cancer That Has Metastasized

This section includes text excerpted from "Metastatic Cancer,"
National Cancer Institute (NCI), March 28, 2013.

What Is Metastatic Cancer?

Metastatic cancer is cancer that has spread from the place where it first started to another place in the body. A tumor formed by metastatic cancer cells is called a metastatic tumor or a metastasis. The process by which cancer cells spread to other parts of the body is also called metastasis.

Metastatic cancer has the same name and the same type of cancer cells as the original, or primary, cancer. For example, breast cancer that spreads to the lung and forms a metastatic tumor is metastatic breast cancer, not lung cancer.

Under a microscope, metastatic cancer cells generally look the same as cells of the original cancer. Moreover, metastatic cancer cells and cells of the original cancer usually have some molecular features in common, such as the expression of certain proteins or the presence of specific chromosome changes.

Although some types of metastatic cancer can be cured with current treatments, most cannot. Nevertheless, treatments are available for all patients with metastatic cancer. In general, the primary goal of these treatments is to control the growth of the cancer or to relieve symptoms caused by it. In some cases, metastatic cancer treatments may help prolong life. However, most people who die of cancer die of metastatic disease.

Can Any Type of Cancer Form a Metastatic Tumor?

Virtually all cancers, including cancers of the blood and the lymphatic system (leukemia, multiple myeloma, and lymphoma), can form metastatic tumors. Although rare, the metastasis of blood and lymphatic system cancers to the lung, heart, central nervous system, and other tissues has been reported.

Where Does Cancer Spread?

The most common sites of cancer metastasis are, in alphabetical order, the bone, liver, and lung. Although most cancers have the ability to spread to many different parts of the body, they usually spread to one site more often than others. The following table shows the most common sites of metastasis, excluding the lymph nodes, for several types of cancer:

Table 48.1. Where Does Cancer Spread

Cancer type	Main sites of metastasis
Bladder	Bone, liver, lung
Breast	Bone, brain, liver, lung
Colorectal	Liver, lung, peritoneum
Kidney	Adrenal gland, bone, brain, liver, lung
Lung	Adrenal gland, bone, brain, liver, other lung
Melanoma	Bone, brain, liver, lung, skin/muscle
Ovary	Liver, lung, peritoneum
Pancreas	Liver, lung, peritoneum
Prostate	Adrenal gland, bone, liver, lung
Stomach	Liver, lung, peritoneum
Thyroid	Bone, liver, lung
Uterus	Bone, liver, lung, peritoneum, vagina

Brain includes the neural tissue of the brain (parenchyma) and the leptomeninges (the two innermost membranes—arachnoid mater and pia mater—of the three membranes known as the meninges that surround the brain and spinal cord; the space between the arachnoid mater and the pia mater contains cerebrospinal fluid). Lung includes the main part of the lung (parenchyma) as well as the pleura (the membrane that covers the lungs and lines the chest cavity).

How Does Cancer Spread?

Cancer cell metastasis usually involves the following steps:

- **Local invasion:** Cancer cells invade nearby normal tissue.

- **Intravasation:** Cancer cells invade and move through the walls of nearby lymph vessels or blood vessels.

- **Circulation:** Cancer cells move through the lymphatic system and the bloodstream to other parts of the body.

- **Arrest and extravasation:** Cancer cells arrest, or stop moving, in small blood vessels called capillaries at a distant location.

They then invade the walls of the capillaries and migrate into the surrounding tissue (extravasation).

- **Proliferation:** Cancer cells multiply at the distant location to form small tumors known as micrometastases.

- **Angiogenesis:** Micrometastases stimulate the growth of new blood vessels to obtain a blood supply. A blood supply is needed to obtain the oxygen and nutrients necessary for continued tumor growth.

Because cancers of the lymphatic system or the blood system are already present inside lymph vessels, lymph nodes, or blood vessels, not all of these steps are needed for their metastasis. Also, the lymphatic system drains into the blood system at two locations in the neck.

The ability of a cancer cell to metastasize successfully depends on its individual properties; the properties of the noncancerous cells, including immune system cells, present at the original location; and the properties of the cells it encounters in the lymphatic system or the bloodstream and at the final destination in another part of the body. Not all cancer cells, by themselves, have the ability to metastasize. In addition, the noncancerous cells at the original location may be able to block cancer cell metastasis. Furthermore, successfully reaching another location in the body does not guarantee that a metastatic tumor will form. Metastatic cancer cells can lie dormant (not grow) at a distant site for many years before they begin to grow again, if at all.

Does Metastatic Cancer Have Symptoms?

Some people with metastatic tumors do not have symptoms. Their metastases are found by X-rays or other tests.

When symptoms of metastatic cancer occur, the type and frequency of the symptoms will depend on the size and location of the metastasis. For example, cancer that spreads to the bone is likely to cause pain and can lead to bone fractures. Cancer that spreads to the brain can cause a variety of symptoms, including headaches, seizures, and unsteadiness. Shortness of breath may be a sign of lung metastasis. Abdominal swelling or jaundice (yellowing of the skin) can indicate that cancer has spread to the liver.

Sometimes a person's original cancer is discovered only after a metastatic tumor causes symptoms. For example, a man whose prostate cancer has spread to the bones in his pelvis may have lower back pain (caused by the cancer in his bones) before he experiences any symptoms from the original tumor in his prostate.

Can Someone Have a Metastatic Tumor without Having a Primary Cancer?

No. A metastatic tumor is always caused by cancer cells from another part of the body.

In most cases, when a metastatic tumor is found first, the primary cancer can also be found. The search for the primary cancer may involve lab tests, X-rays, computed tomography (CT) scans, magnetic resonance imaging (MRI) scans, positron emission tomography (PET) scans, and other procedures.

However, in some patients, a metastatic tumor is diagnosed but the primary tumor cannot be found, despite extensive tests, because it either is too small or has completely regressed. The pathologist knows that the diagnosed tumor is a metastasis because the cells do not look like those of the organ or tissue in which the tumor was found. Doctors refer to the primary cancer as unknown or occult (hidden), and the patient is said to have cancer of unknown primary origin (CUP).

Because diagnostic techniques are constantly improving, the number of cases of CUP is going down.

If a Person Who Was Previously Treated for Cancer Gets Diagnosed with Cancer a Second Time, Is the New Cancer a New Primary Cancer or Metastatic Cancer?

The cancer may be a new primary cancer, but, in most cases, it is metastatic cancer.

What Treatments Are Used for Metastatic Cancer?

Metastatic cancer may be treated with systemic therapy (chemotherapy, biological therapy, targeted therapy, hormonal therapy), local therapy (surgery, radiation therapy), or a combination of these treatments. The choice of treatment generally depends on the type of primary cancer; the size, location, and number of metastatic tumors; the patient's age and general health; and the types of treatment the patient has had in the past. In patients with CUP, it is possible to treat the disease even though the primary cancer has not been found.

Are New Treatments for Metastatic Cancer Being Developed?

Yes, researchers are studying new ways to kill or stop the growth of primary cancer cells and metastatic cancer cells, including new ways to boost the strength of immune responses against tumors. In addition, researchers are trying to find ways to disrupt individual steps in the metastatic process.

Before any new treatment can be made widely available to patients, it must be studied in clinical trials (research studies) and found to be safe and effective in treating disease. NCI and many other organizations sponsor clinical trials that take place at hospitals, universities, medical schools, and cancer centers around the country. Clinical trials are a critical step in improving cancer care. The results of previous clinical trials have led to progress not only in the treatment of cancer but also in the detection, diagnosis, and prevention of the disease. Patients interested in taking part in a clinical trial should talk with their doctor.

Section 48.2

Recurrent Breast Cancer

This section includes text excerpted from "When Cancer Returns,"
National Cancer Institute (NCI), September 2014.

When Cancer Returns

Maybe in the back of your mind, you feared that your cancer might return. Now you might be thinking, "How can this be happening to me again? Haven't I been through enough?"

You may be feeling shocked, angry, sad, or scared. Many people have these feelings. But you have something now that you didn't have before—experience. You've lived through cancer once. You know a lot about what to expect and hope for.

Also remember that treatments may have improved since you had your first cancer. New drugs or methods may help with your treatment or in managing side effects. In fact, cancer is now often thought of as a chronic disease, one which people manage for many years.

Why and Where Cancer Returns

When cancer comes back, doctors call it a **recurrence** (or **recurrent cancer**). Some things you should know are:

- A recurrent cancer starts with cancer cells that the first treatment didn't fully remove or destroy. Some may have been too small to be seen in follow-up. This doesn't mean that the treatment you received was wrong. And it doesn't mean that you did anything wrong, either. It just means that a small number of cancer cells survived the treatment. These cells grew over time into **tumors** or cancer that your doctor can now detect.

- When cancer comes back, it doesn't always show up in the same part of the body. For example, if you had colon cancer, it may come back in your liver. But the cancer is still called colon cancer. When the original cancer spreads to a new place, it is called a metastasis

- It is possible to develop a completely new cancer that has nothing to do with your original cancer. But this doesn't happen very often. Recurrences are more common.

Where Cancer Can Return

Doctors define recurrent cancers by where they develop. The different types of recurrence are:

- **Local recurrence**. This means that the cancer is in the same place as the original cancer or is very close to it.

- **Regional recurrence**. This is when tumors grow in lymph nodes or tissues near the place of the original cancer.

- **Distant recurrence**. In these cases, the cancer has spread (metastasized) to organs or tissues far from the place of the original cancer.

Local cancer may be easier to treat than **regional** or **distant cancer**. But this can be different for each patient. Talk with your doctor about your options.

Taking Control: Your Care and Treatment

Cancer that returns can affect all parts of your life. You may feel weak and no longer in control. But you don't have to feel that way. You can take part in your care and in making decisions. You can also talk with your healthcare team and loved ones as you decide about your care. This may help you feel a sense of control and well-being.

Talking with Your Healthcare Team

Many people have a treatment team of health providers who work together to help them. This team may include doctors, nurses, oncology social workers, dietitians, or other specialists. Some people don't like to ask about treatment choices or side effects. They think that doctors don't like being questioned. But this is not true. Most doctors want their patients to be involved in their own care. They want patients to discuss concerns with them.

Here are a few topics you may want to discuss with your healthcare team:

- **Pain or Other Symptoms**. Be honest and open about how you feel. Tell your doctors if you have pain and where. Tell them what you expect in the way of pain relief.

- **Communication**. Some people want to know details about their care. Others prefer to know as little as possible. Some people with cancer want their family members to make most of their decisions. What would you prefer? Decide what you want to know, how much you want to know, and when you've heard enough. Choose what is most comfortable for you. Then tell your doctor and family members. Ask that they follow through with your wishes.

- **Family Wishes**. Some family members may have trouble dealing with cancer. They don't want to know how far the disease has advanced. Find out from your family members how much they want to know. And be sure to tell your doctors and nurses. Do this as soon as possible. It will help avoid conflicts or distress among your loved ones.

Other Tips for Talking with Your Healthcare Team

- Speak openly about your needs, questions, and concerns. Don't be embarrassed to ask your doctor to repeat or explain something.

- Keep a file or notebook of all the papers and test results that your doctor has given you. Take this file to your visits. Also keep records or a diary of all your visits. List the drugs and tests you have taken. Then you can refer to your records when you need to. Many patients say this is helpful, especially when you meet with a new doctor for the first time.

- Write down your questions before you see your doctors so you will remember them.

- Ask a family member or friend to go to the doctor's office with you. They can help you ask questions to get a clear sense of what to expect. This can be an emotional time. You may have trouble focusing on what the doctor says. It may be easier for someone else to take notes. Then you can review them later.

- Ask your doctor if it's okay to tape-record your talks.

- Tell your doctor if you want to get dressed before talking about your results. Wearing a gown or robe is distracting for some patients. They find it harder to focus on what the doctor is saying.

Treatment Choices

There are many treatment choices for recurrent cancer. Your treatment will depend partly on the type of cancer and the treatment you had before. It will also depend on where the cancer has recurred. For example:

- A local recurrence may be best treated by surgery or radiation therapy. This means that the doctor removes the tumor or destroys it with radiation.

- A distant recurrence may need chemotherapy, biological therapy, or radiation therapy.

It's important to ask your doctor questions about all your treatment choices. You may want to get a second opinion as well. You may also want to ask whether a clinical trial is an option for you.

Should I Get a Second Opinion?

Some patients worry that doctors will be offended if they ask for a second opinion. Usually the opposite is true. Most doctors welcome a second opinion. And many health insurance companies will pay for them.

If you get a second opinion, the doctor may agree with your first doctor's treatment plan. Or the second doctor may suggest another approach. Either way, you have more information and perhaps a greater sense of control. You can feel more confident about the decisions you make, knowing that you've looked at your options.

Chapter 49

Breast Cancer Treatment: FAQs

If I Do Need to Seek Treatment for Breast Cancer, What Are Some of My Options?

You can seek conventional treatment from a specialized cancer doctor, called an oncologist. The oncologist will usually assemble a team of specialists to guide your therapy. Besides the oncologist, the team may include a surgeon, a radiation oncologist who is a specialist in radiation therapy, and others.

Before starting treatment, you may want another doctor to review the diagnosis and treatment plan. Some insurance companies require a second opinion. Others may pay for a second opinion if you request it. You might also be eligible to enroll in a clinical trial to receive treatment that conventional therapies may not offer.

What Is a Clinical Trial and How Do I Know If It Is Right for Me?

Clinical trials are research studies on people to find out whether a new drug or treatment is both safe and effective. New therapies are tested on people only after laboratory and animal studies show promising results. The Food and Drug Administration sets strict rules to

This chapter includes text excerpted from "Frequently Asked Questions," NIHSeniorHealth, National Institute on Aging (NIA), April 2015.

make sure that people who agree to be in the studies are treated as safely as possible.

Clinical trials are taking place in many parts of the country. Information about clinical trials can be found at http://www.cancer.gov/clinicaltrials on the website of the National Cancer Institute (NCI). Check NCI's list of cancer clinical trials for breast cancer prevention trials that are now accepting patients.

Before Treatment Begins, I Have Heard That the Doctor Will Stage the Cancer. What Is Staging?

Once breast cancer has been found, it is staged. Staging means determining how far the cancer has progressed. Through staging, the doctor can tell if the cancer has spread and, if so, to what parts of the body. More tests may be performed to help determine the stage. Knowing the stage of the disease helps the doctor plan treatment. Staging will let the doctor know

- the size of the tumor and exactly where it is in the breast
- if the cancer has spread within the breast
- if cancer is present in the lymph nodes under the arm
- If cancer is present in other parts of the body

What Are the Standard Types of Treatment for Breast Cancer?

Standard treatments for breast cancer include

- surgery that takes out the cancer and some surrounding tissue
- radiation therapy that uses high-energy beams to kill cancer cells and shrink tumors and some surrounding tissue.
- chemotherapy that uses anti-cancer drugs to kill cancer most cells
- hormone therapy that keeps cancer cells from getting most of the hormones they need to survive and grow.

What Kinds of Surgery Are Available for Women with Breast Cancer?

Surgery, as opposed to chemotherapy or radiation, is the most common treatment for breast cancer. The kind of surgery a woman has is based on the type and stage of the cancer. Most women can choose between breast-conserving surgery that removes the cancer but not the breast, or surgery that removes the entire breast and sometimes the surrounding tissue.

What Is Involved in Breast-Conserving Surgery?

There are two types of breast-conserving surgery—lumpectomy and partial mastectomy.

- Lumpectomy is the removal of the tumor and a small amount of normal tissue around it. A woman who has a lumpectomy almost always has radiation therapy as well. Most surgeons also take out some of the lymph nodes under the arm.

- Partial or segmental mastectomy is removal of the cancer, some of the breast tissue around the tumor, and the lining over the chest muscles below the tumor. Often, surgeons remove some of the lymph nodes under the arm. In most cases, radiation therapy follows.

What Does a Mastectomy Involve?

Surgery to remove the entire breast and sometimes the surrounding tissue is called a mastectomy. There are three types:

1. A total or simple mastectomy is removal of the whole breast. Sometimes the surgeon takes out lymph nodes under the arm as well.

2. A modified radical mastectomy is removal of the breast, many of the lymph nodes under the arm, and the lining over the chest muscles. Sometimes, the surgeon removes part of the chest wall muscles, too.

3. A radical mastectomy, sometimes called the Halsted radical mastectomy, is removal of the breast, chest muscles, and all of the lymph nodes under the arm. This surgery is used only when the tumor has spread to the chest muscles.

Are There Any Treatments That Follow Surgery?

Even if the surgeon removes all of the cancer that can be seen at the time of surgery, a woman may still receive follow-up treatment. This may include radiation therapy, chemotherapy, or hormone therapy to try to kill any cancer cells that may be left. Treatment that a patient receives after surgery to increase the chances of a cure is called adjuvant therapy.

How and When Is Breast Reconstruction Done?

Breast reconstruction, surgery to rebuild a breast's shape, is often an option after mastectomy. Some health insurance plans pay for all or part of the cost of breast reconstruction. Often, they will pay for surgery to the other breast so that both breasts are about the same shape and size.

If you are thinking about reconstruction, you should talk with a plastic surgeon before your mastectomy. Some women begin reconstruction at the same time as they have the mastectomy done. Others wait several months or even years. Although the reconstructed breast will not have natural sensation, the surgery can give you a result that looks like a breast.

The reconstructed breast may be made with the patient's own, non-breast tissue or by using implants filled with saline or silicone gel. The Food and Drug Administration has decided that breast implants filled with silicone gel may be used only in clinical trials.

How Is Radiation Therapy Used to Treat Breast Cancer?

Radiation therapy uses high-energy X-rays or other types of radiation to kill cancer cells and shrink tumors. This therapy often follows a lumpectomy, and is sometimes used after mastectomy. During radiation therapy, a machine outside the body sends high-energy beams to kill the cancer cells that may still be present in the affected breast or in nearby lymph nodes. Doctors sometimes use radiation therapy along with chemotherapy, or before or instead of surgery.

How Is Chemotherapy Used to Treat Breast Cancer?

Chemotherapy is the use of drugs to kill cancer cells. A patient may take chemotherapy by mouth in pill form, or it may be put into the body by inserting a needle into a vein or muscle. Chemotherapy is called whole body or systemic treatment if the drug(s) enter the bloodstream, travel through the body, and kill cancer cells throughout the body. Treatment with standard chemotherapy can be as short as two months or as long as two years. Targeted therapies, usually in pill form, have become more common and focus on either a gene or protein abnormality and usually have few adverse side-effects as they directly affect the abnormality and not other cells or tissues in the body.

Sometimes chemotherapy is the only treatment the doctor will recommend. More often, however, chemotherapy is used in addition to surgery, radiation therapy, and/or biological therapy.

How Is Hormonal Therapy Used to Treat Breast Cancer?

Hormonal therapy keeps cancer cells from getting the hormones they need to grow. This treatment may include the use of drugs that change the way hormones work. Sometimes it includes surgery to remove the ovaries, which make female hormones. Like chemotherapy, hormonal therapy can affect cancer cells throughout the body.

Often, women with early-stage breast cancer and those with metastatic breast cancer—meaning cancer that has spread to other parts of the body—receive hormone therapy in the form of tamoxifen. Hormone therapy with tamoxifen or estrogens can act on cells all over the body. However, it may increase the chance of developing endometrial cancer. If you take tamoxifen, you should have a pelvic examination every year to look for any signs of cancer. A woman should report any vaginal bleeding, other than menstrual bleeding, to her doctor as soon as possible.

What Drugs Are Available to Treat Breast Cancer?

Certain drugs that have been used successfully in other cancers are now being used to treat some breast cancers. A mix of drugs may increase the length of time you will live, or the length of time you will live without cancer.

In addition, certain drugs like Herceptin® and Tykerb® taken in combination with chemotherapy, can help women with specific genetic breast cancer mutations better than chemotherapy alone.

Part Six

Managing Side Effects and Complications of Breast Cancer Treatment

Part Six

Chapter 50

Fatigue after Cancer Treatment

Fatigue after Cancer Treatment Ends

Fatigue continues to be a problem for many cancer survivors long after treatment ends and the cancer is gone. Studies show that some patients continue to have moderate-to-severe fatigue years after treatment. Long-term therapies such as tamoxifen can also cause fatigue. In children who were treated for brain tumors and cured, fatigue may continue after treatment.

The causes of fatigue after treatment ends are different than the causes of fatigue during treatment. Treating fatigue after treatment ends also may be different from treating it during cancer therapy.

Since fatigue may greatly affect the quality of life for cancer survivors, long-term follow-up care is important.

Fatigue in Cancer Patients Is Often Treated by Relieving Related Conditions Such as Anemia and Depression

Treatment of fatigue depends on the symptoms and whether the cause of fatigue is known. When the cause of fatigue is not known, treatment is usually given to relieve symptoms and teach the patient ways to cope with fatigue.

This chapter includes text excerpted from "Fatigue–Patient Version (PDQ®)," National Cancer Institute (NCI), May 7, 2015.

Treatment of Anemia

Treating anemia may help decrease fatigue. When known, the cause of the anemia is treated. When the cause is not known, treatment for anemia is supportive care and may include the following:

Change in Diet

Eating more foods rich in iron and vitamins may be combined with other treatments for anemia.

Transfusions of Red Blood Cells

Transfusions work well to treat anemia. Possible side effects of transfusions include an allergic reaction, infection, graft-versus-host disease, immune system changes, and too much iron in the blood.

Medicine

Drugs that cause the bone marrow to make more red blood cells may be used to treat anemia-related fatigue in patients receiving chemotherapy. Epoetin alfa and darbepoetin alfa are two of these drugs. This type of drug may shorten survival time, increase the risk of serious heart problems, and cause some tumors to grow faster or recur. The U.S. Food and Drug Administration (FDA) has not approved these drugs for the treatment of fatigue. Discuss the risks and benefits of these drugs with your doctor.

Treatment of Pain

If pain is making fatigue worse, the patient's pain medicine may be changed or the dose may be increased. If too much pain medicine is making fatigue worse, the patient's pain medicine may be changed or the dose may be decreased.

Treatment of Depression

Fatigue in patients who have depression may be treated with antidepressant drugs. Psychostimulant drugs may help some patients have more energy and a better mood, and help them think and concentrate. The use of psychostimulants for treating fatigue is still being studied.

The FDA has not approved psychostimulants for the treatment of fatigue.

Psychostimulants have side effects, especially with long-term use. Different psychostimulants have different side effects. Patients who have heart problems or who take anticancer drugs that affect the heart may have serious side effects from psychostimulants. These drugs have warnings on the label about their risks. Talk to your doctor about the effects these drugs may have and use them only under a doctor's care. Some of the possible side effects include the following:

- Trouble sleeping

- Euphoria (feelings of extreme happiness)

- Headache

- Nausea

- Anxiety

- Mood changes

- Loss of appetite

- Nightmares

- Paranoia (feelings of fear and distrust of other people)

- Serious heart problems

The doctor may prescribe low doses of a psychostimulant to be used for a short time in patients with advanced cancer who have severe fatigue. Talk to your doctor about the risks and benefits of these drugs.

Certain Drugs Are Being Studied for Fatigue Related to Cancer

The following drugs are being studied for fatigue related to cancer:

- Bupropion is an antidepressant that is being studied to treat fatigue in patients with or without depression.

- Dexamethasone is an anti-inflammatory drug being studied in patients with advanced cancer. In one clinical trial, patients who received dexamethasone reported less fatigue than the group that received a placebo. More trials are needed to study the link between inflammation and fatigue.

Certain Dietary Supplements Are Being Studied for Fatigue Related to Cancer

The following dietary supplements are being studied for fatigue related to cancer:

- L-carnitine is a supplement that helps the body make energy and lowers inflammation that may be linked to fatigue.

- Ginseng is an herb used to treat fatigue which may be taken in capsules of ground ginseng root. In a clinical trial, cancer patients who were either in treatment or had finished treatment, received either ginseng or placebo. The group receiving ginseng had less fatigue than the placebo group.

Treatment of Fatigue May Include Teaching the Patient Ways to Increase Energy and Cope with Fatigue in Daily Life

Exercise

Exercise (including walking) may help people with cancer feel better and have more energy. The effect of exercise on fatigue in cancer patients is being studied. One study reported that breast cancer survivors who took part in enjoyable physical activity had less fatigue and pain and were better able to take part in daily activities. In clinical trials, some patients reported the following benefits from exercise:

- More physical energy
- Better appetite
- More able to do the normal activities of daily living
- Better quality of life
- More satisfaction with life
- A greater sense of well-being
- More able to meet the demands of cancer and cancer treatment

Moderate activity for 3 to 5 hours a week may help cancer-related fatigue. You are more likely to follow an exercise plan if you choose a type of exercise that you enjoy. The health care team can help you plan the best time and place for exercise and how often to exercise.

Patients may need to start with light activity for short periods of time and build up to more exercise little by little. Studies have shown that exercise can be safely done during and after cancer treatment.

Mind and body exercises such as qi gong, tai chi, and yoga may help relieve fatigue. These exercises combine activities like movement, stretching, balance, and controlled breathing with spiritual activity such as meditation.

A Schedule of Activity and Rest

Changes in daily routine make the body use more energy. A regular routine can improve sleep and help the patient have more energy to be active during the day. A program of regular times for activity and rest help to make the most of a patient's energy. A health care professional can help patients plan an exercise program and decide which activities are the most important to them.

The following sleep habits may help decrease fatigue:

- Lie in bed for sleep only

- Take naps for no longer than one hour

- Avoid noise (like television and radio) during sleep

Cancer patients should not try to do too much. Health professionals have information about support services to help with daily activities and responsibilities.

Talk Therapy

Therapists use talk therapy (counseling) to treat certain emotional or behavioral disorders. This kind of therapy helps patients change how they think and feel about certain things. Talk therapy may help decrease a cancer patient's fatigue by working on problems related to cancer that make fatigue worse, such as:

- Stress from coping with cancer

- Fear that the cancer may come back

- Feeling hopeless about fatigue

- Not enough social support

- A pattern of sleep and activity that changes from day to day

Self-Care for Fatigue

Fatigue is often a short-term side effect of treatment, but in some patients it becomes chronic (continues as a long-term condition). Managing chronic fatigue includes adjusting to life with fatigue. Learning the facts about cancer-related fatigue may help you cope with it better and improve quality of life. For example, some patients in treatment worry that having fatigue means the treatment is not working. Anxiety over this can make fatigue even worse. Some patients may feel that reporting fatigue is complaining. Knowing that fatigue is a normal side effect that should be reported and treated may make it easier to manage.

Working with the health care team to learn about the following may help patients cope with fatigue:

- How to cope with fatigue as a normal side effect of treatment

- The possible medical causes of fatigue such as not enough fluids, electrolyte imbalance, breathing problems, or anemia

- How patterns of rest and activity affect fatigue

- How to schedule important daily activities during times of less fatigue, and give up less important activities

- The kinds of activities that may help you feel more alert (walking, gardening, bird-watching)

- The difference between fatigue and depression

- How to avoid or change situations that cause stress

- How to avoid or change activities that cause fatigue

- How to change your surroundings to help decrease fatigue

- Exercise programs that are right for you and decrease fatigue

- The importance of eating enough food and drinking enough fluids

- Physical therapy for patients who have nerve problems or muscle weakness

- Respiratory therapy for patients who have trouble breathing

- How to tell if treatments for fatigue are working

Chapter 51

Managing Infections during Chemotherapy

Information for Patients and Caregivers

Cancer patients who are treated with chemotherapy are more likely to get infections. Each year in the United States, 60,000 cancer patients are hospitalized because their low white blood cell count led to a serious infection. One in 14 of these patients dies.

What Is an Infection?

You get an infection when germs enter your body and multiply, causing illness, organ and tissue damage, or disease. Bacteria and viruses cause infections.

- You can get *bacteria* from the air, water, soil, or food during the course of your medical treatment. Most bacteria come from your own body. Common bacterial infections include pneumonia, bronchitis, and ear infections.

- *Viruses* are passed from one person to another. Common viral infections include the common cold, herpes, and the flu.

This chapter includes text excerpted from "Information for Patients and Caregivers," Centers for Disease Control and Prevention (CDC), November 18, 2015.

How Does the Body Normally Fight Infections?

The immune system helps your body protect itself from getting an infection. Cancer and chemotherapy can damage this system, reducing your numbers of infection-fighting white blood cells and making it harder for your body to fight infections. An infection can lead to sepsis, the body's overwhelming and life-threatening response to an infection.

What Should I Do If I Think I Have an Infection?

Call your doctor right away, even if this happens in the middle of the night. This is considered an emergency. Don't wait until morning. Keep your doctor's phone numbers with you at all times. Make sure you know what number to call during your doctor's office hours, as well as after hours.

Prepare: Watch out for Fever

How Can I Prevent Infections during Chemotherapy?

1. Prepare: Watch Out for Fever

2. Prevent: Clean Your Hands

3. Protect: Know the Signs and Symptoms of Infection

If you get a fever during your chemotherapy treatment, it's a medical emergency. Fever may be the only sign that you have an infection, and an infection during chemotherapy can be life-threatening.

You should take your temperature any time you feel warm, flushed, chilled, or not well. If you have a fever, call your doctor right away, even if it happens in the middle of the night. You should also—

- Find out from your doctor when your white blood cell count is likely to the be the lowest, since this is when you're most at risk for infection.

- Keep a working thermometer in a convenient location and know how to use it.

- Keep your doctor's phone numbers with you at all times. Make sure you know what number to call when their office is open and closed.

- If you have to go to the emergency room, tell the person checking you in that you are a cancer patient undergoing chemotherapy. If you have a fever, you might have an infection. This is a life-threatening condition, and you should be seen quickly.

Prevent: Clean Your Hands

Clean hands help prevent infections. Many diseases are spread by not cleaning your hands, which is especially dangerous when you're getting chemotherapy treatment because your body may not be able to fight off infections like it used to. You and anyone who comes around you, including all members of your household, your doctors, and nurses, should clean their hands frequently. Don't be afraid to ask people to clean their hands. Use soap and water to wash your hands. If soap and water aren't available, it's OK to use an alcohol-based hand sanitizer.

Be sure to clean your hands—

- Before, during, and after cooking food
- Before you eat
- After going to the bathroom
- After changing diapers or helping a child use the bathroom
- After blowing your nose, coughing, or sneezing
- After touching or cleaning up after your pet
- After touching trash
- Before and after treating a cut or wound or caring for your catheter, port, or other access device

Protect: Know the Signs and Symptoms of Infection

During your chemotherapy treatment, your body may not be able to fight off infections like it used to. When your white blood cell counts are low, you must take infection symptoms seriously. Infection during chemotherapy can lead to hospitalization or death. Call your doctor right away if you notice any of the following signs and symptoms of an infection—

- Fever (this is sometimes the only sign of an infection)
- Chills and sweats
- Change in cough or a new cough

- Sore throat or new mouth sore

- Shortness of breath

- Nasal congestion

- Stiff neck

- Burning or pain with urination

- Unusual vaginal discharge or irritation

- Increased urination

- Redness, soreness, or swelling in any area, including surgical wounds and ports

- Diarrhea

- Vomiting

- Pain in the abdomen or rectum

- New onset of pain

Find out from your doctor when your white blood cell count is likely to be the lowest, since this is when you're most at risk for infection. This usually occurs between 7 and 12 days after you finish each chemotherapy dose, and may last up to one week.

Chapter 52

Lymphedema

Lymphedema Is the Build-Up of Fluid in Soft Body Tissues When the Lymph System Is Damaged or Blocked

Lymphedema occurs when the lymph system is damaged or blocked. Fluid builds up in soft body tissues and causes swelling. It is a common problem that may be caused by cancer and cancer treatment. Lymphedema usually affects an arm or leg, but it can also affect other parts of the body. Lymphedema can cause long-term physical, psychological, and social problems for patients.

The Lymph System Is a Network of Lymph Vessels, Tissues, and Organs That Carry Lymph throughout the Body

The parts of the lymph system that play a direct part in lymphedema include the following:

- Lymph: A clear fluid that contains lymphocytes (white blood cells) that fight infection and the growth of tumors. Lymph also contains plasma, the watery part of the blood that carries the blood cells.

This chapter includes text excerpted from "Lymphedema–Patient Version (PDQ®)," National Cancer Institute (NCI), May 29, 2015.

- Lymph vessels: A network of thin tubes that helps lymph flow through the body and returns it to the bloodstream.

- Lymph nodes: Small, bean-shaped structures that filter lymph and store white blood cells that help fight infection and disease. Lymph nodes are located along the network of lymph vessels found throughout the body. Clusters of lymph nodes are found in the underarm, pelvis, neck, abdomen, and groin.

The spleen, thymus, tonsils, and bone marrow are also part of the lymph system but do not play a direct part in lymphedema.

Lymphedema Occurs When Lymph Is Not Able to Flow through the Body the Way That It Should

When the lymph system is working as it should, lymph flows through the body and is returned to the bloodstream.

- Fluid and plasma leak out of the capillaries (smallest blood vessels) and flow around body tissues so the cells can take up nutrients and oxygen.

- Some of this fluid goes back into the bloodstream. The rest of the fluid enters the lymph system through tiny lymph vessels. These lymph vessels pick up the lymph and move it toward the heart. The lymph is slowly moved through larger and larger lymph vessels and passes through lymph nodes where waste is filtered from the lymph.

- The lymph keeps moving through the lymph system and collects near the neck, then flows into one of two large ducts:

- The right lymph duct collects lymph from the right arm and the right side of the head and chest.

- The left lymph duct collects lymph from both legs, the left arm, and the left side of the head and chest.

- These large ducts empty into veins under the collarbones, which carry the lymph to the heart, where it is returned to the bloodstream.

When part of the lymph system is damaged or blocked, fluid cannot drain from nearby body tissues. Fluid builds up in the tissues and causes swelling.

There Are Two Types of Lymphedema

Lymphedema may be either primary or secondary:

- Primary lymphedema is caused by the abnormal development of the lymph system. Symptoms may occur at birth or later in life.

- Secondary lymphedema is caused by damage to the lymph system. The lymph system may be damaged or blocked by infection, injury, cancer, removal of lymph nodes, radiation to the affected area, or scar tissue from radiation therapy or surgery.

This summary is about secondary lymphedema in adults that is caused by cancer or cancer treatment.

Possible Signs of Lymphedema Include Swelling of the Arms or Legs

Other conditions may cause the same symptoms. A doctor should be consulted if any of the following problems occur:

- Swelling of an arm or leg, which may include fingers and toes.
- A full or heavy feeling in an arm or leg.
- A tight feeling in the skin.
- Trouble moving a joint in the arm or leg.
- Thickening of the skin, with or without skin changes such as blisters or warts.
- A feeling of tightness when wearing clothing, shoes, bracelets, watches, or rings.
- Itching of the legs or toes.
- A burning feeling in the legs.
- Trouble sleeping.
- Loss of hair.

Daily activities and the ability to work or enjoy hobbies may be affected by lymphedema.

These symptoms may occur very slowly over time or more quickly if there is an infection or injury to the arm or leg.

Cancer and Its Treatment Are Risk Factors for Lymphedema

Lymphedema can occur after any cancer or treatment that affects the flow of lymph through the lymph nodes, such as removal of lymph nodes. It may develop within days or many years after treatment. Most lymphedema develops within three years of surgery. Risk factors for lymphedema include the following:

- Removal and/or radiation of lymph nodes in the underarm, groin, pelvis, or neck. The risk of lymphedema increases with the number of lymph nodes affected. There is less risk with the removal of only the sentinel lymph node (the first lymph node to receive lymphatic drainage from a tumor).

- Being overweight or obese.

- Slow healing of the skin after surgery.

- A tumor that affects or blocks the left lymph duct or lymph nodes or vessels in the neck, chest, underarm, pelvis, or abdomen.

- Scar tissue in the lymph ducts under the collarbones, caused by surgery or radiation therapy.

Lymphedema often occurs in breast cancer patients who had all or part of their breast removed and axillary (underarm) lymph nodes removed. Lymphedema in the legs may occur after surgery for uterine cancer, prostate cancer, lymphoma, or melanoma. It may also occur with vulvar cancer or ovarian cancer.

Tests That Examine the Lymph System Are Used to Diagnose Lymphedema

It is important to make sure there are no other causes of swelling, such as infection or blood clots. The following tests and procedures may be used to diagnose lymphedema:

- **Physical exam and history:** An exam of the body to check general signs of health, including checking for signs of disease, such as lumps or anything else that seems unusual. A history of the patient's health habits and past illnesses and treatments will also be taken.

- **Lymphoscintigraphy:** A method used to check the lymph system for disease. A very small amount of a radioactive substance that flows through the lymph ducts and can be taken up by lymph nodes is injected into the body. A scanner or probe is used to follow the movement of this substance. Lymphoscintigraphy is used to find the sentinel lymph node (the first node to receive lymph from a tumor) or to diagnose certain diseases or conditions, such as lymphedema.

- **MRI (magnetic resonance imaging):** A procedure that uses a magnet, radio waves, and a computer to make a series of detailed pictures of areas inside the body. This procedure is also called nuclear magnetic resonance imaging (NMRI).

The swollen arm or leg is usually measured and compared to the other arm or leg. Measurements are taken over time to see how well treatment is working.

A grading system is also used to diagnose and describe lymphedema. Grades 1, 2, 3, and 4 are based on size of the affected limb and how severe the signs and symptoms are.

Stages May Be Used to Describe Lymphedema

- **Stage I:** The limb (arm or leg) is swollen and feels heavy. Pressing on the swollen area leaves a pit (dent). This stage of lymphedema may go away without treatment.

- **Stage II:** The limb is swollen and feels spongy. A condition called tissue fibrosis may develop and cause the limb to feel hard. Pressing on the swollen area does not leave a pit.

- **Stage III:** This is the most advanced stage. The swollen limb may be very large. Stage III lymphedema rarely occurs in breast cancer patients. Stage III is also called lymphostatic elephantiasis.

Chapter 53

Pain after Cancer Treatment

Pain

Cancer itself and the side effects of cancer treatment can sometimes cause pain. Pain is not something that you have to "put up with." Controlling pain is an important part of your cancer treatment plan. Pain can suppress the immune system, increase the time it takes your body to heal, interfere with sleep, and affect your mood.

Talk with your healthcare team about pain, especially if:

- the pain isn't getting better or going away with pain medicine

- the pain comes on quickly

- the pain makes it hard to eat, sleep, or perform your normal activities

- you feel new pain

- you have side effects from the pain medicine such as sleepiness, nausea, or constipation

Your doctor will work with you to develop a pain control plan that is based on your description of the pain. Taking pain medicine is an

---

This chapter contains text excerpted from the following sources: Text beginning with the heading "Pain" is excerpted from "Pain," National Cancer Institute (NCI), April 29, 2015; Text beginning with the heading "Cancer, Treatment for Cancer, or Diagnostic Tests May Cause You to Feel Pain" is excerpted from "Cancer Pain–Patient Version (PDQ®)," National Cancer Institute (NCI), March 11, 2016.

important part of the plan. Your doctor will talk with you about using drugs to control pain and prescribe medicine (including opioids and nonopioid medicines) to treat the pain.

Ways to Treat or Lessen Pain

Here are some steps you can take, as you work with your healthcare team to prevent, treat, or lessen pain:

- **Keep track of your pain levels.** Each day, write about any pain you feel. Writing down answers to the questions below will help you describe the pain to your doctor or nurse.

- What part of your body feels painful?

- What does the pain feel like (is it sharp, burning, shooting, or throbbing) and where do you feel the pain?

- When does the pain start? How long does the pain last?

- What activities (such as eating, sleeping, or other activities) does pain interfere with?

- What makes the pain feel better or worse? For example, do ice packs, heating pads, or exercises help? Does pain medicine help? How much do you take? How often do you take it?

- How bad is the pain, on a scale of 1 to 10, where "10" is the most pain and "1" is the least pain?

- **Take the prescribed pain medicine.** Take the right amount of medicine at the right time. Do not wait until your pain gets too bad before taking pain medicine. Waiting to take your medicine could make it take longer for the pain to go away or increase the amount of medicine needed to lower pain. Do not stop taking the pain medicine unless your doctor advises you to. Tell your doctor or nurse if the medicine no longer lowers the pain, or if you are in pain, but it's not yet time to take the pain medicine.

- **Meet with a pain specialist.** Specialists who treat pain often work together as part of a pain or palliative care team. These specialists may include a neurologist, surgeon, physiatrist, psychiatrist, psychologist, or pharmacist. Talk with your healthcare team to find a pain specialist.

- **Ask about integrative medicine.** Treatments such as acupuncture, biofeedback, hypnosis, massage therapy and physical therapy may also be used to treat pain.

Talking With Your Healthcare Team

Prepare for your visit by making a list of questions to ask. Consider adding these questions to your list:

- What problems or levels of pain should I call you about?

- What is most likely causing the pain?

- What can I do to lessen the pain?

- What medicine should I take? If the pain doesn't go away, how much more medicine can I take, and when can I take it?

- What are the side effects of this pain medicine? How long will they last?

- Is there a pain specialist I could meet with to get more support to lower my pain?

Cancer, Treatment for Cancer, or Diagnostic Tests May Cause You to Feel Pain

Pain is one of the most common symptoms in cancer patients. Pain can be caused by cancer, treatment for cancer, or a combination of factors. Tumors, surgery, intravenous chemotherapy, radiation therapy, targeted therapy, supportive care therapies such as bisphosphonates, and/or diagnostic procedures may cause you pain.

Younger patients are more likely to have cancer pain and pain flares than older patients. Patients with advanced cancer have more severe pain, and many cancer survivors have pain that continues after cancer treatment ends.

Pain Control Can Improve Your Quality of Life

Pain can be controlled in most patients with cancer. Although cancer pain cannot always be relieved completely, there are ways to lessen pain in most patients. Pain control can improve your quality of life all through your cancer treatment and after it ends.

Pain Can Be Managed before, during, and after Diagnostic and Treatment Procedures

Many diagnostic and treatment procedures are painful. It helps to start pain control before the procedure begins. Some drugs may be used to help you feel calm or fall asleep. Treatments such as imagery or relaxation can also help control pain and anxiety related to treatment. Knowing what will happen during the procedure and having a relative or friend stay with you may also help lower anxiety.

Different Cancer Treatments May Cause Specific Types of Pain

Patients may have different types of pain depending on the treatments they receive, including:

- Spasms, stinging, and itching caused by intravenous chemotherapy.
- Mucositis (sores or inflammation in the mouth or other parts of the digestive system) caused by chemotherapy or targeted therapy.
- Skin pain, rash, or hand-foot syndrome (redness, tingling, or burning in the palms of the hands and/or the soles of feet) caused by chemotherapy or targeted therapy.
- Pain in joints and muscles throughout the body caused by paclitaxel or aromatase inhibitor therapy.
- Osteonecrosis of the jaw caused by bisphosphonates given for cancer that has spread to the bone.
- Pain syndromes, including mucositis, inflammation in areas receiving radiation therapy, pain flares, and dermatitis, caused by radiation.

Cancer Pain May Affect Quality of Life and Ability to Function Even after Treatment Ends

Pain that is severe or continues after cancer treatment ends increases the risk of anxiety and depression. Patients may be disabled by their pain, unable to work, or feel that they are losing support once their care moves from their oncology team back to their primary care team. Feelings of anxiety and depression can worsen cancer pain and make it harder to control.

Each Patient Needs a Personal Plan to Control Cancer Pain

Each person's diagnosis, cancer stage, response to pain, and personal likes and dislikes are different. For this reason, each patient needs a personal plan to control cancer pain. You, your family, and your healthcare team can work together to manage your pain. As part of your pain control plan, your healthcare provider can give you and your family members written instructions to control your pain at home. Find out who you should call if you have questions.

Chapter 54

Sexuality and Fertility Issues in People with Cancer

Sexual and Fertility Problems (Men)

Many cancer treatments and some types of cancer can cause sexual and fertility-related side effects. Whether you have these problems depends on the type of treatment(s) you receive, your age at time of treatment, and how long it has been since you had treatment.

It is important to learn how the treatment recommended for you may affect your fertility *before* you start treatment. Many men also find it helpful to talk with their doctor or nurse about sexual problems they may have during treatment. Learning about these issues will help you make decisions that are best for you.

Treatments That May Cause Sexual and Fertility Problems

- Radiation therapy to the pelvic area (such as to the anus, bladder, penis, or prostate) may make it difficult to get or keep an erection.

This chapter contains text excerpted from the following sources: Text beginning with the heading "Sexual and Fertility Problems (Men)" is excerpted from "Sexual and Fertility Problems (Men)," National Cancer Institute (NCI), April 29, 2015; Text beginning with the heading "Sexual and Fertility Problems (Women)" is excerpted from "Sexual and Fertility Problems (Women)," National Cancer Institute (NCI), April 29, 2015.

It may also cause infertility, which may be temporary or permanent. Some men notice that changes in sexual function occur slowly over the period of about a year. Smoking, heart disease, high blood pressure, and diabetes can make some problems worse.

- Hormone therapy may cause mood changes, decreased sexual desire, erectile dysfunction, and trouble reaching orgasm.

- Some types of chemotherapy may cause low testosterone levels and lower your sexual desire. Chemotherapy may also cause infertility, which may be temporary or permanent.

- Surgery for penile, rectal, prostate, testicular, and other pelvic cancers may affect sexual function and fertility.

- Other side effects of cancer and its treatment, such as fatigue and anxiety, can also lower your interest in sexual activity.

Learn What to Expect

Before starting treatment talk with your healthcare team to learn what to expect based on the type of treatment you will be receiving. Get answers to questions about:

- **Sexual activity.** Ask your doctor or nurse if it is okay for you to be sexually active during your treatment period. Most men can, but you will want to confirm this with your doctor or nurse.

- **Infertility.** Ask if your treatment could affect your fertility or make you infertile. If you would like to have children after treatment, talk with your doctor or nurse before you start treatment. Learn ahead of time about your options, such as sperm banking. Procedures such as testicular sperm extraction, testicular tissue freezing and testicular tissue cryopreservation (for young boys) are available. Talk with your doctor or a fertility specialist to learn more about these procedures and other that may be available through a clinical trial.

- **Birth control.** It is important to prevent pregnancy during treatment and for some time after treatment. Ask your doctor or nurse about different methods of birth control to choose one that may be best for you and your partner.

- **Condom use.** If you receive chemotherapy you will most likely be advised to use a condom during intercourse, even if your partner is on birth control or cannot have children. This is because your semen may have traces of the chemotherapy drugs.

Talking with Your Healthcare Team

Prepare for your visit by making a list of questions to ask. Consider adding these questions to your list:

Sexual and Sexuality-Related Questions

- What problems or changes might I have during or after treatment?

- How long might these problems last? Will any of these problems be permanent?

- How can these problems be treated or managed?

- Could you give me the name of a specialist who I can talk with to learn more?

- What precautions do I need to take during treatment? For example, do I need to use a condom?

- Is there a support group for men that you would recommend for me?

Fertility-Related Questions

- Will the treatment I receive make me infertile (unable to have children in the future)?

- What are all of my options now if I would like to have children in the future?

- Could you give me the name of a fertility specialist who I can talk with to learn more?

- After treatment, how long should I use some method of birth control?

Sexual and Fertility Problems (Women)

Many cancer treatments and some types of cancer can cause sexual and fertility-related side effects. Whether or not you have these problems depends on the type of treatment(s) you receive, your age at time of treatment, and the length of time since treatment.

It is important to get information about how the treatment recommended for you may affect your fertility *before* you start treatment.

Many women also find it helpful to talk with their doctor or nurse about sexual problems they may have during treatment. Learning about these issues will help you make decisions that are best for you.

Treatments That May Cause Sexual and Fertility Problems

- Some types of chemotherapy may cause symptoms of early menopause (hot flashes, vaginal dryness, irregular or no periods, and feeling irritable) or lead to vaginal infections. It may also cause temporary or permanent infertility.

- Hormone therapy can stop or slow the growth of certain cancers, such as breast cancer. However, lower hormone levels can cause problems (hot flashes, vaginal discharge or pain, and trouble reaching orgasm). These problems are more likely in women over the age of 45.

- Radiation therapy to the pelvic area (vagina, uterus, or ovaries) can cause:

  - infertility

  - symptoms of menopause (hot flashes, vaginal dryness, and no periods)

  - pain or discomfort during sex

  - increased risk of birth defects; use a method of birth control to avoid pregnancy

  - vaginal stenosis (less elastic, narrow, shorter vagina)

  - vaginal itching, burning, or dryness

  - vaginal atrophy (weak vaginal muscles and thin vaginal wall)

- Surgery for cancers of the uterus, bladder, vulvar, endometrium, cervix, or ovaries may cause sexual and infertility-related side effects, depending on the size and location of the tumor.

- Other side effects of cancer and its treatment, such as fatigue and anxiety, can also lower your interest in sexual activity.

What to Expect

Before starting treatment talk with your healthcare team to learn what to expect, based on the type of treatment you will be receiving. Get answers to questions about:

440

- **Infertility.** Ask if treatment could lower your fertility or make you infertile. If you would like to have children after treatment, talk with your doctor or nurse before you start treatment. Learn ahead of time about options such as embryo banking, ovarian tissue banking, ovarian transposition, and clinical trials for egg banking. Talk with your doctor or a fertility specialist to learn more about these procedures and others that may be available through a clinical trial.

- **Pregnancy.** It is important to prevent pregnancy during treatment and for some time after treatment. Ask your doctor or nurse about different methods of birth control, to choose one that may be best for you and your partner.

- **Sexual activity.** Ask your doctor or nurse if it is okay for you to be sexually active during your treatment period. Most women can be sexually active, but you will want to confirm this with your healthcare team.

Talking with Your Healthcare Team

Prepare for your visit by making a list of questions. Consider adding these questions to your list:

Sexual and Sexuality-Related Questions

- What problems or changes might I have during treatment?
- How long might these problems last? Will any be permanent?
- Is there treatment for these problems?
- Would you give me the name of a specialist that I could meet with?
- Is there a support group for women that you would recommend?

Fertility-Related Questions

- Will my fertility be affected by the treatment I receive?
- What are all of my options now if I would like to have children in the future?
- Could you give me the name of a fertility specialist who I can talk with to learn more?
- After treatment, how long should I use birth control?

Chapter 55

Hot Flashes and Night Sweats

Overview

Hot flashes and night sweats are common in cancer survivors, particularly women, but they can also occur in men. Pathophysiologic mechanisms are complex. Treatment options are broad-based, including hormonal agents, nonhormonal pharmacotherapies, and diverse integrative medicine modalities.

Hot flashes occur in approximately two-thirds of postmenopausal women with a breast cancer history and are associated with night sweats in 44%. For most breast cancer and prostate cancer patients, hot flash intensity is moderate to severe. Sweating can be part of the hot flash complex that characterizes the vasomotor instability of menopause. Physiologically, sweating mediates core body temperature by producing transdermal evaporative heat loss. Hot flashes accompanied by sweating that occur during the sleeping hours are often called *night sweats*. Another synonym found in the literature is *hot flushes*.

Approximately 20% of women without breast cancer seek medical treatment for postmenopausal symptoms, including symptoms related

---

This chapter includes text excerpted from "Hot Flashes and Night Sweats–Patient Version (PDQ®)," National Cancer Institute (NCI), October 15, 2014.

to vasomotor instability. Vasomotor symptoms resolve spontaneously in most patients in this population, with only 20% of affected women reporting significant hot flashes 4 years after the last menses. There are no comparable data for women with metastatic breast cancer. Three-quarters of men with locally advanced or metastatic prostate cancer treated with medical or surgical orchiectomy experience hot flashes.

Hot Flashes and Night Sweats May Be Side Effects of Cancer or Its Treatment

Sweating is the body's way of lowering body temperature by causing heat loss through the skin. In patients with cancer, sweating may be caused by fever, a tumor, or cancer treatment.

Hot flashes can also cause too much sweating. They may occur in natural menopause or in patients who have been treated for breast cancer or prostate cancer.

Hot flashes combined with sweats that happen while sleeping are often called night sweats or hot flushes.

Hot Flashes and Night Sweats Affect Quality of Life in Many Patients with Cancer

A treatment plan to help manage hot flashes and night sweats is based on the patient's condition and goals of care. For some patients, relieving symptoms and improving quality of life is the most important goal.

This chapter describes the causes and treatment of hot flashes and night sweats in cancer patients.

Causes

In patients with cancer, hot flashes and night sweats may be caused by the tumor, its treatment, or other conditions

Sweating happens with disease conditions such as fever and may occur without disease in warm climates, during exercise, and during hot flashes in menopause. Sweating helps balance body temperature by allowing heat to evaporate through the skin.

Hot flashes and night sweats are common in patients with cancer and in cancer survivors. They are more common in women but can also occur in men.

Many Patients Treated for Breast Cancer and Prostate Cancer Have Hot Flashes

Menopause in women can have natural, surgical, or chemical causes. Chemical menopause in women with cancer is caused by certain types of chemotherapy, radiation, or hormone therapy with androgen (a male hormone).

"Male menopause" in men with cancer can be caused by orchiectomy (surgery to remove one or both testicles) or hormone therapy with gonadotropin-releasing hormone or estrogen.

Treatment for breast cancer and prostate cancer can cause menopause or menopause-like effects, including severe hot flashes.

Certain Types of Drugs Can Cause Night Sweats

Drugs that may cause night sweats include the following:

- Tamoxifen
- Aromatase inhibitors
- Opioids
- Tricyclic antidepressants
- Steroids

Treatment

Sweats Are Controlled by Treating Their Cause

Sweats caused by fever are controlled by treating the cause of the fever. Sweats caused by a tumor are usually controlled by treatment of the tumor.

Hot Flashes May Be Controlled with Estrogen Replacement Therapy

Hot flashes during natural or treatment-related menopause can be controlled with estrogen replacement therapy. However, many women are not able to take estrogen replacement (for example, women who have or had breast cancer). Hormone replacement therapy that combines estrogen with progestin may increase the risk of breast cancer or breast cancer recurrence.

Treatment of hot flashes in men who have been treated for prostate cancer may include estrogens, progestin, antidepressants, and

445

anticonvulsants. Certain hormones (such as estrogen) can make some cancers grow.

Other Drugs May Be Useful in Some Patients

Studies of non-estrogen drugs to treat hot flashes in women with a history of breast cancer have reported that many of them do not work as well as estrogen replacement or have side effects. Megestrol (a drug like progesterone), certain antidepressants, anticonvulsants, and clonidine (a drug used to treat high blood pressure) are non-estrogen drugs used to control hot flashes. Some antidepressants may change how other drugs, such as tamoxifen, work in the body. Side effects of drug therapy may include the following:

- Antidepressants used to treat hot flashes over a short period of time may cause nausea, drowsiness, dry mouth, and changes in appetite.

- Anticonvulsants used to treat hot flashes may cause drowsiness, dizziness, and trouble concentrating.

- Clonidine may cause dry mouth, drowsiness, constipation, and insomnia.

Patients may respond in different ways to drug therapy. It is important that the patient's health care providers know about all medicines, dietary supplements, and herbs the patient is taking.

Treatments That Help Patients Cope with Stress and Anxiety May Help Manage Hot Flashes

Treatments that change how patients deal with stress, anxiety, and negative emotions may help manage hot flashes. These are called psychological interventions. Psychological interventions help patients gain a sense of control and develop coping skills to manage symptoms. Staying calm and managing stress may lower levels of a hormone called serotonin that can trigger hot flashes.

Psychological interventions may help hot flashes and related problems when used together with drug treatment.

Hypnosis May Help Relieve Hot Flashes

Hypnosis is a trance-like state that allows a person to be more aware, focused, and open to suggestion. Under hypnosis, the person can concentrate more clearly on a specific thought, feeling, or sensation without becoming distracted.

Hypnosis is a newer treatment for hot flashes that has been shown to be helpful. In hypnosis, a therapist helps the patient to deeply relax and focus on cooling thoughts. This may lower stress levels, balance body temperature, and calm the heart rate and breathing rate.

Comfort Measures May Help Relieve Night Sweats Related to Cancer

Comfort measures may be used to treat night sweats related to cancer. Since body temperature goes up before a hot flash, doing the following may control body temperature and help control symptoms:

- Wear loose-fitting clothes made of cotton

- Use fans and open windows to keep air moving

- Practice relaxation training and slow, deep breathing

Herbs and Dietary Supplements Should Be Used with Caution

Studies of vitamin E for the relief of hot flashes show that it is only slightly better than a placebo (pill that has no effect). Most studies of soy and black cohosh show they are no better than a placebo in reducing hot flashes. Soy contains estrogen-like substances; the effect of soy on the risk of breast cancer growth or recurrence is not clear. Studies of ground flaxseed to treat hot flashes have shown mixed results.

Claims are made about several other plant-based and natural products as remedies for hot flashes. These include dong quai, milk thistle, red clover, licorice root extract, and chaste tree berry. Since little is known about how these products work or whether they affect the risk of breast cancer, women should be cautious about using them.

Acupuncture May Be Used to Treat Hot Flashes

Pilot studies of acupuncture and randomized clinical trials that compare true acupuncture and sham (inactive) treatment have been done in patients with hot flashes. Results are not clear and more studies are needed.

Chapter 56

Dealing with Hair Loss Related to Breast Cancer Treatment

Hair Loss (Alopecia)

Some types of chemotherapy cause the hair on your head and other parts of your body to fall out. Radiation therapy can also cause hair loss on the part of the body that is being treated. Hair loss is called alopecia. Talk with your healthcare team to learn if the cancer treatment you will be receiving causes hair loss. Your doctor or nurse will share strategies that have help others, including those listed below.

Ways to Manage

Talk with your healthcare team about ways to manage before and after hair loss:

- **Treat your hair gently.** You may want to use a hairbrush with soft bristles or a wide-tooth comb. Do not use hair dryers, irons, or products such as gels or clips that may hurt your scalp. Wash your hair with a mild shampoo. Wash it less often and be very gentle. Pat it dry with a soft towel.

This chapter includes text excerpted from "Hair Loss (Alopecia)," National Cancer Institute (NCI), April 29, 2015.

- **You have choices.** Some people choose to cut their hair short to make it easier to deal with when it starts to fall out. Others choose to shave their head. If you choose to shave your head, use an electric shaver so you won't cut yourself. If you plan to buy a wig, get one while you still have hair so you can match it to the color of your hair. If you find wigs to be itchy and hot, try wearing a comfortable scarf or turban.

- **Protect and care for your scalp.** Use sunscreen or wear a hat when you are outside. Choose a comfortable scarf or hat that you enjoy and that keeps your head warm. If your scalp itches or feels tender, using lotions and conditioners can help it feel better.

- **Talk about your feelings.** Many people feel angry, depressed, or embarrassed about hair loss. It can help to share these feelings with someone who understands. Some people find it helpful to talk with other people who have lost their hair during cancer treatment. Talking openly and honestly with your children and close family members can also help you all. Tell them that you expect to lose your hair during treatment.

Ways to Care for Your Hair When It Grows Back

- **Be gentle.** When your hair starts to grow back, you will want to be gentle with it. Avoid too much brushing, curling, and blow-drying. You may not want to wash your hair as frequently.

- **After chemotherapy.** Hair often grows back in 2 to 3 months after treatment has ended. Your hair will be very fine when it starts to grow back. Sometimes your new hair can be curlier or straighter—or even a different color. In time, it may go back to how it was before treatment.

- **After radiation therapy.** Hair often grows back in 3 to 6 months after treatment has ended. If you received a very high dose of radiation your hair may grow back thinner or not at all on the part of your body that received radiation.

Talking with Your Healthcare Team

Prepare for your visit by making a list of questions to ask. Consider adding these questions to your list:

- Is treatment likely to cause my hair to fall out?

- How should I protect and care for my head? Are there products that you recommend? Ones I should avoid?

- Where can I get a wig or hairpiece?

- What support groups could I meet with that might help?

- When will my hair grow back?

Chapter 57

Other Side Effects and Complications of Breast Cancer Treatment

Chapter Contents

Section 57.1

Anemia

This section includes text excerpted from "Anemia,"
National Cancer Institute (NCI), April 29, 2015.

What Is Anemia?

Anemia is a condition that can make you feel very tired, short of breath, and lightheaded. Other signs of anemia may include feeling dizzy or faint, headaches, a fast heartbeat, and/or pale skin.

Cancer treatments, such as chemotherapy and radiation therapy, as well as cancers that affect the bone marrow, can cause anemia. When you are anemic, your body does not have enough red blood cells. Red blood cells are the cells that that carry oxygen from the lungs throughout your body to help it work properly. You will have blood tests to check for anemia. Treatment for anemia is also based on your symptoms and on what is causing the anemia.

What Are the Ways to Manage Anemia?

Here are some steps you can take if you have fatigue caused by anemia:

Save your energy and ask for help. Choose the most important things to do each day. When people offer to help, let them do so. They can take you to the doctor, make meals, or do other things you are too tired to do.

Balance rest with activity. Take short naps during the day, but keep in mind that too much bed rest can make you feel weak. You may feel better if you take short walks or exercise a little every day.

Eat and drink well. Talk with your doctor, nurse, or a registered dietitian to learn what foods and drinks are best for you. You may need to eat foods that are high in protein or iron.

Talking with Your Healthcare Team

Prepare for your visit by making a list of questions to ask. Consider adding these questions to your list:

- What is causing the anemia?

- What problems should I call you about?

- What steps can I take to feel better?

- Would medicine, iron pills, a blood transfusion, or other treatments help me?

- Would you give me the name of a registered dietitian who could also give me advice?

Section 57.2

Appetite Loss

This section includes text excerpted from "Appetite Loss," National Cancer Institute (NCI), April 29, 2015.

What Is Appetite Loss?

Cancer treatments may lower your appetite or change the way food tastes or smells. Side effects such as mouth and throat problems, or nausea and vomiting can also make eating difficult. Cancer-related fatigue can also lower your appetite.

Talk with your healthcare team if you are not hungry or if your find it difficult to eat. Don't wait until you feel weak, have lost too much weight, or are dehydrated, to talk with your doctor or nurse. It's important to eat well, especially during treatment for cancer.

What Are the Ways to Manage Appetite Loss?

Take these steps to get the nutrition you need to stay strong during treatment:

- **Drink plenty of liquids.** Drinking plenty of liquids is important, especially if you have less of an appetite. Losing fluid can lead to dehydration, a dangerous condition. You may become weak or dizzy and have dark yellow urine if you are not drinking enough liquids.

- **Choose healthy and high-nutrient foods.** Eat a little, even if you are not hungry. It may help to have five or six small meals throughout the day instead of three large meals. Most people need to eat a variety of nutrient-dense foods that are high in protein and calories.

- **Be active.** Being active can actually increase your appetite. Your appetite may increase when you take a short walk each day.

Talking with Your Healthcare Team

Prepare for your visit by making a list of questions to ask. Consider adding these questions to your list:

- What symptoms or problems should I call you about?

- What steps can I take to feel better?

- What food and drink choices are best for me?

- Do you recommend supplemental nutrition drinks for me?

- Are there vitamins and supplements that I should avoid? Are there any I should take?

- Would you recommend a registered dietitian who could also help me?

Section 57.3

Bleeding and Bruising (Thrombocytopenia)

This section includes text excerpted from "Bleeding and Bruising,"
National Cancer Institute (NCI), April 29, 2015.

What Are Bleeding and Bruising?

Some cancer treatments, such as chemotherapy and targeted therapy, can increase your risk of bleeding and bruising. These treatments can lower the number of platelets in the blood. Platelets are the cells that help your blood to clot and stop bleeding. When your platelet count is low, you may bruise or bleed a lot or very easily and have tiny purple or red spots on your skin. This condition is called thrombocytopenia. It is important to tell your doctor or nurse if you notice any of these changes.

Call your doctor or nurse if you have more serious problems, such as:

- Bleeding that doesn't stop after a few minutes; bleeding from your mouth, nose, or when you vomit; bleeding from your vagina when you are not having your period (menstruation); urine that is red or pink; stools that are black or bloody; or bleeding during your period that is heavier or lasts longer than normal.

- Head or vision changes such as bad headaches or changes in how well you see, or if you feel confused or very sleepy.

What Are the Ways to Manage Bleeding and Bruising?

Steps to take if you are at increased risk of bleeding and bruising:

- **Avoid certain medicines.** Many over-the-counter medicines contain aspirin or ibuprofen, which can increase your risk of bleeding. When in doubt, be sure to check the label. Get a list of medicines and products from your healthcare team that you should avoid taking. You may also be advised to limit or avoid alcohol if your platelet count is low.

457

- **Take extra care to prevent bleeding.** Brush your teeth gently, with a very soft toothbrush. Wear shoes, even when you are inside. Be extra careful when using sharp objects. Use an electric shaver, not a razor. Use lotion and a lip balm to prevent dry, chapped skin and lips. Tell your doctor or nurse if you are constipated or notice bleeding from your rectum.

- **Care for bleeding or bruising.** If you start to bleed, press down firmly on the area with a clean cloth. Keep pressing until the bleeding stops. If you bruise, put ice on the area.

Talking with Your Healthcare Team

Prepare for your visit by making a list of questions to ask. Consider adding these questions to your list:

- What steps can I take to prevent bleeding or bruising?

- How long should I wait for the bleeding to stop before I call you or go the emergency room?

- Do I need to limit or avoid things that could increase my risk of bleeding, such as alcohol or sexual activity?

- What medicines, vitamins, or herbs should I avoid? Could I get a list from you of medicines to avoid?

Section 57.4

Constipation

This section includes text excerpted from "Constipation,"
National Cancer Institute (NCI), April 29, 2015.

What Is Constipation?

Constipation is when you have infrequent bowel movements and stool that may be hard, dry, and difficult to pass. You may also have stomach cramps, bloating, and nausea when you are constipated.

Cancer treatments such as chemotherapy can cause constipation. Certain medicines (such as pain medicines), changes in diet, not drinking enough fluids, and being less active may also cause constipation.

There are steps you can take to prevent constipation. It is easier to prevent constipation than to treat its complications which may include fecal impaction or bowel obstruction.

What Are the Ways to Prevent or Treat Constipation?

Take these steps to prevent or treat constipation:

- **Eat high-fiber foods.** Adding bran to foods such as cereals or smoothies is an easy way to get more fiber in your diet. Ask your healthcare team how many grams of fiber you should have each day. If you have had an intestinal obstruction or intestinal surgery, you should not eat a high-fiber diet.

- **Drink plenty of liquids.** Most people need to drink at least 8 cups of liquid each day. You may need more based on your treatment, medications you are taking, or other health factors. Drinking warm or hot liquids may also help.

- **Try to be active every day.** Ask your healthcare team about exercises that you can do. Most people can do light exercise, even in a bed or chair. Other people choose to walk or ride an exercise bike for 15 to 30 minutes each day.

- **Learn about medicine.** Use only medicines and treatments for constipation that are prescribed by your doctor, since some may lead to bleeding, infection, or other harmful side effects in people being treated for cancer. Keep a record of your bowel movements to share with your doctor or nurse.

Talking with Your Healthcare Team

Prepare for your visit by making a list of questions to ask. Consider adding these questions to your list:

- What problems should I call you about?

- What information should I keep track of and share with you? (For example, you may be asked to keep track of your bowel movements, meals that you have, and exercise that you do each day.)

- How much liquid should I drink each day?

- What steps can I take to feel better?

- Would you give me the name of a registered dietitian who can tell me about foods that might help?

- Should I take medicine for constipation? If so, what medicine should I take? What medicine should I avoid?

Section 57.5

Delirium

This section includes text excerpted from "Delirium,"
National Cancer Institute (NCI), April 29, 2015.

What Is Delirium?

Delirium is a confused mental state that includes changes in awareness, thinking, judgment, sleeping patterns, as well as behavior. Although delirium can happen at the end of life, many episodes of delirium are caused by medicine or dehydration and are reversible.

The symptoms of delirium usually occur suddenly (within hours or days) over a short period of time and may come and go. Although delirium may be mistaken for depression or dementia, these conditions are different and have different treatments.

What Are the Types of Delirium?

The three main types of delirium include:

1. **Hypoactive delirium:** The patient seems sleepy, tired, or depressed

2. **Hyperactive delirium:** The patient is restless, anxious, or suddenly agitated and uncooperative

3. **Mixed delirium:** The patient changes back and forth between hypoactive delirium and hyperactive delirium

What Are the Causes of Delirium?

Your health care team will work to find out what is causing delirium, so that it can be treated. Causes of delirium may include:

- advanced cancer
- older age
- brain tumors
- dehydration
- infection
- taking certain medicines, such as high doses of opioids
- withdrawal from or stopping certain medicines
- Early monitoring of someone with these risk factors for delirium may prevent it or allow it to be treated more quickly

Changes caused by delirium can be upsetting for family members and dangerous to the person with cancer, especially if judgment is affected. People with delirium may be more likely to fall, unable to control their bladder and/or bowels, and more likely to become dehydrated. Their confused state may make it difficult to talk with others about their needs and make decisions about care. Family members may need to be more involved in decision-making.

What Are the Ways to Treat Delirium?

Steps that can be taken to treat symptoms related to delirium include:

Treat the causes of delirium: If medicines are causing delirium, then reducing the dose or stopping them may treat delirium. If conditions such as dehydration, poor nutrition, and infections are causing the delirium, then treating these may help.

Control surroundings: If the symptoms of delirium are mild, it may help to keep the room quiet and well lit, with a clock or calendar and familiar possessions. Having family members around and keeping the same caregivers, as much as possible, may also help.

Consider medicines: Medicines are sometimes given to treat the symptoms of delirium. However, these medicines have serious side effects and patients receiving them require careful observation by a doctor.

Sometimes sedation may help: After discussion with family members, sedation is sometimes used for delirium at the end of life, if it does not get better with other treatments. The doctor will discuss the decisions involved in using sedation to treat delirium with the family.

Talking with Your Health Care Team

Prepare for the visit by making a list of questions to ask. Consider adding these questions to your list:

- Is my family member at risk for delirium?

- What is causing the delirium?

- What problems should we call you about?

- What treatments are advised for my family member?

Section 57.6

Diarrhea

This section includes text excerpted from "Diarrhea,"
National Cancer Institute (NCI), April 29, 2015.

What Is Diarrhea?

Diarrhea means having bowel movements that are soft, loose, or watery more often than normal. If diarrhea is severe or lasts a long time, the body does not absorb enough water and nutrients. This can cause you to become dehydrated or malnourished. Cancer treatments, or the cancer itself, may cause diarrhea or make it worse. Some medicines, infections, and stress can also cause diarrhea. Tell your health care team if you have diarrhea.

Diarrhea that leads to dehydration (the loss of too much fluid from the body) and low levels of salt and potassium (important minerals needed by the body) can be life threatening. Call your health care team if you feel dizzy or light headed, have dark yellow urine or are not urinating, or have a fever of 100.5°F (38°C) or higher.

What Are the Ways to Manage Diarrhea?

You may be advised to take steps to prevent complications from diarrhea:

- **Drink plenty of fluid each day.** Most people need to drink 8 to 12 cups of fluid each day. Ask your doctor or nurse how much fluid you should drink each day. For severe diarrhea, only clear liquids or IV (intravenous) fluids may be advised for a short period.

- **Eat small meals that are easy on your stomach.** Eat six to eight small meals throughout the day, instead of three large meals. Foods high in potassium and sodium (minerals you lose when you have diarrhea) are good food choices, for most people. Limit or avoid foods and drinks that can make your diarrhea worse.

- **Check before taking medicine.** Check with your doctor or nurse before taking medicine for diarrhea. Your doctor will prescribe the correct medicine for you.

- **Keep your anal area clean and dry.** Try using warm water and wipes to stay clean. It may help to take warm, shallow baths. These are called sitz baths.

Talking With Your Health Care Team

Prepare for your visit by making a list of questions to ask. Consider adding these questions to your list:

- What is causing the diarrhea?

- What symptoms should I call you about?

- How much liquid should I drink each day?

- Can I speak to a registered dietitian to learn more about foods and drinks that are best for me?

- What medicine or other steps can I take to prevent diarrhea and to decrease rectal pain?

Section 57.7

Edema

This section includes text excerpted from "Edema,"
National Cancer Institute (NCI), April 29, 2015.

What Is Edema?

Edema, a condition in which fluid builds up in your body's tissues, may be caused by some types of chemotherapy, certain cancers, and conditions not related to cancer.

What Are the Signs of Edema?

Signs of edema may include:

- swelling in your feet, ankles, and legs
- swelling in your hands and arms
- swelling in your face or abdomen
- skin that is puffy, shiny, or looks slightly dented after being pressed
- shortness of breath, a cough, or irregular heartbeat

Tell your healthcare team if you notice swelling. Your doctor or nurse will determine what is causing your symptoms, advise you on steps to take, and may prescribe medicine.

- Some problems related to edema are serious. Call your doctor or nurse if you feel short of breath, have a heartbeat that seems different or is not regular, have sudden swelling or swelling that is getting worse or is moving up your arms or legs, you gain weight quickly, or you don't urinate at all or urinate only a little.

What Are the Ways to Prevent or Lessen Edema?

Steps you can take to prevent or lessen edema-related swelling include:

- **Get comfortable.** Wear loose clothing and shoes that are not too tight. When you sit or lie down, raise your feet with a stool or pillows. Avoid crossing your legs when you sit. Talk with your healthcare team about wearing special stockings, sleeves, or gloves that help with circulation if your swelling is severe.

- **Exercise.** Moving the part of your body with edema can help. Your doctor may give you specific exercises, including walking, to improve circulation. However, you may be advised not to stand or walk too much at one time.

- **Limit salt (sodium) in your diet.** Avoid foods such as chips, bacon, ham, and canned soup. Check food labels for the sodium content. Don't add salt or soy sauce to your food.

- **Take your medicine.** If your doctor prescribes a medicine called a diuretic, take it exactly as instructed. The medicine will help move the extra fluid and salt out of your body.

Talking with Your Healthcare Team

Prepare for your visit by making a list of questions to ask. Consider adding these questions to your list:

- Are my medications or treatment likely to increase my risk of developing edema?

- Are there steps I can take to prevent edema?

- What symptoms or problems should I call you about?

- What steps can I take to feel better if I notice swelling?

- Are there foods, drinks, or activities I should avoid?

Section 57.8

Memory or Concentration Problems

This section includes text excerpted from "Memory or Concentration Problems," National Cancer Institute (NCI), April 29, 2015.

What Are Memory or Concentration Problems?

Whether you have memory or concentration problems (sometimes described as a mental fog or chemo brain) depends on the type of treatment you receive, your age, and other health-related factors. Cancer treatments such as chemotherapy may cause difficulty with thinking, concentrating, or remembering things. So can some types of biological therapies and radiation therapy to the brain.

These cognitive problems may start during or after cancer treatment. Some people notice very small changes, such as a bit more difficulty remembering things, whereas others have much greater memory or concentration problems.

Your doctor will assess your symptoms and advise you about ways to manage or treat these problems. Treating conditions such as poor nutrition, anxiety, depression, fatigue, and insomnia may also help.

What Are the Ways to Manage Memory or Concentration Problems?

It's important for you or a family member to tell your healthcare team if you have difficulty remembering things, thinking, or concentrating. Here are some steps you can take to manage minor memory or concentration problems:

- **Plan your day.** Do things that need the most concentration at the time of day when you feel best. Get extra rest and plenty of sleep at night. If you need to rest during the day, short naps of less than 1 hour are best. Long naps can make it more difficult to sleep at night. Keep a daily routine.

- **Exercise your body and mind.** Exercise can help to decrease stress and help you to feel more alert. Exercise releases endorphins, also known as "feel-good chemicals,"which give people a feeling of well-being. Ask what light physical exercises may be helpful for you. Mind–body practices such as meditation or mental exercises such as puzzles or games also help some people.

- **Get help to remember things.** Write down and keep a list handy of important information. Use a daily planner, recorder, or other electronic device to help you remember important activities. Make a list of important names and phone numbers. Keep it in one place so it's easy to find.

Talking with Your Healthcare Team

It's important for you or a family member to talk with your doctor or nurse about any memory or cognitive changes you may have. Prepare for your visit by making a list of questions to ask. Consider adding these questions to your list:

- Am I at increased risk of cognitive problems based on the treatment I am receiving?

- When might these problems start to occur? How long might they last?

- Are there steps I can take to decrease these problems?

- What symptoms or other problems should I, or a family member, call you about?

- Could I meet with a social worker to get ideas about additional support and resources?

- Are there specialists who could assess, treat, or advise me on these problems (such as neuropsychologists, occupational therapists, vocational therapists, and others)?

Section 57.9

Mouth and Throat Problems

This section includes text excerpted from "Mouth and Throat Problems," National Cancer Institute (NCI), April 29, 2015.

What are Mouth and Throat Problems?

Cancer treatments may cause dental, mouth, and throat problems. Radiation therapy to the head and neck may harm the salivary glands and tissues in your mouth and/or make it hard to chew and swallow safely. Some types of chemotherapy and biological therapy can also harm cells in your mouth, throat, and lips. Drugs used to treat cancer and certain bone problems may also cause oral complications.

Mouth and throat problems may include:

- changes in taste (dysgeusia) or smell
- dry mouth (xerostomia)
- infections and mouth sores
- pain or swelling in your mouth (oral mucositis)
- sensitivity to hot or cold foods
- swallowing problems (dysphagia)
- tooth decay (cavities)

Mouth problems are more serious if they interfere with eating and drinking because they can lead to dehydration and/or malnutrition. It's important to call your doctor or nurse if you have pain in your mouth, lips, or throat that makes it difficult to eat, drink, or sleep or if you have a fever of 100.5 °F (38 °C) or higher.

What Are the Ways to Prevent Mouth and Dental Problems?

Your doctor or nurse may advise you to take these and other steps:

- **Get a dental check-up before starting treatment.** Before you start treatment, visit your dentist for a cleaning and

468

check-up. Tell the dentist about your cancer treatment and try to get any dental work completed before starting treatment.

- **Check and clean your mouth daily.** Check your mouth every day for sores or white spots. Tell your doctor or nurse as soon as you notice any changes, such as pain or sensitivity. Rinse your mouth throughout the day with a solution of warm water, baking soda, and salt. Ask your nurse to write down the mouth rinse recipe that is recommended for you. Gently brush your teeth, gums, and tongue after each meal and before going to bed at night. Use a very soft toothbrush or cotton swabs. If you are at risk of bleeding, ask if you should floss.

What Are the Ways to Manage Mouth and Throat Problems?

Your healthcare team may suggest that you take these and other steps to manage these problems:

- **For a sore mouth or throat:** Choose foods that are soft, wet, and easy to swallow. Soften dry foods with gravy, sauce, or other liquids. Use a blender to make milkshakes or blend your food to make it easier to swallow. Ask about pain medicine, such as lozenges or sprays that numb your mouth and make eating less painful. Avoid foods and drinks that can irritate your mouth; foods that are crunchy, salty, spicy, or sugary; and alcoholic drinks. Don't smoke or use tobacco products.

- **For a dry mouth:** Drink plenty of liquids because a dry mouth can increase the risk of tooth decay and mouth infections. Keep water handy and sip it often to keep your mouth wet. Suck on ice chips or sugar-free hard candy, have frozen desserts, or chew sugar-free gum. Use a lip balm. Ask about medicines such as saliva substitutes that can coat, protect, and moisten your mouth and throat. Acupuncture may also help with dry mouth.

- **For changes to your sense of taste:** Foods may seem to have no taste or may not taste the way they used to or food may not have much taste at all. Radiation therapy may cause a change in sweet, sour, bitter, and salty tastes. Chemotherapy drugs may cause an unpleasant chemical or metallic taste in your mouth. If you have taste changes it may help to try different foods to find ones that taste best to you. Trying cold foods may also help. Here are some more tips to consider:

- If food tastes bland, marinate foods to improve their flavor or add spices to foods.

- If red meat tastes strange, switch to other high-protein foods such as chicken, eggs, fish, peanut butter, turkey, beans, or dairy products.

- If foods taste salty, bitter, or acidic, try sweetening them.

- If foods taste metallic, switch to plastic utensils and non-metal cooking dishes.

- If you have a bad taste in your mouth, try sugar-free lemon drops, gum, or mints.

Talking with Your Healthcare Team

Prepare for your visit by making a list of questions to ask. Consider adding these questions to your list:

- When might these problems start to occur? How long might they last?

- What steps can I take to feel better?

- What medicines can help?

- What symptoms or problems should I call the doctor about?

- What pain medicine and/or mouthwashes could help me?

- Would you recommend a registered dietitian who I could see to learn about good food choices?

- For people receiving radiation therapy to the head and neck: Should I take supplements such as zinc, to help my sense of taste come back after treatment?

Section 57.10

Nausea and Vomiting

This section includes text excerpted from "Nausea and Vomiting,"
National Cancer Institute (NCI), April 29, 2015.

What Are Nausea and Vomiting?

Nausea is when you feel sick to your stomach, as if you are going to throw up. Vomiting is when you throw up. There are different types of nausea and vomiting caused by cancer treatment, including anticipatory, acute, and delayed nausea and vomiting. Controlling nausea and vomiting will help you to feel better and prevent more serious problems such as malnutrition and dehydration.

Your doctor or nurse will determine what is causing your symptoms and advise you on ways to prevent them. Medicines called anti-nausea drugs or antiemetics are effective in preventing or reducing many types of nausea and vomiting. The medicine is taken at specific times to prevent and/or control symptoms of nausea and vomiting. There are also practical steps you may be advised to take to feel better, including those listed below.

What Are the Ways to Manage Nausea and Vomiting?

You may be advised to take these steps to feel better:

- **Take an anti-nausea medicine.** Talk with your doctor or nurse to learn when to take your medicine. Most people need to take an anti-nausea medicine even on days when they feel well. Tell your doctor or nurse if the medicine doesn't help. There are different kinds of medicine and one may work better than another for you.

- **Drink plenty of water and fluids.** Drinking will help to prevent dehydration, a serious problem that happens when your body loses too much fluid and you are not drinking enough. Try to sip on water, fruit juices, ginger ale, tea, and/or sports drinks throughout the day.

- **Avoid certain foods.** Don't eat greasy, fried, sweet, or spicy foods if you feel sick after eating them. If the smell of food bothers you, ask others to make your food. Try cold foods that do not have strong smells, or let food cool down before you eat it.

- **Try these tips on treatment days.** Some people find that it helps to eat a small snack before treatment. Others avoid eating or drinking right before or after treatment because it makes them feel sick. After treatment, wait at least 1 hour before you eat or drink.

- **Learn about complementary medicine practices that may help.** Acupuncture relieves nausea and/or vomiting caused by chemotherapy in some people. Deep breathing, guided imagery, hypnosis, and other relaxation techniques (such as listening to music, reading a book, or meditating) also help some people.

Talking with Your Healthcare Team

Prepare for your visit by making a list of questions to ask. Consider adding these questions to your list:

- What symptoms or problems should I call you about?

- What medicine could help me? When should I take this medicine?

- How much liquid should I drink each day? What should I do if I throw up?

- What foods would be easy on my stomach? What foods should I avoid?

- Could I meet with a registered dietitian to learn more?

- What specialists could I see to learn about acupuncture and other practices that could help to lower my symptoms?

Section 57.11

Nerve Problems (Peripheral Neuropathy)

This section includes text excerpted from "Nerve Problems (Peripheral Neuropathy)," National Cancer Institute (NCI), April 29, 2015.

What Are Nerve Problems?

Some cancer treatments cause peripheral neuropathy, a result of damage to the peripheral nerves. These nerves carry information from the brain to other parts of the body. Side effects depend on which peripheral nerves (sensory, motor, or autonomic) are affected.

Damage to sensory nerves (nerves that help you feel pain, heat, cold, and pressure) can cause:

- tingling, numbness, or a pins-and-needles feeling in your feet and hands that may spread to your legs and arms

- inability to feel a hot or cold sensation, such as a hot stove

- inability to feel pain, such as from a cut or sore on your foot

Damage to motor nerves (nerves that help your muscles to move) can cause:

- weak or achy muscles. You may lose your balance or trip easily. It may also be difficult to button shirts or open jars.

- muscles that twitch and cramp or muscle wasting (if you don't use your muscles regularly).

- swallowing or breathing difficulties (if your chest or throat muscles are affected)

Damage to autonomic nerves (nerves that control functions such as blood pressure, digestion, heart rate, temperature, and urination) can cause:

- digestive changes such as constipation or diarrhea

- dizzy or faint feeling, due to low blood pressure

- sexual problems; men may be unable to get an erection and women may not reach orgasm

- sweating problems (either too much or too little sweating)

- urination problems, such as leaking urine or difficulty emptying your bladder

If you start to notice any of the problems listed above, talk with your doctor or nurse. Getting these problems diagnosed and treated early is the best way to control them, prevent further damage, and to reduce pain and other complications.

What Are the Ways to Prevent or Manage Problems Related to Nerve Changes?

You may be advised to take these steps:

- **Prevent falls.** Have someone help you prevent falls around the house. Move rugs out of your path so you will not trip on them. Put rails on the walls and in the bathroom, so you can hold on to them and balance yourself. Put bathmats in the shower or tub. Wear sturdy shoes with soft soles. Get up slowly after sitting or lying down, especially if you feel dizzy.

- **Take extra care in the kitchen and shower.** Use potholders in the kitchen to protect your hands from burns. Be careful when handling knives or sharp objects. Ask someone to check the water temperature, to make sure it's not too hot.

- **Protect your hands and feet.** Wear shoes, both inside and outside. Check your arms, legs, and feet for cuts or scratches every day. When it's cold, wear warm clothes to protect your hands and feet.

- **Ask for help and slow down.** Let people help you with difficult tasks. Slow down and give yourself more time to do things.

- **Ask about pain medicine and integrative medicine practices.** You may be prescribed pain medicine. Sometimes practices such as acupuncture, massage, physical therapy, yoga, and others may also be advised to lower pain. Talk with your healthcare team to learn what is advised for you.

Talking with Your Healthcare Team

Prepare for your visit by making a list of questions to ask. Consider adding these questions to your list:

- What symptoms or problems might I have? Which ones should I call you about?

- When will these problems start? How long might they last?

- What medicine, treatments, and integrative medicine practices could help me to feel better?

- What steps can I take to feel better? What precautions should I take to stay safe?

- Could you refer me to a specialist who could give me additional advice?

Section 57.12

Skin and Nail Changes

This section includes text excerpted from "Skin and Nail Changes," National Cancer Institute (NCI), April 29, 2015.

What Are Skin and Nail Changes?

Cancer treatments may cause a range of skin and nail changes. Talk with your healthcare team to learn whether or not you will have these changes, based on the treatment you are receiving.

- Radiation therapy can cause the skin on the part of your body receiving radiation therapy to become dry and peel, itch (called pruritus), and turn red or darker. It may look sunburned or tan and be swollen or puffy.

- Chemotherapy may damage fast growing skin and nail cells. This can cause problems such as skin that is dry, itchy, red, and/ or that peels. Some people may develop a rash or sun sensitivity, causing you to sunburn easily. Nail changes may include dark, yellow, or cracked nails and/or cuticles that are red and hurt. Chemotherapy in people who have received radiation therapy in the past can cause skin to become red, blister, peel, or hurt on the part of the body that received radiation therapy; this is called radiation recall.

- Biological therapy may cause itching (pruritus).

- Targeted therapy may cause a dry skin, a rash, and nail problems.

These skin problems are more serious and need urgent medical attention:

- Sudden or severe itching, a rash, or hives during chemotherapy. These may be signs of an allergic reaction.

- Sores on the part of your body where you are receiving treatment that become painful, wet, and/or infected. This is called a moist reaction and may happen in areas where the skin folds, such as around your ears, breast, or bottom.

Your doctor or nurse will talk with about possible skin and nail changes and advise you on ways to treat or prevent them.

What Are the Ways to Manage Skin and Nail Changes?

Depending on what treatment you are receiving, you may be advised to take these steps to protect your skin, prevent infection, and reduce itching:

- **Use only recommended skin products.** Use mild soaps that are gentle on your skin. Ask your nurse to recommend specific lotions and creams. Ask when and how often to use them. Ask what skin products to avoid. For example, you may be advised to not use powders or antiperspirants before radiation therapy.

- **Protect your skin.** Ask about lotions or antibiotics for dry, itchy, infected or swollen skin. Don't use heating pads, ice packs, or bandages on the area receiving radiation therapy. Shave less often and use an electric razor or stop shaving if your skin is sore. Wear sunscreen and lip balm or a loose-fitting long-sleeved shirt, pants, and a hat with a wide brim when outdoors.

- **Prevent or treat dry, itchy skin (pruritus).** Your doctor will work to assess the cause of pruritus. There are also steps you can take to feel better. Avoid products with alcohol or perfume, which can dry or irritate your skin. Take short showers or baths in lukewarm, not hot, water. Put on lotion after drying off from a shower, while your skin is still slightly damp. Keep your home cool and humid. Eat a healthy diet and drink plenty of fluids to help keep your skin moist and healthy. Applying a cool washcloth or ice to the affected area may also help. Acupuncture also helps some people.

- **Prevent or treat minor nail problems.** Keep your nails clean and cut short. Wear gloves when you wash the dishes, work in the garden, or clean the house. Check with your nurse about products that can help your nails.

If your skin hurts in the area where you get treatment, tell your doctor or nurse. Your skin might have a moist reaction. Most often this happens in areas where the skin folds, such as behind the ears or under the breasts. It can lead to an infection if not properly treated. Ask your doctor or nurse how to care for these areas.

Talking with Your Healthcare Team

Prepare for your visit by making a list of questions to ask. Consider adding these questions to your list:

- What symptoms or problems should I call you about?
- What steps can I take to feel better?
- What brands of soap and lotion are best for me to use? What products can help my nails stay healthy?
- What skin and nail products should I avoid?
- When will these problems go away?

Section 57.13

Sleep Problems

This section includes text excerpted from "Sleep Problems,"
National Cancer Institute (NCI), April 29, 2015.

What Are Sleep Problems?

Sleeping well is important for your physical and mental health.
A good night's sleep not only helps you to think clearly, it also lowers your blood pressure, helps your appetite, and strengthens your immune system.

However, sleep problems are common among people being treated for cancer. Studies show that as many as half of all patients have sleep-related problems. These problems may be caused by the side effects of treatment, medicine, long hospital stays, or stress.

Talk with your healthcare team if you have difficulty sleeping, so you can get help you need. Sleep problems that go on for a long time may increase the risk of anxiety or depression. Your doctor will do an assessment, which may include a polysomnogram (recordings taken during sleep that show brain waves, breathing rate, and others activities such as heart rate) to correctly diagnose and treat sleep problems. Assessments may be repeated from time to time, since sleeping problems may change over time.

What Are the Ways to Manage Sleep Problems?

There are steps that you and your healthcare team can take to help you sleep well again.

- **Tell your doctor about problems that interfere with sleep.** Getting treatment to lower side effects such as pain or bladder or gastrointestinal problems may help you sleep better.

- **Cognitive behavioral therapy (CBT) and relaxation therapy may help.** Practicing these therapies can help you to relax. For example, a CBT therapist can help you learn to change negative thoughts and beliefs about sleep into positive ones. Strategies such as muscle relaxation, guided imagery, and self-hypnosis may also help you.

- **Set good bedtime habits.** Go to bed only when sleepy, in a quiet and dark room, and in a comfortable bed. If you do not fall asleep, get out of bed and return to bed when you are sleepy. Stop watching television or using other electrical devices a couple of hours before going to bed. Don't drink or eat a lot before bedtime. While it's important to keep active during the day with regular exercise, exercising a few hours before bedtime may make sleep more difficult.

- **Sleep medicine may be prescribed.** Your doctor may prescribe sleep medicine, for a short period if other strategies don't work. The sleep medicine prescribed will depend on your specific problem (such as trouble falling asleep or trouble staying asleep) as well as other medicines you are taking.

Talking with Your Healthcare Team

Prepare for your visit by making a list of questions to ask. Consider adding these questions to your list:

- Why am I having trouble sleeping?

- What problems should I call you about?

- What steps can I take to sleep better?

- Would you recommend a sleep therapist who could help with the problems I am having?

- Would sleep medicine be advised for me?

Section 57.14

Urinary and Bladder Problems

This section includes text excerpted from "Urinary and Bladder Problems," National Cancer Institute (NCI), April 29, 2015.

What Are Urinary and Bladder Problems?

Some cancer treatments, such as those listed below, may cause the urinary and bladder problems:

- Radiation therapy to the pelvis (including reproductive organs, the bladder, colon and rectum) can irritate the bladder and urinary tract. These problems often start several weeks after radiation therapy begins and go away several weeks after treatment has been completed.

- Some types of chemotherapy and biological therapy can also affect or damage cells in the bladder and kidneys.

- Surgery to remove the prostate (prostatectomy), bladder cancer surgery, and surgery to remove a woman's uterus, the tissue on the sides of the uterus, the cervix, and the top part of the vagina (radical hysterectomy) can also cause urinary problems. These types of surgery may also increase the risk of a urinary tract infection.

What Are the Symptoms of a Urinary Problem?

Talk with your doctor or nurse to learn what symptoms you may experience and ask which ones to call about. Some urinary or bladder changes may be normal, such as changes to the color or smell of your urine caused by some types of chemotherapy. Your healthcare team will determine what is causing your symptoms and will advise on steps to take to feel better.

Irritation of the bladder lining (radiation cystitis):

- pain or a burning feeling when you before or after you urinate

- blood in your urine
- trouble starting to urinate
- trouble emptying your bladder completely
- feeling that you need to urinate urgently or frequently
- leaking a little urine when you sneeze or cough
- bladder spasms, cramps, or discomfort in the pelvic area

Urinary tract infection (UTI):

- pain or a burning feeling when you urinate
- urine that is cloudy or red
- a fever of 100.5 °F (38 °C) or higher, chills, and fatigue
- pain in your back or abdomen
- difficulty urinating or not being able to urinate

In people being treated for cancer, a UTI can turn into a serious condition that needs immediate medical care. Antibiotics will be prescribed if you have a bacterial infection.

Symptoms that may occur after surgery:

- leaking urine (incontinence)
- trouble emptying your bladder completely

What Are the Ways to Prevent or Manage and Bladder Problems?

Here are some steps you may be advised to take to feel better and to prevent problems:

- **Have plenty of liquids.** Drink plenty of liquids. Most people need to drink at least 8 cups of fluid each day, so that urine is light yellow or clear. You'll want to stay away from things that can make bladder problems worse. These include caffeine, drinks with alcohol, spicy foods, and tobacco products.

- **Prevent urinary tract infections.** Your doctor or nurse will talk with you about ways to lower your chances of getting a urinary tract infection. These may include going to the bathroom often, wearing cotton underwear and loose fitting pants, learning about safe and sanitary practices for catheterization, taking showers instead of baths, and checking with your nurse before using products such as creams or lotions near your genital area.

Talking with Your Healthcare Team

Prepare for your visit by making a list of questions to ask. Consider adding these questions to your list:

- What symptoms or problems should I call you about?
- What steps can I take to feel better?
- How much should I drink each day? What liquids are best for me?
- Are there certain drinks or foods that I should avoid?

Chapter 58

Complementary and Alternative Medicine (CAM) Therapies Used for the Side Effects of Breast Cancer and Its Treatment

Chapter Contents

Section 58.1

Complementary and Alternative Medicine—Overview

This section includes text excerpted from
"Complementary and Alternative Medicine" National
Cancer Institute (NCI), April 10, 2015.

Complementary and alternative medicine (CAM) is the term for medical products and practices that are not part of standard medical care.

- **Standard medical care** is medicine that is practiced by health professionals who hold an M.D. (medical doctor) or D.O. (doctor of osteopathy) degree. It is also practiced by other health professionals, such as physical therapists, physician assistants, psychologists, and registered nurses. Standard medicine may also be called biomedicine or allopathic, Western, mainstream, orthodox, or regular medicine. Some standard medical care practitioners are also practitioners of CAM.

- **Complementary medicine** is treatments that are used along with standard medical treatments but are not considered to be standard treatments. One example is using acupuncture to help lessen some side effects of cancer treatment.

- **Alternative medicine** is treatments that are used instead of standard medical treatments. One example is using a special diet to treat cancer instead of anticancer drugs that are prescribed by an oncologist.

- **Integrative medicine** is a total approach to medical care that combines standard medicine with the CAM practices that have shown to be safe and effective. They treat the patient's mind, body, and spirit.

NCI provides evidence-based PDQ information for many CAM therapies in versions for both the patient and health professional.

Are CAM Approaches Safe?

Some CAM therapies have undergone careful evaluation and have found to be safe and effective. However there are others that have been found to be ineffective or possibly harmful. Less is known about many CAM therapies, and research has been slower for a number of reasons:

- Time and funding issues
- Problems finding institutions and cancer researchers to work with on the studies
- Regulatory issues

CAM therapies need to be evaluated with the same long and careful research process used to evaluate standard treatments. Standard cancer treatments have generally been studied for safety and effectiveness through an intense scientific process that includes clinical trials with large numbers of patients.

Natural Does Not Mean Safe

CAM therapies include a wide variety of botanicals and nutritional products, such as dietary supplements, herbal supplements, and vitamins. Many of these "natural" products are considered to be safe because they are present in, or produced by, nature. However, that is not true in all cases. In addition, some may affect how well other medicines work in your body. For example, the herb St. John's wort, which some people use for depression, may cause certain anticancer drugs not to work as well as they should.

Herbal supplements may be harmful when taken by themselves, with other substances, or in large doses. For example, some studies have shown that kava kava, an herb that has been used to help with stress and anxiety, may cause liver damage.

Vitamins can also have unwanted effects in your body. For example, some studies show that high doses of vitamins, even vitamin C, may affect how chemotherapy and radiation work. Too much of any vitamin is not safe, even in a healthy person.

Tell your doctor if you're taking any dietary supplements, no matter how safe you think they are. This is very important. Even though there may be ads or claims that something has been used for years, they do not prove that it's safe or effective.

Supplements do not have to be approved by the federal government before being sold to the public. Also, a prescription is not needed to buy them. Therefore, it's up to consumers to decide what is best for them.

National Cancer Institute (NCI) and the National Center for Complementary and Integrative Health (NCCIH) are currently sponsoring or cosponsoring various clinical trials that test CAM treatments and therapies in people. Some study the effects of complementary approaches used in addition to conventional treatments, and some compare alternative therapies with conventional treatments. Find all cancer CAM clinical trials.

What Should Patients Do When Using or Considering CAM Therapies?

Cancer patients who are using or considering using complementary or alternative therapy should talk with their doctor or nurse. Some therapies may interfere with standard treatment or even be harmful. It is also a good idea to learn whether the therapy has been proven to do what it claims to do.

To find a CAM practitioner, ask your doctor or nurse to suggest someone. Or ask if someone at your cancer center, such as a social worker or physical therapist can help you. Choosing a CAM practitioner should be done with as much care as choosing a primary care provider.

Patients, their families, and their health care providers can learn about CAM therapies and practitioners from the following government agencies:

- National Center for Complementary and Integrative Health

- NCI Office of Cancer Complementary and Alternative Medicine

- Office of Dietary Supplements

Section 58.2

Traditional Chinese Medicine

This section includes text excerpted from "Traditional Chinese Medicine: In Depth," National Center for Complementary and Integrative Health (NCCIH), October 2013.

History

Traditional Chinese medicine (TCM) originated in ancient China and has evolved over thousands of years. TCM practitioners use herbal medicines and various mind and body practices, such as acupuncture and tai chi, to treat or prevent health problems. In the United States, people use TCM primarily as a complementary health approach. This fact sheet provides a general overview of TCM and suggests sources for additional information.

Is It Safe?

- Acupuncture is generally considered safe when performed by an experienced practitioner using sterile needles. Improperly performed acupuncture can cause potentially serious side effects.

- Tai chi and qi gong, two mind and body practices used in TCM, are generally safe.

- There have been reports of Chinese herbal products being contaminated with drugs, toxins, or heavy metals or not containing the listed ingredients. Some of the herbs used in Chinese medicine can interact with drugs, have serious side effects, or be unsafe for people with certain medical conditions.

Is It Effective?

- For most conditions, there is not enough rigorous scientific evidence to know whether TCM methods work for the conditions for which they are used.

Side Effects and Risks

- Herbal medicines used in TCM are sometimes marketed in the United States as dietary supplements. The U.S. Food and Drug Administration (FDA) regulations for dietary supplements are not the same as those for prescription or over-the-counter drugs; in general, the regulations for dietary supplements are less stringent. For example, manufacturers don't have to prove to the FDA that most claims made for dietary supplements are valid; if the product were a drug, they would have to provide proof.

- Some Chinese herbal products may be safe, but others may not be. There have been reports of products being contaminated with drugs, toxins, or heavy metals or not containing the listed ingredients. Some of the herbs used in Chinese medicine can interact with drugs, can have serious side effects, or may be unsafe for people with certain medical conditions. For example, the Chinese herb ephedra (ma huang) has been linked to serious health complications, including heart attack and stroke. In 2004, the FDA banned the sale of ephedra-containing dietary supplements, but the ban does not apply to TCM remedies.

- The FDA regulates acupuncture needles as medical devices and requires that the needles be sterile, nontoxic, and labeled for single use by qualified practitioners only. Relatively few complications from the use of acupuncture have been reported. However, adverse effects—some of them serious—have resulted from the use of non-sterile needles or improper delivery of acupuncture treatments.

- Tai chi and qi gong are considered to be generally safe practices.

- Information on the safety of other TCM methods is limited. Reported complications of moxibustion include allergic reactions, burns, and infections, but how often these events occur is not known. Both moxibustion and cupping (applying a heated cup to the skin to create a slight suction) may mark the skin, usually temporarily. The origin of these marks should be explained to health care providers so that they will not be mistaken for signs of disease or physical abuse.

TCM in the United States

TCM practitioners use a variety of techniques in an effort to promote health and treat disease. In the United States, the most commonly used approaches include Chinese herbal medicine, acupuncture, and tai chi.

- **Chinese herbal medicine.** The Chinese Materia Medica (a pharmacological reference book used by TCM practitioners) describes thousands of medicinal substances—primarily plants, but also some minerals and animal products. Different parts of plants, such as the leaves, roots, stems, flowers, and seeds, are used. In TCM, herbs are often combined in formulas and given as teas, capsules, liquid extracts, granules, or powders.

- **Acupuncture.** Acupuncture is a family of procedures involving the stimulation of specific points on the body using a variety of techniques. The acupuncture technique that has been most often studied scientifically involves penetrating the skin with thin, solid, metal needles that are manipulated by the hands or by electrical stimulation.

- **Tai chi.** Tai chi is a centuries-old mind and body practice. It involves gentle, dance-like body movements with mental focus, breathing, and relaxation.

If You Are Thinking about Using TCM

- Do not use TCM to replace effective conventional care or as a reason to postpone seeing a health care provider about a medical problem.

- Look for published research studies on TCM for the health condition that interests you.

- It is better to use TCM herbal remedies under the supervision of your health care provider or a professional trained in herbal medicine than to try to treat yourself.

- Ask about the training and experience of the TCM practitioner you are considering. You can find information about the credentials and licensing of complementary health practitioners on the NCCIH Web site.

- If you are pregnant or nursing, or are thinking of using TCM to treat a child, you should be especially sure to consult your (or the child's) health care provider.

- Tell all your health care providers about any complementary health approaches you use. Give them a full picture of what you do to manage your health. This will help ensure coordinated and safe care.

Section 58.3

Spirituality in Cancer Care

This section includes text excerpted from "Spirituality
in Cancer Care–Patient Version (PDQ®)," National
Cancer Institute (NCI), May 18, 2015.

Religious and Spiritual Values Are Important to Patients Coping with Cancer

Studies have shown that religious and spiritual values are important to Americans. Most American adults say that they believe in God
and that their religious beliefs affect how they live their lives. However, people have different ideas about life after death, belief in mira-
cles, and other religious beliefs. Such beliefs may be based on gender,
education, and ethnic background.

Many patients with cancer rely on spiritual or religious beliefs and
practices to help them cope with their disease. This is called spiritual
coping. Many caregivers also rely on spiritual coping. Each person may
have different spiritual needs, depending on cultural and religious
traditions. For some seriously ill patients, spiritual well-being may
affect how much anxiety they feel about death. For others, it may affect
what they decide about end-of-life treatments. Some patients and their
family caregivers may want doctors to talk about spiritual concerns,
but may feel unsure about how to bring up the subject.

Some studies show that doctors' support of spiritual well-being in
very ill patients helps improve their quality of life. Healthcare providers
who treat patients coping with cancer are looking at new ways to help
them with religious and spiritual concerns. Doctors may ask patients
which spiritual issues are important to them during treatment as well
as near the end of life. When patients with advanced cancer receive
spiritual support from the medical team, they may be more likely to
choose hospice care and less aggressive treatment at the end of life.

Spirituality and Religion May Have Different Meanings

The terms spirituality and religion are often used in place of each
other, but for many people they have different meanings. Religion

may be defined as a specific set of beliefs and practices, usually within an organized group. Spirituality may be defined as an individual's sense of peace, purpose, and connection to others, and beliefs about the meaning of life. Spirituality may be found and expressed through an organized religion or in other ways. Patients may think of themselves as spiritual or religious or both.

Serious Illness, Such as Cancer, May Cause Spiritual Distress

Serious illnesses like cancer may cause patients or family caregivers to have doubts about their beliefs or religious values and cause much spiritual distress. Some studies show that patients with cancer may feel that they are being punished by God or may have a loss of faith after being diagnosed. Other patients may have mild feelings of spiritual distress when coping with cancer.

Section 58.4

Yoga May Help Women with Breast Cancer Conquer Physical and Emotional Pain

This section includes text excerpted from "Yoga Shows Benefits to Quality of Life in Some Breast Cancer Patients," National Cancer Institute (NCI), August 12, 2013.

Yoga Shows Benefits to Quality of Life in Some Breast Cancer Patients

While some recent research has shown that yoga is associated with improvements in overall quality of life (QOL) and other emotional symptoms, Alyson B. Moadel, Ph.D., Associate Professor of Clinical Medicine at Albert Einstein College of Medicine, and colleagues, wanted to look specifically at a multiethnic sample of breast cancer patients. In a study published in the *Journal of Clinical Oncology* and supported by a grant from the National Cancer Institute, Dr. Moadel examined whether yoga can support and/or preserve QOL better than standard care using standard based QOL measures with an ethnically diverse group of breast cancer patients in an underserved area of New York City.

Participants were randomized in a 2:1 ratio to either a yoga intervention group or a waitlist control. QOL was examined at baseline, 1 month, 3 months, and 6 months. The yoga intervention, based on Hatha techniques, consisted of 1.5 hour classes once a week for 12 weeks, which is a schedule that has been found efficacious in other studies. Participants were 42% African American, 31% Hispanic, and 23% White.

The yoga intervention consisted of physical stretches and poses, breathing exercises, and meditation. Patients were also asked to practice yoga at home daily and were given materials for guidance. Study measures were assessed using several well established reporting tools. The Functional Assessment of Cancer Therapy (FACT) was used to measure patients' reports of QOL in the areas of physical, social, emotional, and functional well being, and was administered in an interview format. Several other measures were used including the Functional Assessment of Chronic Illness for Fatigue and Spirituality to assess change in those components. The Distressed Mood Index was used to measure distressed mood symptoms in domains such as "anxious/sad," "irritable," and "confused." Participants' attendance at yoga classes was recorded by instructors, while home practice was self-reported.

Results showed that participants in the control group reported a greater decrease in social well being than participants in the intervention group (13% vs. 2%). This lack of improvement in social well-being notwithstanding, study authors noted that yoga may serve to promote a sense of social support and connection in participants. Given that many of the patients were receiving cancer treatment, the authors speculated that the effects of the intervention may have been obscured by the relatively impaired QOL of the participants, as compared to other comparable groups of patients.

Secondary analyses of patients not on chemotherapy indicated that those in the yoga group showed improvement in emotional well being and decreased distress after 3 months. The control group experienced marked deterioration in overall QOL, social well-being, and distressed mood.

Throughout the study, weekly class adherence was low. Of the 108 participants included in the final sample for analysis (84 intervention and 44 waitlist control) class attendance ranged from zero to 19 classes attended. One third of intervention group participants did not attend any classes, though eight of these patients reported practicing yoga at home at least a few times per week. The mean number of classes attended by participants was 7, and 61% practiced yoga at home at least a few times per week. The authors shared that this data does reflect natural adherence as no compensation was provided, but the lack of attendance could show that this type of program is not feasible for some patient groups.

At 3 month follow-up, it was found that high class adherers (> 6 classes; n=33) were found to have higher energy levels and physical well being than low adherers (1 to 6 classes; n=24) and non-adherers (0 classes; n=27). There was also significant interaction between adherence and baseline distressed mood. "Attending the intervention at any level was related to improved mood regardless of one's initial distress level, whereas not attending among those with low distress was related to worsening mood," the authors noted.

While this study led to low class adherence, participants still chose to practice at home and did show some benefits in emotional wellbeing, especially for participants not receiving chemotherapy. Authors stated that future studies could use comparison control groups such as a support group or an exercise group to help discern what therapeutic factors are operating in yoga, such as social support, poses, or meditation. Given the low cost of yoga and the ability to practice at home at any time of day, it is an intervention that could have interesting impacts on cancer care and merits future study.

Part Seven

Living with Breast Cancer

Chapter 59

Life after Breast Cancer Treatment

Chapter Contents

Section 59.1

Daily Routine

This section includes text excerpted from "Keep up with Your Daily
Routine," National Cancer Institute (NCI), December 2, 2014.

Keep up with Your Daily Routine

If you feel well enough, keep up with your daily routine. This
includes:

- Going to work

- Spending time with family and friends

- Taking part in activities

- Going on trips

Think about how you want to spend your time and who you like to
be with. What makes you happy? What types of things do you enjoy
the most?

Have Fun

You can still have joy in your life while having cancer. Sometimes
people with cancer try new, fun things that they have never done
before. For instance, have you always wanted to ride in a hot air balloon or go on a boat cruise? What fun things have you always wanted
to try, but have never taken the time to do?

Try to do something just for fun, not because you have to do it. But
be careful not to tire yourself out. Some people get depressed when
they are too tired. Make sure to get enough rest so you feel strong and
can enjoy these fun activities.

Finding Humor and Laughing

If you like to joke with your friends and family don't stop now. For
many people, humor is a way to gain a sense of control. Laughter can
help you relax. When you laugh, your brain releases chemicals that

produce pleasure and relax your muscles. Even a smile can fight off stressful thoughts. Of course, you may not always feel like laughing, but other people have found that these ideas can help:

- Ask people to send you funny cards
- Enjoy the funny things children and pets do
- Watch funny movies or TV shows
- Listen to comedy recordings
- Buy a funny desk calendar
- Read humor-related books or articles
- Check out websites and videos on the Internet. If you don't own a computer, use one at your local library

You may even find that you can laugh at yourself. "I went by to help a friend this summer, and it was really hot, so I took my wig off," one woman said. "I got ready to go and I couldn't find it. After searching high and low, I found it hanging from her dog's mouth. But I just stuck it on my head and went home. My husband said, 'What happened?' Needless to say that wig has never been the same."

Physical Activities

Research shows many people find they have more energy when they take part in physical activities such as swimming, walking, yoga, and biking. They find that these types of activities help them keep strong and make them feel good. A bit of exercise every day:

- Improves your chances of feeling better
- Keeps your muscles toned
- Speeds your healing
- Decreases fatigue
- Controls stress
- Increases appetites
- Decreases constipation
- Helps free your mind of bad thoughts

Even if you have never done physical activities before, you can start now. Choose something you think you'd like to do, and get your doctor's okay to try it. There are exercises you can do even if you have to stay in bed.

Set Goals

You may find it helpful to look beyond your treatment and think about what you want to do when you feel well again. Many people set goals so that they can work toward something. For example, they research and plan a trip, or they think about classes and learning things they've always meant to learn. They may look forward to going to a wedding or meeting a new grandchild.

Section 59.2

Body Changes and Intimacy

This section includes text excerpted from "Facing Forward: Life after Cancer Treatment," National Cancer Institute (NCI), May 2014.

Overview

Some body changes are short-term, and others will last forever. Either way, your looks may be a big concern after treatment. For example, people with ostomies after colon or rectal surgery are sometimes afraid to go out. They may feel ashamed or afraid that others will reject them. They may worry about the idea of having an "accident" in social situations.

Others don't like people being able to see treatment effects such as scars, skin changes, loss of limbs, and changes in weight. Even if your treatment doesn't show, your body changes may trouble you. Feelings of anger and grief are natural. Feeling bad about your body can also lower your sex drive. This loss of or reduction in your sex life may make you feel even worse about yourself.

Changes in the way you look can also be hard for your loved ones, which can be hard on you. Parents and grandparents often worry about how they look to a child or grandchild. They fear that changes in their appearance may scare the child or get in the way of their staying close.

Getting Help

How do you cope with body changes?

- Mourn your losses. They are real, and you have a right to grieve.

- Try to focus on the ways that coping with cancer has made you stronger, wiser, and more realistic.

- If you find that your skin has changed from radiation, ask your doctor about ways you can care for it.

- Look for new ways to enhance your appearance. A new haircut, hair color, makeup, or clothing may give you a lift.

- If you choose to wear a breast form (prosthesis), make sure it fits you well. Your health insurance plan may pay for it.

- Try to recognize that you are more than your cancer. Know that you have worth—no matter how you look or what happens to you in life.

Changes in Sex Life

You may have changes in your sex life after cancer treatment—many people do. Depending on the cancer you had, these problems may be short-term or long-term. For example, about half of women who have had long-term treatment for breast and reproductive organ cancers and more than half of men treated for prostate cancer report long-term sexual problems. Many cancer survivors say they were not prepared for the changes in their sex lives.

Sexual problems after cancer treatment are often caused by changes to your body—from surgery, chemotherapy, or radiation, or by the effects of certain medicines. Sometimes emotional issues can be the cause of sexual problems. Some examples include anxiety, depression, feelings of guilt about how you got cancer, changes in body image after surgery, and stress between you and your partner. Your past sex life is not related to your current sexual problems.

What types of problems occur? People report these main concerns:

- **Worrying about intimacy after treatment.** Some may struggle with their body image after treatment. Even thinking about being seen without clothes may be stressful. People may worry that having sex will hurt or that they won't be able to perform or will feel less attractive. Pain, loss of interest, depression, or cancer medicines can also affect sex drive.

501

- **Not being able to have sex as you did before.** Some cancer treatments cause changes in sex organs that also change your sex life.

  - Some men can no longer get or keep an erection after treatment for prostate cancer, cancer of the penis, or cancer of the testes. Some treatments can also weaken a man's orgasm or make it dry.

  - Some women find it harder, or even painful, to have sex after cancer treatment. Some cancer treatments can cause these problems; sometimes, there is no clear cause. Some women also have a loss of sensation in their genital area.

- **Having menopause symptoms.** When women stop getting their periods, they can get hot flashes, dryness or tightness in the vagina, and/or other problems that can affect their desire to have sex.

- **Losing the ability to have children.** Some cancer treatments can cause infertility, making it impossible for cancer survivors to have children. Depending on type of treatment, age, and length of time since treatment, you may still be able to have children.

Getting Help

Often, sexual problems will not get better on their own. To get help with many of these problems, it's important to tell your doctor about any changes in your sex life. Sometimes there can be an underlying medical problem that causes changes, such as:

- **Vaginal dryness.** Dryness or tightness in the vagina can be caused by menopause. Ask whether using a water-based lubricant during sex, using vaginal dilators before sex, and/or taking hormones or using a hormone cream are options for you.

- **Muscle weakness.** You can help strengthen muscles in your genital area by doing Kegel exercises. Practice by controlling your muscles to stop the flow of urine. You can do these exercises even when you are not urinating. Just tighten and relax the muscles as you sit, stand, or go about your day.

Other issues you may want to discuss include:

- **Concerns about having children.** Discuss family planning concerns with your doctor. If you're a woman, ask if you still need to use birth control, even if you are not getting your period.

- **Talking with a counselor or a psychologist.** You may feel that some of your sexual problems are due to your emotions, like stress or body image. Some people find that sexual problems related to cancer start to strain their relationship with their partner. If this is the case, ask a nurse or social worker if you can talk to a counselor. Talking to someone alone, or with your partner, may help.

- **Seeing a sex therapist.** He or she may be able to help you talk openly about your problems, work through your concerns, and come up with new ways to help you and your partner.

Talking with Your Partner

Even for a couple that has been together a long time, staying connected can be a major challenge at first. It may be comforting to learn that very few committed relationships end because of ostomies, scars, or other body changes. Divorce rates are about the same for people with and without a cancer history.

Tell your partner how you feel about your sex life and what you would like to change. You might want to talk about your concerns, your beliefs about why your sex life is the way it is, your feelings, and what would make you feel better.

Approaching it openly avoids blame, stays positive, and gives your partner a better sense of how you are feeling. Here is an example of how you might start your discussion:

"I know it's tough to talk about, but I think we should discuss our sex life. We've only made love a few times lately. I miss being close to you. I worry that my scars might be a problem. Can you tell me how you feel?"

Try to be open minded as you listen to your partner's point of view:

- Focus on your partner's comments, not on what you plan to say in response.

- Repeat what he or she says in your own words.

- Ask questions to better understand your partner's concerns.

- Acknowledge that your partner's views matter to you. Say things like "I see why you might think that" or "I never thought of it that way before."

Feeling Intimate after Treatment

- Be proud of your body. It got you through treatment!

- Think of things that help you feel more attractive and confident.

- Focus on the positive. Try to be aware of your thoughts, since they can affect your sex life.

- Touch each other. Kiss, hug, and cuddle, even if you cannot have the kind of sex that you used to have.

- Be open to change. You may find new ways to enjoy intimacy.

Dating

If you're single, body changes and concerns about sex can affect how you feel about dating. As you struggle to accept the changes yourself, you may also worry about how someone else will react to physical things, such as scars or ostomies. Or you may find it awkward to bring up sexual problems or loss of fertility, which can make feeling close even harder.

You may wonder how and when to tell a new person in your life about your cancer and body changes. For some, the fear of being rejected keeps them from seeking the social life they would like to have. Others who choose not to date may face pressure from friends or family to be more sociable. Here are some ideas that can make it easier to get back into social situations:

- Focus on activities that you have time to enjoy, such as taking a class or joining a club.

- Try not to let cancer be an excuse for not dating or trying to meet people.

- Wait until you feel a sense of trust and friendship before telling a new date about your cancer. Practice what you will say to someone if you are worried about how you will handle it. Think about how he or she might react, and be ready with a response.

- Think about dating as a learning process with the goal of having a social life you enjoy. Not every date has to be perfect. If some people reject you (which can happen with or without cancer), you have not failed. Try to remember that not all dates worked out before you had cancer.

Section 59.3

Getting Follow-Up Medical Care

This section includes text excerpted from "Facing Forward: Life after Cancer Treatment," National Cancer Institute (NCI), May 2014.

Finishing Your Cancer Treatment

The end of cancer treatment is often a time to rejoice. You are probably relieved to be finished with the demands of treatment and are ready to put the experience behind you. Yet at the same time, you may feel sad and worried. It's common to be concerned about whether the cancer will come back and what you should do after treatment.

When treatment ends, you may expect life to return to the way it was before you were diagnosed with cancer. But it can take time to recover. You may have permanent scars on your body, or you may not be able to do some things you once did easily. Or you may even have emotional scars from going through so much. You may find that others think of you differently now—or you may view yourself in a different way.

One of the hardest things after treatment is not knowing what happens next.

What Is "Normal" after Cancer Treatment?

Those who have gone through cancer treatment describe the first few months as a time of change. It's not so much "getting back to normal" as it is finding out what's normal for you now. People often say that life has new meaning or that they look at things differently now. You can also expect things to keep changing as you begin your recovery.

Getting Follow-Up Medical Care

All cancer survivors should have follow-up care. Knowing what to expect after cancer treatment can help you and your family make plans, lifestyle changes, and important decisions.

Some common questions you may have are:

- Should I tell the doctor about symptoms that worry me?
- Which doctors should I see after treatment?
- How often should I see my doctor?
- What tests do I need?
- What can be done to relieve pain, fatigue, or other problems after treatment?
- How long will it take for me to recover and feel more like myself?
- Is there anything I can or should be doing to keep cancer from coming back?
- Will I have trouble with health insurance?
- Are there any support groups I can go to?

Coping with these issues can be a challenge. Yet many say that getting involved in decisions about their medical care and lifestyle was a good way for them to regain some of the control they felt they lost during cancer treatment. Research has shown that people who feel more in control feel and function better than those who do not. Being an active partner with your doctor and getting help from other members of your healthcare team is the first step.

What Is Follow-up Care?

Once you have finished your cancer treatment, you should receive a follow-up cancer care plan. Follow-up care means seeing a doctor for regular medical checkups. Your follow-up care plan depends on the type of cancer and type of treatment you had, along with your overall health. It is usually different for each person who has been treated for cancer.

In general, survivors usually return to the doctor every 3 to 4 months during the first 2 to 3 years after treatment, and once or twice a year after that. At these visits, your doctor will look for side effects from treatment and check if your cancer has returned (recurred) or spread (metastasized) to another part of your body.

At these visits, your doctor will:

- Review your medical history
- Give you a physical exam

Your doctor may run follow-up tests such as:

- Blood tests

- MRI or CT scans. These scans take detailed pictures of areas inside the body at different angles.

- Endoscopy. This test uses a thin, lighted tube to examine the inside of the body.

At your first follow-up visit, talk with your doctor about your follow-up care plan.

Follow-up care can also include home care, occupational or vocational therapy, pain management, physical therapy, and support groups.

Keeping a Personal Medical Record

Be sure to ask your oncologist for a written summary of your treatment. In the summary, he or she can suggest what aspects of your health need to be followed. Then, share this summary with any new doctors you see, especially your primary care doctor, as you discuss your follow-up care plan.

Many people keep their medical records in a binder or folder and refer to them as they see new doctors. This keeps key facts about your cancer treatment in the same place. Other kinds of health information you should keep include:

- The date you were diagnosed

- The type of cancer you were treated for

- Pathology report(s) that describe the type and stage of cancer

- Places and dates of specific treatment, such as:

- Details of all surgeries

- Sites and total amounts of radiation therapy

- Names and doses of chemotherapy and all other drugs

- Key lab reports, X-ray reports, CT scans, and MRI reports

- List of signs to watch for and possible long-term effects of treatment

- Contact information for all health professionals involved in your treatment and follow-up care

- Any problems that occurred during or after treatment

- Information about supportive care you received (such as special medicines, emotional support, and nutritional supplements)

Be sure to give any new doctors that you see a copy of your treatment summary or medical records.

Which Doctor Should I See Now? How Often?

You will need to decide which doctor will provide your follow-up cancer care and which one(s) you will see for other medical care. For follow-up cancer care, this may be the same doctor who provided your cancer treatment. For regular medical care, you may decide to see your main provider, such as a family doctor. For specific concerns, you may want to see a specialist. This is a topic you can discuss with your doctors. They can help you decide how to make transitions in care.

Depending on where you live, it may make more sense to get follow-up cancer care from your family doctor, rather than your oncologist. It's important to note that some insurance plans pay for follow-up care only with certain doctors and for a set number of visits.

In coming up with your schedule, you may want to check your health insurance plan to see what follow-up care it allows. No matter what your health coverage situation is, try to find doctors you feel comfortable with.

Always tell any new doctors you see about your history of cancer. The type of cancer you had and your treatment can affect decisions about your care in the future. They may not know about your cancer unless you tell them.

A Survivor's Wellness Plan

After cancer treatment, many survivors want to find ways to reduce the chances of their cancer coming back. Some worry that the way they eat, the stress in their lives, or their exposure to chemicals may put them at risk. Cancer survivors find that this is a time when they take a good look at how they take care of themselves. This is an important start to living a healthy life.

When you meet with your doctor about follow-up care, you should also ask about developing a wellness plan that includes ways you can take care of your physical, emotional, social, and spiritual needs. If you find that it's hard to talk with your doctor about these issues, it may be helpful to know that the more you do it, the easier it becomes. And your doctor may suggest other members of the healthcare team for you to talk with, such as a social worker, clergy member, or nurse.

Changes You May Want to Think about Making

- **Quit smoking.** Research shows that smoking can increase the chances of getting cancer at the same site or another site.

- **Cut down on how much alcohol you drink.** Research shows that drinking alcohol increases your chances of getting certain types of cancers.

- **Eat well.** Healthy food choices and physical activity may help reduce the risk of cancer or recurrence. Talk with your doctor or a nutritionist to find out about any special dietary needs that you may have. The American Cancer Society and the American Institute for Cancer Research have developed similar diet and fitness guidelines that may help reduce the risk of cancer:

  - Eat a plant-based diet and have at least 5–9 servings of fruit and vegetables daily. Try to include beans in your diet, and eat whole grains (such as cereals, breads, and pasta) several times daily.

  - Choose foods low in fat and low in salt.

  - Get to and stay at a healthy weight.

- **Exercise and stay active.** Several recent reports suggest that staying active after cancer can help lower the risk of recurrence and can lead to longer survival. Moderate exercise (walking, biking, swimming) for about 30 minutes every—or almost every—day can:

  - Reduce anxiety and depression

  - Improve mood and boost self-esteem

  - Reduce fatigue, nausea, pain, and diarrhea

It is important to start an exercise program slowly and increase activity over time, working with your doctor or a specialist (such as a physical therapist) if needed. If you need to stay in bed during your recovery, even small activities like stretching or moving your arms or legs can help you stay flexible, relieve muscle tension, and help you feel better. Some people may need to take special care in exercising. Talk with your doctor before you begin any exercise program.

Talking with Your Doctor

During cancer treatment, you had a lot of practice in getting the most out of every doctor's visit. These same skills now apply to you as a survivor and are especially helpful if you are changing doctors or going back to a family or primary care doctor you may not have seen for a while.

It is important to be able to talk openly with your doctor. Both of you need information to manage your care. Be sure to tell your doctor if you are having trouble doing everyday activities, and talk about new symptoms to watch for and what to do about them. If you are concerned that the treatment you had puts you at a higher risk for having health problems, be sure to discuss this with your doctor as you develop your follow-up plan.

At each visit, mention any health issues you are having, such as:

- New symptoms

- Pain that troubles you

- Physical problems that get in the way of your daily life or that bother you, such as fatigue, trouble sleeping, sexual problems, or weight gain or loss

- Other health problems you have, such as heart disease, diabetes, or arthritis

- Medicines, vitamins, or herbs you are taking and other treatments you are using

- Emotional problems, such as anxiety or depression, that you may have now or that you've had in the past

- Changes in your family's medical history, such as relatives with cancer

- Things you want to know more about, such as new research or side effects

Just because you have certain symptoms, it doesn't always mean the cancer has come back. Symptoms can be due to other problems that need to be addressed.

Considering Complementary and Alternative Medicine

Complementary and alternative medicine includes many different healing approaches that people use to prevent illness, reduce stress, prevent or reduce side effects and symptoms, or control or cure disease. An approach is generally called "complementary" when it is used in addition to treatments prescribed by a doctor. When it is used instead of treatments prescribed by a doctor, it is often called "alternative." Research has shown that more than half of all people with a history of cancer use one or more of these approaches.

Some common methods include imagery or relaxation, acupressure and massage, homeopathy, vitamins or herbal products, special diets, psychotherapy, prayer, yoga, and acupuncture.

Even though you have finished your cancer treatment, if you are thinking about using any of these methods, discuss it with your doctor or nurse first. Some complementary and alternative therapies may interfere or be harmful when used with medicines normally prescribed by a doctor.

Asking about Your Family's Cancer Risk

You may worry that having cancer might increase your children's risk. It's important to know that most cancer is not passed down through families. Only about 5–10 percent of the most common cancers (such as breast, colon, and prostate) are inherited. In most of the families that have inherited cancers, researchers have found relatives who may have had:

- Cancer before they were 50 years old

- Cancer in two of the same body parts (like both kidneys or both breasts)

- Other risk factors for cancer (such as colon polyps or skin moles)

If you think that your cancer may be inherited, talking with a cancer genetic counselor can help answer your questions and those of your family. He or she can also help you and your doctor decide on the medical care that you and your family might need if a genetic link is found. Genetic testing can determine whether the cancers that occur in your family are due to genes or to other factors.

Getting the Most from Your Follow-Up Visits

Here are some ideas that helped others with their follow-up care.

Before You Go:

- Bring paper, so you can take notes, or ask if you can tape-record the answers.

- Ask someone to come with you to your doctor visits. A friend or family member can help you think about and understand what was said. He or she also may think of new questions to ask.

- Make a list of questions ahead of time and bring it with you.

At Your Visit:

- Ask to talk with the doctor or nurse in a private room with the door closed

- Ask your most important questions first, in case the doctor runs out of time

- Express yourself clearly

- Describe your problem or concern briefly

- Tell the doctor how your problem or concern makes you feel.

- Ask for what you want or need, for example, "I am tired most of the time each day. I've tried napping, but it doesn't help. My fatigue gets in the way of my daily life. What can be done to help me with this problem?"

- Ask the doctor to explain what he or she said in terms you understand

- Repeat back in your own words what you think the doctor meant

- Tell your doctor if you need more information

Before You Leave:

- Ask your doctor or pharmacist about the best way to take your medicine and about possible side effects

- Don't be afraid to ask for more time when you make your next appointment. Or ask the doctor to suggest a time when you could call and get answers to your questions.

- Ask if there are any survivor support groups in the area

- Ask for booklets or other materials to read at home

- Keep your own set of records about any follow-up care you have

Section 59.4

Going Back to Work

This section includes text excerpted from "Going Back to Work,"
National Cancer Institute (NCI), December 2, 2014.

Overview

People with cancer often want to get back to work. Their jobs not only give them an income but also a sense of routine. Work helps people feel good about themselves.

Before you go back to work, talk with your doctor as well as your boss. You will all want to make sure you're well enough to do your job. You may need to work fewer hours or do your job in a different way. Some people feel well enough to work while they're having chemo or radiation treatment. Others need to take time off until their treatments are over.

Talking with Your Boss and Coworkers

The response of coworkers about your cancer treatment may differ. Some people may be a huge source of support, while others may be a source of anger or frustration. Some people mean well, but they don't know the right thing to say. Maybe they just don't know how to offer support. Others don't want to deal with your cancer at all. They may think that you aren't able to work as hard as before.

If coworkers seem unsupportive, it could be because they're anxious for you or for themselves. Your cancer experience may threaten them because it reminds them that cancer can happen to anyone. Try to understand their fears and be patient as you try to regain a good relationship. But some people with cancer say that they get tired of trying to act cheerful around others. Many say that friendships change as they let go of their casual ones and give more time to the meaningful ones.

Relating to Others at Work

How do you relate to other people in your life when you go back to work? Does it feel good to return or do you worry how others will react? Here are some tips for returning to work:

- **Accept help.** When people offer to help, say yes, and have in mind some things that they could do to make your life easier. In this way, you will get the support you need, and they will feel helpful.

- **Talk to others.** If you find that a coworker's feelings about cancer are hurting you, try to resolve the problem with that person face-to-face. If it's still affecting your work after that, your manager, employee assistance counselor, or personnel office may be able to help.

- **Address problems that come up from the start.** Supervisors or coworkers may be able to help those around you understand how you want to be treated.

- **Try to keep up contacts during your recovery.** Coworkers will worry about you. But if they are kept up-to-date about your progress, they will be less anxious and scared. Talk to them on the phone, send email, or appoint a trusted friend or family member to do this for you. Your return to work or other activities will be easier for you and others if you stay in touch.

- **Plan what you'll say about your cancer.** There is no right way to deal with others about your illness, but you do need to think about what you'll say when you're back on the job. Some people don't want to focus on their cancer or be linked in people's minds with the disease. Others are very open about it, speaking frankly with their boss or other workers to air concerns, correct wrong ideas, and decide how to work together. The best approach is the one that feels right to you.

Your Legal Rights at Work

Some people with cancer face roadblocks when they try to go back to work or get a new job. Even people who had cancer many years ago may still have trouble. Employers may not treat them fairly because of false beliefs about cancer. For example, an employer may think cancer can be spread from person to person or that people with cancer take too many sick days. Some employers also think that people with cancer are poor insurance risks.

It is against the law to discriminate against (treat unfairly) workers who have disabilities such as cancer. There are national laws that protect your rights as a worker. And if you're looking for a new job, you have no legal obligation to talk about your cancer history unless your past health has a direct impact on the job you seek.

Handling Problems at Work

- Decide how to handle the problem.

- What are your rights as an employee?

- Are you willing to take action to correct a problem?

- Do you still want to work there? Or would you rather look for a new job?

- If necessary, ask your employer to adjust to your needs.

- Start by talking informally to your supervisor, personnel office, employee assistance counselor, shop steward, or union representative.

- Ask for a change that would make it easier for you to keep your job (for example, flextime, working at home, special equipment at work).

- Document each request and its outcome for your records.

- Get help working with your employer if you need it.

- Ask your doctor or nurse to find times for follow-up visits that don't conflict with your other responsibilities.

- Gct your doctor to write a letter to your employer or personnel officer explaining how, if at all, your cancer may affect your work or your schedule.

Talk with your social worker about laws in your state. Your social worker can give you the name of the state agency that protects your rights as an employee. You may also want to ask about benefits you can get as a person with cancer.

Chapter 60

Nutrition and Cancer

Good Nutrition Is Important for Cancer Patients

Nutrition is a process in which food is taken in and used by the body for growth, to keep the body healthy, and to replace tissue. Good nutrition is important for good health. Eating the right kinds of foods before, during, and after cancer treatment can help the patient feel better and stay stronger. A healthy diet includes eating and drinking enough of the foods and liquids that have the important nutrients (vitamins, minerals, protein, carbohydrates, fat, and water) the body needs.

When the body does not get or cannot absorb the nutrients needed for health, it causes a condition called malnutrition or malnourishment.

This summary is about nutrition in adults with cancer.

Healthy Eating Habits Are Important during Cancer Treatment

Nutrition therapy is used to help cancer patients get the nutrients they need to keep up their body weight and strength, keep body tissue healthy, and fight infection. Eating habits that are good for cancer patients can be very different from the usual healthy eating guidelines.

This chapter includes text excerpted from "Nutrition in Cancer Care–Patient Version (PDQ®)," National Cancer Institute (NCI), January 8, 2016.

Healthy eating habits and good nutrition can help patients deal with the effects of cancer and its treatment. Some cancer treatments work better when the patient is well nourished and gets enough calories and protein in the diet. Patients who are well nourished may have a better prognosis (chance of recovery) and quality of life.

Cancer Can Change the Way the Body Uses Food

Some tumors make chemicals that change the way the body uses certain nutrients. The body's use of protein, carbohydrates, and fat may be affected, especially by tumors of the stomach or intestines. A patient may seem to be eating enough, but the body may not be able to absorb all the nutrients from the food.

Cancer and Cancer Treatments May Affect Nutrition

For many patients, the effects of cancer and cancer treatments make it hard to eat well. Cancer treatments that affect nutrition include:

- Surgery
- Chemotherapy
- Radiation therapy
- Immunotherapy
- Stem cell transplant

When the head, neck, esophagus, stomach, or intestines are affected by the cancer treatment, it is very hard to take in enough nutrients to stay healthy.

The side effects of cancer and cancer treatment that can affect eating include:

- Anorexia (loss of appetite)
- Mouth sores
- Dry mouth
- Trouble swallowing
- Nausea
- Vomiting
- Diarrhea
- Constipation
- Pain
- Depression
- Anxiety

Cancer and cancer treatments may affect taste, smell, appetite, and the ability to eat enough food or absorb the nutrients from food. This can cause malnutrition (a condition caused by a lack of key nutrients). Malnutrition can cause the patient to be weak, tired, and unable to fight infections or get through cancer treatment. Malnutrition may be made worse if the cancer grows or spreads. Eating too little protein and calories is a very common problem for cancer patients. Having enough protein and calories is important for healing, fighting infection, and having enough energy.

Anorexia and Cachexia Are Common Causes of Malnutrition in Cancer Patients

Anorexia (the loss of appetite or desire to eat) is a common symptom in people with cancer. Anorexia may occur early in the disease or later, if the cancer grows or spreads. Some patients already have anorexia when they are diagnosed with cancer. Almost all patients who have advanced cancer will have anorexia. Anorexia is the most common cause of malnutrition in cancer patients.

Cachexia is a condition marked by a loss of appetite, weight loss, muscle loss, and general weakness. It is common in patients with tumors of the lung, pancreas, and upper gastrointestinal tract. It is important to watch for and treat cachexia early in cancer treatment because it is hard to correct.

Cancer patients may have anorexia and cachexia at the same time. Weight loss can be caused by eating fewer calories, using more calories, or both.

It Is Important to Treat Weight Loss Caused by Cancer and Its Treatment

It is important that cancer symptoms and side effects that affect eating and cause weight loss are treated early. Both nutrition therapy and medicine can help the patient stay at a healthy weight. Medicine may be used for the following:

- To help increase appetite
- To help digest food
- To help the muscles of the stomach and intestines contract (to keep food moving along)
- To prevent or treat nausea and vomiting
- To prevent or treat diarrhea
- To prevent or treat constipation

- To prevent and treat mouth problems (such as dry mouth, infection, pain, and sores)

- To prevent and treat pain

Nutrition Therapy in Cancer Care

Screening and Assessment Are Done before Cancer Treatment Begins, and Assessment Continues during Treatment

Screening is used to look for nutrition risks in a patient who has no symptoms. This can help find out if the patient is likely to become malnourished, so that steps can be taken to prevent it.

Assessment checks the nutritional health of the patient and helps to decide if nutrition therapy is needed to correct a problem.

Screening and assessment may include questions about the following:

- Weight changes over the past year.

- Changes in the amount and type of food eaten compared to what is usual for the patient.

- Problems that have affected eating, such as loss of appetite, nausea, vomiting, diarrhea, constipation, mouth sores, dry mouth, changes in taste and smell, or pain.

- Ability to walk and do other activities of daily living (dressing, getting into or out of a bed or chair, taking a bath or shower, and using the toilet).

A physical exam is also done to check the body for general health and signs of disease. The doctor will look for loss of weight, fat, and muscle, and for fluid buildup in the body.

Finding and Treating Nutrition Problems Early May Improve the Patient's Prognosis (Chance of Recovery)

Early nutrition screening and assessment help find problems that may affect how well the patient's body can deal with the effects of cancer treatment. Patients who are underweight or malnourished may not be able to get through treatment as well as a well-nourished patient. Finding and treating nutrition problems early can help the patient gain weight or prevent weight loss, decrease problems with the treatment, and help recovery.

A Healthcare Team of Nutrition Specialists Will Continue to Watch for Nutrition Problems

A nutrition support team will check the patient's nutritional health often during cancer treatment and recovery. The team may include the following specialists:

- Physician

- Nurse

- Registered dietitian

- Social worker

- Psychologist

A patient whose religion doesn't allow eating certain foods may want to talk with a religious advisor about allowing those foods during cancer treatment and recovery.

There Are Three Main Goals of Nutrition Therapy for Cancer Patients in Active Treatment and Recovery

The main goals of nutrition therapy for patients in active treatment and recovery are to provide nutrients that are missing, maintain nutritional health, and prevent problems. The health care team will use nutrition therapy to do the following:

- Prevent or treat nutrition problems, including preventing muscle and bone loss

- Decrease side effects of cancer treatment and problems that affect nutrition

- Keep up the patient's strength and energy

- Help the immune system fight infection

- Help the body recover and heal

- Keep up or improve the patient's quality of life

Good nutrition continues to be important for patients who are in remission or whose cancer has been cured.

The Goal of Nutrition Therapy for Patients Who Have Advanced Cancer Is to Help with the Patient's Quality of Life

The goals of nutrition therapy for patients who have advanced cancer include the following:

- Control side effects

- Lower the risk of infection

- Keep up strength and energy

- Improve or maintain quality of life

Effects of Cancer Treatment on Nutrition

Surgery and Nutrition

Surgery Increases the Body's Need for Nutrients and Energy

The body needs extra energy and nutrients to heal wounds, fight infection, and recover from surgery. If the patient is malnourished before surgery, it may cause problems during recovery, such as poor healing or infection. For these patients, nutrition care may begin before surgery.

Surgery to the Head, Neck, Esophagus, Stomach, or Intestines May Affect Nutrition

Most cancer patients are treated with surgery. Surgery that removes all or part of certain organs can affect a patient's ability to eat and digest food. The following are nutrition problems caused by specific types of surgery:

- Surgery to the head and neck may cause problems with:
  - Chewing
  - Swallowing
  - Tasting or smelling food
  - Making saliva
  - Seeing
- Surgery that affects the esophagus, stomach, or intestines may keep these organs from working as they should to digest food and absorb nutrients.

All of these can affect the patient's ability to eat normally. Emotional stress about the surgery itself also may affect appetite.

Nutrition Therapy Can Help Relieve Nutrition Problems Caused by Surgery

Nutrition therapy can relieve or decrease the side effects of surgery and help cancer patients get the nutrients they need. Nutrition therapy may include the following:

- Nutritional supplement drinks

- Enteral nutrition (feeding liquid through a tube into the stomach or intestines)

- Parenteral nutrition (feeding through a catheter into the bloodstream)

- Medicines to increase appetite

It is common for patients to have pain, tiredness, and/or loss of appetite after surgery. For a short time, some patients may not be able to eat what they usually do because of these symptoms. Following certain tips about food may help. These include:

- Stay away from carbonated drinks (such as sodas) and foods that cause gas, such as:

  - Beans

  - Peas

  - Broccoli

  - Cabbage

  - Brussels sprouts

  - Green peppers

  - Radishes

  - Cucumbers

- Increase calories by frying foods and using gravies, mayonnaise, and salad dressings. Supplements high in calories and protein can also be used.

- Choose high-protein and high-calorie foods to increase energy and help wounds heal. Good choices include:

- Eggs

- Cheese

- Whole milk

- Ice cream

- Nuts

- Peanut butter

- Meat

- Poultry

- Fish

- If constipation is a problem, increase fiber by small amounts and drink lots of water. Good sources of fiber include:

  - Whole-grain cereals (such as oatmeal and bran)

  - Beans

  - Vegetables

  - Fruit

  - Whole-grain breads

Chemotherapy and Nutrition

Chemotherapy Affects Cells All through the Body

Chemotherapy affects fast-growing cells and is used to treat cancer because cancer cells grow and divide quickly. Healthy cells that normally grow and divide quickly may also be killed. These include cells in the mouth, digestive tract, and hair follicles.

Chemotherapy May Affect Nutrition

Chemotherapy may cause side effects that cause problems with eating and digestion. When more than one anticancer drug is given, more side effects may occur or they may be more severe. The following side effects are common:

- Loss of appetite

- Inflammation and sores in the mouth

- Changes in the way food tastes

- Feeling full after only a small amount of food
- Nausea
- Vomiting
- Diarrhea

Nutrition Therapy Can Help Relieve Nutrition Problems Caused by Chemotherapy

Patients who have side effects from chemotherapy may not be able to eat normally and get all the nutrients they need to restore healthy blood counts between treatments. Nutrition therapy can help relieve these side effects, help patients recover from chemotherapy, prevent delays in treatment, prevent weight loss, and maintain general health. Nutrition therapy may include the following:

- Nutrition supplement drinks between meals
- Enteral nutrition (tube feedings)
- Changes in the diet, such as eating small meals throughout the day

Radiation Therapy and Nutrition

Radiation Therapy Can Affect Cancer Cells and Healthy Cells in the Treatment Area

Radiation therapy can kill cancer cells and healthy cells in the treatment area. The amount of damage depends on the following:

- The part of the body that is treated
- The total dose of radiation and how it is given

Radiation Therapy May Affect Nutrition

Radiation therapy to any part of the digestive system often has side effects that cause nutrition problems. Most of the side effects begin a few weeks after radiation therapy begins and go away a few weeks after it is finished. Some side effects can continue for months or years after treatment ends.

The following are some of the more common side effects:

- For radiation therapy to the head and neck

- Loss of appetite

- Changes in the way food tastes

- Pain when swallowing

- Dry mouth or thick saliva

- Sore mouth and gums

- Narrowing of the upper esophagus, which can cause choking, breathing, and swallowing problems

- For radiation therapy to the chest

  - Infection of the esophagus

  - Trouble swallowing

  - Esophageal reflux (a backward flow of the stomach contents into the esophagus)

- For radiation therapy to the abdomen or pelvis

  - Diarrhea

  - Nausea

  - Vomiting

  - Inflamed intestines or rectum

  - A decrease in the amount of nutrients absorbed by the intestines

Radiation therapy may also cause tiredness, which can lead to a decrease in appetite.

Nutrition Therapy Can Help Relieve the Nutrition Problems Caused by Radiation Therapy

Nutrition therapy during radiation treatment can help the patient get enough protein and calories to get through treatment, prevent weight loss, help wound and skin healing, and maintain general health. Nutrition therapy may include the following:

- Nutritional supplement drinks between meals

- Enteral nutrition (tube feedings)

- Changes in the diet, such as eating small meals throughout the day

Patients who receive high-dose radiation therapy to prepare for a bone marrow transplant may have many nutrition problems and should see a dietitian for nutrition support.

Biologic Therapy and Nutrition

Biologic Therapy May Affect Nutrition

The side effects of biologic therapy are different for each patient and each type of biologic agent. The following nutrition problems are common:

- Fever
- Nausea
- Vomiting
- Diarrhea
- Loss of appetite
- Tiredness
- Weight gain

Nutrition Therapy Can Help Relieve Nutrition Problems Caused by Biologic Therapy

The side effects of biologic therapy can cause weight loss and malnutrition if they are not treated. Nutrition therapy can help patients receiving biologic therapy get the nutrients they need to get through treatment, prevent weight loss, and maintain general health.

Stem Cell Transplant and Nutrition

Stem Cell Transplant Patients Have Special Nutrition Needs

Chemotherapy, radiation therapy, and medicines used for a stem cell transplant may cause side effects that keep a patient from eating and digesting food as usual. Common side effects include the following:

- Changes in the way food tastes
- Dry mouth or thick saliva
- Mouth and throat sores
- Nausea

- Vomiting

- Diarrhea

- Constipation

- Weight loss and loss of appetite

- Weight gain

Nutrition Therapy Is Very Important for Patients Who Have a Stem Cell Transplant

Transplant patients have a very high risk of infection. High doses of chemotherapy or radiation therapy decrease the number of white blood cells, which fight infection. It is especially important that transplant patients avoid getting infections.

Patients who have a transplant need plenty of protein and calories to get through and recover from the treatment, prevent weight loss, fight infection, and maintain general health. It is also important to avoid infection from bacteria in food. Nutrition therapy during transplant treatment may include the following:

- A diet of cooked and processed foods only, because raw vegetables and fresh fruit may carry harmful bacteria

- Guidelines on safe food handling

- A specific diet based on the type of transplant and the part of the body affected by cancer

- Parenteral nutrition (feeding through the bloodstream) during the first few weeks after the transplant, to give the patient the calories, protein, vitamins, minerals, and fluids they need to recover

Chapter 61

Exercise and Cancer

There is growing recognition and acceptance of the beneficial role of exercise following a breast cancer diagnosis. Studies have suggested that exercise improves symptom control and may be associated with reductions in cancer-related and overall death rates in women with breast cancer. NCI is currently supporting a pilot research study in women with metastatic breast cancer (MBC) as a first step in determining the feasibility of launching large-scale clinical trials investigating the effects of exercise on breast cancer outcomes.

Lee Jones, Ph.D., Associate Professor and Scientific Director of the Duke University Center for Cancer Survivorship, who is the principal investigator of the study, commented, "There are a lot of research studies that look at the role of exercise in women with early stage breast cancer, but few studies have looked at the role of exercise in patients with metastatic disease."

Jones and his team are conducting a randomized phase II clinical trial in women with MBC. Half of the patients will participate in a treadmill walking program, while the remainder of patients will be in a control group, doing only low-intensity stretching exercises.

The study focuses on the safety and feasibility of exercise training as opposed to the potential role of exercise to improve disease outcomes in women with metastatic disease. Before addressing these types of questions, it is first of crucial importance to determine if exercising by

---

This chapter includes text excerpted from "Exercise Study for Metastatic Breast Cancer Patients May Offer Benefits," National Cancer Institute (NCI), March 27, 2013.

these individuals is safe or possible "because MBC is a totally different clinical scenario than those with early-stage disease," Dr. Jones noted. Women with MBC face many additional challenges from advanced disease and its treatments, including drug toxicities, infections, and hospitalizations, he added. "We have to be on our toes because their situations can change week-to-week."

Dr. Jones reported they have enrolled about 30 women into the study so far and have identified two distinct groups of MBC patients. "There is a group who essentially do very well with exercise," he said. "And then there is another group who really want to exercise but they're just not able to because of toxicity, disease progression, and other factors. I believe this study is going to be extremely informative in terms of working out the characteristics of individuals with advanced disease who may be able to tolerate and benefit from an exercise program."

"That is a simple question but it's an important first step towards moving ahead with larger clinical trials to really get to some of the biology of what's going on," Dr. Jones continued. "It's not just what can we do to help these patients feel better as they go through all these treatments, but can we also impact clinical and disease outcomes in these patients?"

If the pilot study shows promising results for exercise in MBC patients in terms of program adherence, adverse events, and safety profile, "that would bode well for future study in a more select population," Dr. Jones noted. "I think exercise is definitely going to be complementary to standard care for these patients in the future."

Chapter 62

Breast Cancer and Your Emotions: Tips for Coping

Feelings and Cancer

Dealing with the different side effects and life changes of cancer treatment can be hard on you emotionally as well as physically. Just as cancer affects your physical health, it can bring up a wide range of feelings you're not used to dealing with. It can also make many feelings seem more intense. They may change daily, hourly, or even minute to minute. This is true whether you're currently in treatment, done with treatment, or a friend or family member. These feelings are all normal.

Often the values you grew up with affect how you think about and deal with cancer. For example some people:

- Feel they have to be strong and protect their friends and families

- Seek support and turn to loved ones or other cancer survivors

- Ask for help from counselors or other professionals

- Turn to their faith to help them cope

Whatever you decide, it's important to do what's right for you and not to compare yourself with others. Your friends and family members

---

This chapter includes text excerpted from "Feelings and Cancer," National Cancer Institute (NCI), December 2, 2014.

may share some of the same feelings. If you feel comfortable, share this information with them.

Overwhelmed

When you first learn that you have cancer, you may feel as if your life is out of control. This could be because:

- You wonder if you're going to live
- Your normal routine is disrupted by doctor visits and treatments
- People use medical terms that you don't understand
- You feel like you can't do the things you enjoy
- You feel helpless and lonely

Even if you feel out of control, there are ways you can take charge. Try to learn as much as you can about your cancer. Ask your doctor questions and don't be afraid to say when you don't understand. Also, many people feel better if they stay busy. You can take part in activities such as music, crafts, reading, or learning something new.

Denial

When you were first diagnosed, you may have had trouble believing or accepting the fact that you have cancer. This is called denial. It can be helpful because it can give you time to adjust to your diagnosis. It can also give you time to feel hopeful and better about the future.

Sometimes, denial is a serious problem. If it lasts too long, it can keep you from getting the treatment you need.

The good news is that most people work through denial. Usually by the time treatment begins, most people accept the fact that they have cancer and move forward. This is true for those with cancer as well as the people they love and care about.

Anger

People with cancer often feel angry. It's normal to ask, "Why me?" and be angry at the cancer. You may also feel anger or resentment towards your healthcare providers, your healthy friends and your loved ones. And if you're religious, you may even feel angry with God.

Anger often comes from feelings that are hard to show, such as fear, panic, frustration, anxiety, or helplessness. If you feel angry, you don't have to pretend that everything is okay. Anger can be helpful in that it may motivate you to take action. Talk with your family and friends about your anger. Or, ask your doctor to refer you to a counselor.

Fear and Worry

It's scary to hear that you have cancer. You may be afraid or worried about:

- Being in pain, either from the cancer or the treatment
- Feeling sick or looking different as a result of your treatment
- Taking care of your family
- Paying your bills
- Keeping your job
- Dying

Some fears about cancer are based on stories, rumors, or wrong information. To cope with fears and worries, it often helps to be informed. Most people feel better when they learn the facts. They feel less afraid and know what to expect. Learn about your cancer and understand what you can do to be an active partner in your care. Some studies even suggest that people who are well-informed about their illness and treatment are more likely to follow their treatment plans and recover from cancer more quickly than those who are not.

Hope

Once people accept that they have cancer, they often feel a sense of hope. There are many reasons to feel hopeful. Millions of people who have had cancer are alive today. Your chances of living with cancer—and living beyond it—are better now than they have ever been before. And people with cancer can lead active lives, even during treatment.

Some doctors think that hope may help your body deal with cancer. So, scientists are studying whether a hopeful outlook and positive attitude helps people feel better. Here are some ways you can build your sense of hope:

- Plan your days as you've always done.
- Don't limit the things you like to do just because you have cancer.
- Look for reasons to have hope. If it helps, write them down or talk to others about them.

- Spend time in nature.

- Reflect on your religious or spiritual beliefs.

- Listen to stories about people with cancer who are leading active lives.

Stress and Anxiety

Both during and after treatment, it's normal to have stress over all the life changes you are going through. Anxiety means you have extra worry, can't relax, and feel tense. You may notice that:

- Your heart beats faster

- You have headaches or muscle pains

- You don't feel like eating. Or you eat more.

- You feel sick to your stomach or have diarrhea

- You feel shaky, weak, or dizzy

- You have a tight feeling in your throat and chest

- You sleep too much or too little

- You find it hard to concentrate

If you have any of these feelings, talk to your doctor. Though they are common signs of stress, you will want to make sure they aren't due to medicines or treatment.

Stress can keep your body from healing as well as it should.

If you're worried about your stress, ask your doctor to suggest a counselor for you to talk to. You could also take a class that teaches ways to deal with stress. The key is to find ways to control your stress and not to let it control you.

Sadness and Depression

Many people with cancer feel sad. They feel a sense of loss of their health, and the life they had before they learned they had the disease. Even when you're done with treatment, you may still feel sad. This is a normal response to any serious illness. It may take time to work through and accept all the changes that are taking place.

When you're sad, you may have very little energy, feel tired, or not want to eat. For some, these feelings go away or lessen over time. But for others, these emotions can become stronger. The painful feelings don't get any better, and they get in the way of daily life. This may be a medical condition called **depression**. For some, cancer treatment may have added to this problem by changing the way the brain works.

Getting Help for Depression

Depression can be treated. Below are common signs of depression. If you have any of the following signs for more than 2 weeks, talk to your doctor about treatment. Be aware that some of these symptoms could be due to physical problems, so it's important to talk about them with your doctor.

Emotional signs:

- Feelings of sadness that don't go away
- Feeling emotionally numb
- Feeling nervous or shaky
- Having a sense of guilt or feeling unworthy
- Feeling helpless or hopeless, as if life has no meaning
- Feeling short-tempered, moody
- Having a hard time concentrating, feeling scatterbrained
- Crying for long periods of time or many times each day
- Focusing on worries and problems
- No interest in the hobbies and activities you used to enjoy
- Finding it hard to enjoy everyday things, such as food or being with family and friends
- Thinking about hurting yourself
- Thoughts about killing yourself

Body changes:

- Unintended weight gain or loss not due to illness or treatment
- Sleep problems, such as not being able to sleep, having nightmares, or sleeping too much
- Racing heart, dry mouth, increased perspiration, upset stomach, diarrhea
- Changes in energy level
- Fatigue that doesn't go away

- Headaches, other aches and pains

If your doctor thinks that you suffer from depression, he or she may give you medicine to help you feel less tense. Or, he or she may refer you to other experts. Don't feel that you should have to control these feelings on your own. Getting the help you need is important for your life and your health.

Guilt

If you feel guilty, know that many people with cancer feel this way. You may blame yourself for upsetting the people you love, or worry that you're a burden in some way. Or, you may envy other people's good health and be ashamed of this feeling. You might even blame yourself for lifestyle choices that you think could have led to your cancer.

These feelings are all very common. It may help you to share them with someone. Let your doctor know if you would like to talk with a counselor or go to a support group.

Loneliness

People with cancer often feel lonely or distant from others. This may be for a number of reasons:

- Friends sometimes have a hard time dealing with cancer and may not visit or call you

- You may feel too sick to take part in the hobbies and activities you used to enjoy

- Sometimes, even when you're with people you care about, you may feel that no one understands what you're going through

It's also normal to feel alone after treatment. You may miss the support you got from your healthcare team. Many people have a sense that their safety net has been pulled away, and they get less attention. It's common to still feel cut off from certain friends or family members. Some of them may think that now that treatment is over, you will be back to normal soon, even though this may not be true. Others may want to help but don't know how.

Look for emotional support in different ways. It could help you to talk to other people who have cancer or to join a support group. Or, you may feel better talking only to a close friend or family member, or counselor, or a member of your faith or spiritual community. Do what feels right for you.

Gratitude

Some people see their cancer as a "wake-up call." They realize the importance of enjoying the little things in life. They go places they've never been. They finish projects they had started but put aside. They spend more time with friends and family. They mend broken relationships.

It may be hard at first, but you can find joy in your life if you have cancer. Pay attention to the things you do each day that make you smile. They can be as simple as drinking a good cup of coffee or talking to a friend.

You can also do things that are more special to you, like being in nature or praying in a place that has meaning for you. Or, it could be playing a sport you love or cooking a good meal. Whatever you choose, embrace the things that bring you joy when you can.

Other Ways to Cope with Your Emotions

Express Your Feelings

People have found that when they express strong feelings like anger or sadness, they're more able to let go of them. Some sort out their feelings by talking to friends or family, other cancer survivors, a support group, or a counselor. But even if you prefer not to discuss your cancer with others, you can still sort out your feelings by thinking about them or writing them down.

Look for the Positive

Sometimes this means looking for the good even in a bad time or trying to be hopeful instead of thinking the worst. Try to use your energy to focus on wellness and what you can do now to stay as healthy as possible.

Don't Blame Yourself for Your Cancer

Some people believe that they got cancer because of something they did or did not do. Remember, cancer can happen to anyone.

Don't Try to Be Upbeat If You're Not

Many people say they want to have the freedom to give in to their feelings sometimes. As one woman said, "When it gets really bad, I just tell my family I'm having a bad cancer day and go upstairs and crawl into bed."

You Choose When to Talk about Your Cancer

It can be hard for people to know how to talk to you about your cancer. Often loved ones mean well, but they don't know what to say or how to act. You can make them feel more at ease by asking them what they think or how they feel.

Find Ways to Help Yourself Relax

Whatever activity helps you unwind, you should take some time to do it. Meditation, guided imagery and relaxation exercises are just a few ways that have been shown to help others, these may help you relax when you feel worried.

Be as Active as You Can

Getting out of the house and doing something can help you focus on other things besides cancer and the worries it brings. Exercise or gentle yoga and stretching can help too.

Look for Things You Enjoy

You may like hobbies such as woodworking, photography, reading, or crafts. Or find creative outlets such as art, music, or dance.

Look at What You Can Control

Some people say that putting their lives in order helps. Being involved in your healthcare, keeping your appointments, and making changes in your lifestyle are among the things you can control. Even setting a daily schedule can give you a sense of control. And while no one can control every thought, some say that they try not to dwell on the fearful ones.

Chapter 63

Guide for Caregivers

Who Is the Caregiver?

Family caregivers may be spouses, partners, children, relatives, or friends who help the patient with activities of daily living and health care needs at home.

Many cancer patients today receive part of their care at home. Hospital stays are shorter than they used to be, and there are now more treatments that don't need an overnight hospital stay or can be given outside of the hospital. People with cancer are living longer and many patients want to be cared for at home as much as possible. This care is often given by family caregivers. These caregivers may be spouses, partners, children, relatives, or friends.

The family caregiver works with the health care team and has an important role in improving the patient's health and quality of life. Today, family caregivers do many things that used to be done in the hospital or doctor's office by health care providers. Caregiving includes everyday tasks such as helping the patient with medicines, doctor visits, meals, schedules, and health insurance matters. It also includes giving emotional and spiritual support, such as helping the patient deal with feelings and making hard decisions.

It is important that the family caregiver is a part of the team right from the start.

This chapter includes text excerpted from "Family Caregivers in Cancer–Patient Version," National Cancer Institute (NCI), July 14, 2015.

The family caregiver has the very important job of watching for changes in the patient's medical condition while giving long-term care at home. Family caregivers can help plan treatment, make decisions, and carry out treatment plans all through the different parts of treatment.

This chapter is about adult family caregivers in cancer.

Caregiver's Point of View

Caregivers need help and emotional support.

A caregiver responds in his or her own way to the cancer patient's diagnosis and prognosis. The caregiver may feel emotions that are as strong as or stronger than those felt by the patient. The caregiver's need for information, help, and support is different from what is needed by the patient.

The life of a family caregiver changes in many ways when cancer is diagnosed. These changes affect most parts of life and continue after treatment ends.

The caregiver's role changes as the patient's needs change during and after cancer treatment.

Key times when the caregiver's role changes and new challenges come up are at diagnosis, during treatment at the hospital, when the patient needs care at home, after treatment ends, and at the patient's end of life.

At Diagnosis

Family caregivers take an active role that begins when the cancer is being diagnosed. The caregiver has to learn about the kind of cancer the patient has and new medical terms. The caregiver also goes with the patient to new places for treatment and helps the patient make treatment decisions.

During Treatment at the Hospital

The patient may ask the caregiver to be the one to talk to the health care team and make important decisions. The relationship between the caregiver and the patient affects how well this works. Disagreements between the patient and caregiver can make important decisions harder to make and affect treatment choices. In addition to talking to the health care team, the caregiver may also do the following:

- Take on many of the patient's household duties

- Schedule hospital visits and plan travel to and from the visits
- Work through the health care system for the patient
- Arrange for home care
- Take care of insurance matters

During the active treatment phase, a caregiver needs to meet the demands of supporting the patient as well as the demands of home, work, and family. This may be physically and emotionally exhausting.

During Care in the Home

When the patient moves from one care setting (such as the hospital) to another (such as the home), it can be stressful for the patient and the caregiver. The patient usually would rather be at home, which is a familiar and comforting place. The return home usually means more work for the caregiver.

In addition to hands-on patient care, the caregiver may also do the following:

- Be a companion to the patient
- Continue doing many of the patient's household duties
- Take care of medicines and meals
- Schedule doctor visits, plan travel to and from the visits, and go with the patient to them
- Arrange for home visits by therapists or other professionals
- Deal with medical emergencies
- Take care of insurance matters
- Work through the health care system for the patient

Caregivers worry about how they'll be able to do all this and also take care of themselves. The caregiver sometimes has to give up social activities and miss work. This can all be very hard and very tiring in a physical and emotional way for both the caregiver and the patient. These demands can be especially hard on older caregivers.

After Treatment Ends

Some patients and caregivers expect life to go back to the way it was before the cancer was diagnosed and this may not happen. Caregiver stress may continue after the patient's treatment ends, as roles change once again. Some caregivers have problems adjusting for the first year after the end of treatment. Part of this is caused by worry that the cancer will come back. When the caregiver is the partner or spouse of the cancer survivor, there may be sexual problems, also. Studies have shown that these adjustment problems usually do not last long. Problems with adjusting that can last a long time include the following:

- Problems in the relationship between the caregiver and the patient

- Poor communication between the caregiver and the patient

- Lack of social support

At the End of Life

Caring for a patient at home at the end of life brings a new set of challenges for the caregiver. The patient depends even more on the caregiver for physical and emotional support. The patient's symptoms also may be more difficult to manage. The caregiver may feel distressed by these new challenges and by not being able to take part in activities and interests that are important to him or her. The caregiver may feel even more distressed if the patient goes into hospice care. Studies have shown that caregivers have a lower quality of life and poorer health when giving the patient end-of-life care than they do during active treatment.

Some hospital or hospice programs offer end-of-life support services to improve the patient's quality of life and help both the caregiver and the patient. End-of-life support services include the following:

- A team approach helping the patient and family with their physical, emotional, social, spiritual, and economic needs in order to improve the quality of life of the patient and caregiver.

- Including the caregiver in medical decisions and managing the patient's symptoms.

- Watching the caregiver for signs of distress and work with him or her to get the kind of help they need.

Roles for the Family Caregiver

The family caregiver has many roles besides giving the patient hands-on care.

Most people think first of the physical care given by a family caregiver, but a caregiver fills many other roles during the patient's cancer experience. In addition to hands-on care, the caregiver may also do the following:

- Manage the patient's medical care, insurance claims, and bill payments

- Be a companion to the patient

- Go with the patient to doctor appointments, run personal errands, cook, clean, and do other housekeeping chores

- Find doctors and specialists needed and get information that may be hard to find

- Help the patient connect with family, friends, neighbors, and community members

A family caregiver faces the tough job of taking on new roles and challenges as the patient's needs change over time. **The caregiver takes on different roles so that the patient gets all the information, support, and treatment he or she needs.** Caregivers may take on the roles of decision maker, patient advocate, and communicator.

Decision Maker

Doctors, caregivers, and patients are partners in making decisions. Making a decision involves getting the right information in a way that it can be understood. Cancer patients have many information needs. They want to know about staying healthy, tests and treatments, side effects and symptoms, and emotional issues.

In order to make treatment decisions, caregivers and patients often want more information and they may look for help and information from sources other than the doctor. It's common for patients and their families to do the following:

- Use the Internet to search for more information on the patient's cancer and its treatment

- Check on the information given by the doctor

- Look into other treatments or complementary or alternative medicine

- Ask for advice from family and friends

Information from outside sources is sometimes wrong or may be different from what the doctor said. It's important to get information that can be trusted and to talk to the doctor about it. Most libraries can help people find articles about cancer in medical journals and cancer information written for patients and the public. Good places to get information include government agencies, cancer centers, and cancer organizations.

Advocate

The family caregiver knows and understands the needs of the patient. The caregiver becomes an advocate for the patient by giving this information to the health care team. Although a caregiver may not have a medical background, daily contact with the patient gives the caregiver important information that helps the health care team help the patient. Information about the patient's symptoms and problems can help the doctor make better treatment plans and improve the patient's chance of getting better.

As the patient's advocate, the family caregiver may do the following:

- Talk with the health care team about the patient's needs and wishes for the patient
- Get information that may be hard to find
- Find doctors and specialists needed
- Watch the patient for changes and problems
- Help the patient follow treatments
- Tell the health care team about any new symptoms or side effects and ask for help to treat them
- Help the patient make healthy changes and follow healthy behaviors
- Pay the patient's bills and take care of insurance claims

Communicator

Good communication between the doctor, patient, and caregiver can improve the patient's health and medical care. The family caregiver will often take on the role of speaking for the patient while keeping the patient included in decision making. Good communication helps both the doctor and the caregiver get the information they need to support the patient. Doctors need to hear about patients' concerns and caregivers need to understand the disease and treatment options. Poor communication may cause confusion about treatment. This can affect choices made about treatment and the patient's chance of getting better.

Cultural differences between the doctors and the caregiver or patient can affect communication. In some cultures, it is the custom to keep a life-threatening diagnosis a secret from the patient and avoid talking about the disease. Sometimes it is left to the caregiver to tell the patient the truth about a serious or terminal illness. This can be stressful for caregivers and increase their feelings of loneliness and responsibility. Caregivers should tell the health care team if they think cultural beliefs may affect how they talk about the cancer and making treatment decisions.

Assessing Caregiver Needs

Caregiver assessment is done to find out if the caregiver needs support in the caregiving role.

Caregiver assessment helps the health care team understand the caregiver's everyday life, recognize the many jobs done by the caregiver, and look for signs of caregiver strain. Caregiver strain occurs when caregivers are not comfortable in their roles or feel they cannot handle everything they need to do. Caregiver strain may lead to depression and general psychological distress. If the caregiver feels too much strain, caregiving is no longer healthy for either the caregiver or the patient.

A caregiver assessment should look at not only what the patient needs the caregiver to do, but also what the caregiver is willing and able to do. Caregiver strain may occur when the family caregiver does not have the knowledge needed to care for the patient. The health care team can support the caregiver in this area.

Family caregivers report many problems with their caregiving experiences. Assessment is done to find out what the problems are, in order to give the caregiver the right kind of support. Support services can help the caregiver stay healthy, learn caregiving skills, and remain in the caregiving role, all of which help the patient as well.

Some of the factors that affect caregiver strain:

- The number of hours spent caregiving

- How prepared the caregiver is for caregiving

- The types of care being given

545

- How much the patient is able to do without help (such as bathing and dressing)

Caregiver well-being is assessed in several areas to find out what type of help is needed.

There is no standard tool for caregiver assessment. It may be different for each caregiver and family. Some of the factors assessed are culture, age, health, finances, and roles and relationships. Support services can then be chosen to help where the caregiver needs it.

Culture

Studies have shown that a family's culture affects how they handle the caregiver role. In some cultures, the family chooses not to get any outside help. Caregivers who have no outside help or help from other family members are usually more depressed than those who receive help from other sources.

Some of the reasons caregivers do not get outside help is that they:

- Don't want to share family matters with others

- Can't find outside help

- Don't trust social service providers

- Don't know how hospice care can help them

Age and Health

Caregivers may have issues related to age and health that increase their risk for caregiver strain:

- For an older adult caregiver, issues that are a part of aging may make caregiving harder to handle. Older caregivers may have health problems, live on fixed incomes, and have little social support. As they try to meet the demands of caregiving, older caregivers may not take care of their own health. This can make their health worse or cause new health problems. Caregiver strain in older caregivers may lead to an earlier death than non-caregivers the same age.

- Middle-aged and younger caregivers who have jobs and children or other family members to care for are often strained by the caregiving role. These caregivers try to meet the needs of work and family and give up much of their social life while caring for the patient.

Costs of Care

Families with low household incomes may not be able to afford the costs of caregiving. When the family cannot pay for costs related to treatment, the patient's recovery may be affected. Caregiver distress increases.

Roles and Relationships

As the number of roles the caregiver must fill increases, the risk of caregiver strain also increases. Given too many roles to fill, the caregiver will not have the time and energy to do them all. For example, caregivers who have a job and also care for children report high levels of stress. However, working while caregiving can also be helpful. Time away from the caregiving role and the social support from co-workers can give the caregiver some relief.

Roles and relationships among family members can be affected by caregiving. A caregiver assessment looks at family relationships to see if there is risk of caregiver strain.

Chapter 64

Medicare Coverage Related to Breast Cancer

How Is Medicare Funded?

The Centers for Medicare and Medicaid Services (CMS), a branch of the U.S. Department of Health and Human Services (HHS), is the federal agency that runs the Medicare Program and monitors Medicaid programs offered by each state.

In 2011, Medicare covered 48.7 million people. Total expenditures in 2011 were $549.1 billion. This money comes from the Medicare Trust Funds.

This chapter contains text excerpted from the following sources: Text beginning with the heading "How Is Medicare Funded?" is excerpted from "How Is Medicare Funded?" Centers for Medicare and Medicaid Services (CMS), July 29, 2012. Reviewed April 2016; Text beginning with the heading "Medicare Coverage on Mammograms" is excerpted from "Mammograms," Centers for Medicare and Medicaid Services (CMS), November 26, 2013; Text beginning with the heading "Medicare Coverage on Chemotherapy" is excerpted from "Chemotherapy," Centers for Medicare and Medicaid Services (CMS), November 26, 2013; Text under the heading "Medicare Coverage on Cosmetic Surgery" is excerpted from "Cosmetic Surgery," Centers for Medicare and Medicaid Services (CMS), December 20, 2006. Reviewed April 2016; Text beginning with the heading "Medicare Coverage on Breast Reconstruction" is excerpted from "Breast Prostheses," Centers for Medicare and Medicaid Services (CMS), November 20, 2014.

Medicare Trust Funds

Medicare is paid for through 2 trust fund accounts held by the U.S. Treasury. These funds can only be used for Medicare.

Hospital Insurance (HI) Trust Fund

How Is It Funded?

- Payroll taxes paid by most employees, employers, and people who are self-employed
- Other sources, like income taxes paid on Social Security benefits, interest earned on the trust fund investments, and Medicare Part A premiums from people who aren't eligible for premium-free Part A

What Does It Pay For?

- Medicare Part A (Hospital Insurance) benefits, like inpatient hospital care, skilled nursing facility care, home health care, and hospice care
- Medicare Program administration, like costs for paying benefits, collecting Medicare taxes, and combating fraud and abuse

Supplementary Medical Insurance (SMI) Trust Fund

How Is It Funded?

- Funds authorized by Congress
- Premiums from people enrolled in Medicare Part B (Medical Insurance) and Medicare prescription drug coverage (Part D)
- Other sources, like interest earned on the trust fund investments

What Does It Pay For?

- Part B benefits
- Part D
- Medicare Program administration, like costs for paying benefits and for combating fraud and abuse

Medicare Coverage on Mammograms

How Often Is It Covered?

- Screening mammogram once every 12 months (11 full months must have passed since the last screening)

- Diagnostic mammogram when medically necessary

Who's Eligible?

- Women with Part B 40 or older are covered

- Women with Part B between 35-39 can get one baseline mammogram

Your Costs in Original Medicare

- **Screening mammogram**: You pay nothing for the screening test if the doctor or other qualified healthcare provider accepts assignment

- **Diagnostic mammogram**: You pay 20% of the Medicare-approved amount, and the Part B deductible applies.

Medicare Coverage on Chemotherapy

How Often Is It Covered?

Medicare covers chemotherapy for cancer patients who are hospital inpatients and outpatients, as well as for patients in a doctor's office or freestanding clinic.

Who's Eligible?

All people with Medicare Part A (Hospital Insurance) and/or Medicare Part B (Medical Insurance) are covered. Part A covers hospital inpatients, and Part B covers hospital outpatients and patients in a doctor's office or freestanding clinic.

Your Costs in Original Medicare

You pay a copayment as a hospital outpatient.

You pay 20% of the Medicare-approved amount if you get your treatment in a doctor's office or freestanding clinic. The Part B deductible applies.

Medicare Coverage on Cosmetic Surgery

How Often Is It Covered?

Medicare doesn't cover cosmetic surgery unless it's needed because of accidental injury or to improve the function of a malformed body part. Medicare covers breast prostheses for breast reconstruction if you had a mastectomy because of breast cancer.

Medicare Coverage on Breast Reconstruction

How Often Is It Covered?

Medicare Part B (Medical Insurance) covers external breast prostheses (including a post-surgical bra) after a mastectomy. Medicare Part A (Hospital Insurance) covers surgically implanted breast prostheses after a mastectomy if the surgery takes place in an inpatient setting, and Part B covers the breast reconstruction surgery if it takes place in an outpatient setting.

Who's Eligible?

All People with Medicare Part a and/or Part B Are Covered.

Your Costs in Original Medicare

You pay 20% of the Medicare-approved amount for the doctor's services and the external breast prostheses. The Part B deductible applies.

For surgeries to implant breast prostheses in a hospital inpatient setting, you pay the Part A hospital care costs.

Chapter 65

Breast Cancer and Your Rights

Chapter Contents

Section 65.1

Women's Health and Cancer Rights Act

This section includes text excerpted from "The Center for Consumer Information and Insurance Oversight," Centers for Medicare and Medicaid Services (CMS), February 2, 2012. Reviewed April 2016.

Women's Health and Cancer Rights Act of 1998 (WHCRA)

The Women's Health and Cancer Rights Act of 1998 (WHCRA) is a federal law that provides protections to patients who choose to have breast reconstruction in connection with a mastectomy.

If WHCRA applies to you and you are receiving benefits in connection with a mastectomy and you elect breast reconstruction, coverage must be provided for:

- All stages of reconstruction of the breast on which the mastectomy has been performed;

- Surgery and reconstruction of the other breast to produce a symmetrical appearance; and

- Prostheses and treatment of physical complications of all stages of the mastectomy, including lymphedema.

This law applies to two different types of coverage:

1. Group health plans (provided by an employer or union)

2. Individual health insurance policies (not based on employment)

Group health plans can either be "insured" plans that purchase health insurance from a health insurance issuer, or "self-funded" plans that pay for coverage directly. How they are regulated depends on whether they are sponsored by private employers, or state or local ("non-federal") governmental employers. Private group health plans are regulated by the Department of Labor. State and local governmental plans, for purposes of WHCRA, are regulated by CMS. If any group health plan buys insurance, the insurance itself is regulated by the State's insurance department.

Contact your employer's plan administrator to find out if your group coverage is insured or self-funded, to determine what entity or entities regulate your benefits.

Health insurance sold to individuals (not through employment) is primarily regulated by State insurance departments.

WHCRA requires group health plans and health insurance companies (including HMOs), to notify individuals regarding coverage required under the law. Notice about the availability of these mastectomy-related benefits must be given:

1. To participants and beneficiaries of a group health plan at the time of enrollment, and to policyholders at the time an individual health insurance policy is issued; and

2. Annually to group health plan participants and beneficiaries, and to policyholders of individual policies.

Contact your State's insurance department to find out whether additional state law protections apply to your coverage if you are in an insured group health plan or have individual (non-employment based) health insurance coverage. WHCRA does not apply to high risk pools since the pool is a means by which individuals obtain health coverage other than through health insurance policies or group health plans.

WHCRA does NOT require group health plans or health insurance issuers to cover mastectomies in general. If a group health plan or health insurance issuer chooses to cover mastectomies, then the plan or issuer is generally subject to WHCRA requirements.

Section 65.2

Your Rights After a Mastectomy

This section contains text excerpted from the following sources: Text
beginning with the heading "Women's Health and Cancer Rights
Act" is excerpted from "Women's Health and Cancer Rights Act," U.S.
Department of Labor (DOL), October 4, 2014; Text under the heading
"Will Health Insurance Pay for Breast Reconstruction?" is excerpted
from "Will Health Insurance Pay for Breast Reconstruction?"
National Cancer Institute (NCI),
February 12, 2013.

Women's Health and Cancer Rights Act

If you have had a mastectomy or expect to have one, you may be
entitled to special rights under the Women's Health and Cancer Rights
Act of 1998 (WHCRA).

The following questions and answers clarify your basic WHCRA
rights. Under WHCRA, if your group health plan covers mastectomies, the plan must provide certain reconstructive surgery and other
post-mastectomy benefits.

Your health plan or health insurance issuer (also commonly referred
to as your health insurance company) is required to provide you with
a notice of your rights under WHCRA when you enroll in the health
plan, and then once each year.

The following information provides answers to frequently asked
questions about WHCRA.

I've Been Diagnosed with Breast Cancer and Plan to Have a Mastectomy. How Will WHCRA Affect My Benefits?

Under WHCRA, group health plans and insurance companies
offering mastectomy coverage also must provide coverage for certain services relating to the mastectomy in a manner determined in
consultation with your attending physician and you. This required
coverage includes all stages of reconstruction of the breast on which
the mastectomy was performed, surgery and reconstruction of the
other breast to produce a symmetrical appearance, prostheses and

treatment of physical complications of the mastectomy, including lymphedema.

I Have Not Been Diagnosed with Cancer. However, Due to Other Medical Reasons I Must Undergo a Mastectomy. Does WHCRA Apply to Me?

Yes, if your group health plan or health insurance company covers mastectomies and you are receiving benefits in connection with a mastectomy. Despite its name, nothing in the law limits WHCRA rights to cancer patients.

Does WHCRA Require All Group Health Plans and Health Insurance Companies to Provide Reconstructive Surgery Benefits?

Generally, group health plans, as well as their insurance companies, that provide coverage for medical and surgical benefits with respect to a mastectomy must comply with WHCRA.

However, if your coverage is provided by a "church plan" or "governmental plan," check with your plan administrator. Certain plans that are church plans or governmental plans may not be subject to this law.

May Group Health Plans or Health Insurance Companies Impose Deductibles or Coinsurance Requirements on the Coverage Specified in WHCRA?

Yes, but only if the deductibles and coinsurance are consistent with those established for other benefits under the plan or coverage.

I Just Changed Jobs and Am Enrolled under My New Employer's Plan. I Underwent a Mastectomy and Chemotherapy Treatment under My Previous Employer's Plan. Now I Want Reconstructive Surgery. Under WHCRA, Is My New Employer's Plan Required to Cover My Reconstructive Surgery?

If your new employer's plan provides coverage for mastectomies and if you are receiving benefits under the plan that are related to your mastectomy, then your new employer's plan generally is required to cover reconstructive surgery if you request it. In addition, your new employer's plan generally is required to cover the other benefits specified in WHCRA. It does not matter that you were not enrolled in your new employer's plan at the time you had the mastectomy.

There are additional protections under the Patient Protection and Affordable Care Act (ACA). For plan years beginning on or after January 1, 2014, a group health plan generally cannot limit or deny benefits relating to a health condition that was present before your enrollment date in your new employer's plan (a preexisting condition).

My Employer's Group Health Plan Provides Coverage through an Insurance Company. Following My Mastectomy, My Employer Changed Insurance Companies. The New Insurance Company Is Refusing to Cover My Reconstructive Surgery. Does WHCRA Provide Me with Any Protections?

Yes, as long as the new insurance company provides coverage for mastectomies, you are receiving benefits under the plan related to your mastectomy, and you elect to have reconstructive surgery. If these conditions apply, the new insurance company is required to provide coverage for breast reconstruction as well as the other benefits required under WHCRA. It does not matter that you were not covered by the new company at the time you had the mastectomy.

I Understand That My Group Health Plan Is Required to Provide Me with a Notice of My Rights under WHCRA When I Enroll in the Plan. What Information Can I Expect to Find in This Notice?

Plans must provide a notice to all employees when they enroll in the health plan describing the benefits that WHCRA requires the plan and its insurance companies to cover. These benefits include coverage of all stages of reconstruction of the breast on which the mastectomy was performed, surgery and reconstruction of the other breast to produce a symmetrical appearance, prostheses, and treatment of physical complications of the mastectomy, including lymphedema.

The enrollment notice also must state that for the covered employee or their family member who is receiving mastectomy-related benefits, coverage will be provided in a manner determined in consultation with the attending physician and the patient.

Finally, the enrollment notice must describe any deductibles and coinsurance limitations that apply to the coverage specified under

WHCRA. Deductibles and coinsurance limitations may be imposed only if they are consistent with those established for other benefits under the plan or coverage.

What Can I Expect to Find in the Annual WHCRA Notice from My Health Plan?

Your annual notice should describe the four categories of coverage required under WHCRA and information on how to obtain a detailed description of the mastectomy-related benefits available under your plan. For example, an annual notice might look like this:

"Do you know that your plan, as required by the Women's Health and Cancer Rights Act of 1998, provides benefits for mastectomy-related services including all stages of reconstruction and surgery to achieve symmetry between the breasts, prostheses, and complications resulting from a mastectomy, including lymphedema? Call your plan administrator [phone number here] for more information."

Your annual notice may be the same notice provided when you enrolled in the plan if it contains the information described above.

My State Requires Health Insurance Companies to Cover the Benefits Required by WHCRA and Also Requires Health Insurance Companies to Cover Minimum Hospital Stays in Connection with a Mastectomy (Which Is Not Required by WHCRA). If I Have a Mastectomy and Breast Reconstruction, Am I Also Entitled to the Minimum Hospital Stay?

If your employer's group health plan provides coverage through an insurance company, you are entitled to the minimum hospital stay required by the state law. Many state laws provide more protections than WHCRA. Those additional protections apply to coverage provided by an insurance company (known as "insured" coverage).

If your employer's plan does not provide coverage through an insurance company (in other words, your employer "self-insures" your coverage), then the state law does not apply. In that case, only the Federal law, WHCRA, applies, and it does not require minimum hospital stays.

To find out if your group health coverage is "insured" or "self-insured," check your health plan's Summary Plan Description or contact your plan administrator.

If your coverage is "insured" and you want to know if you have additional state law protections, check with your state insurance department.

My Health Coverage Is through an Individual Policy, Not through an Employer. What Rights, If Any, Do I Have under WHCRA?

WHCRA rights apply to individual coverage as well. These requirements are generally within the jurisdiction of the state insurance department. Call your state insurance department or the Department of Health and Human Services toll free at 1-877-267-2323, extension 61565, for further information.

Do I Have a Right to Preventive Services Related to the Detection of Breast Cancer?

Under the ACA, you may receive recommended preventive services, such as breast cancer mammography screenings for women 40 years of age and older, with no copayment, coinsurance or deductible (or other cost-sharing).

WHCRA does not require coverage for preventive services related to the detection of breast cancer.

Will Health Insurance Pay for Breast Reconstruction?

Since 1999, the Women's Health and Cancer Rights Act (WHCRA) has required group health plans, insurance companies, and HMOs that offer mastectomy coverage to also pay for reconstructive surgery after mastectomy. This coverage must include reconstruction of the other breast to give a more balanced look, breast prostheses, and treatment of all physical complications of the mastectomy, including lymphedema.

WHCRA does not apply to Medicare and Medicaid recipients. Some health plans sponsored by religious organizations and some government health plans may also be exempt from WHCRA. More information about WHCRA can be found through the Department of Labor.

A woman considering breast reconstruction may want to discuss costs and health insurance coverage with her doctor and insurance company before choosing to have the surgery. Some insurance companies require a second opinion before they will agree to pay for a surgery.

Chapter 66

Cancer and the Americans with Disabilities Act

The Americans with Disabilities Act (ADA)

The Americans with Disabilities Act (ADA), which was amended by the ADA Amendments Act of 2008 ("Amendments Act" or "ADAAA"), is a federal law that prohibits discrimination against qualified individuals with disabilities. Individuals with disabilities include those who have impairments that substantially limit a major life activity, have a record (or history) of a substantially limiting impairment, or are regarded as having a disability.

Title I of the ADA covers employment by private employers with 15 or more employees as well as state and local government employers. Section 501 of the Rehabilitation Act provides similar protections related to federal employment. In addition, most states have their own laws prohibiting employment discrimination on the basis of disability. Some of these state laws may apply to smaller employers and may provide protections in addition to those available under the ADA.

This chapter includes text excerpted from "Questions and Answers about Cancer in the Workplace and the Americans with Disabilities Act (ADA)," U.S. Equal Employment Opportunity Commission (EEOC), May 15, 2013.

The U.S. Equal Employment Opportunity Commission (EEOC) enforces the employment provisions of the ADA. This document, which is one of a series of question-and-answer documents addressing particular disabilities in the workplace, explains how the ADA applies to job applicants and employees who have or had cancer. In particular, this document explains:

- when an employer may ask an applicant or employee questions about his cancer and how it should treat voluntary disclosures;

- what types of reasonable accommodations employees with cancer may need;

- how an employer should handle safety concerns about applicants and employees with cancer; and

- how an employer can ensure that no employee is harassed because of cancer or any other disability.

General Information about Cancer

Cancer is a group of related diseases characterized by the out-of-control growth of abnormal cells caused by both external and internal factors, such as chemicals, radiation, immune conditions, and inherited mutations. In 2008, the last year for which incidence data is available, more than 12 million Americans were living with cancer. Some of these individuals had cancers that were not "active," or in remission, while others still had evidence of cancer and may have been undergoing treatment.

Cancer's effect on an individual depends on many factors, including the primary site of the cancer, stage of the disease, age and health of the individual, and type of treatment(s). The most common symptoms and side effects of cancer and/or treatment are pain, fatigue, problems related to nutrition and weight management, nausea, vomiting, hair loss, low blood counts, memory and concentration loss, depression, and respiratory problems.

Despite significant gains in cancer survival rates, people with cancer still experience barriers to equal job opportunities. Often, employees with cancer face discrimination because of their supervisors' and co-workers' misperceptions about their ability to work during and after cancer treatment. Even when the prognosis is excellent, some employers expect that a person diagnosed with cancer will take long absences from work or be unable to focus on job duties.

As a result of changes made by the ADAAA, people who currently have cancer, or have cancer that is in remission, should easily be found to have a disability within the meaning of the first part of the ADA's definition of disability because they are substantially limited in the major life activity of normal cell growth or would be so limited if cancer currently in remission was to recur. Similarly, individuals with a history of cancer will be covered under the second part of the definition of disability because they will have a record of an impairment that substantially limited a major life activity in the past. Finally, an individual is covered under the third ("regarded as") prong of the definition of disability if an employer takes a prohibited action (for example, refuses to hire or terminates the individual) because of cancer or because the employer believes the individual has cancer.

Obtaining, Using, and Disclosing Medical Information

Title I of the ADA limits an employer's ability to ask questions related to cancer and other disabilities and to conduct medical examinations at three stages: pre-offer, post-offer, and during employment.

Job Applicants

Before an Offer of Employment Is Made
1. May an Employer Ask a Job Applicant Whether He Has or Had Cancer or about His Treatment Related to Cancer Prior to Making a Job Offer?

No. An employer may not ask questions about an applicant's medical condition or require an applicant to have a medical examination before it makes a conditional job offer. This means that an employer cannot legally ask an applicant questions such as:

- whether she has or ever had cancer;

- whether she is undergoing chemotherapy or radiation or taking medication used to treat or control cancer (for example, Tamoxifen) or ever has done so in the past; or

- whether she ever has taken leave for surgery or medical treatment, or how much sick leave she has taken in the past year.

Of course, an employer may ask questions pertaining to the qualifications for, or performance of, the job, such as:

- whether the applicant can lift up to 50 pounds;
- whether he can travel out of town; or
- whether he can work rotating shifts.

2. Does the ADA Require an Applicant to Disclose That She Has or Had Cancer or Some Other Disability before Accepting a Job Offer?

No. The ADA does not require applicants to voluntarily disclose that they have or had cancer or another disability unless they will need a reasonable accommodation for the application process (for example, additional time to take a pre-employment test due to fatigue caused by radiation treatments). Some individuals with cancer, however, choose to disclose their condition to dispel any rumors or speculation about their appearance, such as emaciation or hair loss.

Sometimes, the decision to disclose depends on whether an individual will need a reasonable accommodation to perform the job (for example, flexible working hours to receive or recover from treatment). A person with cancer, however, may request an accommodation after becoming an employee even if she did not do so when applying for the job or after receiving the job offer.

3. May an Employer Ask Any Follow-Up Questions If an Applicant Voluntarily Reveals That He Has or Had Cancer?

No. An employer generally may not ask an applicant who has voluntarily disclosed that he has cancer any questions about the cancer, its treatment, or its prognosis. However, if an applicant voluntarily discloses that he has cancer **and the employer reasonably believes that he will require an accommodation to perform the job because of his cancer or treatment,** the employer may ask whether the applicant will need an accommodation and what type. The employer must keep any information an applicant discloses about his medical condition confidential.

After an Offer of Employment Is Made

After making a job offer, an employer may ask questions about the applicant's health (including questions about the applicant's disability) and may require a medical examination, as long as all applicants for the same type of job are treated equally (that is, all applicants are asked the same questions and are required to take the same examination).

After an employer has obtained basic medical information from all individuals who have received job offers, it may ask specific individuals for more medical information if it is medically related to the previously obtained medical information.

4. What May an Employer Do When It Learns That an Applicant Has or Had Cancer after She Has Been Offered a Job but before She Starts Working?

When an applicant discloses after receiving a conditional job offer that she has or had cancer, an employer may ask the applicant additional questions, such as whether she is undergoing treatment or experiencing any side effects that could interfere with the ability to do the job or that might require a reasonable accommodation. The employer also may send the applicant for a follow-up medical examination or ask her to submit documentation from her doctor answering questions specifically designed to assess the applicant's ability to perform the job's functions safely. Permissible follow-up questions at this stage differ from those at the pre-offer stage when an employer only may ask an applicant who voluntarily discloses a disability whether she needs an accommodation to perform the job and what type.

An employer may not withdraw an offer from an applicant with cancer or a history of cancer if the applicant is able to perform the essential functions of a job, with or without reasonable accommodation, without posing a direct threat (that is, a significant risk of substantial harm) to the health or safety of himself or others that cannot be eliminated or reduced through reasonable accommodation. ("Reasonable accommodation" is discussed in Questions 10 through 15. "Direct threat" is discussed in Questions 6 and 16.)

Employees

The ADA strictly limits the circumstances under which an employer may ask questions about an employee's medical condition or require the employee to have a medical examination. Once an employee is on the job, his actual performance is the best measure of ability to do the job.

5. When May an Employer Ask an Employee If Cancer, or Some Other Medical Condition, May Be Causing Her Performance Problems?

Generally, an employer may ask disability-related questions or require an employee to have a medical examination when it knows about a particular employee's medical condition, has observed performance problems, and reasonably believes that the problems are related to a medical condition. At other times, an employer may ask for medical information when it has observed symptoms, such as extreme fatigue or irritability, or has received reliable information from someone else (for example, a family member or co-worker) indicating that the employee may have a medical condition that is causing performance problems. Often, however, poor job performance is unrelated to a medical condition and generally should be handled in accordance with an employer's existing policies concerning performance.

6. May an Employer Require an Employee on Leave Because of Cancer to Provide Documentation or Have a Medical Exam before Allowing Her to Return to Work?

Yes. If the employer has a reasonable belief that the employee may be unable to perform her job or may pose a direct threat to herself or others, the employer may ask for medical information. However, the employer may obtain only the information needed to make an assessment of the employee's present ability to perform her job and to do so safely.

7. Are There Any Other Instances When an Employer May Ask an Employee with Cancer about Her Condition?

Yes. An employer also may ask an employee about cancer when it has a reasonable belief that the employee will be unable to safely perform the essential functions of her job because of cancer. In addition, an employer may ask an employee about her cancer to the extent the information is necessary:

- to support the employee's request for a reasonable accommodation needed because of her cancer;

- to verify the employee's use of sick leave related to her cancer if the employer requires all employees to submit a doctor's note to justify their use of sick leave; or

- to enable the employee to participate in a voluntary wellness program.

Keeping Medical Information Confidential

With limited exceptions, an employer must keep confidential any medical information it learns about an applicant or employee. Under the following circumstances, however, an employer may disclose that an employee has cancer:

- to supervisors and managers, if necessary to provide a reasonable accommodation or meet an employee's work restrictions;

- to first aid and safety personnel if an employee may need emergency treatment or require some other assistance at work;

- to individuals investigating compliance with the ADA and similar state and local laws; and

- where needed for workers' compensation or insurance purposes (for example, to process a claim).

8. May an Employer Tell Employees Who Ask Why Their Co-Worker Is Allowed to Do Something That Generally Is Not Permitted (Such as Work at Home or Take Periodic Rest Breaks) That She Is Receiving a Reasonable Accommodation?

No. Telling co-workers that an employee is receiving a reasonable accommodation amounts to a disclosure that the employee has a disability. Rather than disclosing that the employee is receiving a reasonable accommodation, the employer should focus on the importance of maintaining the privacy of all employees and emphasize that its policy is to refrain from discussing the work situation of any employee with co-workers. Employers may be able to avoid many of these kinds of questions by training all employees on the requirements of equal employment laws, including the ADA.

Additionally, an employer will benefit from providing information about reasonable accommodations to all of its employees. This can be done in a number of ways, such as through written reasonable accommodation procedures, employee handbooks, staff meetings, and periodic training. This kind of proactive approach may lead to fewer questions from employees who misperceive co-worker accommodations as "special treatment."

9. If an Employee Has Lost a Lot of Weight or Appears Fatigued, May an Employer Explain to Co-Workers That the Employee Has Cancer?

No. Although the employee's co-workers and others in the workplace may be concerned about the employee's health, an employer may not reveal that the employee has cancer. An employee, however, may voluntarily choose to tell her co-workers and others that she has cancer and about her treatment. However, even when an employee voluntarily discloses that she has cancer, the employer must keep this information confidential consistent with the ADA. An employer also may not explain

567

to other employees why an employee with cancer has been absent from work if the absence is related to his cancer or another disability.

Accommodating Employees with Cancer

The ADA requires employers to provide adjustments or modifications—called reasonable accommodations—to enable applicants and employees with disabilities to enjoy equal employment opportunities unless doing so would be an undue hardship (that is, a significant difficulty or expense). Accommodations vary depending on the needs of the individual with a disability. Not all employees with cancer will need an accommodation or require the same accommodations, and most of the accommodations a person with cancer might need will involve little or no cost. An employer must provide a reasonable accommodation that is needed because of the limitations caused by the cancer itself, the side effects of medication or treatment for the cancer, or both.

10. What Other Types of Reasonable Accommodations May Employees with Cancer Need?

Some employees may need one or more of the following accommodations:

- leave for doctors' appointments and/or to seek or recuperate from treatment
- periodic breaks or a private area to rest or to take medication
- modified work schedule or shift change
- permission to work at home
- modification of office temperature
- permission to use work telephone to call doctors where the employer's usual practice is to prohibit personal calls
- reallocation or redistribution of marginal tasks to another employee
- reassignment to a vacant position when the employer is no longer able to perform her current job

11. How Does an Employee with Cancer Request a Reasonable Accommodation?

There are no "magic words" that a person has to use when requesting a reasonable accommodation. A person simply has to tell the employer that she needs an adjustment or change at work because of her cancer. A request for reasonable accommodation also can come from a family member, friend, health professional, or other representative on behalf of a person with cancer.

12. May an Employer Request Documentation When an Employee Who Has Cancer Requests a Reasonable Accommodation?

Yes. An employer may request reasonable documentation where a disability or the need for reasonable accommodation is not known or obvious. An employer, however, is entitled only to documentation sufficient to establish that the employee has cancer and to explain why an accommodation is needed. A request for an employee's entire medical record, for example, would be inappropriate, as it likely would include information about conditions other than the employee's cancer.

13. Does an Employer Have to Grant Every Request for a Reasonable Accommodation?

No. An employer does not have to provide an accommodation if doing so will be an undue hardship. Undue hardship means that providing the reasonable accommodation will result in significant difficulty or expense. An employer also does not have to eliminate an essential function of a job as a reasonable accommodation, tolerate performance that does not meet its standards, or excuse violations of conduct rules that are job-related and consistent with business necessity and that the employer applies consistently to all employees (such as rules prohibiting violence, threatening behavior, theft, or destruction of property).

If more than one accommodation would be effective, the employee's preference should be given primary consideration, although the employer is not required to provide the employee's first choice of reasonable accommodation. If a requested accommodation is too difficult or expensive, an employer may choose to provide an easier or less costly accommodation as long as it is effective in meeting the employee's needs.

14. May an Employer Be Required to Provide More than One Accommodation for the Same Employee with Cancer?

Yes. The duty to provide a reasonable accommodation is an ongoing one. Although some employees with cancer may require only one reasonable accommodation, others may need more than one. For example, an employee with cancer may require leave for surgery and subsequent recovery but may be able to return to work on a part-time or modified schedule while receiving chemotherapy. An employer must consider each request for a reasonable accommodation and determine whether it would be effective and whether providing it would pose an undue hardship.

15. May an Employer Automatically Deny a Request for Leave from Someone with Cancer Because the Employee Cannot Specify an Exact Date of Return?

No. Granting leave to an employee who is unable to provide a fixed date of return may be a reasonable accommodation. Although many types of cancer can be successfully treated—and often cured—the treatment and severity of side effects often are unpredictable and do not permit exact timetables. An employee requesting leave because of cancer, therefore, may be able to provide only an approximate date of return (for example, "in six to eight weeks," "in about three months"). In such situations, or in situations in which a return date must be postponed because of unforeseen medical developments, employees should stay in regular communication with their employers to inform them of their progress and discuss the need for continued leave beyond what originally was granted. The employer also has the right to require that the employee provide periodic updates on his condition and possible date of return. After receiving these updates, the employer may reevaluate whether continued leave constitutes an undue hardship.

Concerns about Safety

When it comes to safety concerns, an employer should be careful not to act on the basis of myths, fears, or stereotypes about cancer. Instead, the employer should evaluate each individual on her skills, knowledge, experience and how having cancer affects her.

16. When May an Employer Refuse to Hire, Terminate, or Temporarily Restrict the Duties of a Person Who Has or Had Cancer Because of Safety Concerns?

An employer only may exclude an individual with cancer from a job for safety reasons when the individual poses a direct threat. A "direct threat" is a significant risk of substantial harm to the individual or others that cannot be eliminated or reduced through reasonable accommodation. This determination must be based on objective, factual evidence, including the best recent medical evidence and advances in the treatment of cancer.

In making a direct threat assessment, the employer must evaluate the individual's present ability to safely perform the job. The employer also must consider:

1. the duration of the risk;

2. the nature and severity of the potential harm;

3. the likelihood that the potential harm will occur; and

4. the imminence of the potential harm.

The harm must be serious and likely to occur, not remote or speculative. Finally, the employer must determine whether any reasonable accommodation (for example, temporarily limiting an employee's duties, temporarily reassigning an employee, or placing an employee on leave) would reduce or eliminate the risk.

Harassment

The ADA prohibits harassment, or offensive conduct, based on disability just as other federal laws prohibit harassment based on race, sex, color, national origin, religion, age, and genetic information. Offensive conduct may include, but is not limited to, offensive jokes, slurs, epithets or name calling, physical assaults or threats, intimidation, ridicule or mockery, insults or put-downs, offensive objects or pictures, and interference with work performance. Although the law does not prohibit simple teasing, offhand comments, or isolated incidents that are not very serious, harassment is illegal when it is so frequent or severe that it creates a hostile or offensive work environment or when it results in an adverse employment decision (such as the victim being fired or demoted).

17. What Should Employers Do to Prevent and Correct Harassment?

Employers should make clear that they will not tolerate harassment based on disability or on any other basis. This can be done in a number of ways, such as through a written policy, employee handbooks, staff meetings, and periodic training. The employer should emphasize that harassment is prohibited and that employees should promptly report such conduct to a manager. Finally, the employer should immediately conduct a thorough investigation of any report of harassment and take swift and appropriate corrective action. For more information on the standards governing harassment under all of the EEO laws, see www. eeoc.gov/policy/docs/harassment.html.

Retaliation

The ADA prohibits retaliation by an employer against someone who opposes discriminatory employment practices, files a charge of employment discrimination, or testifies or participates in any way in an investigation, proceeding, or litigation related to a charge of employment discrimination. It is also unlawful for an employer to retaliate against someone for requesting a reasonable accommodation. Persons who believe that they have been retaliated against may file a charge of retaliation as described below.

How to File a Charge of Employment Discrimination

Against Private Employers and State/Local Governments

Any person who believes that his or her employment rights have been violated on the basis of disability and wants to make a claim against an employer must file a charge of discrimination with the EEOC. A third party may also file a charge on behalf of another person who believes he or she experienced discrimination. For example, a family member, social worker, or other representative can file a charge on behalf of someone who is incapacitated because of cancer. The charge must be filed by mail or in person with the local EEOC office within 180 days from the date of the alleged violation. The 180-day filing deadline is extended to 300 days if a state or local anti-discrimination agency has the authority to grant or seek relief as to the challenged unlawful employment practice.

The EEOC will send the parties a copy of the charge and may ask for responses and supporting information. Before formal investigation, the EEOC may select the charge for EEOC's mediation program. Both parties have to agree to mediation, which may prevent a time consuming investigation of the charge. Participation in mediation is free, voluntary, and confidential.

If mediation is unsuccessful, the EEOC investigates the charge to determine if there is "reasonable cause" to believe discrimination has occurred. If reasonable cause is found, the EEOC will then try to resolve the charge with the employer. In some cases, where the charge cannot be resolved, the EEOC will file a court action. If the EEOC finds no discrimination, or if an attempt to resolve the charge fails and the EEOC decides not to file suit, it will issue a notice of a "right to sue," which gives the charging party 90 days to file a court action. A charging party can also request a notice of a "right to sue" from the EEOC 180 days after the charge was first filed with the Commission, and may then bring suit within 90 days after receiving the notice. For a detailed description of the process, you can visit the website at www.eeoc.gov/employees/howtofile.cfm.

Against the Federal Government

If you are a federal employee or job applicant and you believe that a federal agency has discriminated against you, you have a right to file a complaint. Each agency is required to post information about how to contact the agency's EEO Office. You can contact an EEO Counselor by calling the office responsible for the agency's EEO complaints program. Generally, you must contact the EEO Counselor within 45 days from the day the discrimination occurred. In most cases the EEO Counselor will give you the choice of participating either in EEO counseling or in an alternative dispute resolution (ADR) program, such as a mediation program.

If you do not settle the dispute during counseling or through ADR, you can file a formal discrimination complaint against the agency with the agency's EEO Office. You must file within 15 days from the day you receive notice from your EEO Counselor about how to file.

Once you have filed a formal complaint, the agency will review the complaint and decide whether or not the case should be dismissed for a procedural reason (for example, your claim was filed too late). If the agency doesn't dismiss the complaint, it will conduct an investigation. The agency has 180 days from the day you filed your complaint to finish the investigation. When the investigation is finished, the agency will issue a notice giving you two choices: either request a hearing before an EEOC Administrative Judge or ask the agency to issue a decision as to whether the discrimination occurred. For a detailed description of the process, you can visit the website at www.eeoc.gov/federal/fed_employees/complaint_overview.cfm.

Part Eight

Breast Cancer Research
and Clinical Trials

Chapter 67

Exploring the Links between Physical Activity and Cancer

How does physical activity influence cancer risk? DCEG scientists are investigating which cancers are affected by physical activity, what type of activity, how much activity makes a difference, effects on survival following a cancer diagnosis, and the biological mechanisms underlying these relationships.

There is strong evidence that physical activity reduces the risk of breast, colon, and endometrial cancer. Associations with other cancers are less clear, but Charles E. Matthews, Ph.D., Steven C. Moore, Ph.D., M.P.H., and colleagues are making strides to expand the current knowledge base on the range of cancer sites associated with physical activity and the relationship between amount of activity and cancer.

Leisure-Time Physical Activity

The focus of research on physical activity has recently shifted from activities associated with one's occupation to leisure-time activity. Dr. Moore is leading a team of investigators who are using pooled data within the NCI Cohort Consortium to study the association between leisure-time physical activity and 26 different types of cancer, some

This chapter includes text excerpted from "Exploring the Links between Leisure-Time Physical Activity, Sedentary Behavior, and Cancer," National Cancer Institute (NCI), March 5, 2015.

rare or not previously studied. According to Dr. Moore, "This is the largest study to date of physical activity and cancer. Our results may broaden the number of cancers linked to physical activity and may suggest new avenues for prevention."

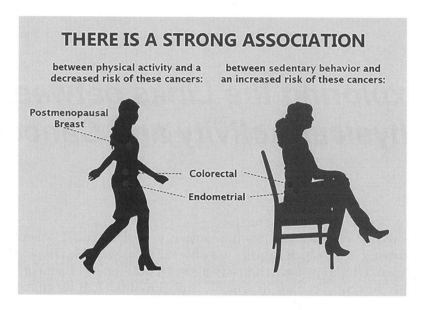

Figure 67.1. *Link between Physical Activity and Cancer*

Scientists are searching for links to many other cancers; in particular, an upcoming NCI study may broaden the number of cancers linked to physical activity.

Research indicates that physical activity also affects overall mortality from all causes combined. In a previous study within the Cohort Consortium, Dr. Moore and colleagues found that leisure-time physical activity was associated with longer life expectancy, even at relatively low levels of activity and regardless of body weight.

"Our findings highlight the important contribution that leisure-time physical activity in adulthood can make to longevity," Dr. Moore said.

Ongoing studies will extend our understanding of the relationship between the amount of physical activity and mortality. DCEG fellow Hannah Arem, Ph.D., M.H.S., is evaluating the association between levels of physical activity beyond the federally recommended minimum and mortality, with particular interest in defining the upper limit of benefit, or possible harm, associated with very high levels of exercise.

Sedentary Behavior: Is Sitting the New Smoking?

In recent years, sedentary behavior has emerged as a risk factor for disease that is distinct from and independent of leisure-time physical activity. Sedentary behavior is linked with diabetes, obesity, and cardiovascular disease; it can also increase the risk of certain cancers, most notably colorectal and endometrial. New insights about the adverse health effects of sitting have helped us understand some of the limitations of the prevailing strategy, regular exercise, to reduce these risks, as well as opportunities to augment this strategy. DCEG investigators have helped define the magnitude of the problem, quantify the health risks associated with sedentary behaviors, and describe the risks associated with reducing sedentary time.

"The average adult spends more than half their day sitting or in sedentary behaviors," Dr. Matthews said. "We're learning that exercise alone may not be enough to reduce the risk of cancer and other diseases."

Using data from the NIH-AARP Diet and Health Study, Dr. Matthews and colleagues found that higher amounts of sitting time and television viewing were associated with mortality, even after adjustment for exercise participation. Dr. Matthews takes this message to heart; he is often seen standing in seminars or walking on the tread-desk in his office.

DCEG investigators are also curious about the tradeoffs between sedentary behavior and physical activity. Dr. Matthews and colleagues recently estimated the mortality benefits associated with reducing sedentary time by an hour and replacing with different types of physical activity.

"We found that replacing sitting time with any type of activity was beneficial for less active adults," Dr. Matthews said. "For more active adults, mortality was only lower for those who replaced sitting time with purposeful exercise." DCEG fellow Sarah Keadle, Ph.D., M.P.H., is examining television viewing as a modifiable risk factor.

Sleep is another health behavior that relates to sedentary behavior and physical activity; researchers are evaluating sleep as part of the full 24-hour measurement period. A recent paper by DCEG fellow Qian Xiao, Ph.D., and Dr. Matthews looked at the interrelationships of sleep, physical activity, sedentary behavior, and body mass index with mortality.

According to Dr. Matthews, "We are finding that sleep, sedentary behavior, and physical activity are all independently associated with mortality. Each behavior seems to have unique physiologic functions and patterns of risk for mortality."

Benefits of Physical Activity for Cancer Survivors

DCEG investigators are also assessing the benefits of physical activity in cancer survivors, a population quickly growing thanks, in part, to improved cancer treatments and early detection. Evidence from observational prospective studies suggests that physical activity after cancer diagnosis may be associated with a reduced risk of cancer recurrence and improved overall mortality among multiple cancer survivor groups, including breast, colorectal, prostate, and ovarian cancer.

Dr. Arem and Dr. Matthews recently published a paper on exercise and television viewing habits (the most prevalent leisure-time sedentary behavior) before and after diagnosis among colorectal cancer survivors. Increasing exercise and minimizing TV viewing both were associated with lower mortality risk among colorectal cancer survivors.

"This study gives us a snapshot of physical activity and sedentary behaviors among colorectal cancer survivors and how these factors might influence mortality," according to Dr. Arem.

Biomarker Studies Give Insight into Mechanisms

Regular physical activity helps maintain a healthy body weight and may prevent cancers directly and indirectly, by mechanisms that include regulating hormones and providing beneficial effects on insulin and glucose metabolism, inflammatory markers, and the immune system.

Using information recorded by a lightweight accelerometer worn by participants in the National Health and Nutritional Examination Survey (NHANES), Dr. Matthews and colleagues reported the first objective data on the amount of time spent in overall sedentary behaviors in a nationally representative sample. After adjusting for the effect of exercise, the amount of daily sedentary time was linked to levels of C-reactive protein, insulin, and other cardio-metabolic biomarkers. Future DCEG metabolomic studies will continue to evaluate associations between accelerometer-based measures of active and sedentary time.

DCEG investigators are leveraging better measurements of physical activity and sedentary behavior with new metabolism assays, like the urinary estrogen assay. Using data and samples collected from premenopausal women in the Nurses' Health Study II, Dr. Matthews,Regina G. Ziegler, Ph.D., M.P.H., and colleagues from Harvard University recently found that greater leisure-time physical activity was associated with lower urinary estradiol and several metabolites in the 16-hydroxylation pathway. Both measures have been associated with reduced risk of breast cancer in previous studies.

Ongoing work will examine the effect of exercise intervention on estrogen metabolism in postmenopausal women. Investigators will also evaluate estrogen metabolism as a potential mediator of the energy balance-breast cancer association.

Measurements Are Key

The validity of etiologic studies is dependent on the breadth, accuracy, and precision of the measured exposures or endpoints. Due to their size, prospective studies of cancer have typically relied on the self-reported questionnaire-based approach to assess physical activity. Though contemporary questionnaires ask for more detailed information about exercise and sedentary behavior, using only questionnaires may impede full understanding of the relationship between physical activity and cancer.

Dr. Matthews reports, "We have developed a new internet-based recall method that does a better job of capturing the full range of daily activities, including sleep, physical activity, and sedentary behaviors, perhaps with more accuracy than our traditional questionnaire-based methods."

In collaboration with Heather Bowles, Ph.D., Amy Subar, Ph.D., M.P.H., R.D., and Gordon Willis, Ph.D., from the NCI Division of Cancer Control and Population Sciences, Dr. Matthews and Dr. Moore created and are testing the new web-based tool Physical Activities Completed over Time in 24 Hours (ACT24) for use in large-scale studies. The tool will be employed in future NIH-AARP Diet and Health Studies as well as in other cohorts. Stephen J. Chanock, M.D., Director of DCEG, states, "In an increasingly sedentary world, it is vital to explore the links between physical activity, sedentary behaviors, and health outcomes like cancer. Research by DCEG investigators continues to add evidence and increase our understanding of how physical activity affects cancer, which will in turn lead to stronger and better recommendations about healthy lifestyle."

Chapter 68

In Triple-Negative
Breast Cancer,
Targeting an Addiction

A new approach to disrupting genes that promote the development and spread of tumors may hold promise for treating an aggressive and difficult-to-treat type of breast cancer, according to results from a new study.

In the study, a drug that blocks the activity of an enzyme called CDK7 halted tumor cell proliferation in cell lines of triple-negative breast cancer, and shrank tumors in mouse models of this cancer type.

Unlike many so-called targeted therapies, the drug does not work by directly targeting cells with specific genetic alterations. Instead, the drug acts indirectly, through CDK7, to interfere with the expression of what the authors, Jean Zhao, Ph.D., of Dana-Farber Cancer Institute and her colleagues, called an "Achilles cluster" of genes—a group of genes on which the cancer cells are highly dependent.

The type of drug tested in the study, the researchers wrote, may represent an especially effective option for treating cancers such as triple-negative breast cancer that don't appear to have individual "driver" genes.

Targeting Transcription

Triple-negative breast cancers, which represent approximately 13 percent of breast cancer cases, often return after initial treatment

This chapter includes text excerpted from "In Triple-Negative Breast Cancer, Targeting an Addiction," National Cancer Institute (NCI), October 26, 2015.

and are highly likely to spread. This type of breast cancer is more frequently diagnosed in African Americans and younger women than in other women.

In addition to being more aggressive than other breast cancer subtypes, triple-negative breast cancers are more challenging to treat. Because their growth is not fueled by hormones, for example, hormone therapies like tamoxifen and aromatase inhibitors are not useful in treating it.

And from a genetic standpoint, most triple-negative breast cancers bear little resemblance to each other. Although they often contain many genetic alterations, few if any of these are shared across all triple-negative breast cancers, and none appears to be primarily responsible for their growth and spread. So, unlike the case with HER2-positive breast cancers, individual driver genes for this cancer type that could potentially be targeted by specific therapies have yet to be identified.

But, Dr. Zhao and her colleagues explained, evidence from other studies indicated that many triple-negative tumors do consistently express a common group of genes that, collectively, appear to promote the development and spread of these cancers. The researchers hypothesized that maintaining the expression of this collection of genes would require continuous transcription—part of the process of decoding the instructions in genes—and that, consequently, triple-negative tumors may "be more sensitive to drugs that target transcription."

Interfering with an Addiction

So the researchers tested a drug, THZ1, which targets a protein called CDK7, in a series of cell line and animal models of triple-negative breast cancer. CDK7 is a member of a family of enzymes known as cyclin-dependent kinases that help to control transcription.

In experiments on cell lines, THZ1 suppressed the proliferation of triple-negative breast cancer cells but had no effect on the proliferation of breast cancer cells that express hormone receptors, even though THZ1 blocked CDK7 activity in both cell lines. This finding indicates that the triple-negative cells "appear to be far more dependent on the activity of CDK7" than the hormone receptor-positive cells, the researchers wrote.

The drug also shrank tumors in several mouse models of triple-negative breast cancer, including tumors derived from tumor fragments from two patients with metastatic disease whose cancers had progressed after multiple lines of treatment.

Further studies in cell lines using gene-editing technologies to block CDK7 activity, including the CRISPR/Cas9 system, provided additional confirmation that triple-negative cancer cells were highly dependent on—or "addicted" to—the gene cluster regulated by CDK7. However, the triple-negative cells were not addicted to genes regulated by other members of the CDK family, Dr. Zhao and her colleagues reported.

Previous studies have found that triple-negative breast cancer and aggressive forms of several other cancers, including ovarian and lung cancers, have similar expression patterns of genes in this Achilles cluster. As a result, they wrote, this treatment approach "may be applicable to other difficult-to-treat cancers."

Promise and Caution

In addition to providing a target for treatment, the gene cluster could be a biomarker to identify patients who may be candidates for THZ1 or other CDK7-targeted drugs, wrote Hector L. Franco, Ph.D., and W. Lee Kraus, Ph.D., of the University of Texas Southwestern Medical Center, in an accompanying editorial.

"However, due to the universal role and biological importance of transcription in all cells, targeting transcription as a therapeutic strategy may be challenging due to the potential lack of selectivity for cancer cells over normal cells," they cautioned. "Therefore, it is imperative to determine if the therapeutic window between efficacy and toxicity for malignant and non-malignant cells is large enough to produce a therapeutically efficacious effect."

The study did not reveal evidence of any off-target effects, said study coauthor Daniel Stover, M.D., in an email. "However, off-target effects cannot be completely ruled out as this [agent] has not been tested in humans," he cautioned. The research team is "hopeful" that they will be able to test CDK7-targeted agents in patients with triple-negative breast cancer, he added.

Chapter 69

Treatment Helps Preserve Fertility for Some Women with Breast Cancer

Results from a clinical trial sponsored by National Cancer Institute (NCI) show that giving some younger women with early-stage breast cancer a hormone-suppressing drug in addition to chemotherapy helps to preserve ovarian function and improves their ability to get pregnant after treatment.

The Prevention of Early Menopause Study (POEMS) trial tested whether administering injections of the drug goserelin (Zoladex) prior to and during standard pre- or post-operative chemotherapy could help to prevent long-term failure of ovarian function—a common side effect of chemotherapy that can leave women infertile. The trial enrolled women between the ages of 18 and 49 who had estrogen-receptor (ER) negative, early-stage breast cancer. By blunting production of hormones that regulate ovarian activity, goserelin temporarily causes the ovaries to become dormant—a form of chemical menopause—protecting them from chemotherapy, which seeks out actively reproducing cells.

Overall, only eight percent of women who received monthly injections of goserelin beginning 1 week prior to chemotherapy experienced

This chapter includes text excerpted from "Treatment Helps Preserve Fertility for Some Women with Breast Cancer," National Cancer Institute (NCI), March 12, 2015.

ovarian failure (as measured by the loss of menstruation and post-menopausal levels of the hormone FSH), compared with 22 percent of women who received chemotherapy alone. Also, 21 percent of women in the goserelin group had at least one pregnancy, compared with just 11 percent in the chemotherapy-alone group.

The trial randomized a smaller population of eligible patients—218 in total—than had originally been planned, explained study co-author Lori Minasian, M.D., of NCI's Division of Cancer Prevention. However, detailed statistical analyses showed a consistent positive benefit of goserelin across multiple different endpoints, she continued, findings that were convincing even with a smaller than planned study sample.

A trial like POEMS was difficult to conduct, Dr. Minasian explained, because it needed to enroll not just younger women, among whom breast cancer is relatively rare, but also women whose cancer was not responsive to hormones. In ER-positive breast cancers, which are much more common than ER-negative breast cancers, extended treatment with hormone-blocking drugs such as tamoxifen are an essential part of therapy and improve survival.

So limiting the trial to ER-negative, premenopausal patients, although challenging, was essential to do the trial, explained its lead investigator Halle Moore, M.D., of the Cleveland Clinic Taussig Cancer Institute.

"We wanted to measure ovarian function at 2 years," Dr. Moore said, "and the extended hormonal treatments [used in hormone recep-tor-positive patients] would interfere with our ability to measure meno-pausal hormones [such as FSH] and whether women were having men-strual periods, which were included in our ovarian failure definition."

"An important feature of this trial is that we not only had a biologic correlate—menstruation and hormone levels—but we also had actual pregnancy outcomes," Dr. Minasian said. "That really is the value of this trial."

The investigators also found that patients who received both gos-erelin and chemotherapy lived longer, both overall and without their disease returning. Given the small number of patients and the excel-lent prognosis of women with early-stage disease, the observed survival differences are by no means definitive, Dr. Minasian stressed.

"At the very least, we can say that this approach doesn't appear to be detrimental in these patients," she said. "But no patient should have this treatment solely because they think it will provide a survival advantage."

By preventing some of the menopausal symptoms caused by chemotherapy-induced ovarian failure, adding goserelin to chemotherapy treatment may also improve patients' quality of life, Dr. Moore added.

The trial findings received substantial attention when they were initially presented last June at the 2014 American Society of Clinical Oncology annual meeting, and they appear to be influencing care for women with breast cancer, Dr. Moore said.

"I think oncologists are beginning to use goserelin routinely, and publication of the results will only increase awareness," she said.

At the Cleveland Clinic, premenopausal women with breast cancer are routinely offered the treatment. Some patients who plan on having children, she continued, have opted to use goserelin and also undergo embryo or egg cryopreservation to optimize their chances of getting pregnant after their cancer treatment.

Dr. Moore described a younger patient with early-stage breast cancer she saw recently who had almost backed out of having chemotherapy because of fertility concerns.

"I discussed [the goserelin] option with her," she said. "Even though she doesn't know for sure if she wants children, just that feeling of being able to improve those prospects was comforting to her, and she went ahead with the treatment."

Chapter 70

Genomic Features of Invasive Lobular Breast Carcinoma

Characteristics of Invasive Lobular Carcinoma (ILC)

Investigators with The Cancer Genome Atlas (TCGA) Research Network have identified molecular characteristics of a type of breast cancer, invasive lobular carcinoma (ILC), that distinguishes it from invasive ductal carcinoma (IDC), the most common invasive breast cancer subtype. The new study—a comprehensive analysis of the genomes of 817 breast tumors—builds on the research network's 2012 analysis of IDC, and provides the first in-depth analysis of the genetic drivers of ILC. Understanding the genomic differences between the two subtypes may enable clinicians to develop more personalized approaches to treating breast cancer.

ILC, which is the second most common subtype of invasive breast cancer, is defined by a lack of adhesiveness between cells, caused by ILC's hallmark loss of the cell-cell adhesion protein E-cadherin. The new analysis confirmed the importance of the loss of E-cadherin function in ILC and identified differences between ILC and IDC in

---

This chapter includes text excerpted from "TCGA Study Identifies Genomic Features of Invasive Lobular Breast Carcinoma," National Cancer Institute (NCI), October 8, 2015.

commonly mutated genes and Akt signaling activity, which affects cell growth. ILC tumors showed *FOXA1* gene mutations more frequently than IDC tumors, whereas mutations of the *GATA3* gene were more common in IDC. Both the *FOXA1* and *GATA3* proteins are key regulators of estrogen receptor function, suggesting that ILC tumors and IDC tumors may rely on different mechanisms to activate estrogen receptor-mediated gene expression programs. In addition, ILC tumors showed greater Akt signaling pathway activity than IDC tumors, and less expression of the tumor suppressor protein PTEN, suggesting that ILC tumors may be more sensitive to drugs that block the Akt pathway. The analysis further identified three subtypes of ILC—*reactive-like, immune-related*, and *proliferative*—that have distinct clinical outcomes, with the reactive-like subtype demonstrating the best outcome and the proliferative subtype the poorest. Finally, the researchers found that tumors that display components of both ILC and IDC were either ILC-like or IDC-like in their molecular features, and do not constitute a distinct subtype of invasive breast cancer. The findings were published October 8, 2015 in *Cell*. The National Cancer Institute and the National Human Genome Research Institute, both parts of the National Institutes of Health, jointly manage the TCGA program.

Chapter 71

TAILORx Trial Shows Women at Low Risk for Breast Cancer Recurrence May Forgo Chemotherapy

Summary

Initial findings from the Trial Assigning Individualized Options for Treatment, or TAILORx, show that, for women with early-stage hormone receptor-positive breast cancer that has a low risk of recurrence based on a test for the expression of 21 genes, 5-year recurrence rates are very low when postoperative treatment consists of hormone therapy alone.

Background

Approximately 125,000 women in the United States were diagnosed with node-negative, estrogen receptor (ER)-positive breast cancer in 2014. Such women generally receive both hormone therapy and chemotherapy after surgery to remove their tumor. Although the use of

This chapter includes text excerpted from "TAILORx Trial Shows Women at Low Risk for Breast Cancer Recurrence May Forgo Chemotherapy," National Cancer Institute (NCI), September 28, 2015.

adjuvant chemotherapy has contributed to lower breast cancer mortality rates overall, it is generally thought that most patients with node-negative, hormone receptor-positive breast cancer can be adequately treated with hormone therapy alone. However, the identification of which women could avoid chemotherapy has been difficult. A molecular test that assesses the expression of 21 genes associated with breast cancer recurrence, called the 21-gene recurrence score (Oncotype DX®), has been found to predict benefit from adjuvant chemotherapy in women with hormone receptor-positive disease. This study was carried out to provide prospective validation in a clinical trial of the test's ability to predict which women can be safely spared from receiving adjuvant chemotherapy

The Study

TAILORx was designed to determine whether a test that analyzes the expression of a group of genes that are associated with risk of recurrence among women with early-stage breast cancer could be used to assign patients to the most appropriate and effective treatment. The study, which began recruiting participants in 2006, has enrolled more than 10,000 women ages 18 to 75 at 1,000 sites in the United States, Australia, Canada, Ireland, New Zealand, and Peru, to various treatment options depending on their score on the 21-gene recurrence test. Women were eligible for the trial if they had been recently diagnosed with hormone receptor-positive, HER2-negative breast cancer that had not spread to the lymph nodes.

Women with the lowest 21-gene recurrence score (0 to 10), who constituted about 16 percent of the participants, were assigned to receive hormone therapy alone; women with a score of 11 to 25, who made up 68 percent of the participants, were randomly assigned to receive hormone therapy alone or hormone therapy plus adjuvant chemotherapy; and women with the highest scores (25 and higher) were assigned to receive hormone therapy plus adjuvant chemotherapy.

The ranges used to define risk in TAILORx are different from those traditionally used in other studies, where low risk is defined as a score of less than 18, intermediate risk is 18 to 30, and high risk is 31or higher. The thresholds used in TAILORx were chosen to minimize the potential for undertreatment of the subjects enrolled in the trial.

More than 1,600 women in the trial had tumors with a 21-gene recurrence score in the lowest range. These women received hormone therapy that consisted of an aromatase inhibitor (used in about 60 percent of patients), tamoxifen (used in one-third of the patients), tamoxifen followed by aromatase inhibitor therapy (used in 1 percent of the patients), treatments that suppressed ovarian function (used in 3 percent of the patients), or other or unknown treatments (used in 3 percent of the patients).

The trial, which was sponsored by NCI, was led by Joseph Sparano, M.D., of Montefiore Medical Center in New York and the ECOG-ACRIN Research Group. All of the adult cancer research groups of the NCI-sponsored National Clinical Trials Network (ECOG-ACRIN, the Alliance for Trials in Clinical Oncology, NCIC-Clinical Trials Group, NRG Oncology, and SWOG) participated in the trial.

Results

Five years after study entry, in the low-risk subset that was the subject of this initial analysis, 93.8 percent of the women were free of invasive disease, 99.3 percent were free of distant relapse, and 98 percent were still alive. Recurrence events were, according to the authors, "far exceeded by second primary breast cancers, other second primary cancer events, and deaths from other causes." These results provide support for the use of the 21-gene panel test to identify a low-risk subset of women that can be spared postsurgical chemotherapy.

Continued follow-up and analysis in the trial is ongoing, with full results expected in several years, to determine whether adjuvant chemotherapy improves outcomes over hormone therapy alone in women with higher recurrence scores.

Limitations

Although this study clearly identifies patients who do not benefit from adjuvant chemotherapy, only 16 percent of those enrolled had a recurrence score of 10 or less. Nearly 70 percent of enrollees had a mid-range score of 11 to 25, and the results to date do not provide information about whether this subset of women can be spared chemotherapy.

Conclusion

"TAILORx is one of the first and most important trials using a gene panel test to determine how to most effectively treat women with breast cancer," said Jo Anne Zujewski, M.D., of NCI's Cancer Therapy Evaluation Program (CTEP). "These excellent results in the low-risk subset of women should help spare a significant number of women from being overtreated with chemotherapy."

Chapter 72

Benefits of Adjuvant Bisphosphonates for Postmenopausal Breast Cancer

Summary

Bisphosphonates can reduce the rate of breast cancer recurrence in bone, according to a meta-analysis of randomized trials of bisphosphonates as adjuvant therapy for women with early-stage breast cancer. Additional analyses showed that adjuvant bisphosphonates can also improve survival among women who are postmenopausal when the treatment begins.

Background

Bisphosphonates are a class of drugs that are used to treat abnormally high blood calcium (hypercalcemia) and bone pain caused by some types of cancer. In breast cancer, bisphosphonates are used primarily to reduce bone loss (osteoporosis) and the risk of fracture among

This chapter includes text excerpted from "Meta-Analysis Finds Benefits of Adjuvant Bisphosphonates for Postmenopausal Breast Cancer," National Cancer Institute (NCI), September 9, 2015.

postmenopausal women with estrogen receptor-positive disease who receive aromatase inhibitors.

Because of their effects on bone, bisphosphonates have been studied for a potential role in reducing the risk of breast cancer recurrence in bone. Cancer cells released into the bloodstream by breast tumors may spread to bone and remain dormant there for extended periods. At some point, in a process that is not well understood, these cells may begin to divide and form small metastases. If bisphosphonates could protect against bone metastases, then these drugs might also improve survival.

Clinical trials of bisphosphonates as adjuvant therapy for women with breast cancer have produced mixed results. Some, but not all, of these studies have suggested that the use of bisphosphonates can reduce rates of recurrence and death in certain women with breast cancer.

For example, a 2009 study found that adding the bisphosphonate zoledronic acid (Zometa®) to adjuvant hormone therapy improved clinical outcomes for premenopausal women with early-stage breast cancer. (Long-term results of this trial published in 2011 showed persistent benefits.) However, results published in 2011 from the AZURE trial showed that adding zoledronic acid to standard adjuvant therapy did not extend disease-free survival for women with stage II or III breast cancer.

The Study

To better understand the potential role of adjuvant bisphosphonate treatment for women with early-stage breast cancer, the Early Breast Cancer Trialists' Collaborative Group (EBCTCG) conducted a meta-analysis of individual patient data for 18,766 participants in 26 randomized trials. These trials compared adjuvant bisphosphonate use for 2 to 5 years with no bisphosphonate use.

The primary endpoints of the study were any recurrence of breast cancer (which included breast cancer in either breast or at a distant site); a distant recurrence of breast cancer, that is, at a site other than in either breast; and death from breast cancer. Secondary outcomes included death without a recurrence of breast cancer; recurrence of the cancer in bone; recurrence in tissues other than bone or either breast; a new primary cancer in the other (contralateral) breast; and any bone fractures.

To determine whether any benefits of adjuvant bisphosphonate use were limited to certain subsets of women, the data were analyzed in groups according to several factors, including the women's menopausal status, the class of bisphosphonate, the duration of treatment, tumor size, whether the cancer had spread to the lymph nodes, and whether the cancer was estrogen-receptor positive.

Results

Overall, the addition of adjuvant bisphosphonates was associated with a significant reduction in 10-year risk of bone recurrence (7.8 percent versus 9.0 percent). Although the authors observed reductions at 10 years for distant recurrence (20.4 percent versus 21.8 percent), and breast cancer mortality (16.6 percent versus 18.4 percent), these differences were of only borderline statistical significance.

When the study authors looked at the findings according to the trial participants' menopausal status, they found that treatment with adjuvant bisphosphonates had no effect on any of the outcomes for premenopausal women. However, among the 11,767 postmenopausal women included in the analysis, the use of bisphosphonates was associated with statistically significant reductions in distant recurrence, in bone recurrence, and in death from breast cancer.

For example, during the first decade after diagnosis, 6.6 percent of postmenopausal women who used a bisphosphonate experienced a recurrence in bone, versus 8.8 percent of women who did not use the drug. During the same period, 14.7 percent of postmenopausal women who used a bisphosphonate died from breast cancer, versus 18.0 percent of women who did not use the drug.

The reductions in bone recurrence and the survival benefit for postmenopausal women did not depend on the class of bisphosphonate used, the duration of treatment, the size of the breast tumor, or whether the cancer had spread to the lymph nodes or was estrogen-receptor positive.

Among all participants, 3,453 women had a recurrence of cancer, and 2,106 women subsequently died of the disease. The risk of a recurrence of cancer and of dying of the disease did not differ between women who received bisphosphonates and those who did not.

Among the 501 women who died from causes other than breast cancer, the risk of death also did not differ between women who received bisphosphonates and those who did not.

Bisphosphonate use did not reduce the incidence of a new breast cancer developing in the contralateral breast. Bone fractures were reduced among women who received bisphosphonates compared with those who did not. Overall, the 5-year risk of fractures was 5.1 percent in women who were assigned to bisphosphonates and 6.3 percent in women who did not use them.

Limitations

Information about the occurrence of bone fractures was available for only 71 percent of the women included in the analysis (13,341 participants).

Additional studies are needed to help researchers determine whether different bisphosphonate regimens have different effects. "Much more reliable comparisons of different bisphosphonate regimens will emerge from ongoing trials that compare them directly," the study authors wrote. The SWOG0307 trial, for example, is comparing three types of bisphosphonates in treating women who have undergone surgery for stage I, stage II, or stage III breast cancer. Reporting their initial results in abstract form, trial investigators said they found no differences in efficacy by type of bisphosphonate but there were differences in toxicities.

More research is also needed to help clarify the relationship between menopausal status and the response to bisphosphonates. "The complex interactions between reproductive hormones, tumor biology, bone cell function, and bone marrow stem cells could well change" as women progress from premenopause to postmenopause, the authors noted.

Conclusion

Jo Anne Zujewski, M.D., of NCI's Cancer Therapy Evaluation Program (CTEP), who was not involved in the meta-analysis, noted that bisphosphonates have bone-protective effects and are generally well tolerated by patients.

"This study provides better evidence for prescribing bisphosphonates for women at an increased risk of a recurrence of breast cancer," Dr. Zujewski commented. Physicians should consider the new results when making treatment decisions and in their discussions with patients about the risks and benefits of using bisphosphonates, she added.

Chapter 73

Clinical Trials

Chapter Contents

Section 73.1

What Are Clinical Trials?

This section includes text excerpted from "What Are Clinical Trials?" National Cancer Institute (NCI), July 1, 2013.

Clinical trials are research studies that involve people. They are the final step in a long process that begins with research in a lab. Most treatments we use today are the results of past clinical trials.

Cancer clinical trials are designed to test new ways to:

- Treat cancer

- Find and diagnose cancer

- Prevent cancer

- Manage symptoms of cancer or side effects from its treatment

Any time you or a loved one needs treatment for cancer, clinical trials are an option to think about. Trials are available for all stages of cancer. It is a myth that they are only for people who have advanced cancer that is not responding to treatment.

Every trial has a person in charge, usually a doctor, who is called the principal investigator. The principal investigator prepares a plan for the trial, called a protocol. The protocol explains what will be done during the trial. It also contains information that helps the doctor decide if this treatment is right for you. The protocol includes information about:

- The reason for doing the trial

- Who can join the trial (called "eligibility requirements")

- How many people are needed for the trial

- Any drugs that will be given, how they will be given, the dose, and how often

- What medical tests will be done and how often

- What types of information will be collected about the people taking part

Why Are Clinical Trials Important?

Clinical trials are key to developing new methods to prevent, detect, and treat cancer. It is through clinical trials that researchers can determine whether new treatments are safe and effective and work better than current treatments. When you take part in a clinical trial, you add to our knowledge about cancer and help improve cancer care.

Section 73.2

How to Find a Cancer Treatment Trial

This section includes text excerpted from "How to Find a Cancer Treatment Trial: A 10-Step Guide," National Cancer Institute (NCI), June 4, 2015.

A 10-Step Guide for Finding a Cancer Treatment Trial

This guide will help you look for a cancer treatment clinical trial. It does not provide medical advice and should not be used in place of advice from your doctor or other members of your healthcare team. If you wish, your healthcare team and your loved ones can assist you in deciding whether or not a clinical trial is right for you. But, the decision to take part in a clinical trial is yours alone to make.

This guide takes you through the following steps:

Step 1: Understand Clinical Trials
Step 2: Talk With Your Doctor
Step 3: Complete the Checklist
Step 4: Find NCI-Supported Clinical Trials
Step 5: Other Lists of Trials
Step 6: Identify Potential Trials
Step 7: Contact the Trial Team
Step 8: Ask Questions
Step 9: Talk to Your Doctor
Step 10: Make an Appointment

A Word about Timing

Some treatment trials will not accept people who have already been treated for their cancer. The researchers conducting these trials are hoping to find improved cancer treatments for people with newly diagnosed disease.

- **If you have just found out that you have cancer**, the time to think about joining a trial is before you have any treatment. Talk with your doctor about how quickly you need to make a treatment decision.

Other treatment trials are looking for people who have already been treated for their cancer.

- **If you have already had cancer treatment** and are looking for a new treatment option, there are still clinical trials for you to think about.

Step 1: Understand Clinical Trials

Clinical trials are research studies that involve people. They are the final step in a long process that begins with laboratory research and testing in animals. Many treatments used today are the result of past clinical trials.

If you would like to learn more about clinical trials, or review your understanding of them before going further, the National Cancer Institute (NCI) booklet Taking Part in Cancer Treatment Research Studies can help you understand what cancer clinical trials are, why they are important, and how they work.

Step 2: Talk with Your Doctor

When thinking about clinical trials, **your best starting point is your doctor or another member of your healthcare team**

Usually, it is a doctor who may know about a clinical trial, or search for one, that could be a good option for you and your type of cancer. He or she can provide information and answer questions while you think about joining a clinical trial.

In some cases, your doctor may not be familiar with clinical trials. If so, you may want to get a second opinion about your treatment options, including taking part in a clinical trial.

Step 3: Complete the Checklist

If you decide to look for a clinical trial, **you must know certain details about your cancer diagnosis**. You will need to compare these details with the eligibility criteria of any trial that interests you. Eligibility criteria are the guidelines for who can and cannot take part in a certain clinical trial. They are also called entry criteria or enrollment criteria.

To help you know which trails you may be eligible to join, **complete the Cancer Details Checklist** as much as possible. This form asks questions about your cancer and provides space to write down your answers. Keep the form with you during your search for a clinical trial.

To get the information you need for the form, **ask your doctor, a nurse, or social worker at your doctor's office for help**. Explain to them that you are interested in looking for a clinical trial and that you need these details before starting to look. They may be able to review your medical records and help you fill out the form. The more information you can find to complete the form, the easier it will be to find a clinical trial to fit your situation.

Step 4: Find NCI-Supported Clinical Trials

Many websites have lists of cancer clinical trials that are taking place in the United States. Some trials are sponsored by nonprofit organizations, including the U.S. federal government. Others are sponsored by for-profit groups, such as drug companies. Hospitals and academic medical centers also sponsor trials conducted by their own researchers. Because of the many types of sponsors, no single list of clinical trials is complete.

This website helps you find NCI-supported clinical trials that are taking place across the United States, Canada, and internationally. The list includes:

- All NCI network trials, including trials supported through the:
  - National Clinical Trials Network (NCTN)
  - NCI Community Oncology Research Program (NCORP)
  - Experimental Therapeutics Clinical Trials Network (ETCTN)
- Trials that are funded in full or in part by NCI, including trials taking place at NCI-designated cancer centers
- Trials at the NIH Clinical Center in Bethesda, Maryland

You can search for NCI trials yourself using NCI's clinical trials search form.

Step 5: Other Lists of Trials

In addition to NCI's list of cancer clinical trials, you may want to check a few other trial lists. Why? Because:

- They may include trials not found in NCI's list.

- You may prefer the way you can search those lists.

Other places to look for lists of cancer clinical trials include the websites of:

- U.S. National Library of Medicine's ClinicalTrials.gov

- Research organizations that conduct clinical trials

- Drug and biotechnology companies

- Clinical trial listing services

- Cancer advocacy groups

- World Health Organization International Clinical Trials Registry Platform (ICTRP)

Helpful Tip: Whichever web site you use to search for clinical trials, be sure to print a copy of the clinical trial summary for every trial that interests you.

A clinical trial summary should tell you what will be done in the trial, how, and why. It should also list the location(s) where the trial is taking place, so you will know where you need to travel to take part in the trial.

U.S. National Library of Medicine's ClinicalTrials.gov

The National Library of Medicine Is Operated by the U.S. Federal Government. It Manages a Website Called ClinicalTrials.gov, Which Lists Clinical Trials for Cancer and Many Other Diseases and Conditions. It Contains Trials That Are in NCI's List of Cancer Trials as Well as Trials Sponsored by Pharmaceutical or Biotech Companies.

Research Organizations That Conduct Cancer Clinical Trials

Many cancer centers across the United States, including NCI-designated Cancer Centers, sponsor or take part in cancer clinical trials.

The websites of these centers usually have a list of the clinical trials taking place at their location. Some of the trials included in these lists may not be in NCI's list.

Keep in mind that the amount of information about clinical trials on these web sites can vary. You may have to contact a cancer center's clinical trials office to get more information about the trials that interest you.

Drug and Biotechnology Companies

Many companies provide lists of the clinical trials that they sponsor on their web sites. Sometimes, a company's web site may refer you to the web site of another organization that helps the company find patients for its trials. The other organization may be paid fees for this service.

The website of the Pharmaceutical Research and Manufacturers of America (PhRMA) includes a list of its member companies, many of which sponsor cancer clinical trials. PhRMA is a trade organization that represents drug and biotechnology companies in the United States.

Clinical Trial Listing Services

Other organizations provide lists of clinical trials as a part of their business. These organizations generally do not sponsor or take part in clinical trials. Some of them may receive fees from drug or biotechnology company sponsors of trials for listing their trials or helping them find patients for their trials.

Keep the following points in mind:

- The trial lists provided by these organizations often rely heavily on trial lists that are available at no cost from the U.S. federal government (NCI and ClinicalTrials.gov).

- The websites of these organizations may not be updated regularly.

- The websites of these organizations may require you to register to search for clinical trials or obtain trial contact information for trials that interest you.

The following list links to the websites of several clinical trial listing services.

- BreastCancerTrials.org

- CenterWatch.com

- eCancerTrials.com

- EmergingMed.com

- EvitiClinicalTrials.com

Cancer Advocacy Groups

Cancer advocacy groups work on behalf of people diagnosed with cancer and their loved ones. They provide education, support, financial assistance, and advocacy to help patients and families who are dealing with cancer, its treatment, and survivorship. These organizations recognize that clinical trials are important to improving cancer care. They work to educate and empower people to find information and obtain access to appropriate treatment.

Advocacy groups work hard to know about the latest advances in cancer research. They will sometimes have information about certain government-sponsored clinical trials, as well as some trials sponsored by cancer centers or drug and biotechnology companies.

To find trials, search the web sites of advocacy groups for specific types of cancer. Many of these websites have lists of clinical trials or refer you to the websites of organizations that match patients to trials. Cancer Action Now, managed by the non-profit Marti Nelson Cancer Foundation, provides a partial list of cancer advocacy groups. Or, you can contact an advocacy group directly for assistance in finding clinical trials.

Step 6: Identify Potential Trials

At this point, you should have completed the Cancer Details Checklist, found one or more trials of interest to you, and printed out or saved a summary for each trial.

This Section Will Help You to:

- take a closer look at the trial summaries

- narrow your list to include only those trials for which you would like to get more information

Key Questions to Ask about Each Trial:

- **Trial objective:** What is the main purpose of the trial? Is it to cure your cancer? To slow its growth or spread? To lessen the severity of cancer symptoms or the side effects of treatment? To determine whether a new treatment is safe and well-tolerated? Read this information carefully to learn whether the trial's main objective matches your goals for treatment.

- **Eligibility criteria:** Do the details of your cancer diagnosis and your current overall state of health match the trial's entry criteria? This may tell you whether or not you can qualify for the trial. If you're not sure, keep the trial on your list for now.

- **Trial location:** Is the location of the trial manageable for you? Some trials take place at more than one location. Look carefully at how often you will need to receive treatment during the course of the trial. Decide how far and how often you are willing to travel. You will also need to ask whether the sponsoring organization will pay for some or all of your travel costs.

- **Study length:** How long will the trial run? Not all clinical trial summaries provide this information. If they do, consider the time involved and whether it will work for you and your family.

After considering these questions, if you are still interested in one or more of the clinical trials you have found, then you are ready for Step 7.

Helpful Tip: Don't worry if you cannot answer all of the questions below just yet. The idea is to narrow your list of trials, if possible. However, don't give up on trials you're not sure about. You may want to talk with your doctor or another healthcare team member during this process, especially if you find the trial summaries hard to understand.

Step 7: Contact the Trial Team

There are many ways to contact the clinical trial team.

- Contact the trial team directly. The clinical trial summary should include the phone number of a person or an office that you can contact for more information. You do not need to talk to the lead researcher (called the "protocol chair" or "principal investigator") at this time, even if his or her name is given along with the telephone number. Instead, call the number and ask to speak with the "trial coordinator," the "referral coordinator," or the "protocol assistant." This person can answer questions from patients and their doctors. It is also this person's job to decide whether you are likely to be eligible to join the trial.

(A final decision will probably not be made until you have had a visit with a doctor who is taking part in the trial.)

- Ask your doctor or another healthcare team member to contact the trial team for you. Because the clinical trial coordinator will ask questions about your cancer diagnosis and your current general health, you may want to ask your doctor or someone else on your healthcare team to contact the clinical trial team for you.

- The trial team may contact you. If you have used the web site of a clinical trial listing service and found a trial that interests you, you may have provided your name, phone number, and e-mail address so the clinical trial team can contact you directly.

You will need to refer to the Cancer Details Checklist during this conversation, so keep it handy.

Step 8: Ask Questions

Whether you or someone from your healthcare team calls the clinical trial team, this is the time to get answers to questions that will help you decide whether or not to take part in this particular clinical trial.

It will be helpful if you can talk about your cancer and your current general health in a manner that is brief and to the point. Before you make the call, you may want to rehearse how you will present key information about your cancer diagnosis and general health with a family member or a friend. This will make you more comfortable when you are talking with the clinical trial team member, and it will help you answer his or her questions more smoothly. Remember to keep your Cancer Details Checklist handy to help you answer some of the questions that may be asked.

Questions to Ask the Trial Coordinator

1. Is the trial still open?

On occasion, clinical trial listings will be out of date and will include trials that are no longer accepting new participants.

2. Am I eligible for this trial?

The trial team member will ask you many, if not all, of the questions listed on your Cancer Details Checklist. This is the time to confirm that you are a candidate for this trial. However, a final decision will likely not be made until you have had your first visit with a doctor who is taking part in the clinical trial (Step 10).

3. Why do researchers think the new treatment might be effective?

Results from previous research have indicated that the new treatment may be effective in people with your type of cancer. Ask about the previous research studies. Results from studies in humans are stronger than results from laboratory or animal studies.

4. What are the potential risks and benefits associated with the treatments I may receive in this trial?

Every treatment has risks, whether you receive the treatment as part of a clinical trial or from your doctor outside of a clinical trial. Be sure you understand the possible risks and side effects of each treatment you may receive as a participant in this trial. Also, ask for a detailed description of how the treatments you may receive could benefit you.

5. Who will watch over my care and safety?

Primary responsibility for the care and safety of people taking part in a cancer clinical trial rests with the clinical trial team. Also, clinical trials are governed by safety and ethical regulations set by the Federal government and the organization sponsoring and carrying out the trial. One of these groups is called the Institutional Review Board (IRB). The trial team will be able to give you more information.

6. Can I get a copy of the trial's protocol document?

A trial's protocol document is an action plan for the trial. It includes the reason(s) for doing the trial, the number of people that will be included, the eligibility criteria for participation, the treatments that will be given, the medical tests that will be done and how often, and what information will be collected. These documents are usually written in highly technical language and are often confidential. In some cases, however, the trial team may be allowed to release the protocol document to you.

7. Can I get a copy of the informed consent document?

Yes. The U.S. Food and Drug Administration (FDA) and the Office for Human Research Protections (OHRP) require that potential participants in a clinical trial receive detailed, understandable information about the trial. This process is known as "informed consent," and it must be in writing. It may be helpful to see a copy of this document before you make your final decision about joining the trial.

8. Is there a chance that I will receive a placebo?

Placebos (sham or inactive treatments) are rarely used alone in cancer treatment trials. When they are used, they are most often given along with a standard (usual) treatment. In such cases, a trial will compare a standard treatment plus a new treatment with the same standard treatment plus a placebo. If a placebo is used alone, it's because no standard treatment exists. In this case, a trial will compare the effects of a new treatment with the effects of a placebo. Be sure you understand the treatments that are being used in any trial you are thinking of joining.

9. Is the trial randomized?

In a randomized clinical trial, participants are assigned by chance to different treatment groups or "arms" of the trial. Neither you nor your doctor can choose which arm you are in. All participants in an arm receive the same treatment. At the end of the trial, the results from the different treatment arms are compared. In a randomized trial, you may or may not receive the new treatment that is being tested.

10. What is the dose and schedule of the treatments given in each arm of the trial?

Dose refers to the amount of treatment given, and schedule refers to when and how often treatment is given. You will want to think about this information when you are discussing your treatment options with your healthcare team. Is the treatment schedule manageable for you?

11. What costs will I or my health insurance plan have to pay?

In many cases, the research costs are paid by the organization sponsoring the trial. Research costs include the treatments being studied and any tests performed purely for research purposes. However, you or your insurance plan would be responsible for paying "routine patient care costs." These are the costs of medical care (for example, doctor visits, hospital stays, X-rays) that you would receive whether or not you were taking part in a clinical trial. Some insurance plans don't cover these costs once you join a trial. Check with your health plan to find out which costs it will and will not pay for.

12. If I have to travel, who will pay for my travel and lodging?

Clinical trials rarely cover travel and lodging expenses. Usually, you will be responsible for these costs. However, you should still ask this question.

13. Will participation in this trial require more time (hours/days) than standard care? Will participation require a hospital stay?

Understanding how much time is involved and whether a hospital stay is required, compared to the usual treatment for your type of cancer, may influence your decision. This information will also be important if you decide to take part in the trial because it will help you in making plans.

14. How will participating in this trial affect my everyday life?

A diagnosis of cancer can disrupt the routine of your everyday life. Many people seek to keep their routine intact as they deal with their cancer and its treatment. This information will be useful in making plans and in determining whether you need any additional help at home.

Step 9: Talk to Your Doctor

To make a final decision, you will want to know the potential risks and benefits of all treatment options available to you. Through the research that you have done, you likely have a good idea about the possible risks and benefits of the treatment(s) in clinical trials that interest you. If you have any remaining questions or concerns, you should discuss them with your doctor. You should also ask your doctor about the risks and benefits of standard, or usual, treatment for your type of cancer. Then, you and your doctor can compare the risks and benefits of standard treatment with those of treatment in a clinical trial. You may decide that joining a trial is your best option, or you may decide not to join a trial. It's your choice.

The Questions to Ask in Step 8 can give you ideas of questions to ask your doctor.

Step 10: Make an Appointment

If you decide to join a clinical trial for which you are eligible, schedule a visit with the trial team. Most likely, the same person you spoke with in Step 8.

Section 73.3

Deciding to Take Part in a Clinical Trial

This section includes text excerpted from "Deciding to Take Part in a Clinical Trial," National Cancer Institute (NCI), July 1, 2013.

Joining a Clinical Trial

When you need treatment for cancer, you may want to think about joining a clinical trial. Like all treatment options, clinical trials have possible benefits and risks. By looking closely at all options, including clinical trials, you are taking an active role in a decision that affects your life. This section has information you can use when making your decision.

Possible Benefits

- You will have access to a new treatment that is not available to people outside the trial.

- The research team will watch you closely.

- If the treatment being studied is more effective than the standard treatment, you may be among the first to benefit.

- The trial may help scientists learn more about cancer and help people in the future.

Possible Risks

- The new treatment may not be better than, or even as good as, the standard treatment.

- New treatments may have side effects that doctors do not expect or that are worse than those of the standard treatment.

- You may be required to make more visits to the doctor than if you were receiving standard treatment. You may have extra expenses related to these extra visits, such as travel and child-care costs.

- You may need extra tests. Some of the tests could be uncomfortable or time consuming.

- Even if a new treatment has benefits in some patients, it may not work for you.

- Health insurance may not cover all patient care costs in a trial.

Who Can Join

Every clinical trial has a protocol, or study plan, that describes what will be done during the trial, how the trial will be conducted, and why each part of the trial is necessary. The protocol also includes guidelines for who can and cannot take part in the trial. These guidelines are called eligibility criteria.

Common eligibility criteria include:

- Having a certain type or stage of cancer

- Having received (or not having received) a certain kind of therapy in the past

- Being in a certain age group

- Medical history

- Current health status

Criteria such as these help reduce the medical differences among people in the trial. When people taking part in a trial are alike in key ways, researchers can be more certain that the results are due to the treatment being tested and not to other factors.

Some people have health problems besides cancer that could be made worse by the treatments in a trial. If you are interested in joining a trial, you will receive medical tests to be sure that you fit for the trial.

Section 73.4

Ongoing Clinical Trials

This section contains text excerpted from the following sources:
Text beginning with the heading "Genomic Testing for Primary
Breast Cancer" is excerpted from "Genomic Testing for Primary
Breast Cancer," ClinicalTrials.gov, U.S. National Institutes of
Health (NIH), January 29, 2016; Text beginning with the heading
"Shorter Course Radiation for the Treatment of Breast Cancer That
Has Spread to Lymph Nodes" is excerpted from "Shorter Course
Radiation for the Treatment of Breast Cancer That Has Spread
to Lymph Nodes," ClinicalTrials.gov, U.S. National Institutes of
Health (NIH), March 1, 2016; Text beginning with the heading
"Changes in Breast Density and Breast Cancer Risk in Women
with Breast Cancer and in Healthy Women" is excerpted from
"Changes in Breast Density and Breast Cancer Risk in Women
with Breast Cancer and in Healthy Women," ClinicalTrials.gov,
U.S. National Institutes of Health (NIH), February 16, 2016.

Genomic Testing for Primary Breast Cancer

Purpose

The goal of this research study is find out if researchers can use
genetic testing on tumor samples to predict if tumors will respond to
breast cancer treatments. The tumor sample will be tested to learn
if certain genes are activated (turned on) in the tumor. Researchers
hope that the activation of these genes may predict if the tumor will
be sensitive or resistant to routine breast cancer treatments, such as
chemotherapy or hormonal therapy.

Detailed Description

This study will involve performing a test on a sample of tumor.
If you agree to take part in this study, you will have a tumor biopsy
before you receive any drugs to treat breast cancer. The sample of the
tumor will be will be taken at one of the following times:

- At the time of a planned biopsy to learn if you have breast
  cancer.

- At the time of planned surgery to remove a known breast cancer.

- If the breast cancer has been previously biopsied and your doctor plans to give you breast cancer treatments before surgery, you will have a biopsy before starting these drugs.

The amount of tumor collected for this study will be about the size of the tip of a pencil.

If you are going to have surgery to remove the breast cancer before receiving breast cancer treatments, a small piece of the tumor will be removed and sent for testing. If you are going to have a planned needle biopsy, an extra core sample and/or fine needle sample will be taken. If you are going to have a research biopsy, an ultrasound or mammogram will be used to find the tumor and a needle will be inserted into the tumor to collect a piece of tissue.

After the genetic testing is complete, researchers will use the results to learn how well this test is able to give results that can be used to predict response to breast cancer drugs and therapy.

Length of Study

You will be off study after the five years of follow-up.

This is an investigational study. The test that will be performed on your breast cancer tumor sample is an investigational test.

Up to 1100 patients will take part in this study. All will be enrolled at MD Anderson.

Shorter Course Radiation for the Treatment of Breast Cancer That Has Spread to Lymph Nodes

Purpose

The proposed study is being done to learn more about a particular dose of radiation treatment for breast cancer that is completed in a shorter amount of time than what has traditionally been used to treat breast cancer. Subjects are being asked to be in this research study because they have already had surgery for breast cancer and some cancer cells were found in their lymph nodes that drain the breast tissue.

Detailed Description

Subjects who join the study will receive a shortened course of radiation treatment that will last approximately four (4) weeks, instead of the traditional six (6) week course that women have typically received in this situation. The shorter course subjects will receive is designed in a way that it is thought to be equivalent to the longer course. This shorter course has already been shown to be very safe and effective when treating breast cancer in the breast tissue only. However, because cancer cells were found in the lymph nodes that drain their breast, subjects require radiation to a larger area of their chest, armpit, and shoulder than has been completely tested with this experimental dose.

Changes in Breast Density and Breast Cancer Risk in Women with Breast Cancer and in Healthy Women

Purpose

RATIONALE: Studying mammograms for breast density changes over time may help doctors predict breast cancer risk.

PURPOSE: This natural history study is looking at changes in breast density and gathering health information over time to assess breast cancer risk in women with breast cancer and in healthy women.

Detailed Description

OBJECTIVES:

- Determine the mammographic density (MD) longitudinal change trajectory in women with breast cancer and in healthy female participants to assess within-individual MD longitudinal change and breast cancer risk.

- Determine whether these patients or healthy participants manifest different patterns of within-individual change in MD and evaluate predictors of across-individual differences.

- Determine whether the developmental profile of MD differs systematically between these patients and healthy participants.

OUTLINE: This is a prospective, retrospective, controlled study. Patients and healthy participants are frequency-matched by age (± 2 years) and ethnicity.

- **Questionnaire**: Patients and healthy participants complete a self-administered questionnaire providing detailed information on breast cancer risk factors, including demographics, behavioral and lifestyle factors, reproductive history, family

618

history of breast cancer, comorbidities, medication and hormone replacement therapy use, and breast cancer screening history. This information is then cross-validated with documented data abstracted from medical records to provide a longitudinal and historical framework for assessing individual risk.

- **Mammographic density (MD) assessment**: Patients and healthy participants are evaluated for patterns of longitudinal change in MD and subsequent breast cancer risk by retrospective review of screening mammograms performed prior to breast cancer diagnosis.

PROJECTED ACCRUAL: A total of 1500 patients and 1500 healthy participants will be accrued for this study.

Part Nine

Additional Help and Information

Chapter 74

Glossary of Breast Cancer Terms

adenosis: A disease or abnormal change in a gland. Breast adenosis is a benign condition in which the lobules are larger than usual.

areola: The area of dark-colored skin on the breast that surrounds the nipple.

atrophy: Thinning or diminishing of tissue or muscle.

atypical ductal hyperplasia: A benign (not cancer) condition in which there are more cells than normal in the lining of breast ducts and the cells look abnormal under a microscope. Having ADH increases your risk of breast cancer.

atypical lobular hyperplasia: A benign (not cancer) condition in which there are more cells than normal in the breast lobules and the cells look abnormal under a microscope. Having ALH increases your risk of breast cancer.

biological therapy: Treatment to boost or restore the ability of the immune system to fight cancer, infections, and other diseases. Also used to lessen certain side effects that may be caused by some cancer treatments.

biopsy: The removal and examination of tissue, cells or fluid from a living body.

This glossary contains terms excerpted from documents produced by several sources deemed reliable.

BRCA1: A gene on chromosome 17 that normally helps to suppress cell growth. A person who inherits certain mutations (changes) in a BRCA1 gene has a higher risk of getting breast, ovarian, prostate, and other types of cancer. BRCA1 is short for (breast cancer 1, early onset gene).

BRCA2: A gene on chromosome 13 that normally helps to suppress cell growth. A person who inherits certain mutations (changes) in a BRCA2 gene has a higher risk of getting breast, ovarian, prostate, and other types of cancer. BRCA2 is short for (breast cancer 2, early onset gene).

breast density: Describes the relative amount of different tissues present in the breast. A dense breast has less fat than glandular and connective tissue.

breast implant: Any surgically implanted artificial device intended to replace missing breast tissue or to enhance a breast.

breast-conserving surgery: An operation to remove the breast cancer but not the breast itself. Also called breast-sparing surgery.

chest wall: The system of structures outside the lungs that move as a part of breathing, including bones (the rib cage) and muscles (diaphragm and abdomen).

core biopsy: The removal of a tissue sample with a wide needle for examination under a microscope.

cryoablation: A procedure in which tissue is frozen to destroy abnormal cells. This is usually done with a special instrument that contains liquid nitrogen or liquid carbon dioxide. Also called cryosurgery.

cyst: A sac or capsule in the body. It may be filled with fluid or other material.

diagnostic mammogram: X-ray of the breasts used to check for cancer after a lump or other sign or symptom of breast cancer has been found.

ductal carcinoma in situ: A noninvasive condition in which abnormal cells are found in the lining of a breast duct. The abnormal cells have not spread outside the duct to other tissues in the breast.

excisional biopsy: A surgical procedure in which an entire lump or suspicious area is removed for diagnosis. The tissue is then examined under a microscope to check for signs of disease.

fat necrosis: A benign condition in which fat tissue in the breast or other organs is damaged by injury, surgery, or radiation therapy.

The fat tissue in the breast may be replaced by a cyst or by scar tissue, which may feel like a round, firm lump.

fibroadenoma: A benign (not cancer) tumor that usually forms in the breast from both fibrous and glandular tissue. Fibroadenomas are the most common benign breast tumors.

fine-needle aspiration biopsy: The removal of tissue or fluid with a thin needle for examination under a microscope. Also called FNA biopsy.

grade: A description of a tumor based on how abnormal the cancer cells look under a microscope and how quickly the tumor is likely to grow and spread.

hematoma: A collection of blood inside the body, for example in skin tissue.

hormonal therapy: Treatment that adds, blocks, or removes hormones. For certain conditions (such as diabetes or menopause), hormones are given to adjust low hormone levels.

implant displacement views: A procedure used to do a mammogram (X-ray of the breasts) in women with breast implants.

in situ: In its original place. For example, in carcinoma in situ, abnormal cells are found only in the place where they first formed. They have not spread.

incisional biopsy: A surgical procedure in which a portion of a lump or suspicious area is removed for diagnosis. The tissue is then examined under a microscope to check for signs of disease.

inflammation/irritation: The response of the body to infection or injury characterized by swelling, redness, warmth and/or pain.

intraductal papilloma: A benign (not cancer), wart-like growth in a milk duct of the breast. It is usually found close to the nipple and may cause a discharge from the nipple. It may also cause pain and a lump in the breast that can be felt.

lactation: The production and secretion of milk by the breast glands.

latissimus dorsi flap reconstruction: Breast reconstruction using a patient's own tissue from the side of the back to create the new breast or provide enough skin and breast tissue to cover a breast implant.

latissimus dorsi: Two triangular muscles running from the spinal column (backbone) to the shoulder.

LCIS (lobular carcinoma in situ): A condition in which abnormal cells are found in the lobules of the breast. LCIS seldom becomes invasive cancer; however, having it in one breast increases the risk of developing breast cancer in either breast.

lobe: A portion of an organ, such as the breast, liver, lung, thyroid, or brain.

lobule: A small lobe or a subdivision of a lobe.

local anesthesia: A temporary loss of feeling in one small area of the body caused by special drugs or other substances called anesthetics. The patient stays awake but has no feeling in the area of the body treated with the anesthetic.

lumpectomy: Surgery to remove abnormal tissue or cancer from the breast and a small amount of normal tissue around it. It is a type of breast-sparing surgery.

lymph node: A rounded mass of lymphatic tissue that is surrounded by a capsule of connective tissue. Lymph nodes filter lymph (lymphatic fluid), and they store lymphocytes (white blood cells). They are located along lymph vessels. Also called a lymph gland.

lymph vessel: A thin tube that carries lymph (lymphatic fluid) and white blood cells through the lymphatic system. Also called lymphatic vessel.

lymph: The clear fluid that travels through the lymphatic system and carries cells that help fight infections and other diseases. Also called lymphatic fluid.

lymphocyte: A type of immune cell that is made in the bone marrow and is found in the blood and in lymph tissue. The two main types of lymphocytes are B lymphocytes and T lymphocytes. B lymphocytes make antibodies, and T lymphocytes help kill tumor cells and help control immune responses. A lymphocyte is a type of white blood cell.

macrocalcification: A small deposit of calcium in the breast that cannot be felt but can be seen on a mammogram. It is usually caused by aging, an old injury, or inflamed tissue and is usually not related to cancer.

mammography: A type of X-ray examination of the breasts used for detection of cancer.

mastectomy: Partial or complete removal of the breast.

menopausal hormone therapy: Hormones (estrogen, progesterone, or both) given to women after menopause to replace the hormones no longer produced by the ovaries. Also called hormone replacement therapy and HRT.

menopause: The time of life when a woman's ovaries stop working and menstrual periods stop. Natural menopause usually occurs around age 50. A woman is said to be in menopause when she hasn't had a period for 12 months in a row.

metastatic disease: A stage of cancer after it has spread from its original site to other parts of the body.

microcalcification: A tiny deposit of calcium in the breast that cannot be felt but can be detected on a mammogram. A cluster of these very small specks of calcium may indicate that cancer is present.

mutation: Any change in the DNA of a cell. Mutations may be caused by mistakes during cell division, or they may be caused by exposure to DNA-damaging agents in the environment.

necrosis: Death of cells or tissues.

needle localization: A procedure used to mark a small area of abnormal tissue so it can be removed by surgery. An imaging device is used to guide a thin wire with a hook at the end through a hollow needle to place the wire in or around the abnormal area.

noninvasive: In cancer, it describes disease that has not spread outside the tissue in which it began. In medicine, it describes a procedure that does not require inserting an instrument through the skin or into a body opening.

perimenopausal: Describes the time in a woman's life when menstrual periods become irregular as she approaches menopause. This is usually three to five years before menopause and is often marked by many of the symptoms of menopause, including hot flashes, mood swings, night sweats, vaginal dryness, trouble concentrating, and infertility.

premalignant: A term used to describe a condition that may (or is likely to) become cancer. Also called precancerous.

premenopausal: Having to do with the time before menopause. Menopause ("change of life") is the time of life when a woman's menstrual periods stop permanently.

prosthesis: Any artificial device used to replace or represent a body part.

raloxifene: The active ingredient in a drug used to reduce the risk of invasive breast cancer in postmenopausal women who are at high risk of the disease or who have osteoporosis. It is also used to prevent and treat osteoporosis in postmenopausal women.

rupture: A hole or tear in the shell of the implant that allows silicone gel filler material to leak from the shell.

saline: Saltwater (A solution made of water and a small amount of salt).

sclerosing adenosis: A benign condition in which scar-like tissue is found in a gland, such as the breast lobules or the prostate. A biopsy may be needed to tell the difference between the abnormal tissue and cancer.

screening: Checking for disease when there are no symptoms. Since screening may find diseases at an early stage, there may be a better chance of curing the disease.

silicone: Silicone is a man-made material that can be found in several forms such as oil, gel, or rubber (elastomer). The exact composition of silicone will be different depending on its use.

sonogram: A computer picture of areas inside the body created by bouncing high-energy sound waves (ultrasound) off internal tissues or organs. Also called an ultrasonogram.

surgical biopsy: The removal of tissue by a surgeon for examination by a pathologist. The pathologist may study the tissue under a microscope.

tamoxifen: A drug used to treat certain types of breast cancer in women and men. It is also used to prevent breast cancer in women who have had ductal carcinoma in situ.

wire localization: A procedure used to mark a small area of abnormal tissue so it can be removed by surgery. An imaging device is used to guide a thin wire with a hook at the end through a hollow needle to place the wire in or around the abnormal area.

Chapter 75

Directory of Organizations That Offer Information and Financial Assistance to People with Breast Cancer

Government Agencies That Provide Information about Breast Cancer

Agency for Healthcare Research and Quality
Office of Communications and Knowledge Transfer
540 Gaither Rd.
Ste. 2000
Rockville, MD 20850
Phone: 301-427-1104
Website: www.ahrq.gov

Centers for Disease Control and Prevention
1600 Clifton Rd.
Atlanta, GA 30333
Toll-Free: 800-CDC-INFO
(800-232-4636)
Phone: 404-639-3311
Toll-Free TTY: 888-232-6348
Fax: 800-232-4636
Website: www.cdc.gov
E-mail: CDC-INFO@cdc.gov

Information in this chapter was compiled from sources deemed accurate. All contact information was verified and updated in April 2016. Text under the heading "Find a Breast Cancer Screening Provider If You Are Uninsured or Underinsured" is excerpted from "Find a Screening Provider Near You," Centers for Disease Control and Prevention (CDC), August 3, 2015.

Federal Trade Commission
600 Pennsylvania Ave. N.W.
Washington, DC 20580
Phone: 202-326-2222
Website: www.ftc.gov
E-mail: webmaster@ftc.gov

Healthfinder®
National Health Information
Center
P.O. Box 1133
Washington, DC 20013-1133
Fax: 301-984-4256
Website: www.healthfinder.gov
E-mail: healthfinder@nhic.org

National Cancer Institute
NCI Office of
Communications and
Education
Public Inquiries Office
6116 Executive Blvd., Ste. 300
Bethesda, MD 20892-8322
Toll-Free: 800-4-CANCER
(800-422-6237)
Toll-Free TTY: 800-332-8615
Fax: 800-422-6237
Website: www.cancer.gov
E-mail: cancergovstaff@mail.nih.
gov

National Center for
Complementary and
Alternative Medicine
National Institutes of Health
NCCAM Clearinghouse, P.O.
Box 7923
Gaithersburg, MD 20898-7923
Toll-Free: 888-644-6226
Toll-Free TTY: 866-464-3615
Toll-Free Fax: 866-464-3616
Website: www.nccam.nih.gov
E-mail: info@nccam.nih.gov

National Center for Health
Statistics
3311 Toledo Rd.
Hyattsville, MD 20782
Toll-Free: 800-CDC-INFO
(800-232-4636)
Fax: 800-232-4636
Website: www.cdc.gov/nchs
E-mail: CDC-INFO@cdc.gov

National Institute on Aging
Bldg. 31, Rm. 5C27
31 Center Dr., MSC 2292
Bethesda, MD 20892
Toll-Free: 800-222-2225
Phone: 301-496-1752
Toll-Free TTY: 800-222-4225
Fax: 301-496-1072
Website: www.nia.nih.gov
E-mail: niaic@nia.nih.gov

National Institutes of Health
9000 Rockville Pike
Bethesda, MD 20892
Phone: 301-496-4000
TTY: 301-402-9612
Website: www.nih.gov
E-mail: NIHinfo@od.nih.gov

National Women's Health
Information Center
Office on Women's Health
200 Independence Ave. S.W.
Rm. 712 E.
Washington, DC 20201
Toll-Free: 800-994-9662
Phone: 202-690-7650
Toll-Free TDD: 888-220-5446
Fax: 202-205-2631
Website: www.womenshealth.
gov

Sister Study
Toll-Free: 877-4SISTER
(877-474-7837)
TTY: 866-TTY-4SIS
(866-889-4747)
Fax: 866-889-4747
Website: www.sisterstudy.niehs.
nih.gov/English/index1.htm
E-mail: postmaster@sisterstudy.
org

**U.S. Department of Health
and Human Services**
200 Independence Ave. S.W.
Washington, DC 20201
Toll-Free: 877-696-6775
Website: www.hhs.gov

**U.S. Food and Drug
Administration**
10903 New Hampshire Ave.
Silver Spring, MD 20993
Toll-Free: 888-INFO-FDA
(888-463-6332)
Website: www.fda.gov

**U.S. National Library of
Medicine**
8600 Rockville Pike
Bethesda, MD 20894
Toll-Free: 888-FIND-NLM
(888-346-3656)
Phone: 301-594-5983
Toll-Free TDD: 800-735-2258
Fax: 301-402-1384
Website: www.nlm.nih.gov
E-mail: custserv@nlm.nih.gov

Private Agencies That Provide Information about Breast Cancer

**African American Breast
Cancer Alliance**
P.O. Box 8981
Minneapolis, MN 55408
Toll-Free: 800-422-6237
Phone: 612-825-3675
Website: www.aabcainc.org
E-mail: aabca@aabcainc.org

American Cancer Society
250 Williams St. N.W.
Atlanta, GA 30303
Toll-Free: 800-227-2345
Toll-Free TTY: 866-228-4327
Website: www.cancer.org

**American College of
Radiology**
1891 Preston White Dr.
Reston, VA 20191
Toll-Free: 800-227-5463
Phone: 703-648-8900
Website: www.acr.org
E-mail: info@acr.org

**American Institute for
Cancer Research**
1759 R St. N.W.
Washington, DC 20009
Toll-Free: 800-843-8114
Phone: 202-328-7744
Fax: 202-328-7226
Website: www.aicr.org
E-mail: aicrweb@aicr.org

American Medical Association
515 N. State St.
Chicago, IL 60654
Toll-Free: 800-621-8335
Website: www.ama-assn.org

American Society for Clinical Oncology
2318 Mill Rd., Ste. 800
Alexandria, VA 22314
Toll-Free: 888-651-3038
Phone: 571-483-1780
Fax: 571-366-9537
Website: www.cancer.net
E-mail: contactus@cancer.net

American Society for Radiation Oncology
8280 Willow Oaks Corporate Dr.
Ste. 500
Fairfax, VA 22031
Toll-Free: 800-962-7876
Phone: 703-502-1550
Fax: 703-502-7852
Website: www.astro.org

American Society of Plastic and Reconstructive Surgeons
444 E. Algonquin Rd.
Arlington Heights, IL 60005
Phone: 847-228-9900
Website: www.plasticsurgery.org

Association of Cancer Online Resources
173 Duane St.
Ste. 3A
New York, NY 10013-3334
Phone: 212-226-5525
Website: www.acor.org
E-mail: feedback@acor.org

Avon Foundation for Women
777 Third Ave.
New York, NY 10017
Phone: 866-505-AVON
(866-505-2866)
Website: www.avonfoundation.org

Breast Cancer Care
5-13 Great Suffolk St.
London, SE1 0NS
United Kingdom
Toll-Free: 808-800-6000
Website: www.breastcancercare.org.uk
E-mail: info@breastcancercare.org.uk

Breast Cancer Research Foundation
60 E. 56th St.
8th Fl.
New York, NY 10022
Toll-Free: 866-FIND-A-CURE
(866-346-3228)
Phone: 646-497-2600
Fax: 646-497-0890
Website: www.bcrfcure.org
E-mail: bcrf@bcrfcure.org

BreastCancerTrials.org
3450 California St.
San Francisco, CA 94118
Phone: 415-476-5777
Website: www.breastcancertrials.org

Breastcancer.org
7 E.Lancaster Ave.
3rd Fl.
Ardmore, PA 19003
Phone: 610-642-6550
Website: www.breastcancer.org

Cancer and Careers, CEW Foundation
159 W.25th St.
8th Fl.
Phone: 646-929-8032
Website: www.cancerandcareers.org
E-mail: cancerandcareers@cew.org

Cancer Support Community
1050 17th St. N.W.
Ste. 500
Washington, DC 20036
Toll-Free: 888-793-9355
Phone: 202-659-9709
Fax: 212-685-3334
Website: www.cancersupportcommunity.org
E-mail: help@cancersupportcommunity.org

CancerCare
275 Seventh Ave.
New York, NY 10001
Toll-Free: 800-813-HOPE (800-813-4673)
Phone: 212-712-8400
Fax: 212-712-8495
Website: www.cancercare.org
E-mail: info@cancercare.org

CancerConnect.com
491 N. Main St.
Ste. 200, P.O. Box 2581
Ketchum, ID 83340
Website: www.cancerconnect.com
E-mail: info@cancerconsultants.com

Caring.com
2600 S. El Camino Real
Ste. 300
San Mateo, CA 94403
Website: www.caring.com

Cleveland Clinic
9500 Euclid Ave.
Cleveland, OH 44195
Toll-Free: 800-223-2273; 866-588-2264 (Info Line)
Phone: 216-636-5860 (Info Line)
TTY: 216-444-0261
Website: www.my.clevelandclinic.org

College of American Pathologists
325 Waukegan Rd.
Northfield, IL 60093-2750
Toll-Free: 800-323-4040
Phone: 847-832-7000
Fax: 847-832-8000
Website: www.cap.org

Facing Our Risk of Cancer Empowered (FORCE)
16057 Tampa Palms Blvd. W.
PMB #373
Tampa, FL 33647
Toll-Free: 866-288-RISK (866-288-7475); 866-824-RISK (866-824-7475)
Fax: 954-827-2200
Website: www.facingourrisk.org
E-mail: info@facingourrisk.org

Family Caregiver Alliance
785 Market St.
Ste. 750
San Francisco, CA 94103
Toll-Free: 800-445-8106
Phone: 415-434-3388
Website: www.caregiver.org
E-mail: info@caregiver.org

Imaginis
25 E.Ct. St.
Ste. 301
Greenville, SC 29601
Website: www.imaginis.com
E-mail: learnmore@imaginis.com

Inflammatory Breast Cancer Research Foundation
P.O. Box 2805
Toll-Free: 1-877-stop-ibc
(1-877-786-7422)
Website: www.ibcresearch.org
E-mail: information@mail.
ibcresearch.org

International Agency for Research on Cancer
150 Cours Albert Thomas
Lyon, 69372 Lyon CEDEX 08
France
Phone: 33 04 72 73 84 85
Fax: 33 04 72 73 85 75
Website: www.iarc.fr

Susan G. Komen for the Cure
5005 LBJ Fwy
Ste. 250
Dallas, TX 75244
Toll-Free: 877-GO-KOMEN
(877-46-56636)
Phone: 877-465-6636
Website: ww5.komen.org

Lab Tests Online
American Association for Clinical Chemistry
900 Seventh St.
NW Ste. 400
Toll-Free: 800-892-1400
Phone: 1202-857-0717
Fax: 1-202-833-4576
Website: www.labtestsonline.org

Living Beyond Breast Cancer
354 W. Lancaster Ave.
Ste. 224
Haverford, PA 19041
Phone: 610-645-4567;
484-708-1550
Fax: 610-645-4573
Website: www.lbbc.org
E-mail: mail@lbbc.org

Lymph Notes
Website: www.lymphnotes.com

Men Against Breast Cancer
P.O. Box 150
Adamstown, MD 21710-0150
Toll-Free: 866-547-MABC
(866-547-6222)
Phone: 866-547-6222
Fax: 301-874-8657
Website: www.
menagainstbreastcancer.org
E-mail: info@
menagainstbreastcancer.org

Metastatic Breast Cancer Network
P.O. Box 1449
New York, NY 10159
Toll-Free: 888-500-0370
Website: www.mbcnetwork.org
E-mail: mbcn@mbcn.org

Mothers Supporting Daughters with Breast Cancer
25235 Fox Chase Dr.
Chestertown, MD 21620
Phone: 410-778-1982
Fax: 410-778-1411
Website: www.
mothersdaughters.org
E-mail: msdbc@verizon.net

National Breast Cancer Coalition
1101 17th St. N.W.
Ste. 1300
Washington, DC 20036
Toll-Free: 800-622-2838
Phone: 202-296-7477
Fax: 202-265-6854
Website: www.
breastcancerdeadline2020.org

National Breast Cancer Foundation, Inc.
2600 Network Blvd.
Ste. 300
Frisco, TX 75034
Website: www.
nationalbreastcancer.org

National Coalition for Cancer Survivorship
1010 Wayne Ave.
Ste. 770
Silver Spring, MD 20910
Toll-Free: 877-NCCS-YES
(877-622-7937)
Phone: 301-650-9127
Website: www.canceradvocacy.
org
E-mail: info@canceradvocacy.org

National Comprehensive Cancer Network
275 Commerce Dr.
Ste. 300
Fort Washington, PA 19034
Phone: 215-690-0300
Fax: 215-690-0280
Website: www.nccn.org

National Hospice and Palliative Care Organization
1731 King St.
Ste. 100
Alexandria, VA 22314
Toll-Free: 800-658-8898
Phone: 703-837-1500
Fax: 703-837-1233
Website: www.nhpco.org
E-mail: nhpco_info@nhpco.org

National Lymphedema Network
116 New Montgomery St.
Ste. 235
San Francisco, CA 94105
Toll-Free: 800-541-3259
Phone: 415-908-3681
Fax: 415-908-3813
Website: www.lymphnet.org
E-mail: nln@lymphnet.org

National Society of Genetic Counselors
330 N. Wabash Ave.
Ste. 2000
Chicago, IL 60611
Phone: 312-321-6834
Website: www.nsgc.org
E-mail: nsgc@nsgc.org

OncoLink The Perelman Center for Advanced Medicine
3400 Civic Center Blvd.
Ste. 2338
Philadelphia, PA 19104
Phone: 215-349-8895
Fax: 215-349-5445
Website: www.oncolink.org
E-mail: hampshire@uphs.upenn.edu

SHARE: Self Help for Women with Breast or Ovarian Cancer
1501 Broadway
Ste. 704A
New York, NY 10036
Toll-Free: 866-891-2392
Phone: 212-719-0364;
212-382-2111
Website: www.
sharecancersupport.org
E-mail: info@
sharecancersupport.org

Sharsheret: Your Jewish Community Facing Breast Cancer
1086 Teaneck Rd.
Ste. 2G
Teaneck, NJ 07666
Toll-Free: 866-474-2774
Phone: 201-833-2341
Fax: 201-837-5025
Website: www.sharsheret.org
E-mail: info@sharsheret.org

Sisters Network Inc.
2922 Rosedale St.
Houston, TX 77004
Toll-Free: 866-781-1808
Phone: 713-781-0255
Fax: 713-780-8998
Website: www.
sistersnetworkinc.org
E-mail: infonet@
sistersnetworkinc.org

Society of Interventional Radiology
3975 Fair Ridge Dr.
Ste. 400 N.
Fairfax, VA 22033
Toll-Free: 800-488-7284
Phone: 703-691-1805
Fax: 703-691-1855
Website: www.sirweb.org

Society of Nuclear Medicine
1850 Samuel Morse Dr.
Reston, VA 20190
Phone: 703-708-9000
Fax: 703-708-9015
Website: www.snm.org
E-mail: feedback@snm.org

Tigerlily Foundation
11654 Plaza America Dr.
#725
Reston, VA 20190
Toll-Free: 888-580-6253
Fax: 703-663-9844
Website: www.
tigerlilyfoundation.org
E-mail: info@tigerlilyfoundation.org

Triple Negative Breast Cancer Foundation
P.O. Box 204
Norwood, NJ 07648
Toll-Free: 877-880-8622
Phone: 646-942-0242
Website: www.tnbcfoundation.org
E-mail: info@tnbcfoundation.org

Well Spouse Foundation
63 W. Main St.
Ste. H
Freehold, NJ 07728
Toll-Free: 800-838-0879
Phone: 732-577-8899
Fax: 732-577-8644
Website: www.wellspouse.org
E-mail: info@wellspouse.org

Y-ME National Breast Cancer Organization
5775 N Glen Park Rd.
Ste. 201
Glendale, WI 53209
Toll-Free: 800-977-4121
Phone: 414-977-1780
Fax: 414-977-1781
Website: www.abcdbreastcancersupport.org
E-mail: abcdinc@abcdmentor.org

Young Survival Coalition
61 Broadway
Ste. 2235
New York, NY 10006
Toll-Free: 877-972-1011
Website: www.youngsurvival.org

Financial Resources for People with Breast Cancer

The following government departments provide financial and income assistance programs for people with breast cancer:

Department of Health and Human Services
Toll-Free: 877-696-6775
Website: www.hhs.gov

Medicare and Medicaid
Toll-Free: 877-267-2323
Website: www.cms.hhs.gov

National Breast and Cervical Cancer Early Detection Program
Toll-Free: 800-CDC-INFO (800-232-4636)
Website: www.cdc.gov/cancer/nbccedp

Social Security
Toll-Free: 800-772-1213
Website: www.ssa.gov

The following private organizations provide financial assistance to people with breast cancer:

American Cancer Society
Toll-Free: 800-227-2345
Website: www.cancer.org/Treatment/SupportProgramsServices

The American Cancer Society offers programs for cancer patients to help pay the costs of transportation, treatment, lodging, and other expenses.

CancerCare Co-Payment Assistance Foundation
Toll-Free: 866-55-COPAY (866–552–6729)
Website: www.cancercarecopay.org

This organization offers help to those who cannot afford their insurance copayments for cancer care.

Fertile Hope
Toll-Free: 866-965-7205 (LIVESTRONG Survivor Care)
Website: www.fertilehope.org

This organization provides financial help to people with cancer whose insurance will not cover fertility treatment.

NeedyMeds
Website: www.needymeds.org
Helpline: 800-503-6897

This website collects information about patient assistance programs for medications and medical supplies sponsored by government agencies, nonprofit organizations, and pharmaceutical companies.

Partnership for Prescription Assistance
Toll-Free 888-4PPA-NOW (888-477-2669)
Website: www.pparx.org

This organization assists patients who do not have coverage for prescription medications to receive free or low-cost medications.

Patient Advocate Foundation
Toll-Free: 800-532-5274
Website: www.patientadvocate.org

This organization assists patients with medical debt, access to insurance issues, and job retention.

Find a Breast Cancer Screening Provider If You Are Uninsured or Underinsured

Centers for Disease Control and Prevention's (CDC) National Breast and Cervical Cancer Early Detection Program (NBCCEDP) provides breast and cervical cancer screenings and diagnostic services to low-income, uninsured, and underinsured women across the United States.

What Services Does the NBCCEDP Provide?

Local NBCCEDP programs offer the following services for eligible women—

- Clinical breast examinations

- Mammograms

- Pap tests

- Pelvic examinations

- Human papillomavirus (HPV) tests

- Diagnostic testing if results are abnormal

- Referrals to treatment

Who Should Get Breast and Cervical Cancer Screenings?

All women are at risk for breast and cervical cancer, but regular screenings can prevent these diseases or find them early. The U.S. Preventive Services Task Force has established the following guidelines for screening, but you should talk with your health care provider how often you should get screened.

- Breast cancer: Women between 50 and 74 years old should get a mammogram every two years. Those under 50 should talk with their provider about when they should be screened.

- Cervical cancer: Women should get their first Pap test at age 21 and continue screening until age 65.

Are You Eligible for Free or Low-Cost Screenings?

You may be eligible for free or low-cost screenings if you meet these qualifications—

- You are between 40 and 64 years of age for breast cancer screening

- You are between 21 and 64 years of age for cervical cancer screening

- You have no insurance, or your insurance does not cover screening exams

- Your yearly income is at or below 250% of the federal poverty level

Index

Index

NIH Study Offers Insight into Why
 Cancer Incidence Increases with Age
 (NIH) 109n
nipple discharge
 breast changes 13
 described 5
 symptoms 25
 warning signs 107
nipples
 clinical breast exam 5
 depicted *24*
 visual examination 216
Nolvadex (tamoxifen)
 overview 359–62
 selective estrogen receptor
  modulators 352
noninvasive cancer
 breast changes 16
 defined 627
 magnetic resonance imaging 242
nonmalignant *see* benign
nutrition
 appetite loss 455
 mouth problems 468
 obesity 143
 personal medical records 507
 radiation therapy 525
Nutrition in Cancer Care–Patient
 Version (NCI) 517n
nutrition therapy, cancer
 treatment 517

O

obesity
 autologous tissue 330
 breast cancer risk 107
 overview 143–5
 radiation therapy 184
 risk factors 106
 see also overweight
"Obesity" (NCI) 143n
"Obesity and Cancer Risk"
 (NCI) 143n
Office of Disease Prevention and
 Health Promotion (ODPHP)
 publication
  mammograms 228n
older adults, caregivers 546

Omnigraphics, Inc.
 publications
  breast (MRI) 242n
  breast self-exam 215n
  estrogen and cancer
   development 33n
  lobular carcinoma in situ
   (LCIS) 81n
  mastectomy 318n
  triple-negative breast
   cancer 99n
OncoLink The Perelman Center for
 Advanced Medicine, contact 636
oncologists, treatment 31
oncology, cancer pain 434
"ONE's Column: Breast Cancer
 Screening for Women with Dense
 Breasts: The Gray Zone (or Actually
 the White Zone)" (NCI) 218n
oophorectomy
 clinical management 38
 described 280
 ovarian ablation 186
 prophylactic surgery 175
 risk reducing surgeries 195
 see also prophylactic oophorectomy
opioids
 delirium 460
 night sweats 445
 pain management 432
oral contraceptives
 breast cancer risk 139
 chemoprevention 176
 estrogen therapy 35
 ovarian cancer risk 140
 risk factors 191
"Oral Contraceptives and Cancer
 Risk" (NCI) 139n
osteoporosis
 bisphosphonates 597
 estrogen therapy 35
 hormones 132
 selective estrogen receptor
  modulators 185
ovarian ablation
 defined 187
 hormone-sensitive breast cancer
  treatment 351
 hormone therapy 304